THE AMERICAN PRESIDENCY
IN ACTION: 1789

THE MACMILLAN COMPANY
NEW YORK · BOSTON · CHICAGO · DALLAS
ATLANTA · SAN FRANCISCO

MACMILLAN AND CO., Limited
LONDON · BOMBAY · CALCUTTA · MADRAS
MELBOURNE

THE MACMILLAN COMPANY
OF CANADA, Limited
TORONTO

THE AMERICAN PRESIDENCY IN ACTION 1789

A Study in Constitutional History

BY
JAMES HART
University of Virginia

THE MACMILLAN COMPANY · NEW YORK
1948

COPYRIGHT, 1948, BY
INSTITUTE FOR RESEARCH IN THE SOCIAL SCIENCES
UNIVERSITY OF VIRGINIA

All rights reserved—no part of this book may be reproduced in any form without permission in writing from the publisher except by a reviewer who wishes to quote brief passages in connection with a review written for inclusion in magazine or newspaper.

First Printing

Acknowledgment is hereby made to the authors, editors, and publishers named, in quoting copyrighted material as indicated below:

Charles A. Beard: *The Economic Origins of Jeffersonian Democracy.* Copyright 1915 by The Macmillan Company and used with its permission.

James Bryce: *The American Commonwealth*, Vols. I and II. Copyright 1893 by Macmillan and Co. Ltd., 1910, 1914 by The Macmillan Company, 1921 and 1920 by the Rt. Hon. Viscount Bryce and used with the permission of Macmillan & Co. Ltd., and The Macmillan Company.

Edward S. Corwin: *The President's Removal Power Under the Constitution.* Published by National Municipal League, New York. Copyright 1927 by Edward S. Corwin and used with his permission.

Max Farrand (ed.): *The Records of the Federal Convention of 1787* (rev. ed.), 4 vols. Copyright 1937 by Yale University Press and used with its permission.

John C. Fitzpatrick (ed.): *The Diaries of George Washington, 1748-1799*, 4 vols. Published by Houghton Mifflin Co., Boston and New York, The Riverside Press, Cambridge. Copyright 1925 by the Mount Vernon Ladies' Association of the Union and used with its permission.

The Journal of William Maclay, ed. Edgar S. Maclay. Copyright 1890 by D. Appleton & Company, 1927 by Albert & Charles Boni, Inc. and used with the permission of the latter.

Charles C. Thach: *The Creation of the Presidency, 1775-1789.* Copyright 1923 by the Johns Hopkins Press and used with its permission.

A. N. Whitehead: *Symbolism: Its Meaning and Effect.* Copyright 1927 by The Macmillan Company and used with its permission.

Ray Stannard Baker and William E. Dodd (eds.): *The Public Papers of Woodrow Wilson: College and State*, Vols. I and II; *The New Democracy*, Vols. I and II; *War and Peace*, Vols. I and II. Published by Harper & Bros., New York and London. Copyright 1925, 1926, 1927 by Edith Bolling Wilson and used with her permission.

PRINTED IN THE UNITED STATES OF AMERICA

To
Thomas and Gertrude FitzHugh

PREFACE

As the subtitle of this volume indicates, it is a study in the constitutional history of the American Presidency. The year 1789 was the year of beginnings for the Presidency in action; and the facets of what may be the greatest office in the political history of mankind are many. In the broadest terms the constitutional [1] roles of the President have become three: his ceremonial role as *chef d'état*; his legal role as the Chief Magistrate of the national government; and his political role as the titular head of his party and potential leader of the nation. In more detail, George Fort Milton has listed "six types of public service" which "Constitution, crisis, and custom, the great architects of our political institutions," have given to the President. He is a modern Pooh-bah, who is at once "Chief of State," "Chief of Foreign Relations," "Commander in Chief of the Army and Navy of the United States," "Chief of Government," "Chief of Party," and leader of public opinion.[2] It is of no little interest to seek the extent to which these several aspects of the office had emerged by the end of 1789, the first year of operations under the Constitution. While the historical materials used in this study are readily available, and have been exploited for various purposes by many historians, and by such historically minded political scientists as Edward S. Corwin, they do not appear to have previously been made the basis of an examination, in one place and in such detail, of all the constitutional aspects of the Presidency in its first year of activity, as these are viewed by the political scientist as distinguished from the professional historian. It seems appropriate, therefore, to offer this volume as an intensive study of the constitutional beginnings of the Presidency in action. It may be added that, if the book is favorably received, it is the author's intention to employ the same method in further studies in the early constitutional history of the Presidency.

The author desires, finally, to call the attention of his readers to Leonard D. White's *The Federalists,* which at this writing is in process of publication by The Macmillan Company.

J. H.

Charlottesville
Christmas, 1947

[1] See below, "A Note on the Use in This Volume of the Terms 'Constitutional' and 'History,'" p. xiii.
[2] George Fort Milton, *The Use of Presidential Power, 1789-1943* (Little, Brown and Co., Boston, 1944) 3-4.

ACKNOWLEDGMENTS

This study is published as a direct result of the stimulus, encouragement and financial aid of Professor Wilson Gee in his capacity as Director of the Institute for Research in the Social Sciences of the University of Virginia. Professor Gee's decisions with respect to the writer have always been just except when they have been more than generous.

The masterful skill of Miss Ruth Ritchie, Secretary of the Institute, enabled the author to turn in a manuscript which was all but perfect in form.

Mr. Harry Clemons, Librarian of the University of Virginia, and various members of his staff in the Alderman Library have placed at the disposal of the writer the facilities and skills necessary to his work, and have done so with that unfailing courtesy which is characteristic of the institution.

While this study was in large measure written directly from the primary sources, into its preparation there went many contributions of various teachers, authors, colleagues, and friends, for which the author is grateful, and which a whole volume could not adequately acknowledge.

J. H.

CONTENTS

CHAPTER I. WASHINGTON: THE UNANIMOUS CHOICE OF HIS COUNTRY ... 1
    The Symbolic Character of Washington's Unanimous Election ... 1
    An Important Opinion of General Washington on the Presidency ... 2
    Washington on the Threshold ... 3

CHAPTER II. THE PRESIDENT AS CHIEF OF STATE ... 10
    The Inaugural Ceremony ... 10
    Style of Living and Line of Conduct ... 11
    Refusal to Accept Pecuniary Compensation ... 16
    A Presidential Tour ... 17
    The Official Precedence of the President ... 18
    Some Pronouncements of the First Inaugural Address ... 20
    Replies to Addresses ... 21
    The Proclamation of a Day of Thanksgiving ... 24
    The Use and Form of Proclamations ... 26
    Imitations of Monarchy ... 28
    Attitude toward Criticism ... 54

CHAPTER III. THE PRESIDENT AND CONGRESS ... 55

CHAPTER IV. THE PRESIDENT AND THE SENATE ... 78
    Treaties and Foreign Relations ... 78
    Nominations and Appointments ... 111
    Politics and Appointments ... 126

CHAPTER V.	THE PRESIDENT AS ADMINISTRATIVE CHIEF	134
CHAPTER VI.	MISCELLANEOUS CONSTITUTIONAL QUESTIONS RAISED IN HOUSE DEBATE	144
CHAPTER VII.	THE ESTABLISHMENT OF THE GREAT DEPARTMENTS	152

Three "Organic" Acts of Congress 152

The Question of a Home Department 153

The Great Debate on the Tenure of Office 155

Comparison of the Treasury with the Other Two Departments . . . 214

An Interpretation of the Administrative Legislation of the First Session in Terms of Its Underlying Administrative Theory 239

Index 249

A NOTE ON THE USE
IN THIS VOLUME
OF THE TERMS
"CONSTITUTIONAL" AND "HISTORY"

WHEN one writes a word, one literally makes ink-marks on paper. The scribblings of a lettered grown-up differ from those of an untutored child in that the grown-up makes ink-marks previously learned and customarily used to symbolize thought references. Yet it is well known that a single verbal symbol may be used in thought or communication to indicate two or more referents.[1] Thus in the current usage of political science the word *constitution* may refer to either of two related but distinct referents: (1) a single written instrument which is formally the source of all legal authority under a given governmental system, and which accordingly creates the principal organs of government and defines their legal competences and the limitations thereof; and (2) the totality of the principles and rules, whether written or unwritten, whether of law or of custom, which define the basic features of the given governmental system.

The British have a constitution only in the latter sense; while the United States has a constitution in both senses. In this study, accordingly, it is a practical necessity to use the verbal symbol *constitution* now with one referent, now with the other. It is hoped that the referent intended will in each instance be clear from the context.

It is important to note that the *scope* of this study is as broad as the second referent listed above. As a study in the *constitutional* history of the Presidency, this volume is concerned not only with constitutional law—indeed, not at all with constitutional law as defined by decisions of the Supreme Court, which had not been organized by the end of 1789—but also with "organic" statutes,[2] "legislative decisions,"[3] constitutional problems and issues, and practices, whether ceremonial, legal, or political, which relate to the basic aspects of the Presidency.

When, however, the word *constitution* is used to symbolize this broad referent, the referent is itself a *class* of objects which includes *some*

[1] C. K. Ogden and I. A. Richards, *The Meaning of Meaning* (Harcourt, Brace and Co., New York, 1927).
[2] This term is defined below (p. 152) in the section of chapter 7 which is entitled, "Three Organic Acts of Congress."
[3] Such as the famous "legislative decision of 1789," which is considered at length below in chapter 7.

statutes, *some* practices, but not all.[4] In such a case all that usage does is to point to *typical* members of the class; and the referent is necessarily fuzzy around the edges.[5] It then becomes a matter of "construction" or "interpretation," often involving choice, to resolve the ambiguity with respect to whether the referent includes this or that particular statute or custom which is on the borderline of the class as defined.[6] This has always been a fact, but it was not fully appreciated until it was realized that classification is not for man a process of passive discovery, but an *a priori* method by which the "big blooming buzzing confusion"[7] of the *given*[8] of experience is so arranged that the human mind can deal with it. It is accordingly no longer to be expected that the members of a class will have *identical class qualities,* but only that they will exhibit varying degrees of *similarity* with respect to the abstract qualities which define the class.[9] That is why the question, where to draw the line, so as to include or exclude objects which might conceivably be included in the class, is often a matter of choice, but of a choice to be made, if made intelligently, in terms of the *purpose* for which the class has been defined as a tool of analysis.[10] What this means in terms of the scope actually given to this study is that what the author has included, excluded, or overlooked with reference to its bearing on the *constitutional* history of the Presidency is, except in the obvious cases, subject to criticism.

As a study in constitutional *history* this book starts with familiar his-

---

[4] Since the term *constitution* in the broad or British sense refers *only* to the *basic* features of the given governmental system, the referent includes only those statutes and practices which are basic to that system. That the first appropriation act enacted by Congress was of the "lump-sum" variety was of constitutional significance; but the specific provisions of the act were not in themselves of such significance. The same is true of customs and practices. Some customs, unimportant in themselves, are of *symbolic* significance, as in connection with the ceremonial role of the President as head of state. Each statute or statutory provision and each practice must be judged in relation to the *purpose* for which the term *constitution* in this sense has come to be employed as a tool of analysis.
[5] *Cf.* Mr. Justice Holmes in his dissenting opinion in *Springer v. Philippine Islands,* 277 U.S. 189, 209–211 (1928).
[6] Walter Wheeler Cook, "Scientific Method and the Law," 15 *Johns Hopkins Alumni Magazine* 213–236 (March, 1927); James Hart, *Tenure of Office Under the Constitution* (The Johns Hopkins Press, Baltimore, 1930) 6–8, 27, note 25, and *An Introduction to Administrative Law With Selected Cases* (F. S. Crofts & Co., New York, 1940) 131–132.
[7] Horace M. Kallen, *The Philosophy of William James* (Modern Library, New York, 1925) 76.
[8] C. I. Lewis, *Mind and the World Order* (Charles Scribner's Sons, New York, Chicago, Boston, 1929).
[9] George Boas, *Our New Ways of Thinking* (Harper & Bros., New York and London, 1930) Part One ("From Truth to Probability").
[10] Those who were privileged to know the late Walter Wheeler Cook, one of whose articles is cited in note 6 above, will remember that, in his favorite capacity as an intellectual gadfly, he constantly asked, "What do you mean?" and "For what purpose?"

torical materials, but selects, arranges and interprets them in terms of their significance for the political scientist. This is also the aim of the contemplated series of volumes mentioned in the Preface. The author thus acts on the dictum of Sir John Robert Seeley that

> "History without political science has no fruit;
> Political science without history has no root." [11]

With all due respect to the professional historians, upon whose splendid efforts this work has been erected as a house is erected upon its foundations, they have all too often treated the events and utterances recorded in the materials of our constitutional history as the events and utterances of a *dead* past. They have not sufficiently brought to their *use* of the sources questions which are meaningful in terms of the general problems of political science, and hence of the constitutional problems of the present in so far as they can be illuminated by a study of political science. Yet if "History is past politics, and . . . politics are present history," [12] the history and politics of the past must find many points of fruitful contact with the history and politics of the present and even of the future as presently viewed. This is not to criticize the professional historians, but to justify the historical method in political science, the purpose of which is properly to make those contacts between the past and the present without indulging either in the fallacy of easy overgeneralization from history or in the time-serving practice of using historical materials merely as an ill-digested reservoir of supporting argument for a crude form of special pleading, as the political alchemists have so often done. It is the hope of the author that this volume will rather stimulate its readers to make history contribute to their own attainment of balanced judgment in the spirit of the Greek ideal of the mean.[13] Perhaps the reader cannot help being temperamentally conservative. Perhaps the author cannot help being temperamentally liberal.[14] Even so, for both alike, the doctrine of the mean is needed as a consciously employed tool of self-correction.

J. H.

---

[11] Sir J. R. Seeley, *Introduction to Political Science* (Macmillan & Co., London and New York, 1896) 4.
[12] Edward A. Freeman, *The Methods of Historical Study* (Macmillan & Co., London, 1886) 44.
[13] See Aristotle as cited in chapter 1, note 2, below, p. 1.
[14] On the use in this study of the terms *conservative* and *liberal*, see below (p. 47) the section of chapter 2 entitled, "An illuminating example of political symbolism."

MEMORANDUM ON CITATIONS

IT is the conviction of the author that citations should be as simple and succinct as clarity allows. Accordingly, he has omitted unnecessary symbols and commas, indicated the volume number of works published in more than one volume by an arabic numeral immediately preceding the name of the author or the title of the publication, and abbreviated the titles of certain works which are frequently cited in ways which may here be indicated.

The citation of *Writings* without further description refers in all cases to the bicentennial edition in 39 volumes of *The Writings of George Washington* (edited from the original manuscript sources by John C. Fitzpatrick, prepared under the direction of the United States George Washington Bicentennial Commission, and published by authority of Congress, Government Printing Office, Washington, 1931–1944).

The citation of *Diaries* without further description refers in all cases to *The Diaries of George Washington, 1748–1799* (Regents' Edition, in 4 volumes, edited by John C. Fitzpatrick for and published by The Mount Vernon Ladies' Association of the Union, Houghton Mifflin Co., Boston and New York, 1925). The Mount Vernon Ladies' Association of the Union has kindly granted the author of this volume permission to make full use of the pertinent parts of the *Diaries*.

The citation of *Journal of William Maclay* refers in all cases to that journal as published in 1927 by Albert and Charles Boni, New York, with an "Introduction" by Charles A. Beard and a "Preface" by Edgar S. Maclay. The Messrs. Boni have kindly granted the author of this volume permission to make full use of the pertinent parts of Maclay.

The citation of *Annals* without further description refers in all cases to the *Annals of Congress*, the full title of which is *The Debates and Proceedings of the Congress of the United States*, compiled by Joseph Gales, Sr., and published by Gales and Seaton, Washington, vol. I in 1834.

The citation of *Laws of the United States* without further description refers in all cases to the publication in 5 volumes in 1815 under that title of the statutes of Congress, under the authority of an act of Congress, by John Bioren and W. John Duane, Philadelphia, and R. C. Weightman, Washington City. The laws of the first session are in the second volume of this compilation.

The citation of *Messages and Papers of the Presidents* refers in all cases to an edition of that collection, originally made by James D. Richardson, which was published in 20 volumes, with additions and changes in pagination, by the Bureau of National Literature, Inc., New York, 1917.

In chapter 7, two works are so frequently cited that after full citation in note 14 they are referred to by abbreviated titles. Charles C. Thach, *The Creation of the Presidency, 1775–1789* (The Johns Hopkins Press, Baltimore, 1922), which is No. 4 of Series XL of the *Johns Hopkins University Studies in Historical and Political Science,* is cited after note 14 of chapter 7 simply as *Thach*. Edward S. Corwin, *The President's Removal Power Under the Constitution* (National Municipal League Monograph Series, National Municipal League, New York, 1927) is cited after note 14 of chapter 7 simply as Corwin's *Removal Power*. Since this brochure is out of print, note 14 of chapter 7 gives two other references to its material for the benefit of the reader.

... *the first transactions of a nation, like those of an individual upon his first entrance into life, make the deepest impression, and are to form the leading traits in its character.*

—George Washington in 1788.[1]

---

[1] 29 *Writings* 465. Washington to John Armstrong. April 25, 1788. While this is obviously an exaggeration, beginnings are important, and the statement shows how acutely aware Washington was of this fact.

Chapter 1

WASHINGTON: THE UNANIMOUS CHOICE OF HIS COUNTRY

. .
.

THE SYMBOLIC CHARACTER OF WASHINGTON'S UNANIMOUS ELECTION

WASHINGTON'S UNIQUE POSITION. A. N. Whitehead has said that the "symbolic function of great men" makes "balanced historical judgment" difficult. At opposite poles are the "hysteria of depreciation" and the "hysteria which dehumanizes in order to exalt."[1] With respect to Washington we passed from idolatry to "debunking," and now need to apply the doctrine of the mean as a method of self-correction.[2] In other words, we need to build, from the half-truths of thesis and antithesis, a synthesis.[3] Even in such a synthesis, however, will not Washington hold a unique place in American history? John Quincy Adams wrote in his diary in 1839:

Among the felicities of Washington's life is the unity of the two great objects which he had to pursue: first, the war of independence; and, secondly, the establishment of the Constitution of the United States. There is the unity of a Grecian drama in both of them—a tragedy and a comedy. No reputation of a great man can be acquired but by the accomplishment of some great object. But perhaps fortune is the great furnisher of occasions. The Revolutionary age

[1] From A. N. Whitehead, *Symbolism, Its Meaning and Effect* (The Macmillan Co., New York, 1927) 77–78.
[2] Aristotle, "Ethica Nicomachea" and "Magna Moralia," in 9 W. D. Ross, ed., *The Works of Aristotle Translated into English* (The Clarendon Press, Oxford, 1925) 1108b, lines 11–13, and 1186b, lines 12–17; Aristotle, *Politics* (Jowett trans., The Clarendon Press, Oxford, 1923) 168–173, 210–211, 213–214.
[3] The present writer repudiates the "speculative idealism" of Hegel. See 2 Dr. Harald Höffding, *A History of Modern Philosophy* (tr. from the German ed. by B. E. Meyer, Macmillan & Co., London and New York, 1900) 180–183. Yet thought seems to proceed by action and reaction between extremes, and the mean (synthesis) seems to be a balanced judgment which rejects both the excess of one extreme (thesis) and the deficiency of the other (antithesis), even while it incorporates the permanent worth of the half-truth of each. The useful applications to political thought and practice are many.

and the Constituent age were the times for great men; the Administrative age is an age of small men and small things.[4]

Washington was Federalist in his thinking, but even so he transcended Federalism as no other Federalist did. As the hero of the tragedy, Washington was a national hero before he began his role in the comedy. As a hero he was not, however, in the sense in which Andrew Jackson and Franklin D. Roosevelt were, a popular idol. He was a *deus ex machina* rather than a leader of the people. Precisely in this fact, however, and in his playing this role in both the great dramas on which our national life is founded, lies his uniqueness; and it was that uniqueness which invested the American Presidency from the start with a heroic quality which has contributed greatly to its possession of perhaps the finest tradition of any civic office in history. That Washington was twice the unanimous choice of his country was a necessary feature of his heroic role.

AN IMPORTANT OPINION OF GENERAL WASHINGTON ON THE PRESIDENCY

WASHINGTON IN 1788 ON THE QUESTION OF THE CONSTITUTIONAL RE-ELIGIBILITY OF THE PRESIDENT. On April 28, 1788, a year before his first inauguration, Washington wrote to Lafayette:

There are other points on which opinions would be more likely to vary. As for instance, on the ineligibility of the same person for President, after he should have served a certain course of years. Guarded so effectually as the proposed Constitution is, in respect to the prevention of bribery and undue influence in the choice of President: I confess, I differ widely myself from Mr. Jefferson and you, as to the necessity or expediency of rotation in that appointment. The matter was fairly discussed in the Convention, and to my full convictions; though I cannot have time or room to sum up the argument in this letter. There cannot, in my judgment, be the least danger that the President will by any practicable intrigue ever be able to continue himself one moment in office, much less perpetuate himself in it; but in the last stage of corrupted morals and political depravity: and even then there is as much danger that any other species of domination would prevail. Though, when a people shall have become incapable of governing themselves and fit for a master, it is of little consequence from what quarter he comes. Under an extended view of this part of the sub-

---

[4] 10 *Memoirs of John Quincy Adams* (J. B. Lippincott & Co., Philadelphia, 1876) 117, under the date of April 25, 1839. In this passage Adams gave no hint of the significant contribution to the Presidency of his contemporary, Andrew Jackson, and no anticipation of the dramas of the future.

ject, I can see no propriety in precluding ourselves from the services of any man, who on some great emergency shall be deemed universally, most capable of serving the Public.[5]

The formal constitutional guards were not so strong as the framers anticipated; but the democratization of the Presidency brought by the party system and the great contribution of Jackson [6] made the latter part of this paragraph sound wise in 1944 to *liberals* as it sounded wise in 1788 to *conservatives*.[7]

WASHINGTON ON THE THRESHOLD

THE QUESTION: TO SERVE OR NOT TO SERVE. On April 20, 1788, Washington wrote to Thomas Johnson expressing the hope that the Maryland Convention should not adjourn to a later period than the decision of the Virginia Convention. He added that if he had exceeded the proper limit,

my motive must excuse me. I have but one public wish remaining. It is, that in *peace* and *retirement,* I may see this Country rescued from the danger which is impending, and rise into respectability maugre the Intrigues of its public and private enemies.[8]

Five days later he wrote to John Armstrong that the "interruption" to his "domestic retirement" involved in going to the Philadelphia Convention had been "repugnant to my feelings, my interests, and my wishes," and that he had gone only at the "earnest and pressing solicitations" of others and because "an absolute refusal to act" at "so critical a moment" might be construed "as a total dereliction of my Country" or worse. He added that, although Armstrong had said he thought another "tour of duty" would fall to his lot, he could but hope he would be disappointed.[9] He so expressed himself to Rochambeau,[10] and more fully to Lafayette, to whom he wrote that the Presidency

has no enticing charms, and no fascinating allurements for me. However, it might not be decent for me to say I would refuse to accept or even to speak much about an appointment, which may never take place: for in so doing, one might

[5] 29 *Writings* 479.
[6] Henry Jones Ford, *The Rise and Growth of American Politics* (The Macmillan Co., New York, 1898) 162–196, 275–293; J. Allen Smith, *The Spirit of American Government* (The Chautauqua Press, Chautauqua, The Macmillan Co., New York, 1911) chap. 8.
[7] On the use in this volume of the terms, *liberals* and *conservatives,* see the section below (p. 47) entitled, "An illuminating example of political symbolism."
[8] 29 *Writings* 462–464.   [9] *Ibid.* 464. April 25, 1788.   [10] *Ibid.* 475. April 28, 1788.

possibly incur the application of the moral resulting from that Fable, in which the Fox is represented as inveighing against the sourness of the grapes, because he could not reach them.

He added that "at my time of life and under my circumstances" "the encreasing infirmities of nature and the growing love of retirement" did not permit him

to entertain a wish beyond that of living and dying an honest man on my own farm.[11]

In August Hamilton wrote to Washington:

I take it for granted, Sir, that you have concluded to comply with what will no doubt be the general call of your country in relation to the new government. You will permit me to say that it is indispensable you should lend yourself to its first operations. It is to little purpose to have *introduced* a system, if the weightiest influence is not given to its firm *establishment,* in the outset.[12]

Washington replied that he could say nothing on the delicate subject; for the event might never happen, and if it did,

it would be a point of prudence to defer forming one's ultimate and irrevocable decision, so long as new data might be afforded for one to act with the greater wisdom and propriety.

His personal desire was to live and die on his farm; but if it became indispensable to do otherwise,

while you and some others who are acquainted with my heart would *acquit,* the world and Posterity might probably accuse me [of] *inconsistency* and *ambition.*

But he hoped always to possess firmness and virtue enough to maintain the character of "an honest man." [13]

In September Washington wrote at length on the subject to Henry Lee. If his election would be thought to strengthen the government, it would for that reason be obnoxious to opposition Electors, of whom he expected many. He feared the imputation of ambition or at least inconsistency in leaving retirement after his strong declarations on the subject; but he was certain that

whenever I shall be convinced the good of my country requires my reputation to be put in risque; regard for my own fame will not come in competition with an object of so much magnitude.

In the last resort, he indicated, if he declined, it would be because of a belief

[11] *Ibid.* 479–480. April 28, 1788.   [13] *Ibid.* 66–67. August 28, 1788.
[12] 30 *Writings* 66–67, note 80.

that some other person, who had less pretence and less inclination to be excused, could execute all the duties fully as satisfactorily as myself.

To say more would be indiscreet. Saying that this was a confidential communication, he concluded the discussion with the general observation that his inclinations were to remain as he was,

unless a clear and insurmountable conviction should be impressed on my mind that some very disagreeable consequences must in all human probability result from the indulgence of my wishes.[14]

When Hamilton wrote again to say that, "It cannot be considered as a compliment" to say a successful beginning might materially depend upon Washington's acceptance, and that his aid was "indispensable,"[15] he answered that the expectation of having ere long to make a decision made him feel "a kind of gloom upon my mind." If he should be appointed and prevailed upon to accept,

the acceptance would be attended with more diffidence and reluctance that I ever experienced before in my life.

And he would do so

in hopes that at a convenient and early period my services might be dispensed with, and that I might be permitted once more to retire, to pass an unclouded evening after the stormy day of life, in the bosom of domestic tranquillity.[16]

To Benjamin Lincoln he wrote that nothing in this world could ever draw him from retirement

unless it be a *conviction* that the partiality of my Countrymen had made my services absolutely necessary, joined to a *fear* that my refusal might induce a belief that I preferred the consolation of my own reputation and private ease, to the good of my Country.

He had naturally supposed that his declarations at the close of the war would have saved him from this embarrassing situation, until "the public papers and private letters from my Correspondents in almost every quarter" made him realize he might soon be obliged to decide whether he would go again into public life or not.[17]

In November he wrote to Gouverneur Morris that if "a kind of inevitable necessity" should impel him to accept, it would be time enough to "yield to its impulse, when it can no longer be resisted."[18] He also commented to Jonathan Trumbull on the question, "which you suppose will certainly be put to me."[19]

[14] *Ibid.* 97–98. September 22, 1788.
[15] *Ibid.* 110, note 31.
[16] *Ibid.* 109–112. October 3, 1788.
[17] *Ibid.* 118–120. October 26, 1788.
[18] *Ibid.* 143. November 28, 1788.
[19] *Ibid.* 149–150. December 4, 1788.

After he had been in office more than three months Washington expressed "heartfelt satisfaction" at

the repeated testimonies of approbation which my conduct in accepting the Presidency of these United States has drawn from every quarter, and particularly from those who I trust, know me well enough to do justice to the motives which induced me once more to embark on the Ocean of public life.[20]

WASHINGTON ON JOHN ADAMS FOR VICE PRESIDENT. October 26, 1788, Washington wrote to Benjamin Lincoln as follows:

... and so little agency do I wish to have in electioneering, that I have never entered into a single discussion with any person nor to the best of my recollection expressed a single sentiment orally or in writing respecting the appointment of a Vice President. From the extent and respectability of Massachusetts it might reasonably be expected, that he would be chosen from that State. But having taken it for granted, that the person selected for that important place would be a true Foederalist; in that case, I was altogether disposed to acquiesce in the prevailing sentiments of the Electors, without giving any unbecoming preference or incurring any unnecessary ill-will. . . .

For this purpose I must speak again hypothetically for argument's sake, and say, supposing I should be appointed to the Administration and supposing I should accept it, I most solemnly declare, that whoever shall be found to enjoy the confidence of the States so far as to be elected Vice President, cannot be disagreeable to me in that office. And even if I had any predilection, I flatter myself, I possess patriotism enough to sacrifice it at the shrine of my country; . . . [21]

On January 1, 1789, Washington wrote with respect to John Adams for Vice President:

From different channels of information, it seemed probable to me (even before the receipt of your letter) that Mr. John Adams would be chosen Vice President. He will doubtless make a very good one: and let whoever may occupy the first seat, I shall be entirely satisfied with that arrangement for filling the second office.[22]

On the last day of the same month he wrote to Benjamin Lincoln that in Maryland and Virginia Adams probably would have a considerable number of electoral votes, and added:

Some of these gentlemen will have been advised that this measure would be entirely agreeable to me, and that I considered it to be the only certain way to prevent the election of an Antifederalist.[23]

In these remarks several things are noteworthy. Washington in effect was already thinking in terms of geographical or sectional balance in

[20] Ibid. 377. August 10, 1789. [22] Ibid. 173-174. Washington to the Secretary of War.
[21] Ibid. 120-121. [23] Ibid. 189-190.

choosing the first two officers of state. He did not want to electioneer because he wanted to stand above party; but he was a Federalist in the sense of the day—a friend of the Constitution—and wanted a Federalist in second place so much that he quietly sent word to Federalist electors in Virginia and Maryland that this objective depended upon a concentration on Adams. It is of course true that the friends of the Constitution liked it for the same conservative reasons which made skeptics of some and Anti-Federalists of others, and which, as time went on, caused men to line up on opposing sides on constitutional construction and public policy.[24]

SOME GENERAL REFLECTIONS OF WASHINGTON IN ANTICIPATION OF THE PRESIDENCY. To Lafayette Washington wrote that, if he had to serve, he would try "(even at the hazard of former fame or present popularity) to extricate my country from the embarrassments in which it is entangled, through want of credit; and to establish a general system of policy." "I think I see a *path,* as clear and direct as a ray of light," he declared, and listed harmony, honesty, industry, and frugality as the "four and essential pillars of public felicity." [25]

". . . no earthly consideration short of so general a call," wrote Washington on March 9, "together with a desire to reconcile contending parties as far as in me lays, could again bring me into public life . . ." [26]

Later in the month he said he accepted the Presidency "in conformity to the voice of my Country and the earnest entreaties of my friends, however contrary it is to my own desires and inclinations." [27]

Writing to the Acting Secretary of War on April 1, he said he was going to the chair of government with feelings "not unlike those of a culprit who is going to the place of his execution." He hated to "quit a peaceful abode for an Ocean of difficulties, without that competency of political skill, abilities, and inclination which is necessary to manage the helm." He thought of himself as embarking the voice of his country and his own good name on the voyage; and added:

Integrity and firmness is all I can promise: these, be the voyage long or short, never shall forsake me although I may be deserted by all men.[28]

[24] See Henry Jones Ford, *The Rise and Growth of American Politics* (The Macmillan Co., New York, 1898); J. Allen Smith, *The Spirit of American Government* (The Chautauqua Press, Chautauqua, The Macmillan Co., New York, 1911); Charles A. Beard, *An Economic Interpretation of the Constitution of the United States* (The Macmillan Co., New York, 1936); Charles A. Beard, *Economic Origins of Jeffersonian Democracy* (The Macmillan Co., New York, 1915).
[25] 30 *Writings* 186. January 29, 1789.
[26] *Ibid.* 224. Washington to Benjamin Harrison.
[27] *Ibid.* 245. March 23, 1789. Washington to George Steptoe Washington.
[28] *Ibid.* 268.

To Charles Thomson, sent to Mount Vernon to notify Washington of his election, he said the "unanimous suffrages" scarcely left him "the alternative for an option," though he felt his own "inability to perform" the task.[29]

In his official farewell to Alexandria, he spoke of the "painful emotions" involved in deciding to accept or refuse, and asked "what possible advantage" it would afford him to accept. He continued:

> The unanimity of the choice, the opinion of my friends, communicated from different parts of Europe, as well as of America, the apparent wish of those, who were not altogether satisfied with the Constitution in its present form, and an ardent desire on my own part, to be instrumental in conciliating the good will of my countrymen towards each other have induced an acceptance.
>
> . . . no earthly consideration, short of a conviction of duty, could have prevailed upon me to depart from my resolution, *"never more to take any share in transactions of a public nature."* [30]

To the Citizens of Baltimore he declared:

> But having undertaken the task, from a sense of duty, no fear of encountering difficulties and no dread of losing popularity, shall ever deter me from pursuing what I conceive to be the true interests of my Country.[31]

In his First Inaugural Address he referred to himself as

> one who, inheriting inferior endowments from nature and unpracticed in the duties of civil administration. . . .[32]

On May 5, when he had been in office less than a week, he expressed this foreboding:

> . . . I greatly apprehend that my Countrymen will expect too much from me. I fear, if the issue of public measures should not correspond with their sanguine expectations, they will turn the extravagant (and I may say undue) praises which they are heaping upon me at this moment, into equally extravagant (though I will fondly hope unmerited) censures.[33]

In like vein he declared in his reply to an official address from the City of New York:

> . . . the partiality of my Countrymen in my favor has induced them to expect too much from the exertions of an individual. It is from their co-operation alone, I derive all my expectations of success.[34]

Washington was fully aware both that he had no precedents to guide him and that his every act would set a precedent for the future. He

[29] *Ibid.* 285–286. April 14, 1789.
[30] *Ibid.* 286–287. April 16, 1789.
[31] *Ibid.* 288. April 17, 1789.
[32] *Ibid.* 292. April 30, 1789.
[33] *Ibid.* 309.
[34] *Ibid.* 317–318. May 9, 1789.

wrote of "the important and untried task which my country has assigned to me" [35] and observed to Madison:

As the first of every thing, in *our situation* will serve to establish a Precedent, it is devoutly wished on my part, that these precedents may be fixed on true principles.[36]

It seems clear that Washington realized that his reputation, which he deeply cherished, had everything to lose in assuming the responsibilities of the Presidency. The "pillars" of public felicity included harmony, by which conservatives sought to avoid the dangers of party strife,[37] and honesty, which meant supporting the public credit and incidentally promoting that "confidence" which, to conservatives of every age, is endangered by "reform" in the interest of the many.[38] The "general call" gave Washington the hope that he could symbolize a concert of interests along Federalist lines. He realized that his election would do more than anything else could to reconcile the skeptics to the new system. Yet when he thought that party strife might tarnish his name, when he realized his inexperience in politics and civil administration,[39] when he saw how much was expected of him, and when he considered that he might be forced to stand firm against a swing of the pendulum back from conservative reaction to Revolutionary populism, he dreaded the task ahead. Duty as he saw it prevailed; but misgivings could not be dissipated.

[35] *Ibid.* 313. May 9, 1789.
[36] *Ibid.* 310–311. May 5, 1789.
[37] J. Allen Smith, *The Spirit of American Government* (The Chautauqua Press, Chautauqua, The Macmillan Co., New York, 1911) 203 ff; Henry Jones Ford, *The Rise and Growth of American Politics* (The Macmillan Co., New York, 1898) 90 ff.
[38] To Rochambeau Washington wrote on January 29, 1789, "We are on the point of seeing the completion of the new Government, which, by giving motives to labour and security to property, cannot fail to augment beyond all former example the *capital Stock;* that is to say, *the aggregate amount of property* in the Country." 30 *Writings* 189.
[39] *Cf.* Henry Jones Ford, *The Rise and Growth of American Politics* (The Macmillan Co., New York, 1898) 101, 103–104, 118.

Chapter 2

THE PRESIDENT AS CHIEF OF STATE

. . .

THE INAUGURAL CEREMONY

THE FIRST INAUGURATION. The first inaugural ceremony could not be compared in grandeur with a British coronation, but it was charged with symbolism, and Adams fussed over ceremony, as Maclay was in time to fuss against it. Maclay recorded in his journal for April 30:

This is a great, important day. Goddess of etiquette, assist me while I describe it. . . . Turned into the Hall. The crowd already great. The Senate met. The Vice President rose in the most solemn manner. . . . "Gentlemen, I wish for the direction of the Senate. The President will, I suppose, address the Congress. How shall I behave? How shall we receive it? Shall it be standing or sitting?"

. . . Mr. Lee began with the House of Commons (as is usual with him), then the House of Lords, then the King, and then back again. The result of his information was, that the Lords sat and the Commons stood on the delivery of the King's speech. Mr. Izard . . . made . . . this sagacious discovery, that the Commons stood because they had no seats to sit on, being arrived at the bar of the House of Lords. It was discovered after some time that the King sat, too, and had his robes and crown on.

. . . Mr. Carroll got up to declare that he thought it of no consequence how it was in Great Britain; they were no rule to us, etc. . . .

. . . The Speaker was introduced, followed by the Representatives. Here we sat an hour and ten minutes before the President arrived—this delay was owing to Lee, Izard, and Dalton, who had stayed with us while the Speaker came in, instead of going to attend the President. The President advanced between the Senate and Representatives, bowing to each. He was placed in the chair by the Vice-President; the Senate with their President on the right, and the Speaker and the Representatives on his left. The Vice-President rose and addressed a short sentence to him. The import of it was that he should now take the oath of office as President. . . . He finished with a bow, and the

President was conducted out of the middle window into the gallery, and the oath was administered by the Chancellor. Notice that the business was done was communicated to the crowd by proclamation, etc., who gave three cheers, and repeated it on the President's bowing to them.

According to the *Annals,* "the Chancellor proclaimed, 'Long live George Washington, President of the United States.'"[1]

As the company returned into the Senate chamber, the President took the chair and the Senators and Representatives their seats. He rose, and all arose also, and addressed them. . . . This great man was agitated and embarrassed more than ever he was by the leveled cannon or pointed musket. . . . I felt hurt that he was not first in everything. He was dressed in deep brown, with metal buttons, with an eagle on them, white stockings, a bag, and sword.

From the hall there was a grand procession to Saint Paul's Church, where prayers were said by the Bishop. . . . The militia were all under arms, lined the street near the church, made a good figure, and behaved well.

. . . In the evening there were grand fireworks. The Spanish Ambassador's house was adorned with transparent paintings; the French Minister's house was illuminated, and had some transparent pieces; the Hall was grandly illuminated, and after all this the people went to bed.[2]

So natural was the symbolism of the occasion that even Maclay did not object in his journal to the analogy between the "proclamation" of the Chancellor of New York and the time-honored formula of Monarchism: "Long live the King!"

STYLE OF LIVING AND LINE OF CONDUCT

THE QUESTION OF AN APPROPRIATE "STYLE OF LIVING" AND "LINE OF CONDUCT" FOR THE PRESIDENT. To Representative Madison Washington had written from Mount Vernon on March 30, 1789:

. . . it is my wish and intention to conform to the public desire and expectation, with respect to the style proper for the Chief Magistrate to live in, . . .

He added it was well to know first what that desire and expectation was.[3]

Before his inauguration the President-elect appears to have called on

---

[1] 1 *Annals* 27.
[2] *Journal of William Maclay* 6–9. Except for the point taken from the *Annals* as cited in note 1, the above account of the inaugural ceremony is all quoted from these pages of Maclay. See Everett S. Brown, "The Inauguration of George Washington," 45 *Michigan Alumnus,* 213–221 (1939).
[3] 30 *Writings* 255.

the members of Congress. Senator Maclay has left this description of the visit to him and Mr. Wynkoop:

28th April.—This day I ought to note with some extraordinary mark. I had dressed and was about to set out, when General Washington, the greatest man in the world, paid me a visit. I met him at the foot of the stairs. Mr. Wynkoop just came in. We asked him to take a seat. He excused himself on account of the number of his visits. We accompanied him to the door. He made us complaisant bows—one before he mounted and the other as he went away on horseback.[4]

Maclay heard from General St. Clair that the President was "neither to entertain nor to receive invitations," and was to be seen only at his Tuesday and Friday levees. He told the General that for the President "to be seen only in public on stated times, like an Eastern Lama," would be as offensive as for him to be "run down" by a "crowd of visitants" would be impracticable. He would be considered a figurehead, and court paid to his supposed favorite.[5]

In May Washington set methodically about forming a "system" with respect to his "line of conduct," and in characteristic fashion defined the problem in a series of questions which he sent to Adams, Jay, Hamilton and Madison.[6] The balanced judgment by which he habitually sought the middle way is indicated by his reference to a course "equally distant from an association with all kinds of company on the one hand and from a total seclusion from Society on the other."[7] He further clarified the mean at which he aimed in these words:

The President in all matters of business and etiquette, can have no object but to demean himself in his public character, in such a manner as to maintain the dignity of Office, without subjecting himself to the imputation of superciliousness or unnecessary reserve.

The President approached this question with the realization that he would be setting a first precedent:

Many things which appear of little importance in themselves and at the beginning, may have great and durable consequences from their having been established at the commencement of a new general government. It will be much easier to commence the administration, upon a well adjusted system, built on tenable grounds, than to correct errors or alter inconveniences after they shall have been confirmed by habit.[8]

His practical sense also taught him that the "primary object" was to "allow him time for all the official duties of his station." The next object

---

[4] *Journal of William Maclay* 4.
[5] *Ibid.* 15. May 4, 1789.
[6] 30 *Writings* 319–321; 321, note 83; 322–323; 323, note 88.
[7] *Ibid.* 319.
[8] *Ibid.* 321.

was to avoid both the charge of superciliousness and "seclusion from information" by too much reserve and too great a withdrawal from company, and the "inconveniences" and "reduction of respectability" by "too free an intercourse" and "too much familiarity." [9]

Hamilton's position was emphatically that:

The public good requires, as a primary object, that the dignity of the office should be supported.

This aim should be sought "at the risk of partial or momentary dissatisfaction." But Hamilton wanted to "avoid extensive disgust or discontent." He wrote:

Men's minds are prepared for a pretty high tone in the demeanor of the executive, but I doubt whether for so high a tone as in the abstract might be desirable. The notions of equality are yet, in my opinion, too general and too strong to admit of such a distance being placed between the President and other branches of the government as might even be consistent with a due proportion. . . .

After discussing levees, formal entertainments, and dinners, Hamilton continued:

It is an important point to consider what persons may have access to your Excellency on business. The heads of departments will, of course, have this privilege. Foreign ministers of some descriptions will also be entitled to it. In Europe, I am informed, ambassadors only have direct access to the chief magistrate. Something very near what prevails there would, in my opinion, be right. . . . I have thought that the members of the Senate should also have a right of *individual* access on matters relative to the *public administration*. In England and France peers of the realm have this right. We have none such in this country, but I believe that it will be satisfactory to the people to know that there is some body of men in the state who have a right of continual communication with the President. It will be considered a safeguard against secret combinations to deceive him.

There was danger that the Representatives would be offended unless granted the same privilege; but Hamilton fell back upon the constitutional prerogatives of the Senate:

But there is a reason for the distinction in the Constitution. The Senate are coupled with the President in certain executive functions, treaties, and appointments. This makes them in a degree his constitutional counsellors, and gives them a *peculiar* claim to the right of access. . . . [10]

[9] *Ibid.* 322–323.
[10] 4 *Works of Hamilton* (John C. Hamilton, ed., Charles S. Francis & Co., New York, 1851) 1–3. For some reason this letter is dated May 5, though it purports to be in reply to a presidential inquiry, and the queries are dated May 10. For Vice President Adams's reply see 8 *The Works of John Adams* (Charles Francis Adams, ed., Little, Brown and

In July David Stuart in a frank letter to the President reported the popular disapproval of imitations of monarchy:

Mr. Henry's description of it [the new government], that it squinted towards monarchy, is in every mouth, and has established him in the general opinion, as a true Prophet.

Stuart thus stated the symbolism involved from the popular, as distinguished from the Hamiltonian, point of view:

As trivial as this may appear, it appears to be more captivating to the generality, than matters of more importance . . . an error of judgment is more easily pardoned, than one of the heart.

In contrast with the "clamor and abuse" against John Adams, Washington was praised for "dispensing with ceremony occasionally, and walking the streets." [11]

In his reply to Stuart the President thought the "motives" of his "system," which had been indispensable on his first coming to New York, had been misunderstood. This system he described as involving three points. The first was "returning *no* visits." The second was appointing certain days to receive them generally, with exceptions in special circumstances. The third was at first entertaining no company, and afterwards only "official characters."

The President then embarked upon a lengthy defense of his system. The first two points had been shown necessary in the first few days; for otherwise

I should have been unable to attend to *any* sort of business unless I had applied the hours allotted to rest and refreshment to this purpose for by the time I had done breakfast, and thence till dinner, and afterwards till bed time I could not get relieved from the ceremony of one visit before I had to attend to another; in a word, I had no leisure to read or to answer the dispatches that were pouring in upon me from all quarters.

As for the third point, he had been early informed through "very respectable channels" that it was no less essential

---

Co., Boston, 1853) 491–493. That the President sought the advice of the Vice President might have developed into an historic precedent.

For a summary of the "system" actually adopted by the President, see Jared Sparks, *The Life of George Washington* (Tappan and Dennet, Boston, 1844) 412–414.

[11] 30 *Writings* 362, note 60. Washington did walk upon occasion. Examples are recorded in the *Diaries*. On various occasions he walked round the Battery. 4 *Diaries* 14, 15, 57, 58. See also *ibid.* 56. Patrick Henry's remark about the new system's squinting toward monarchy had been made in the Virginia ratifying convention. 3 *Elliot's Debates* (J. B. Lippincott Co., Philadelphia, 1937 printing in 5 volumes) 58. David Stuart, who wrote the letter to Washington which is quoted and digested in the text above, had also been a member of that convention. *Ibid.* 654, 662.

if the President was to preserve the dignity and respect that was due to the first Magistrate, for that a contrary conduct had involved the late President of Congress in insuperable difficulties, and the office (in this respect) in perfect contempt. for the table was considered as a public one, and every person, who could get introduced, conceived that he had a *right* to be invited to it. This, although the table was always crowded (and with mixed company, and the President considered in no better light than as a Maitre d'Hôtel) was in its nature impracticable and as many offences given as if no table had been kept.

The citizens of New York knew this, and the principal members of both houses had been so convinced of "the degrading situation of their President" that it was "the general opinion" that the President of the United States should "neither give or receive invitations." Some advocated this policy from a belief "that it was fundamentally right in order to acquire respect."

Washington, however, had had two powerful objections to so rigid a rule: (1) its novelty would be considered "an ostentatious shew of mimicry of sovereignty"; and (2) "so great a seclusion would have stopped the avenues to useful information from the many, and make me more dependent on that of the few."

Yet a "discriminating medium" was difficult; "for if the citizens at large were begun upon no line could be drawn." On the whole, then, he had thought it best to confine *his* invitations to official characters and strangers of distinction. This had been his practice hitherto, but whether to depart from it in some measure had to be the result of "experience and information."

So strongly had the local citizens imbibed the idea of the impropriety of his accepting invitations to dinner, that he had received none except for dining with the Governor on the day of his arrival:

so that, if this should be adduced as an article of impeachment there can be at least *one* good reason adduced for my not dining out; to wit never having been asked to do so.[12]

[12] 30 *Writings* 360–362. July 26, 1789. Washington had no rule against making informal visits to official characters. Thus on October 14, 1789, before starting his New England tour, he called with his lady upon the Count de Moustier and Madame Brehan. 4 *Diaries* 20. On November 23 he called on the Dutch minister and Mr. Adams. *Ibid.* 54. Two days later he called on Jay and Knox on matters of business, made informal calls on Governor George Clinton and others, and then went with his wife to the "dancing assembly." *Ibid.* 55. On December 2 he visited the Vice President and his family and then walked to see Senator Rufus King. *Ibid.* 56. December 15 he called on Knox to give him "the heads" of letters to Westerners, mainly on Indian affairs. *Ibid.* 58. December 16 he and his family *dined* with Governor George Clinton along with the Vice President and Mrs. Adams, the Mayor, and others. *Ibid.* 59. However, on November 15, Washington declined an invitation to attend the funeral of Mrs. Isaac

Maclay was invited to share the President's box at the theater.[13] He deplored the presidential levees as interfering with Senate business and tending toward court etiquette.[14] Invited to one of the President's dinners, he found the food excellent, the room warm, and the solemnity oppressive.[15]

In October Washington wrote to ask Gouverneur Morris, who was abroad, to get him mirrors for a table, "with neat and fashionable but not expensive ornaments for them." The frames might be "plated ware, or any thing else more fashionable but not more expensive." He also wanted wine coolers of plated ware for dinner and after-dinner wines:

One idea however I must impress you with and that is in whole or part to avoid extravagance. For extravagance would not comport with my own inclination, nor with the example which ought to be set.[16]

The style of living and line of conduct were made delicate problems by the difference of opinion between those who would promote imitations of monarchy and those who wanted to cultivate republican simplicity. As the spokesman of the latter view Senator Maclay doubtless represented the masses. The difference was symbolic of the difference between the revolutionary trend toward democracy and the Federalist reaction. The problem was intensified by the experimental character of the American Presidency. For the framers had projected into a monarchist world an officer who was neither a king nor a prime minister, but whose position as the *chef d'état* and chief executive was, as Theodore Roosevelt once put it, "almost that of a king and a prime minister rolled into one."[17]

REFUSAL TO ACCEPT PECUNIARY COMPENSATION

WASHINGTON'S REFUSAL TO ACCEPT A PRESIDENTIAL SALARY. In his First Inaugural Address Washington, directing his remarks particularly to the House of Representatives, declared that, when first called by his

---

Roosevelt, wife of a New York senator, because he questioned the propriety, and because, if it were proper in this case, he might find it hard to "discriminate" thereafter. *Ibid.* 52. Interestingly enough, December 29 was such a snowy day that not a soul attended the levee! *Ibid.* 61.
[13] *Journal of William Maclay* 29–30. May 11, 1789.
[14] *Ibid* 67. See index for references to levees.
[15] *Ibid.* 134–135. August 27, 1789.
[16] 30 *Writings* 443–445. October 13, 1789.
[17] From a letter from Theodore Roosevelt to Lady Delamere, March 7, 1911, reproduced in facsimile at the end of Lord Charnwood, *Theodore Roosevelt* (Atlantic Monthly Press, Little, Brown and Co., Boston, 1923) 223.

Country, "the high light in which I contemplated my duty required that I should renounce every pecuniary compensation." From this he had never departed, and he "must decline as inapplicable to myself, any share in the personal emoluments, which may be indispensably included in a permanent provision for the Executive Department." So he asked that the estimates, while he was in office, be "limited to such actual expenditures as the public good may be thought to require."[18] An editor's note points out that for the eight years of his incumbency the expenditures were almost exactly what the salary at the prevailing rate would have been.[19] Even so, however, the refusal of Washington to accept "pecuniary compensation" was symbolic of his conscious role as what Lord Byron so well called the "Cincinnatus of the West."[20] In symbolic terms it set a standard of service for all future Presidents.

A PRESIDENTIAL TOUR

WASHINGTON'S TOUR OF NEW ENGLAND. As early as May, 1789, Washington had in mind the possibility of a tour after the adjournment of Congress. In his queries on a line of conduct he asked:

8th. Whether, during the recess of Congress, it would not be advantageous to the interests of the Union for the President to make the tour of the United States, in order to become better acquainted with their principal Characters and internal Circumstances, as well as to be more accessible to numbers of well-informed persons, who might give him useful information and advices on political subjects?[21]

In October Hamilton, Knox, and Jay approved the contemplated tour of New England, and Madison saw nothing improper in it. Jay said the South would expect a tour of that section.[22]

[18] 30 *Writings* 295-296.   [19] *Ibid.* 296, note 49.
[20] "Where may the wearied eye repose
When gazing on the Great;
Where neither guilty glory glows,
Nor despicable state?
Yes—one—the first—the last—the best—
The Cincinnatus of the West,
Whom envy dared not hate,
Bequeath'd the name of Washington,
To make man blush there was but one!"
—"Ode to Napoleon Buonaparte," stanza xix. 2 *Poetical Works of Lord Byron* (in 6 vols., John Murray, London, 1855) 9.
[21] 30 *Writings* 320. See 5 *The Writings of Thomas Jefferson* (Washington ed., Derby & Jackson, New York, 1859) 101-102, for President Jefferson's reaction in 1807 to the suggestion that he make a northern tour.
[22] 4 *Diaries* 14-17 (October 5-8, 1789).

On October 12, Washington wrote to his sister that he proposed

> in two or three days to set out for Boston by way of relaxation from business and reestablishment of my health after the long and tedious complaint with which I have been afflicted, . . .[23]

The next day he wrote Gouverneur Morris that

> in the morning I commence a tour, though rather late in the season, through the States eastward of this.[24]

In offering Mr. Jefferson the position of Secretary of State he wrote:

> Being on the eve of a journey through the Eastern States, with a view to observe the situation of the Country, and in a hope of perfectly reestablishing my health, . . .[25]

The constitutional significance of the tour was that it was a visit of the ceremonial head of state to one of the principal sections of the Union.[26] His progress from Mount Vernon to New York for his inauguration had taken him on a triumphal march through the middle states;[27] and he was later to visit Rhode Island,[28] after it joined the Union, and to make a tour of the South.[29] On the present tour he did not visit Rhode Island or Vermont.[30]

THE OFFICIAL PRECEDENCE OF THE PRESIDENT

THE OFFICIAL PRECEDENCE OF THE PRESIDENT: THE HANCOCK INCIDENT. The official precedence of the President of the United States was dramatized in a great precedent when Washington visited Boston, the principal town in New England and the capital of the great State of Massachusetts. A few miles from Brookfield a letter was delivered to

---

[23] 30 *Writings* 436.   [24] *Ibid.* 445.   [25] *Ibid.* 446–447.
[26] For a list of complimentary addresses to the President on this tour and of his replies, see *Ibid.* 453, note 14.
[27] Everett S. Brown, "The Inauguration of George Washington," 45 *Michigan Alumnus* 213, 215–218 (1939).
[28] 31 *Writings* 94–95, note 65. August, 1790. See *Ibid.* 47–48.
[29] *Ibid.* 250–292. March-June, 1791. See Jared Sparks, *The Life of George Washington* (Tappan and Dennet, Boston, 1844) 421, 429, 434. Sparks said the southern tour covered 1887 miles "with the same horses, without a single accident, and practically according to an original schedule." P. 434. *Cf.* 31 *Writings* 294.
[30] 30 *Writings* 453, note 14. See *ibid.* 455–456 for a generous gesture to the children of a household where he stopped on his New England tour, and the remark in sending the gifts: "As I do not give these things with a view to have it talked of, or even to its being known, the less there is said about the matter the better you [the father] will please me." Thus did Washington spurn the wiles of the seeker of popular favor.

the President from Governor John Hancock of Massachusetts. Washington replied that he was highly sensible of the honor intended him, but would wish to visit Boston without any parade or extraordinary ceremony. He had determined on leaving New York to decline the honor of any invitation for quarters on his journey, in order to avoid troubling private families, and so had requested that lodgings be engaged for him in Boston.[31]

The next day Washington acknowledged from Weston another letter from the Governor, informed him of a change of plans made at the suggestion of gentlemen from Boston and the Deputy Adjutant General, and added:

I will do myself the honor to accept your Excellency's polite invitation of taking an informal dinner with you.[32]

When the President finally got to Boston, he found that Lieutenant Governor Samuel Adams had been sent by the Governor to welcome him at the town limits; but his entrance was delayed by a dispute between the Lieutenant Governor and the town officials as to who had the right to welcome him to the town. The town authorities won the argument.[33]

Since the Governor failed to pay Washington the first visit, the latter called off the dinner engagement and dined at his lodgings, having at dinner with him Vice President John Adams.[34] By this action Washington asserted the official precedence of the President of the United States over the Governor of a State, the only possible rival for such precedence in the whole governmental system of the country.

On Sunday[35] the Governor sent a note to the President saying if the President was at home and at leisure he would call in half an hour, and that he would have done so sooner

had his health in any degree permitted. He now hazards every thing as it respects his health, for the desirable purpose.[36]

The President's reply, written at 1 o'clock, presented his best respects to the Governor, stated he would be at home till 2 o'clock, and added:

The President of the United States need not express the pleasure it will give him to see the Governor; but, at the same time, he most earnestly begs that the Governor will not hazard his health on the occasion.[37]

[31] Ibid. 451–452. October 22, 1789.
[32] Ibid. 452–453.
[33] Ibid. 452, note 13.
[34] Ibid. 453, note 14.
[35] An editorial note speaks of Sunday, October 25, but the exchange of notes is as of October 26. See Ibid. 453–454 and notes 14 and 16.
[36] Ibid. 453–454, note 16.
[37] Ibid. 453.

An editorial note states that "Hancock claimed to have a severe attack of the gout and was carried by retainers into Washington's presence."[38] If this was a face-saving device, it merely emphasized the triumph of the Presidency in this battle of official etiquette.

The *Diaries* leave no doubt that the President stood expressly on his precedence. Washington recorded that he had accepted Hancock's invitation to an informal dinner "under a full persuasion that he would have waited upon me so soon as I should have arrived," and that, when the Governor sent word through his Secretary that he was too indisposed to do so, he excused himself, "being resolved to receive the visit." When the Governor sent the Lieutenant Governor and two of his Council to express his "concern" that he had not been able to call upon the President "so soon as I came to Town,"

I informed them in explicit terms that I should not see the Gov'r unless it was at my own lodgings.

The Governor was received on Sunday between attendance at the Episcopal church in the forenoon and at the Congregational church in the afternoon.[39] This denominational impartiality was in itself symbolic.

It is an interesting study to follow the accumulation over the years of other forms in which the position of the President as the first citizen of the Republic has been given official or customary recognition.

SOME PRONOUNCEMENTS OF THE FIRST INAUGURAL ADDRESS

PRESIDENTIAL INVOCATION OF THE DEITY. Presidential invocation of the Deity began with George Washington's First Inaugural Address:

... it would be peculiarly improper to omit in this first official act, my fervent supplications to that Almighty Being who rules over the Universe, ... that his benediction may consecrate to the liberties and happiness of the People of the United States, a Government instituted by themselves for these essential purposes: ...

---

[38] *Ibid.* 453-454, note 16.
[39] 4 *Diaries* 35-36. Monday evening the President had tea with the Governor. *Ibid.* 36. On Tuesday he received addresses, including one from the Governor and Council, and in the evening was given a dinner at "Fanuiel [sic] Hall" by the Governor and Council. *Ibid.* 37.
   Washington himself was careful of the proprieties. On October 23 he said that when he went to Boston it would be improper for him to *review* the militia or see them maneuver except as a "private man," and hence he could do no more than pass along the line, which might, if General Brooks thought proper, be under arms to receive him. *Ibid.* 32.

He continued:

No People can be bound to acknowledge and adore the invisible hand, which conducts the Affairs of men more than the People of the United States. Every step, by which they have advanced to the character of an independent nation, seems to have been distinguished by some token of providential agency.

In the recent revolution in the system of their United Government, he went on,

the tranquil deliberations and voluntary consent of so many distinct communities, from which the event has resulted, cannot be compared with the means by which most Governments have been established, without some return of pious gratitude. . . .[40]

This was the first official pronouncement in the deliberate process by which the Constitution was in a remarkably short time made the Ark of our Covenant.[41]

WASHINGTON ON THE AMERICAN EXPERIMENT AS THE TEST OF REPUBLICANISM. In his First Inaugural Address as President of the newly reorganized American system of government, which was a republic in a monarchist world, Washington also solemnly declared:

. . . the preservation of the sacred fire of liberty, and the destiny of the Republican model of government, are justly considered as *deeply,* perhaps as *finally* staked, on the experiment entrusted to the hands of the American people.[42]

In so saying he seemed to imply, though delicately, that if republican excesses led to a monarchist reaction in America, it would tend to show that our dream was but an illusion.

REPLIES TO ADDRESSES

THE CONSTITUTIONAL SIGNIFICANCE OF REPLIES TO ADDRESSES. An address to the President became a mode by which organizations and official bodies of various sorts complimented the President or expressed to him their views; and his replies became a form of pronouncement by the President as chief of state. Even when the replies were perfunctory,

[40] 30 *Writings* 292–293.
[41] See below, p. 22, Washington's reference to the Constitution as our "Magna-Charta."
[42] 30 *Writings* 294–295. April 30, 1789.

they represented the symbolic aspect of the President as head of the nation. Some of Washington's replies contained sentiments which are worthy of being recorded.

WASHINGTON ON AMERICA'S MISSION. The idea that the United States has a world mission, to be fulfilled by her political example, has persisted from the first. President Washington gave his form of the idea in his reply to an address of the Legislature of Pennsylvania:

It should be the highest ambition of every American to extend his views beyond himself, and to bear in mind that his conduct will not only affect himself, his country, and his immediate posterity; but that its influence may be coextensive with the world, and stamp political happiness or misery on ages yet unborn. To establish this desirable end; and to establish the government of *laws,* the union of these States is absolutely necessary; therefore in every proceeding, this great, this important object should ever be kept in view; and, so long as our measures tend to this; and are marked with the wisdom of a well-informed and enlightened people, we may reasonably hope, under the smiles of Heaven, to convince the world that the happiness of nations can be accomplished by pacific revolutions in their political systems, without the destructive intervention of the sword.[43]

WASHINGTON ON RELIGION AND GOVERNMENT. Some time after October 9 Washington said in his reply to the address of the Synod of the Dutch Reformed Church in North America:

I readily join with you that "while just government protects all in their religious rights, true religion affords to government its surest support." [44]

In the reply made on his tour of New England to an address from the ministers and elders representing the Massachusetts and New Hampshire churches of the First Presbytery of the Eastward, Newburyport, he stated:

I am persuaded, you will permit me to observe that the path of true piety is so plain as to require but little political direction. To this consideration we ought to ascribe the absence of any regulation, respecting religion, from the Magna-Charta of our country. To the guidance of the ministers of the gospel this important object is, perhaps, more properly committed. It will be your care to instruct the ignorant, and to reclaim the devious, and, in the progress of morality and science, to which our government will give every furtherance, we may confidently expect the advancement of true religion, and the completion of our happiness.[45]

[43] *Ibid.* 395, note 13. The date of the address to which the reply was sent was September 5, 1789.
[44] *Ibid.* 432, note 83. [45] *Ibid.* 453, note 14.

WASHINGTON ON RELIGIOUS LIBERTY AND CONSCIENTIOUS OBJECTION. In his reply to an address from an annual regional meeting of Quakers, the President said:

> Government being, among other purposes, instituted to protect the persons and consciences of men from oppression, it certainly is the duty of rulers, not only to abstain from it themselves, but, according to their stations, to prevent it in others.
>
> The liberty enjoyed by the people of these States, of worshipping Almighty God agreeably to their consciences, is not only among the choicest of their *blessings,* but also of their *rights.* While men perform their social duties faithfully, they do all that society or the state can with propriety demand or expect; and remain responsible only to their Maker for the religion, or modes of faith, which they may prefer or profess.
>
> Your principles and conduct are well known to me; and it is doing the people called Quakers no more than justice to say, that (except their declining to share with others the burthen of the common defense) there is no denomination among us, who are more exemplary and useful citizens.
>
> I assure you very explicitly, that in my opinion the conscientious scruples of all men should be treated with great delicacy and tenderness; and it is my wish and desire, that the laws may always be as extensively accommodated to them, as a due regard to the protection and essential interests of the nation may justify and permit.[46]

REPLY TO THE ADDRESS OF THE GENERAL ASSEMBLY OF GEORGIA. An address to the President from the General Assembly of Georgia under the date of December 22, 1789, after the failure to make a treaty with the Creeks, mentioned also the escape of slaves into Spanish territory, which, it said, "if not speedily restrained may grow into an evil of national magnitude." In his reply the President said:

> I am not ignorant how much the local situation of your State exposed its inhabitants to suffer the distresses of the late war in a severe manner; nor how manfully they exerted themselves in the common cause during the struggle which established our independence. Wasted as your country was at the return of peace, and exposed as your frontiers have since been to the ravages of the Indians, I cannot but flatter myself that you will ere long realize the blessings, which were to be expected from your natural resources, and find a compensation from your sufferings in the benefits of an efficient general government.
>
> It will not be expected I presume, on this occasion, that I should enter into the merits of the delicate subject to which you allude. It may be sufficient to say, that, while I regret extremely the failure of the late negociation for peace with the Creek-Indians; I am satisfied that the explanations which have been

[46] *Ibid.* 416, note 54. The address to which this was the reply was dated September 28, 1789.

received through authentic channels will be of eminent service. I am also convinced that nothing will be wanting on your part to concur in the accomplishment of a pacification; and I still hope that under the influence of the general Government that desirable object may be effected. With respect to this subject in general, as well as to the other calamity which you mention as resulting from your being the south frontier of the Union, I request you will be persuaded, that I shall make such use of the powers vested in me by the constitution as may appear to me best calculated to promote the public good.[47]

THE PROCLAMATION OF A DAY OF THANKSGIVING

"THE FIRST NATIONAL THANKSGIVING DAY PROCLAMATION UNDER THE CONSTITUTION."[48] On September 25 Boudinot moved in the House a resolution calling for a joint committee of both houses to wait on the President, to request him to recommend to the people of the United States a day of public thanksgiving and prayer,

to be observed by acknowledging, with grateful hearts, the many signal favors of Almighty God, especially by affording them an opportunity peaceably to establish a Constitution of government for their safety and happiness.

Immediately Burke said he

did not like this mimicking of European customs, where they made a mere mockery of thanksgivings. Two parties at war frequently sung *Te Deum* for the same event, though to one it was a victory, and to the other a defeat.

Boudinot distinguished the use of a good thing from its abuse, and considered the measure to be "both prudent and just." But Tucker objected:

Why should the President direct the people to do what, perhaps, they have no mind to do? They may not be inclined to return thanks for a Constitution until they have experienced that it promotes their safety and happiness. We do not yet know but they may have reason to be dissatisfied with the effects it has already produced; but whether this be so or not, it is a business with which Congress have nothing to do; it is a religious matter, and, as such, is proscribed to us. If a day of thanksgiving must take place, let it be done by the authority of the several States; . . .

Sherman came to Boudinot's support by appealing to precedents in holy writ for thanksgiving on any signal event, citing as an example the

---

[47] *Ibid.* 481, note 61. For the report of the commissioners on their failure to effect a treaty with the Creek Nation see 1 *American State Papers, Indian Affairs* (Gales and Seaton, Washington, 1832) 68 ff.
[48] 30 *Writings* 428, note 79.

thanksgiving and rejoicing in the time of Solomon after the building of the temple. Then after Boudinot quoted precedents from the practice of the late Congress, the question on the resolution was carried in the affirmative.[49] The resolution was adopted by the Senate on the following day.[50]

The result was the first Thanksgiving proclamation under the Constitution, which was apparently also the first presidential proclamation. The President noted that both houses had made the request, and said he did "recommend and assign" Thursday, November 26, "to be devoted" to the purpose. He mentioned as one of the causes of thanksgiving

the peaceable and rational manner in which we have been enabled to establish constitutions of government for our safety and happiness, and particularly the national One now lately instituted, . . .

Another cause was "the civil and religious liberty with which we are blessed." Among the supplications, which extended to "all Sovereigns and Nations (especially such as have shown kindness unto us)" and finally to "all Mankind," was one to beseech "the great Lord and Ruler of Nations"

to pardon our national and other transgressions, to enable us all, whether in public or private stations, to perform our several and relative duties properly and punctually, to render our national government a blessing to all the People, by constantly being a government of wise, just and constitutional laws, discreetly and faithfully executed and obeyed, . . .[51]

Thanksgiving Day has become a national holiday which derives some of its tradition from the fact that the first Thanksgiving Day under the Constitution was proclaimed by the father of his country in the first year of his Presidency. Boudinot, the mover of the House resolution, pretty evidently wanted thanksgiving for the establishment of government under the Constitution to be emphasized. Tucker, on the other hand, thought such a move premature, and seemed to sense the purpose to sanctify the Constitution in the eyes of the people. When it is considered that in the minds of many of them the new system was still on trial, that purpose can scarcely be doubted; and the text of the proclamation tended to promote it. According to their premises, the approaches of Boudinot and Tucker were both natural.

[49] 1 *Annals* 949–950.
[50] *Ibid.* 92, 958–959.
[51] 30 *Writings* 427–428. The proclamation was dated October 3, 1789. On November 26 Washington attended the thanksgiving service at St. Paul's; but the weather was bad, and few persons were there. 4 *Diaries* 55.

THE USE AND FORM OF PROCLAMATIONS

THE USE AND FORM OF PRESIDENTIAL PROCLAMATIONS. The resolution of Congress asking the President to recommend a day of public thanksgiving and prayer did not specify the mode in which the recommendation was to be made;[52] but it was natural for the mode employed to be a proclamation. For many thanksgiving proclamations had been issued from colonial days. The first one known to be extant is said to bear the date of 1676.[53] Merely for example, one was issued by the acting governor of New York in 1760,[54] and another by the United States in Congress assembled in 1783, recommending it to the several states to set aside a stated day for the purpose.[55] It is said that the *Journals* of the Continental Congress record eight such recommendations.[56]

With this background the first presidential proclamation of a thanksgiving day is scarcely to be put down as an imitation of monarchy; though the proclamation was a mode by which English kings had long made things known to their subjects in the most solemn, formal manner; the power of proclamations had played an important part in English constitutional history;[57] and the short-lived Statute of Proclamations probably remains the most far-reaching delegation of legislative power to the executive in the whole history of Anglo-American jurisprudence.[58] A thanksgiving proclamation is but a hortatory[59] proclamation, and does not purport to have legislative force or indeed any legal effects. Such a proclamation is appropriately issued by any head of state.

[52] See the preceding section of this study.
[53] Robert F. Roden, *The Cambridge Press, 1638–1692* (Dodd, Mead & Co., New York, 1905) 177.
[54] *Proclamations for Thanksgiving, issued by the Continental Congress, Pres't. Washington, etc.* (Franklin B. Hough, ed., Munsell & Rowland, Albany, 1858) 1–3. A copy of this publication is in the Tracy W. McGregor Library of the University of Virginia.
[55] *Ibid.* 23–25.
[56] *Ibid.* viii.
[57] George Burton Adams, *Constitutional History of England* (Henry Holt and Co., New York, 1921) 252, 274 ff; 1 Sir William R. Anson, *The Law and Custom of the Constitution* (The Clarendon Press, Oxford, 1911) 243–245, 320–325; A. V. Dicey, *Introduction to the Study of the Law of the Constitution* (8th ed., Macmillan & Co., London, 1920) 48–52; 12 Co. Rep. 74 (1610); George Burton Adams and H. Morse Stephens, *Select Documents of English Constitutional History* (The Macmillan Co., New York, 1908) 334–337.
[58] A. V. Dicey, *Introduction to the Study of the Law of the Constitution* (8th ed., Macmillan & Co., London, 1920) 48–51; George Burton Adams and H. Morse Stephens, *Select Documents of English Constitutional History* (The Macmillan Co., New York, 1908) 247–250.
[59] James Hart, *The Ordinance Making Powers of the President* (The Johns Hopkins Press, Baltimore, 1925) 316.

THE PRESIDENT AS CHIEF OF STATE 27

The form of presidential proclamations has been much the same from the Administration of Washington.[60] That form bears resemblance to the form used by His Britannic Majesty;[61] but it is not to be inferred that it was itself an imitation of monarchy by the first President. It may be that proclamations of all sorts took their form from the royal form; but the form was already more or less standardized in America before 1789.[62]

The presidential form may be briefly indicated. First comes the heading:

> "By the President of the United States of America.
> "A Proclamation."

The first proclamation does not have this heading in the *Writings of Washington*[63] or *Messages and Papers of the Presidents*;[64] but it was so published in both the *Pennsylvania Gazette*[65] and the *Maryland Gazette*.[66] This form of heading appeared in the congressional proclamation of 1783 mentioned above. Next comes the preamble, which has one or more of the well-known "Whereas" clauses. These appeared in the first proclamation. Next comes the body of the document, which opens with, "Now, therefore, I . . ." In the proclamation of September 15, 1792, the opening words first took the form, "Now, therefore, I, George Washington, President of the United States."[67] Lastly, comes the formula of attestation, the signature of the President, and the countersignature of the Secretary of State below the seal. The formula is not given in *Writings of Washington* for the first proclamation, but

[60] Cf. ibid. 316–317.
[61] 1 Sir William R. Anson, *The Law and Custom of the Constitution* (The Clarendon Press, Oxford, 1911) 53–54. Note the use of the royal "we" instead of the presidential "I." See also 3 William Stubbs, *The Constitutional History of England* (5th ed., The Clarendon Press, Oxford, 1903) 481–483; 1 Michael MacDonagh, *The Pageant of Parliament* (T. Fisher Unwin, Ltd., London, 1921) 34.
[62] See in *Proclamations for Thanksgiving*, cited above, the form of the proclamations of the acting governor of New York in 1760 and of the Congress in 1783. The heading of the latter was:
> "By the United States in Congress assembled.
> "A Proclamation."

[63] 30 *Writings* 427–428.
[64] 1 *Messages and Papers of the Presidents* 56.
[65] *Pennsylvania Gazette*, October 14, 1789, p. 3. This was examined from a microfilm copy in the Tracy W. McGregor Library of the University of Virginia.
[66] *Maryland Gazette*, October 15, 1789, p. 3. This was examined from a microfilm copy in the Tracy W. McGregor Library of the University of Virginia. In the *Proclamations for Thanksgiving* cited above, the first proclamation of Washington is printed on pp. 30–32, with the heading "Proclamation."
[67] 1 *Messages and Papers of the Presidents* 116–117. This form of the opening words of the body does not, however, appear in some later proclamations. Cf. ibid. 129, 148, 149, with ibid. 152, 153, 172.

appears in the form in which the proclamation was published in the two newspapers mentioned above, and in *Messages and Papers of the Presidents*. In the latter it reads for this first proclamation:

Given under my hand, at the city of New York, the 3d day of October, A.D. 1789.[68]

This formula was first used in what became a more or less standardized form in a proclamation of January 24, 1791:

In testimony whereof I have caused the seal of the United States to be affixed to these presents and signed the same with my hand. Done at the City of Philadelphia the 24th day of January, A.D. 1791, and of the Independence of the United States of America the fifteenth.[69]

There may be variation of detail from time to time; but the statement of the date in terms of the Independence of the United States as well as of Our Lord has become traditional.[70] Nor did this originate with presidential proclamations. It was so done in the congressional proclamation of 1783 mentioned above. The first proclamation had no countersignature; but a proclamation of the next August had at the left, below the seal:

"By the President:
Th: Jefferson." [71]

IMITATIONS OF MONARCHY

THE SPEECH AND THE ADDRESSES IN REPLY. The address to the second session of Congress, delivered in the Senate Chamber on January 8, 1790, is listed as the first annual address of Washington.[72] The address which he delivered immediately after taking the oath of office on April 30, 1789, however, served in effect as an inaugural address and annual message rolled into one. It was delivered to both houses, and both houses made addresses in reply, to which the President responded by his replies. The analogy to the speech from the throne and the address in reply in the British monarchy is unmistakable.[73]

[68] *Ibid.* 56. [69] *Ibid.* 93.
[70] It appeared in a proclamation of Washington dated August 14, 1790, with reference to the "Sovereignty and Independence of the United States." *Ibid.* 72. *Cf. ibid.* 93, 94, 95.
[71] *Ibid.* 72. [72] 30 *Writings* 491.
[73] See 1 Michael MacDonagh, *The Pageant of Parliament* (T. Fisher Unwin, Ltd., London, 1921) 201–223 (chaps. XVII and XVIII). See p. 219 for reference to "most gracious speech."

The next day the analogy was brought into sharp relief in the Senate. In Maclay's own words,

May 1st.—Attended at the Hall at eleven. The prayers were over and the minutes reading. When we came to the minute of the speech it stood, *His most gracious speech*. I looked all around the Senate. Every countenance seemed to wear a blank. The Secretary was going on; I must speak or nobody would. "Mr. President, we have lately had a hard struggle for our liberty against kingly authority. The minds of men are still heated: everything related to that species of government is odious to the people. The words prefixed to the President's speech are the same that are usually placed before the speech of his Britannic Majesty. I know they will give offense. I consider them as improper. I therefore move that they be struck out, and that it stand simply address or speech, as may be judged most suitable."

The Vice President "rose in his chair" and expressed surprise that there should be objection to following the practice of that government "under which we had lived so long and happily formerly." Adams said he was for "a dignified and respectable government," and as far as he knew, the people thought as he did;

that for his part he was one of the first in the late contest [the Revolution] and, if *he could have thought of this, he never would have drawn his sword.*

"Painful as it was," Maclay had to argue with the Chair. He said there had been a "revolution" in popular sentiments respecting government; that "even the modes" of British monarchy were now "abhorred"; that the enemies of the Constitution had made the objection that under it there could with facility be a transition to "kingly government and all the trappings and splendor of royalty," and would point to this phrase in the Senate minutes as "the first step of the ladder in the ascent to royalty."

Adams rose again and said he had mentioned it to the Secretary and could not possibly conceive that any person could take offense at it. Maclay got up again to say his opposition sprang solely from a sense of duty. Adams remained standing, and said he had been long abroad, and did not know the present temper of the people. Reed favored the phrase, and said the Senate would be at a loss to do business if it avoided British words. "I had to reply," says Maclay. Lee had said a word or two on Maclay's side, but when Adams said he had been responsible, Lee got up and informed the chair he had not known that fact.

Maclay won out:

The question was put and carried for erasing the words without a division.

After adjournment Adams took Maclay aside and talked at length on efficient government and respect for General Washington. Maclay said he "would yield to no person" in respect for Washington and favored efficient government, and that nothing but a sense of duty could have forced him to oppose the chair. Adams then made Maclay a long talk on "checks to government and the balance of power," and since he seemed to expect an answer,

I caught at the last word, and said undoubtedly without a balance there could be no equilibrium, and so left him hanging in geometry.

In his journal Maclay made the incident the occasion for reflections on the American Revolution:

The unequivocal declaration that he would never have drawn his sword, etc., has drawn my mind to the following remarks: that the motives of the actors in the late Revolution were various can not be doubted. The abolishing of royalty, the extinguishment of patronage and dependencies attached to that form of government, were the exalted motives of many revolutionists, and these were the improvements meant by them to be made of the war which was forced on us by British aggression—in fine, the amelioration of government and bettering the condition of mankind. These ends and none other were publicly avowed, and all our constitutions and public acts were formed in this spirit. Yet there were not wanting a party whose motives were different. They wished for the loaves and fishes of government, and cared for nothing else but a translation of the diadem and scepter from London to Boston, New York, or Philadelphia; or, in other words, the creation of a new monarchy in America, and to form niches for themselves in the temple of royalty.

This spirit manifested itself strongly among the officers at the close of the war, and I have been afraid the army would not have been disbanded if the common soldiers could have been kept together. This spirit they developed in the Order of Cincinnati, where I trust it will spend itself in a harmless flame and soon become extinguished. That Mr. Adams should, however, so unequivocally avow this motive, at a time when a republican form of government is secured to every State in the Union, appears to me a mark of extreme folly.[74]

On May 7 the Senate committee reported an answer to the President's speech. There was objection to the part which stated

the United States had been in *anarchy* and *confusion,* and the President stepping in and *rescuing* them.

This led to a long debate, in which the words were struck out. Lee offered part of a sentence which Maclay thought proper, but which

[74] *Journal of William Maclay* 9–12.

THE PRESIDENT AS CHIEF OF STATE 31

lost. Patterson's phrase, "rescued us from evils *im*pending *over* us," was carried, "but half the Senate nearly made sour faces at it." Ellsworth said it was tautological, but was at a loss to amend it. Maclay said the tautology would be eliminated by changing "impending" to "pending," but he would not say the language would be eloquent. Then, since he was up, he could not help remarking that he thought the whole clause improper. It would fix a stain on the annals of America. Wyngate wanted the clause struck out. Maclay said he would second reconsideration. It was reconsidered, amended, and then recommitted to the same committee, who retired "for the purpose of dressing it." While they were out, Adams raised the question of the manner of delivering the answer to the President, and a committee was appointed to confer on this and other subjects with the House. Lee

got up and said something on the propriety of having a seat with a canopy for the President.

Finally the committee returned with what Maclay thought a vastly better text of the address. But when it spoke, with reference to the government, of "dignity and *splendor*" the Pennsylvanian wanted to substitute "respectability" for "splendor." Discussion followed, in which Maclay delivered himself of his dislike of "sounding names and pompous expressions," and discoursed on "splendor" as follows:

that different men had a train of different ideas raised by the same word; that "splendor," when applied to government, brought into my mind, instead of the highest perfection, all the faulty finery, brilliant scenes, and expensive trappings of royal government, and impressed my mind with an idea quite the reverse of republican respectability, which I thought consisted in firm and prudent councils, frugality, and economy.

But the word was not deleted, and the answer was agreed to. Adams

rose in the chair and repeated twice, with more joy in his face than I had ever seen him assume before, he hoped the Government would be supported with *dignity* and *splendor*. I thought he did it by way of triumph over me for a former defeat I gave him, but may be I was mistaken.[75]

The Senate address was not delivered to the President until May 18, the delay having been apparently due to the dispute between the two houses over a title for the President.[76] The Senate finally decided to address him for the present under the same style and title as the House had already given him in its address;[77] namely, the simple constitutional

[75] *Ibid.* 19–22.
[76] See generally 1 *Annals* 31–38 and *Journal of William Maclay* 19–38.
[77] 1 *Annals* 36; *Journal of William Maclay* 32–37.

designation of President of the United States. The committee was then ordered to wait on the President to know the time when he would be pleased to receive the address of the Senate.[78] On the 18th the Senate met and proceeded in carriages to the President's, where they were received in the antechamber, which lacked enough seats. After about three minutes it was signified to them to wait upon the President in his levee-room. The Vice President went first, with senators following in no particular order. They bowed upon entering, and after a bow the Vice President read the address, at first very badly and then with more assurance. The President took his reply out of his coat pocket, but between the paper, his hat, and his spectacles, he did no little fumbling. At the end he delivered his reply to the Vice President, bowed around to the company, and desired them to be seated. Adams neither accepted nor declined, but stood so long the President repeated the request. Adams then declined with a low bow and retired. The other senators then made their bows, and went out to the door, where Colonel Humphreys waited on them until their carriages took them up.[79]

Meanwhile, the House, which opposed titles, had on May 1 committed the President's speech to committee of the whole, which resolved that an address to the President ought to be prepared, expressing House congratulations on his unanimous election, approbation of the patriotic sentiments and enlightened policy of his speech, and assurance of their disposition to concur in every measure tending to "secure the liberties, promote the harmony, and advance the happiness and prosperity of their country." The House then ordered that a committee of five, headed by Madison, prepare the address.[80] The draft reported by that committee was adopted without amendment; and it was resolved that the Speaker, attended by the members, do present it to the President. A committee of three was ordered to wait upon the President to know when it would be convenient for him to receive it.[81] This committee reported on May 7 that the President had designated 12 o'clock on the next day, at such place as the House might appoint. The House then appointed the chamber adjoining that in which it met.[82] It was so done, with the President making a brief answer.[83] An editorial note in *Writings of Washington* states, however, that the President replied on May 9, probably not in person.[84]

These events set a precedent followed under Washington and

[78] 1 *Annals* 37; *Journal of William Maclay* 37.
[79] *Journal of William Maclay* 40–41.
[80] 1 *Annals* 241–242.
[81] *Ibid.* 257–258. May 5, 1789.
[82] *Ibid.* 293.
[83] *Ibid.* 302. May 8, 1789.
[84] 30 *Writings* 310, note 66.

THE PRESIDENT AS CHIEF OF STATE 33

Adams [85] but deliberately broken by Mr. Jefferson when he notified Congress at the beginning of his Presidency that he would communicate with them only by written messages.[86] When Woodrow Wilson startled the country by delivering messages in person,[87] this long-neglected precedent was revived, though without the addresses in reply, and indeed not as a ceremonial at the opening of Congress but as a means by which a popular leader spoke to the country over the heads of his "colleagues" in Congress.

It should be added that in July, 1789, both houses agreed upon a resolution worded as follows:

That when the Senate and House of Representatives shall judge it proper to make a joint address to the President, it shall be presented to him in his audience chamber, by the President of the Senate, and in the presence of the Speaker and both Houses.[88]

MRS. KNOX AND THE WICKED SHORT SOFA. Mr. Jefferson ridiculed the early ceremonial efforts by picturing them as comic opera. Four years after the alleged event he penned in his *Anas* a hearsay description of "the following specimen of the phrenzy which prevailed at New York on the opening of the new government." The occasion was "the first public ball which took place after the President's arrival there." According to Mr. Jefferson's informant, a Mr. Brown,

These arrangements were as follows: a sofa at the head of the room, raised on several steps, whereon the President and Mrs. Washington were to be seated. The gentlemen were to dance in swords. Each one, when going to dance, was to lead his partner to the foot of the sofa, make a low obeisance to the President and his lady, then go and dance, and when done, bring his partner again to the foot of the sofa for new obeisances, and then retire to their chairs.

This comic opera imitation of a royal ball was, alas! for a moment reduced to farce when Mrs. Knox, who had been on the committee of arrangements, followed George and Martha to the sofa, with the ap-

[85] See 1 *Messages and Papers of the Presidents* 57–62, 73–79, 95–102, 117–124, 130–137, 154–164, 174–181, 191–202, 223–235, 240–248, 261–270, 279–287, 288–290, 295–303; Jared Sparks, *The Life of George Washington* (Tappan and Dennet, Boston, 1844) 409–410, 423–424; 12 *The Writings of Washington* (Jared Sparks, ed., Little, Brown and Co., 1858) vii–viii, 1–77; 9 *The Works of John Adams* (Charles Francis Adams, ed., Little, Brown and Co., Boston, 1854) 105–149.
[86] 1 *Messages and Papers of the Presidents* 313. December 8, 1801.
[87] 4 Ray Stannard Baker, *Woodrow Wilson: Life and Letters* (Doubleday, Doran & Co., Garden City, 1931) 104–113; Ray Stannard Baker and William E. Dodd, eds., *The Public Papers of Woodrow Wilson: 1 The New Democracy* (Harper & Bros., New York and London, 1926) 32, 37, etc.
[88] 1 *Annals* 56, 697–698.

parent "design of forcing an invitation from the President to a seat" thereon. Without saying, as he might have done, that this move belied the implication of the whole arrangement, Mr. Jefferson went on to tell with evident relish—but from hearsay—what happened:

She mounted up the steps after them unbidden, but unfortunately the wicked sofa was so short, that when the President and Mrs. Washington were seated, there was not room for a third person; she was obliged, therefore, to descend in the face of the company, and sit where she could.[89]

THE ISSUE OVER WHETHER THE PRESIDENT SHOULD BE GIVEN A TITLE. This issue deserves full examination, since the views expressed on both sides are illustrative of the deep significance of symbolism in politics.[90] A week before Washington's inauguration the Senate appointed a committee to confer with a like House committee and report on what style or title it would be proper to annex to the offices of President and Vice President, if any other than those given in the Constitution.[91] Maclay heard that the title "selected from all the potentates of the earth for our President was to have been" the Polish title of *Elective Majesty*.[92] The joint committee reported, however, "That it is not proper to annex any style or title to the respective styles or titles of office expressed in the Constitution." [93]

The House adopted this report, but the Senate rejected it after an interesting debate which may be summarized from Maclay:

Lee declared

... all the world, civilized and savage, called for titles; that there must be something in human nature that occasioned this general consent; that, therefore, he conceived it was right.

Ellsworth

declared that the sentence in the primer of *fear God and honor the king* was of great importance; that kings were of divine appointment; that Saul, the head and shoulders taller than the rest of the people, was elected by God and anointed by his appointment.

Maclay countered

that within the space of twenty years back more light had been thrown on the subject of governments and on human affairs in general than for several

[89] 9 *Writings of Thomas Jefferson* (Washington ed., Derby & Jackson, New York, 1859) 147–148. From *The Anas*, under the date of June 10, 1793.
[90] See Karl Loewenstein, "The Influence of Symbols in Politics," in Roy V. Peel and Joseph S. Roucek, eds., *Introduction to Politics* (Thomas Y. Crowell Co., New York, 1942) 62–84.
[91] 1 *Annals* 24. April 23 and 24, 1789.   [93] 1 *Annals* 200 (April 24), 257 (May 5).
[92] *Journal of William Maclay* 17. May 4, 1789.

generations before; that this light of knowledge had diminished the veneration for titles, . . . that the abuse of power and the fear of bloody masters had extorted titles as well as adoration, in some instances from the trembling crowd; that the impression now on the minds of the citizens of these States was that of horror for kingly authority.

Izard "dwelt almost entirely on the antiquity of kingly government," but Carroll "spoke against kings."

Maclay observed in his journal that the Vice President "repeatedly helped the speakers for titles." When Ellsworth was "enumerating how common the appellation of President was," Adams "Put him in mind that there were presidents of fire companies and of a cricket club." When Lee was saying that he believed some of the states authorized titles, Adams from the chair "told him that Connecticut did it." Maclay "collected" himself "for a last effort":

I read the clause in the Constitution against titles of nobility; . . . that as to kingly government, it was equally out of the question, as a republican government was guaranteed to every State in the Union; that they were both equally forbidden fruit of the Constitution . . . gentlemen seemed to court a rupture with the other House. . . . Our conduct would mark us to the world as actuated by the spirit of dissention, and the characters of the Houses would be as aristocratic and democratical.

After the Senate rejected the report against titles, the motion was made by Izard, and either defeated or withdrawn,[94] to call the President *His Excellency*. Lee suggested *Highness* with some prefatory word. *Elective* was proposed as the prefatory word. It was "insisted that such a dignified title would add greatly to the weight and authority of the Government both at home and abroad." Lee "read over a list of the titles of all the princes and potentates of the earth, marking where the word 'highness' occurred." But Maclay in refutation urged that

at present it was impossible to add to the respect entertained for General Washington; that if you gave him the title of any foreign prince or potentate, a belief would follow that the manners of that prince and his modes of government would be adopted by the President. . . . That particularly "elective highness," which sounded nearly like "electoral highness," would have a most ungrateful sound to many thousands of industrious citizens who had fled from German oppression; that "highness" was part of the title of a prince or princes of the blood, and was often given to dukes; that it was degrading our President to place him on a par with any prince of any blood in Europe, nor was there one of them that could enter the list of true glory with him.

[94] Maclay says it was withdrawn, the *Annals* that it was defeated.

Despite Maclay's effective thrusts, a committee was appointed to consider a title for the President. Maclay blamed Adams and Lee for this "wholly silly business." To him the Senate seemed determined on a court, and he reflected that he had lost "every particle of court favor." [95]

On the next day, as Maclay goes on to record, the committee reported a title: *His Highness the President of the United States of America and Protector of the Rights of the Same.* Meanwhile the clerk of the House appeared, to announce officially House adoption of the report of the joint committee against titles. Maclay asked for postponement of the report before the Senate and the request for a conference on the differences between the houses. In a forty minute "harangue" Vice President Adams finally "got to his favorite topic of titles" and their "immense advantage" and "absolute necessity." He said the President had to be something that included all the dignities of the diplomatic corps and something greater still:

What will the common people of foreign countries, what will the sailors and soldiers say, "George Washington, President of the United States"? They will despise him *to all eternity*. This is all nonsense to the philosopher, but so is all government whatever.

This brought Maclay to his feet again. He quoted the constitutional appellation of the *President of the United States of America,* and said this was his title of office, nor could they alter, add to, or diminish it without infringing the Constitution. The terms given to nobility in the Old World were "contraband language in the United States." Since foreigners did not understand our language, we should have to use *Hohen Mogende* to a Dutchman, *Beylerbey* to a Turk or Algerine, and so of the rest. If we borrowed from the English terms not wholly unintelligible to our citizens, would not the "plagiarism" produce "contempt" among them? He denied Adams's assertion that government was nonsense to the philosopher, but was ready to admit that "every high-sounding, pompous appellation, descriptive of qualities which the object does not possess, must appear bombastic nonsense in the eyes of every wise man."

In the end the report was postponed, and a conference requested; but the old committee [96] was reappointed, and the minute of rejection went down with the appointment of the conferees.[97]

On May 11 the House took under consideration the Senate's request for a conference. Parker moved that the House, having accepted the

[95] *Journal of William Maclay* 22–24. Cf. 1 *Annals* 33–34. May 8, 1789.
[96] That is, the same one which had just reported in favor of a title.
[97] *Journal of William Maclay* 25–28. Cf. 1 *Annals* 34. May 9, 1789.

joint report against titles and having proceeded accordingly in its address in response to the President's speech, deemed it improper to accede to a conference. He was seconded by Page, who thought the House had no power to interfere in the business, and "did not conceive the real honor or dignity" of the President or Vice President to "consist in high sounding titles."

Lee was against any title, but wanted a committee to confer. Tucker made a speech in which he said:

Does the dignity of a nation consist in the distance between the first magistrate and his citizens? Does it consist in the exaltation of one man, and the humiliation of the rest? If so, the most despotic Government is the most dignified; and to make our dignity complete, we must give a high title, an embroidered robe, a princely equipage, and finally, a crown and hereditary succession. . . . And whom, sir, do we mean to gratify? Is it our present President? Certainly, if we expect to please him, we shall be greatly disappointed. He has a real dignity of character, and is above such little vanities. . . . This spirit of imitation, sir, this spirit of mimicry and apery will be the ruin of our country. . . .

Madison wanted a conference for due respect to the Senate and to give weight and dignity to the opinion of the House. He did not conceive titles to be "so pregnant with danger as some gentlemen apprehend. . . . We have seen superb and august titles given, without conferring power and influence, or even without obtaining respect." He himself was against them "because they are not very reconcilable with the nature of our Government or the genius of the people." So in any event they would not be very proper at that juncture:

But my strongest objection is founded in principle; instead of increasing, they diminish the true dignity and importance of a republic, . . . If we give titles, we must either borrow or invent them. . . . The more truly honorable shall we be, by showing a total neglect and disregard to things of this nature; the more simple, the more republican we are in our manners, the more rational dignity we shall acquire.

In the course of further discussion, White mentioned that the prior vote of the House had been unanimous; while Jackson asked if styling Washington His Serene Highness, His Grace, or Mightiness would add one tittle to the solid properties he possessed. Clymer said the most impotent potentates generally assumed the most lofty titles. He wished to check the notorious propensity in this country to shower down titles upon a man as soon as he was elected to public office. He would venture to affirm there were more honorable esquires here than in all the world besides. Page feared the time might come when the President would be made the fountain of honor,[98] and contended that a title must be followed by robe and diadem.

The upshot was to appoint a committee headed by Madison to confer with the Senate committee.[99] Meanwhile Maclay was committing to his journal his dislike of Adams:

He takes on him to school the members from the chair. His grasping after titles has been observed by everybody. Mr. Izard, after describing his air, manner, deportment, and personal figure in the chair, concluded with applying the title of *Rotundity* to him.[100]

Maclay continues the story:

On May 14 Mr. Lee reported from the joint committee that the House committee "had adhered in the strictest manner to their former resolution." He moved that the report in favor of titles be entered on the files of the Senate, and that the Senate resolve that it had decided in favor of titles, but would, in conformity to the practice of the House, for the present address the President without title. In opposition to this Maclay tried ridicule: "If all men were of one stature, there would be neither high nor low." *Highness* denoted excess of stature over other men. Saul, head and shoulders above anybody else, and greased to boot with a great horn of oil, must have been *highly* conspicuous. On this principle, let America be searched, and the honor would probably fall upon some "huge Patagonian." Men should see where Nature leads before adopting her as a guide. If the term high was metaphorical, and the high station of the President entitled him to it, nevertheless, since nothing could be true metaphorically which was not so naturally, the proposed title belonged to the man in the moon, as his station was the most elevated known. As for Protector, the organ of protection was the war power, which was vested in Congress.

Although a general postponement of the report on the title was carried, to the disgust of Maclay Lee had his way about putting it on the files of the Senate and about informing the House that the Senate, while it favored a title for the President, would for the present conform to the practice of the other body.[101] Nevertheless, Maclay correctly sensed

[98] Cf. 1 Sir William Blackstone, *Commentaries on the Laws of England* (W. E. Dean, New York, 1851) Bk. I, § 272.
[99] 1 *Annals* 331–337. May 11, 1789.
[100] *Journal of William Maclay* 29. May 11, 1789. The present account is confined to the question of a title for the President, but Adams wanted a whole system of titles to make the government high-toned. See, for example, *ibid.* 2, 37, 63.
[101] *Journal of William Maclay* 32–36. The last statement in the text above is brought out quite clearly in 1 *Annals* 36, according to which the Senate resolved that the

the fact that victory was his. "I have, by plowing with the heifer of the other House, completely defeated them." [102] "And now I hope we have disposed of a business which in one shape or other has engaged almost the whole time of the Senate from the 23d of April" until May 14.[103] "But, with all their art, I have balked them for once." [104]

Suspicious by nature, Maclay speculated on the game of Lee, who "has acted as a high priest through the whole of this idolatrous business." Adams came in for his especial disgust: "Our Vice President's doctrine is that all honors and titles should flow from the President and Senate only." [105]

Adams for his part was still unconvinced. Some days later he said to Maclay:

You are against titles. But there are no people in the world so much in favor of titles as the people of America; and the Government will never be properly administered until they are adopted in the fullest manner.

To this Maclay made the manly reply:

... I am convinced that were we to adopt them in the fashion of Europe we would ruin all. You have told us, sir, that they are idle in a philosophic point of view. Governments have been long at odds with common sense. I hope the conduct of America will reconcile them. Instead of adding respect to government, I consider that they will bring the personages who assume them into contempt and ridicule.[106]

On May 11, while the subject of titles was still pending, Maclay was invited by the President of the United States to sit in his box at the theater, to see the "School for Scandal," which Maclay thought "an indecent representation before ladies of character and virtue." [107] Later, he noted that "through the whole of this base business [of titles] I have endeavored to mark the conduct of General Washington." He had "no clew" to his view. It was "scarce possible, but he must have dropped

---

"present" address "be 'To the President of the United States,' without addition of title," and preceded its decision to conform "for the present" to House practice with these words:

"From a decent respect for the opinion and practice of civilized nations, whether under monarchical or republican forms of Government, whose custom is to annex titles of respectability to the office of their Chief Magistrate; and that, on intercourse with foreign nations, a due respect for the majesty of the people of the United States may not be hazarded by an appearance of singularity, the Senate have been induced to be of opinion, that it would be proper to annex a respectable title to the office of President of the United States; . . ."
This was May 14, 1789.
[102] *Journal of William Maclay* 34.
[103] *Ibid.* 35–36.
[104] *Ibid.* 37.
[105] *Ibid.* 36.
[106] *Ibid.* 49. May 26, 1789.
[107] *Ibid.* 29–30.

something on the subject," but if it had been on his side he would, he thought, have heard it.[108]

In July, David Stuart wrote to Washington:

> Nothing could equal the ferment and disquietude occasioned by the proposition respecting titles. As it is believed to have originated from Mr. Adams and Lee, they are not only unpopular in the extreme, but highly odious. Neither I am convinced, will ever get a vote from this State again.[109]

Washington replied it was to be "lamented" that the question of titles had been stirred. It had given him "much uneasiness lest it should be supposed by some (unacquainted with facts) that the object they had in view was not displeasing to me." He said the question had been moved before he arrived,

> without any privity or knowledge of it on my part, and urged after I was apprized of it contrary to my opinion; for I foresaw and predicted the reception it has met with, and the use that would be made of it by the adversaries of the government. Happily the matter is now done with, I hope never to be revived.[110]

THE PROPOSAL IN THE SENATE THAT THE PRESIDENT'S NAME APPEAR IN THE ENACTING CLAUSE OF STATUTES. The form of the enacting clause of statutes—those magic words, as the late Jesse Reeves used to say, that make not-law law—had to be worked out by the two houses of Congress. Should laws be enacted by the Congress or by the Senate and House of Representatives? There was at first some maneuvering between the two houses,[111] but the formula settled upon was:

> Be it enacted by the senate and house of representatives of the United States of America in congress assembled.[112]

---

[108] *Ibid.* 34.   [109] 30 *Writings* 363, note 61.
[110] *Ibid* 359, 362–363. July 26, 1789. An editorial note points out that Washington arrived in New York the day before the original committee was appointed on April 23, though he was not inaugurated until April 30. *Ibid.* 363, note 61.

In September, when the salary bill was up, Maclay was astonished at the disposition of some senators to give "princely" incomes to all Federal officers: "Can it be that they wish to surround the President with a set of lordly and pompous officers, and thus having provided the furniture of a court, nothing but the name of majesty, highness, or some such title will be wanted to step into all the forms of royalty?" *Journal of William Maclay* 141. September 1, 1789.

It is interesting to note that in a letter dated November 1, 1789, Joseph Barrell wrote from Boston to General Webb that they had been preparing for "the Visit of the best of Men," whom he designated in the letter as "His majesty the President" and "His Majesty." Barrell gave an account of the reception of Washington in Boston on his eastern tour. 3 *Correspondence and Journals of Samuel Blachley Webb* (collected and edited by Worthington Chauncey Ford, New York; Wickersham Press, Lancaster, Pa., 1894) 142–144.

[111] See 1 *Annals* 30, 276–282, and *Journal of William Maclay,* 15–16, 18–19.
[112] 2 *Laws of the United States* 1.

When the first bill to be enacted under the Constitution[113] went to the Senate from the House, it stood, *Be it enacted by the Congress of the United States*. The first amendment in the Senate was to change the enacting clause to read, *by the Senate and Representatives*. "Mr. Izard gave us a kind of dissenting speech from both original and amendment. He wanted the President's name in it. Our Vice-President rose in the chair to deliver sentiments to the same purpose, and upon this principle he was rather against the amendment, because it did not mention the President." But the amendment carried.[114]

Ellsworth took the position on the third reading of the bill

that the great and dignified station of the President and the conspicuous part he would act in the field of legislation, as all laws must pass in review before him, and were subject to his revision and correction, etc., entitled him to have his name or place marked in the enacting clause of all laws; or at least he should be brought into view among the component parts of Congress.

Ellsworth developed this theme for "nearly a quarter of an hour" but made no motion; "indeed," thought Maclay, "the spirit of his address was reducible to this: 'I will make no motion; if any of you are foolish enough to do it, you may.'" It seems, therefore, that this imitation of monarchy died aborning. But the incident left Maclay wondering what Ellsworth's motive could be: "Solely to play the courtier?" [115]

THE QUESTION WHETHER FEDERAL WRITS SHOULD RUN IN THE NAME OF THE PRESIDENT. In the First Session the Senate originated not only the judiciary bill [116] but also a bill for regulating process in the federal courts.[117] As passed by the Senate, the first clause of this latter bill declared that "all writs or processes, issuing out of the Supreme or Circuit Courts, should be in the name of the President of the United States." The House of Representatives voted 25 to 18 to strike out the words, "the President thereof," so that writs would issue only in the name of the United States.[118]

The Senate agreed to the House amendments except this one on the style of the writ.[119] By a vote of 28 to 22 the House decided to adhere to the amendment. Before this vote was taken,

[113] *Ibid.* The act was entitled, "An act to regulate the time and manner of administering certain oaths." Approved June 1, 1789.
[114] *Journal of William Maclay* 15–16. May 4, 1789. The story of how the Senate amendment for enactment by the *Senate and Representatives* was changed finally to enactment by the Senate and *House of* Representatives is told in Henry von Hasseln, *The Work of the First Congress in 1789* (1946) 11–12. This work is an unpublished M.A. thesis written under the present author at the University of Virginia.
[115] *Journal of William Maclay* 18–19. May 5, 1789.
[116] 1 *Annals* 47. June 12, 1789.
[117] *Ibid.* 82. September 17, 1789.
[118] *Ibid.* 949. September 24, 1789.
[119] *Ibid.* 91. September 25, 1789.

Mr. Stone hoped the House would insist upon their amendment. He thought substituting the name of the President, instead of the name of the United States, was a declaration that the sovereign authority was vested in the Executive. He did not believe this to be the case. The United States were sovereign; they acted by an agency, but could remove such agency without impairing their own capacity to act. He did not fear the loss of liberty by this single mark of power; but he apprehended that an aggregate, formed of one inconsiderable power, and another inconsiderable authority, might, in time, lay a foundation for pretensions it would be troublesome to dispute, and difficult to get rid of. A little prior caution was better than much future remedy.[120]

The Senate still persisted, and asked for a conference.[121] The House appointed managers, who reported no agreement. But the Senate sent the bill to the House with a proposed amendment. The House vote on agreeing was a tie which the Speaker broke for the affirmative.[122]

The bill, as enacted, apparently left the door open, but said nothing about writs running in the name of the President.[123] On the morning after the House had voted to adhere, Maclay entered the Senate chamber to find Vice President Adams, Ellsworth, and Ames "railing against the House vote of adherence." Maclay thought them wrong, but they were so opinionated he did not contradict them. However, he noted in his journal:

. . . This is only a part of their old system of giving the President as far as possible every appendage of royalty. The original reason of the English writs running in the King's name was his being personally in court, and English jurisprudence still supposes him to be so. But with us it seems rather confounding the executive and judicial branches.[124]

The matter did not rest here, however. For at its first term, the February Term, 1790, the Supreme Court adopted the following quoted rule:

[120] *Ibid.* 951. September 25, 1789.
[121] *Ibid.* 92, 952. September 26, 1789.
[122] *Ibid* 94, 962. September 28, 1789.
[123] 2 *Laws of the United States* 72. Approved September 29, 1789. This act, which was to expire at the end of the next session, provided that the forms of writs and executions, "except their style," in the circuit and district courts, in suits at common law, should follow those of the states; that the "forms and modes of proceedings" in equity and admiralty and maritime cases should be "according to the course of the civil law." It further provided that all writs and processes from a supreme or circuit court should "bear the teste of the chief justice," and those from a district court should bear the teste of the judge of that court; and that they should all be under the seal of the respective courts and signed by the clerk thereof. Did this leave the *style* of its writs to each court?
[124] *Journal of William Maclay* 163. September 26, 1789.

4. *Ordered,* That (unless, and until, it shall be otherwise provided by law) all process of this court shall be in the name of "the President of the United States."[125]

At the August Term, 1795, for example, in the case of *United States v. Richard Peters, District Judge,* the form of the writ of prohibition issued by the Supreme Court to Judge Peters was as follows:

United States, ss.
The President of the United States to the honorable Richard Peters, Esquire, judge of the district court of the United States, in and for the Pennsylvania district: It is shown to the judges of the supreme court of the United States . . . You, therefore, are hereby prohibited, . . .[126]

From this style of process the Supreme Court of the United States appears never to have departed. The Revised Rules adopted in 1939 provide in Rule 6 as follows:

1. All process of this court shall be in the name of the President of the United States, and shall contain the given names, as well as the surnames of the parties.

For example, a subpoena in an original action in 1945 began as follows:

The United States of America, SS:
The President of the United States,
To the State of Indiana
Greetings:

(Seal)

....

Again, the form of mandate used by the Supreme Court at the present time begins as follows:

UNITED STATES OF AMERICA, SS:
The President of the United States of America,

To the Honorable the Judges of the.............................
Court of the United States for the..........................
District of ....

GREETING:
Whereas, etc.[127]

---

[125] 2 U.S. (2 Dallas) 400 (1790).
[126] 3 U.S. 120, 129, 131 (1795).
[127] This information was furnished the present writer by the Office of the Clerk, Supreme Court of the United States, Washington 13, D.C., per Mr. E. P. Cullinan, Assistant. When this bit of history was recounted to an attorney, friend of the present writer, he exclaimed that it is an illustration of an inertia in the law which is analogous to the inertia of matter in the classical physics.

THE QUESTION WHETHER THE PRESIDENT IS PERSONALLY IMMUNE TO JUDICIAL PROCESS. On September 26, 1789, before the Senate convened, Maclay got into an argument with Vice President Adams and Ellsworth. In the course of the argument they said

... The President, personally, was not the subject to any process whatever; could have no action whatever brought against him; was above the power of all judges, justices, etc. For what, said they, would you put it in the power of a common justice to exercise any authority over him and stop the whole machine of Government?

Maclay countered that, although President, he was not above the laws; but both of them insisted "you could only impeach him, and no other process whatever lay against him." Suppose, persisted Maclay, the President committed murder in the street, and ran away, before being removed on impeachment and thus made liable to indictment. Or suppose he continued his murders daily and neither house was sitting to impeach him. To the reply that the people would then rise up, he rejoined that this meant allowing the mob to do what legal justice had to abstain from. Adams said this was arguing from cases nearly impossible; none of the hundreds of crowned heads of Europe in the last two centuries had committed murder. Maclay's answer was that except for Charles IX this was very true "in the retail," but that they generally did these things on a great scale. His cases, he maintained, were possible, if improbable. General Schuyler then joining the circle, Maclay asked his opinion. As he thought the President "a kind of sacred person," Maclay put him down in his journal as a *jure divino* man. He thought the incident not worth recording, but it

shows clearly how amazingly fond of the old leaven many people are. I needed no index, however, of this kind with respect to John Adams.[128]

SUMMARY AND COMMENT. To make a ceremony out of the inauguration of the head of any state is entirely natural; and this ceremony may symbolize the elevation of the tribune of the people as well as the accession to the throne of a sovereign. In writing to David Stuart of his "system" of official conduct Washington gave as his aim a "discriminating medium" between "lowering the dignity and respect that was due to the first Magistrate" and "an ostentatious shew of mimicry of sovereignty." His refusal to accept a presidential salary symbolized his unique position, even then recognized by him and the world, as the first American hero. His New England tour, his enforcement of presi-

[128] *Journal of William Maclay* 163–164.

dential precedence over a state governor, his First Inaugural Address's invocation of the Deity and assertion that the American experiment was a great if not the final test of republicanism, his pronouncements in replies to addresses, and his first thanksgiving proclamation were all incidents of his position as the head of state.

The speech and addresses in reply certainly resembled the ceremonies at the opening of Parliament.[129] Yet the speech, if not the addresses, was so appropriate for one who was at once the head of state and the chief executive charged with the constitutional duty of giving to Congress from time to time information of the state of the Union and recommending measures to their consideration,[130] that it seems to have been taken as a matter of course. When Mr. Jefferson as President eliminated at one stroke this whole business, it may have been in part because he realized he could guide the House better by informal negotiation and political management, at which he was a past master, than by a formal speech, which he could not make effectively; yet this discarding of ceremonial was officially explained on the ground of

principal regard to the convenience of the Legislature, to the economy of their time, to their relief from the embarrassment of immediate answers on subjects not yet fully before them, and to the benefits thence resulting to the public affairs.[131]

It was also consistent with the Jeffersonian idea and practice of republican simplicity and *pêle-mêle*.[132] The attempt of the Vice President in 1789 to incorporate in the Senate minutes a reference to *His most gracious speech* was clearly an imitation of monarchy.

The imitation of court etiquette at the first public ball described from hearsay by Mr. Jefferson enabled him to paint it as a comic opera which Mrs. Knox reduced to farce. Senate insistence upon giving the President a high-sounding title was the most overt attempt of all to imitate monarchy; but even in 1789 the House would have none of it, Maclay spent his best sarcasm in the Senate in ridiculing the idea, and the President wrote David Stuart he had not approved because he had

[129] See the description of this ancient ceremony in Frederick Austin Ogg, *English Government and Politics* (2d ed., The Macmillan Co., New York, 1936) 370–374.
[130] See Article II, section 3, of the Constitution.
[131] From the letter accompanying Mr. Jefferson's First Annual Message of December 8, 1801. 1 *Messages and Papers of the Presidents* 313.
[132] 1 Henry Adams, *History of the United States* (Charles Scribner's Sons, New York, 1889) 247–248; 4 *The Writings of Thomas Jefferson* (Washington ed., Derby & Jackson, New York, 1859) 396–397, 423–424, 426; 5 *ibid.* 101–102; 2 *Letters and Other Writings of James Madison* (published by order of Congress, R. Worthington, New York, 1884), 189, 195–199.

foreseen the popular reaction. The question soon ceased to be a question, and the incident passed into historical oblivion.

The proposal in the Senate that the President's name appear in the enacting clause of statutes was an obvious imitation of monarchy, but got nowhere even in the Senate. The House blocked the Senate's move to specify in the law that federal writs should run in the name of the President, as British writs ran in the name of the King; though the compromise language enabled the Supreme Court, in its politically irresponsible position, to play at this imitation of monarchy in a manner which persists to this very day.

Maclay's conversational argument with Adams and Ellsworth over whether the President was personally immune to judicial process illustrates a 1789 version of republicanism versus monarchist tradition. Yet it is now generally understood that the President is immune, while in office, to all judicial process except notice of the trial of his impeachment before the Senate.[133] In the trial of Aaron Burr in Richmond, Chief Justice Marshall issued a *subpoena duces tecum* to President Jefferson. The story is complicated and somewhat confused; but President Jefferson never appeared in court in response to the subpoena. Beveridge significantly says that for once most Republicans thought Marshall right;[134] but Mr. Jefferson cannot be accused of deliberate imitation of monarchy as such; and his letter to George Hay giving his objections to being ordered to appear before a court as a witness elaborated the grounds stated in 1789 by John Adams to Maclay, which seem to be the basis of the supposed rule of general presidential immunity to judicial process:

But if the Constitution enjoins on a particular officer to be always engaged in a particular set of duties imposed on him, does not this supersede the general law, subjecting him to minor duties inconsistent with these? The Constitution enjoins his constant agency in the concerns of six millions of people. Is the law paramount to this, which calls on him on behalf of a single one? Let us apply the Judge's own doctrine to the case of himself and his brethren. The sheriff of Henrico summons him from the bench, to quell a riot somewhere in his county. The federal judge is by the general law, a part of the *posse* of the State sheriff. Would the judge abandon major duties to perform lesser ones? Again; the court of Orleans or Maine commands, by subpoenas, the attendance of all the judges of the Supreme Court. Would

[133] *Cf.* James Hart, *The Ordinance Making Powers of the President* (The Johns Hopkins Press, Baltimore, 1925) 297–299, 302 ff; Edward S. Corwin, *The President: Office and Powers* (2d ed., New York University Press, New York, 1941) 297–298, 438–440.
[134] 3 Albert J. Beveridge, *The Life of John Marshall* (Houghton Mifflin Co., Boston and New York, 1919) 407, 433–447, 450, 454–456, 468, 518–522.

they abandon their posts as judges, and the interests of millions committed to them, to serve the purposes of a single individual? The leading principle of our Constitution is the independence of the Legislature, executive and judiciary of each other, and none are more jealous of this than the judiciary. But would the executive be independent of the judiciary, if he were subject to the *commands* of the latter, and to imprisonment for disobedience; if the several courts could bandy him from pillar to post, keep him constantly trudging from north to south and east to west, and withdraw him entirely from his constitutional duties? The intention of the Constitution, that each branch should be independent of the others, is further manifested by the means it has furnished to each, to protect itself from enterprises of force attempted on them by the others, and to none has it given more effectual or diversified means than to the executive. Again; because ministers can go into a court in London as witnesses, without interruption to their executive duties, it is inferred that they would go to a court one thousand or one thousand five hundred miles off, and that ours are to be dragged from Maine to Orleans by every criminal who will swear that their testimony "may be of use to him." The judge says, "*it is apparent* that the President's duties as chief magistrate do not demand his whole time, and are not unremitting." If he alludes to our annual retirement from the seat of government, during the sickly season, he should be told that such arrangements are made for carrying on the public business, at and between the several stations we take, that it goes on as unremittingly there, as if we were at the seat of government. I pass more hours in public business at Monticello than I do here, every day; and it is much more laborious, because all must be done in writing. Our stations being known, all communications come to them regularly, as to fixed points. It would be very different were we always on the road, or placed in the noisy and crowded taverns where courts are held. . . .[135]

In short, any evil consequences which may result from presidential immunity are immeasurably outweighed by the public necessity that he be at all times free to attend to the continuous duties of his high office.

AN ILLUMINATING EXAMPLE OF POLITICAL SYMBOLISM. In net result the imitations of monarchy were for the most part nipped in the bud in 1789, as their remnants were, with one curious exception, summarily torn up by the roots in 1801. It by no means follows, however, that the debates which occurred on the subject in 1789 are without present interest. Rather is this whole episode an illuminating example of political symbolism. In a brilliant chapter on "Uses of Symbolism" A. N. Whitehead says:

[135] 5 *The Writings of Thomas Jefferson* (Washington ed., Derby & Jackson, New York, 1859) 103–104. June 20, 1807.

The attitude of mankind towards symbolism exhibits an unstable mixture of attraction and repulsion. . . . Hard-headed men want facts and not symbols. . . . The repulsion from symbolism stands out as a well-marked element in the cultural history of civilized people. . . .

. . . the symbolic elements in life have a tendency to run wild. . . . The life of humanity can easily be overwhelmed by its symbolic accessories. A continuous process of pruning, and of adaptation to a future ever requiring new forms of expression, is a necessary function in every society. The successful adaptation of old symbols to changes of social structure is the final mark of wisdom in sociological statesmanship. Also an occasional revolution in symbolism is required.

There is, however, a Latin proverb. . . . In English it reads thus:— Nature, expelled with a pitchfork, ever returns. This proverb is exemplified by the history of symbolism. However you may endeavour to expel it, it ever returns. Symbolism is no mere idle fancy or corrupt degeneration; it is inherent in the very texture of human life. Language itself is a symbolism. And, as another example, however you reduce the functions of your government to their utmost simplicity, yet symbolism remains. It may be a healthier, manlier ceremonial, suggesting finer notions. But still it is symbolism. You abolish the etiquette of a royal court, with its suggestion of personal subordination, but at official receptions you ceremonially shake the hand of the Governor of your State. Just as the feudal doctrine of a subordination of classes, reaching up to the ultimate overlord, requires its symbolism; so does the doctrine of human equality obtain its symbolism. Mankind, it seems, has to find a symbol in order to express itself. Indeed 'expression' is 'symbolism.'

. . . The object of symbolism is the enhancement of the importance of what is symbolized.

In a discussion of instances of symbolism, our first difficulty is to discover exactly what is being symbolized. The symbols are specific enough, but it is often extremely difficult to analyze what lies behind them, even though there is evidently some strong appeal beyond the mere ceremonial acts.

....

My main thesis is that a social system is kept together by the blind force of instinctive actions, and of instinctive emotions clustered around habits and prejudices. It is therefore not true that any advance in the scale of culture inevitably tends to the preservation of society. On the whole, the contrary is more often the case, . . . This essay [136] is practically written round the thesis that advances in the art of civilization are apt to be destructive of the social system. Burke conceived this conclusion to be a *reductio ad absurdum*. But it is the truth. . . .

[136] Whitehead here refers to Edmund Burke's work entitled, *A Vindication of Natural Society*.

THE PRESIDENT AS CHIEF OF STATE

Burke surveys [137] the standing miracle of the existence of an organized society, culminating in the smooth unified action of the state. . . . He asks what is the force which leads this throng of separate units to coöperate in the maintenance of an organized state, in which each individual has his part to play, . . . His answer to the riddle is that the magnetic force is 'prejudice,' or in other words, 'use and wont.' . . . Burke was well ahead of his time in drawing attention to the importance of precedence as a political force. Unfortunately, in the excitement of the moment, Burke construed the importance of precedence as implying the negation of progressive reform.

. . . .

When a revolution has sufficiently destroyed this common symbolism leading to common actions for usual purposes, society can only save itself from dissolution by means of a reign of terror. Those revolutions which escape a reign of terror have left intact the fundamental efficient symbolism of society. For example, . . . the American revolution of the eighteenth century . . .
. . . A national hero, such as George Washington . . . is a symbol of the common purpose which animates American life. . . .

. . . .

It is the first step in sociological wisdom, to recognize that the major advances in civilization are processes which all but wreck the societies in which they occur:—like unto an arrow in the hands of a child. The art of free society consists first in the maintenance of the symbolic code; and secondly in fearlessness of revision, to secure that the code serves those purposes which satisfy an enlightened reason. Those societies which cannot combine reverence to their symbols with freedom of revision, must ultimately decay either from anarchy, or from the slow atrophy of a life stifled by useless shadows.[138]

Whitehead thus ends with the paradox or dilemma of social change, and bids us follow the mean[139] between anarchy and stagnation. In 1789 John Adams, after the manner of Edmund Burke, was acutely conscious of the role of "use and wont" in producing and preserving social solidarity. History records, however, that the symbolic revision which he feared did not reduce American society to anarchy. That society preserved enough of its basic code of symbolism even to effect the Jacksonian revolution without a violent upheaval. Maclay stood for a symbolic revolution in that part of the old symbolism which he realized the popular mind had already discarded. In so doing he symbolized the Revolutionary trend toward democracy which the Federalist reaction had sought to restrain by those paper checks of the Constitution its leaders

---

[137] Whitehead here refers to Burke's *Reflections on the French Revolution*.
[138] From A. N. Whitehead, *Symbolism: Its Meaning and Effect* (The Macmillan Co., New York, 1927) 60–88.
[139] See Aristotle as cited above, chapter 1, note 2.

were now determined to make effective in practice, just as he anticipated the "changes of social structure"[140] to be brought by Jeffersonian Republicanism and Jacksonian Democracy.[141]

The matter appeared in its clearest light in the Senate debate over a presidential title. Lee said there must be something in human nature that made all the world call for titles. If for *titles* he had substituted *symbolism*, he would have stated a general truth. Indeed, symbolism was not all on the side of the advocates of titles. It was equally evident in the position of Maclay. For the very republican simplicity which he cherished was itself symbolic of the civic virtues connoted for him by the symbol, *republic*. Lee's error, however, in mistaking the particular for the universal, was almost as natural in a monarchist world as was that of the philosopher of Langley's imaginary society of ephemeral insects whose life span was an hour, when just before sunset he told the frightened nation assembled under a mushroom that when the sun fell behind the horizon the world would come to an end.[142]

Ellsworth correctly sensed *habit* as the basis of political obedience, but made the same mistake as Lee when he feared that social anarchy would result from failure to find a *closely analogous* substitute for the words of the primer, *fear God and honor the king*.

Vice President Adams could not conceive of dignity and respectability attaching to the presidency of the *United States,* with no further high title to distinguish it from the presidency of a *fire company* or a *cricket club*. Yet history has made the President of the United States *the* President among all presidents, and not least because the tradition of the office centers about tribunes of the people like Andrew Jackson[143] and Franklin D. Roosevelt. Just as in former times men might honor kingship even while they despised the man who at the moment was king, so today American citizens can feel awe and respect for the greatest political office within the gift of any great people even while they hate the man in the White House. The Presidency has risen to this position without the prop of any high-sounding title. Indeed, such a prop was symbolically repulsive to the people in the beginning and would today

---

[140] These are the words of Whitehead in the quotation made above.
[141] *Journal of William Maclay* v (*Introduction* by Charles A. Beard), xvii (*Preface* by Edgar S. Maclay).
[142] This imaginative story in enforcement of the relativity of human thought is quoted from Samuel Pierpont Langley, *The New Astronomy* (Ticknor and Co., Boston, 1888) 250–251, by Walter Wheeler Cook, "Scientific Method and the Law," 15 *Johns Hopkins Alumni Magazine* 213–236 (March, 1927).
[143] Henry Jones Ford, *The Rise and Growth of American Politics* (The Macmillan Co., New York, 1898) 162–196, 275–293; James Hart, "Classical Statesmanship," 32 *Sewanee Review* 396–403 (1925).

be incongruous with an office which is a symbol of popular government.

That Maclay sensed this is evident from his speeches. A title would detract from rather than enhance popular respect for General Washington, who was already a national hero of unique symbolic meaning.[144] In the House also Tucker turned away from "the exaltation of one man" as implying "the humiliation of another."

Today we recognize England for a popularly governed country in which the monarch is but a head of state who, in presiding for life and by hereditary succession, but symbolizes the glory of the national past.[145] Nor are we shocked today to have our President described as a king elected by the American people for four years.[146] Why, then, did Adams and Maclay both take their differences so seriously? If "the object of symbolism is the enhancement of the importance of what is symbolized,"[147] what exactly was being symbolized by these two men which was so important to them as to stir their emotions?

The hypothesis [148] may be advanced that the clash between Adams and Maclay over titles, like practically every clash recorded in these pages, represented a dichotomy which runs like a thread through American history. This dichotomy is hard to define, in part because it takes on different forms from age to age and even from year to year, and in part because, while it always has its roots in a conflict of concrete economic interests which divide the few from the many, the few find it expedient to deny its class basis, and accuse the country squires who unite the many of fomenting class differences even while they denounce these

---

[144] Cf. 1 Homer Carey Hockett, *Constitutional History of the United States* (The Macmillan Co., New York, 1939) 259. The present writer is indebted generally to this work, to Andrew C. McLaughlin, *A Constitutional History of the United States* (student ed., D. Appleton-Century Co., New York and London, 1935), and to his former history professor, the late John Holladay Latané.

[145] In an address in response to King George at Buckingham Palace on December 27, 1918, President Wilson referred to "the great nation over which you preside," and went on to say: "For you and I, sir—I temporarily—embody the spirit of two great nations; and whatever strength I have, and whatever authority, I possess only so long and so far as I express the spirit and purpose of the American people." *The Public Papers of Woodrow Wilson: 1 War and Peace* (Ray Stannard Baker and William E. Dodd, eds., Harper & Bros., New York and London, 1927) 337. By permission of Mrs. Woodrow Wilson.

[146] Bryce said the framers "made an enlarged copy of the State Governor, or to put the same thing differently, a reduced and improved copy of the English king. He [the President] is George III. shorn of a part of his prerogative . . . , while his dignity as well as his influence are diminished by his holding office for four years instead of for life." 1 James Bryce, *The American Commonwealth* (The Macmillan Co., New York, 1910 ed., 1912) 39.

[147] These are the words of Whitehead in the quotation made above.

[148] In the quotation made above from Whitehead, he says: "In a discussion of instances of symbolism, our first difficulty is to discover exactly what is being symbolized."

squires as traitors to their class. Yet in its most general terms it is the eternal conflict between Jefferson and Hamilton, between Jackson and the Whigs and Biddles, between Franklin D. Roosevelt and the economic royalists, between the leaders of the poor and uninfluential and the spokesmen of the rich and well born, between those who stress the basic rights of the many and those who seek to preserve the vested interests and special privileges of the few, between *liberals* and *conservatives* [149] in the only meaningful sense of those terms, in which they refer to a divergence of view *within* the framework of *free* government [150] which is basically the same but varies in its particular manifestations in relation to the problems of the day. The hypothesis is admittedly a gross over-generalization; but it is none the less a necessary starting point for an understanding of the history of our politics.

The issue over titles was but a particular and highly symbolic phase of this eternal struggle. In 1789 we were an infant republic in a monarchist world. To the conservative mentality this fact signified a dangerous experiment which might put the bottom rail on top; while to the liberal mind it signified a glorious opportunity for popular government.

To the liberal, *republicanism* meant much more than the absence of a king. To him monarchy implied the right of rulership, and republicanism popular sovereignty; monarchy furnished a basis for class distinctions, and republicanism symbolized recognition that all men were created equal and endowed by their Creator with certain unalienable rights.

[149] It is natural for those who still adhere to nineteenth century Liberalism to resent the appropriation of their name by the "liberals" of today; but it is equally natural for the Liberalism of the last century to become the conservatism of today. The terms *liberal* and *conservative* are used in this study in relation both to the basic difference indicated in the text above and to the relativity of the expression of that basic difference to the problems of the day. In 1789 liberals and conservatives had just divided over the ratification of the Constitution and were already beginning tentatively to divide over the interpretation and application of that instrument. In 1793 they were to divide over our attitude to the gigantic struggle which in that year broke out between England and France.

Liberals and conservatives alike need the idea of the mean as a self-corrective. For neither the interest of the few nor that of the many is identifiable with the public good. The good of each group in the community is a factor in the common good; but the public good is also a factor in any enlightened view of the long-run interest of each group. Liberals, in particular, tend too often to become "professional" liberals who side automatically with the demands of every vocal *part* of the many, including in these latter days the demands of powerful trade unionists for irresponsible economic power.

[150] This qualification is necessary to avoid the confusion of *liberal* with *communist* and *conservative* with *fascist*. While some liberals become communists, and some conservatives become fascists, they do so in both cases by abandoning the basic tenets of free government. To every believer in those basic tenets every communist and every fascist is alike the enemy of his most cherished values.

To the conservative, the British constitution was the model[151] even though he realized that under American conditions and sentiments it could be only approximated. To him government by the gentry could be preserved and radical majority rule prevented only by emphasizing the symbolism of authority. To him democracy, if it did not end in mob violence, would at least undermine by stay laws and cheap money the vested rights of property and contract which he regarded as the only foundation of a stable and prosperous society in which the best would have their rightful place.[152] To him the only tolerable solution was a strong government with coercive power and with the popular branch checked[153] by the Senate, the courts, and an independent Executive.

Against the background of monarchist abuse in the Old World, one-man power under any other name was to the republican still suspect; while to the conservative, "Energy in the Executive is a leading character in the definition of good government,"[154] and that energy could be enhanced as a protection against mobocracy by various imitations of the trappings of monarchy calculated to attach to the Presidency the same sort of awesome symbolism.

Each in terms of his own values, Adams and Maclay were both right; though Adams failed to see that it was too late to use the device of monarchist trappings as a means to his ends.

Though the imitations of monarchy are now a dead issue, the basic clash between what we now call Jeffersonians and Hamiltonians goes on in terms of the problems of each succeeding period. As the twentieth century student views less symbolic aspects of this clash as they appeared in the early days of the republic, he cannot but have divided loyalties. For while Jeffersonian ends are the same today as a hundred and fifty years ago, and Hamiltonian ends likewise have not changed in a century and a half, the industrial revolution has brought it about that the means by which the respective ends may best be implemented have in notable instances been interchanged.[155] State rights, for example, which for Mr. Jefferson were a bulwark of popular government, are for modern trusts a

[151] J. Allen Smith, *The Spirit of American Government* (The Chautauqua Press, Chautauqua, The Macmillan Co., New York, 1907) 3–85; Henry Jones Ford, *The Rise and Growth of American Politics* (The Macmillan Co., New York, 1898) 1–120.
[152] Charles Austin Beard, *An Economic Interpretation of the Constitution of the United States* (The Macmillan Co., New York, 1936).
[153] J. Allen Smith, *The Spirit of American Government* (The Chautauqua Press, Chautauqua, The Macmillan Co., New York, 1907) chap. 6.
[154] *The Federalist* (Lodge ed., G. P. Putnam's Sons, New York and London, 1888) No. LXX, p. 436.
[155] For this thesis the present writer is indebted to Robert Kent Gooch, "Were Jefferson Alive," a special article in the Washington *Post*, September 1, 1936. See also James Hart, "The Presidency in Action" (book review), 20 *Va. Q. Rev.* 445, 447–448 (1944).

bulwark of their special privileges. The Presidency, which in 1789 Tucker sought by constitutional amendment to curb, is today the principal potential focal point for the leadership of political democracy in forcing responsibility to the community upon irresponsible economic power.

ATTITUDE TOWARD CRITICISM

WASHINGTON ON WHY A PRESIDENT SHOULD WELCOME KNOWLEDGE OF CRITICISM. When on July 14, 1789, David Stuart reported to Washington the unfavorable reaction to such things as the proposal to give the President a title,[156] he replied that he should like to be informed through so good a medium "of the public opinion of both men and measures," and especially of himself and more particularly on the critical side. In a few wise words he then made an observation which all Presidents would do well to remember:

The man who means to commit no wrong, will never be guilty of enormities; consequently can never be unwilling to learn what is ascribed to him as foibles. If they are really such the knowledge of them in a well disposed mind will go half way toward a reform. If they are not errors he can explain and justify the motives of his actions.[157]

The appropriateness of this attitude derives from the fact that the President is "prime minister" as well as "king" and, even in his capacity as "king," is the symbol but not the sovereign of the nation.

[156] 30 *Writings* 362, note 60, 363, note 61.
[157] *Ibid*. 360. Washington to David Stuart. July 26, 1789.

Chapter 3

THE PRESIDENT AND CONGRESS

. .
.

LEGISLATIVE RECOMMENDATIONS OF WASHINGTON IN THE FIRST SESSION (1789). In his First Inaugural Address Washington said the present occasion called only for reference to "the Great Constitutional Charter . . . which, in defining your powers, designates the objects to which your attention is to be given." So he substituted, "in place of a recommendation of particular measures, the tribute that is due to the talents, the rectitude, and the patriotism" of the members of Congress. The sole specific reference was to constitutional amendments; and here he said it was for Congress to decide, though he assured himself it would follow the middle way.[1]

It is worth noting, however, that there remain fragments of a proposed address to Congress which was never delivered but which was in the handwriting of the President,[2] and that this address made specific reference to various legislative functions of Congress. It may be that these references were so general that Washington decided it was better to confine himself to the over-all statement of his First Inaugural Address.

On August 5 the President consulted Madison. He had two matters to communicate to Congress, he said, the substance of which was in the enclosed paper. One was for decision before adjournment, the other "only to fix the attention, and to promote inquiry against the next meeting." He asked Madison whether oral or written communication would be best, and if the former, what mode should be adopted to effect it? Please amend the enclosed address, he concluded, by adding to or striking out.[3]

The apparent outcome was a written message to Congress of August 7 on Indian affairs and the militia. Indian disputes with some states and frontier hostilities "seem to require the immediate interposition of the general Government." So he had "directed" that papers submitted by

[1] 30 *Writings* 293–295. See also 1 *Annals* 27–29.
[2] 30 *Writings* 296–308. It is dated April (?), 1789. See p. 296, note 51.
[3] *Ibid.* 369–370.

55

Knox be "laid before you for your information." "If it should be the judgment of Congress" to have a treaty with the Southern Indians,

I think proper to suggest the consideration of the expediency of instituting a temporary Commission for that purpose, to consist of three persons whose authority should expire with the occasion.

How far this step was enough "unassisted by Posts" was also "a matter which merits your serious consideration."

In the second place, the President was "induced to suggest" "some uniform and effective system for the Militia of the United States." The "honor, safety and well being" of the country depended on this measure, and he was anxious for it to receive "an early attention as circumstances will admit." For it was now possible to avail ourselves of the military knowledge of trained officers and men, a resource which was daily diminished by deaths and other causes.[4] These general terms were doubtless designed merely to "fix attention" and "promote inquiry."

On August 10 the President sent another message. He had "directed" that a statement of troops in the service of the United States be laid before them for their information. These troops had been raised under congressional resolves of 1784 and 1787 to protect the frontiers against Indians, prevent intrusions on the public lands, and facilitate surveying and selling said lands to reduce the public debt. As these objects still needed troops,

it is necessary that the establishment thereof should in all respects, be conformed by Law, to the Constitution of the United States.[5]

On the same day Washington wrote a note to Pierce Butler, senator from South Carolina, thanking him for giving him the perusal of certain letters. The Indian business, he said, was now before Congress, and it would be well if the information about fugitive Negroes could come forward specifically.[6]

On September 16 the President laid before Congress a letter from the governor of the Western territory telling of "reciprocal hostilities" on the Ohio river frontier. In his special message on this occasion he said that acts of 1787 and 1788 had made provisional arrangement for calling forth the militia of Virginia and Pennsylvania, and

[4] *Ibid.* 371–373. See also 1 *Annals* 59–60, 710–711.
[5] 30 *Writings* 376. It is here given as addressed to the Senate. See also 1 *Messages and Papers of the Presidents* 52; 1 *Annals* 62, 715. On the last-cited page the message is addressed to the House of Representatives.
[6] 30 *Writings* 379. See above, chapter 2, Washington's reply to the address of the General Assembly of Georgia.

As the circumstances which occasioned the said arrangement continue nearly the same, I think proper to suggest to your consideration the expediency of making some temporary provision for calling forth the militia of the United States for the purposes stated in the Constitution, which would embrace the cases apprehended by the governor of the Western territory.[7]

A message sent to both houses under the date of September 29 stated that the President had been informed the day before by a joint committee that the two houses had agreed to recess from this day to the first Monday in January, and that in view of the long and laborious session and the reasons he presumed for this resolution,

it does not appear to me expedient to recommend any measures to their consideration at present, or now to call your attention, Gentlemen, to any of those matters in my department, which require your advice and consent and yet remain to be dispatched.[8]

The last clause was omitted from the message to the House.[9]

From this record it is evident that in the first session there was neither a presidential assertion of strong legislative leadership nor even a large number of legislative recommendations. Aside from his suggestion of pursuit of the mean in handling the delicate problem of constitutional amendments and his effort to raise for future consideration the problem of the establishment of a militia system, his only formal legislative proposals were for a temporary commission to treat with the Southern Indians, a law to bring the existing military establishment into conformity with the Constitution, and a temporary provision for calling forth the militia for constitutional purposes, with hostilities on the Ohio river particularly in view. It is not without significance that, with the exception of proposals of amendment, all these matters were cognate to the constitutional powers of the President in treaty making or as commander in chief. Most of them, moreover, concerned military matters which were peculiarly within the personal competence of George Washington.

THE SUCCESS OF WASHINGTON'S LEGISLATIVE PROPOSALS. Although the President kept his legislative proposals almost wholly within the province of his personal and constitutional concern, every suggestion which he made for immediate [10] action was followed. The amendments

---

[7] *Ibid.* 405, where it is reproduced from Richardson, and appears as addressed to the Senate. See 1 *Messages and Papers of the Presidents* 53; 1 *Annals* 82, 927. On the last-cited page it appears as addressed to the House of Representatives.
[8] 30 *Writings* 423–424. See p. 423, note 68. See also 1 *Annals* 95, 964.
[9] See 1 *Messages and Papers of the Presidents* 55; 1 *Annals* 95, 964.
[10] This does not include his incidental suggestion that whether a treaty with the Southern Indians would suffice if "unassisted by Posts" merited the serious consideration of Congress.

proposed to the states were calculated to allay disquietude without undermining the strength of the new government. The commission to negotiate with the Southern Indians was provided for.[11] The military establishment was brought into the new constitutional framework.[12] A temporary measure for calling forth the militia was enacted,[13] and a House committee was appointed to prepare and bring in a bill "providing a proper system of regulation for the militia of the United States."[14] The latter subject remained unfinished business when the session adjourned;[15] but Washington's intention had been only to "fix attention" and "promote inquiry." Congress followed his cautious lead without exception, though it should be added that it narrowed his proposal to provide for calling forth the militia for all constitutional purposes to the single purpose of "protecting the inhabitants of the frontiers of the United States from the hostile incursions of the Indians."[16]

PRESIDENT WASHINGTON AND REPRESENTATIVE MADISON IN THE FIRST SESSION. In November of 1788 Washington wrote to Benjamin Lincoln of the political situation in Virginia, and said the Federalists were mortified that Madison had failed of election to the Senate of the United States by 8 or 9 votes.[17] At about the same time he wrote to Madison that the accounts from Richmond were "indeed very impropitious to foederal measures," Patrick Henry having only to say, let this be law, and it was law.[18] The next month he wrote to David Stuart:

Sorry indeed should I be, if Mr. Madison meets the same fate in the district of which Orange composes a part, as he has done in the Assembly; and to me it seems not at all improbable.[19]

In February, however, Washington wrote Madison that he had heard of his election to the House.[20]

In the first session of the First Congress Washington was apparently

[11] 2 *Laws of the United States* 34–35. Approved August 20, 1789.
[12] *Ibid.* 74. Approved September 29, 1789.
[13] *Ibid.* These proposals were incorporated into the same statute.
[14] 1 *Annals* 714. August 8, 1789.
[15] 4 *Diaries* 60 (December 18, 1789); 1 *Annals* 1082–1083 (January 11, 1790, the 2d sess. of the 1st Cong. having convened January 4).
[16] 2 *Laws of the United States* 74. On the day before adjournment the House refused (16 yeas, 25 nays) to disagree to a Senate amendment which struck out "all that respected the number of the militia to be called into service for the defense of the frontiers, from the States of Pennsylvania, Virginia, and Georgia," and inserted "a clause instead thereof, empowering the President to call out the militia generally, for the purpose of protecting the frontiers against the hostile invasion of the Indians." 1 *Annals* 962–964; 2 *Laws of the United States* 74. Even so, the statute was much narrower than the President had suggested. See Constitution, Article I, section 8, §15.
[17] 30 *Writings* 125–126. November 14, 1788.
[18] *Ibid.* 131. November 17, 1788.   [20] *Ibid.* 203–204. February 16, 1789.
[19] *Ibid.* 146–147. December 2, 1788.

THE PRESIDENT AND CONGRESS 59

in frequent contact with Representative Madison. It was to Madison that he wrote ahead to hire lodgings for him in New York.[21] He corresponded with Madison about such matters as his reply to the address of the House,[22] the "line of conduct" to be pursued by the President,[23] communications to Congress,[24] the mode of communication with the Senate and appointments,[25] and again appointments.[26] In a communication already cited he suggested that Madison come for an interview that afternoon.[27] In another letter already cited he enclosed written points and asked Madison to "suffer them to run through your mind between this and tomorrow afternoon when I shall expect to see you at the appointed time." [28] In this same confidential communication, he asked:

Being clearly of opinion that there ought to be a difference in the wages of the members of the two branches of the Legislature would it be politic or prudent in the President when the Bill comes to him to send it back with his reasons for non-concurring? [29]

In reporting to Madison his further reflections, following a conversation the night before, about nominations for judges and Attorney General, Washington introduced a note of warmth:

I am very troublesome, but you must excuse me. Ascribe it to friendship and confidence, and you will do justice to my motives. . . .[30]

Maclay thought Madison guilty of "urging the doctrine of taking away the right of removals of officers from the Senate in order to pay court to the President," and then added in his journal these significant words, "whom, I am told, he already affects to govern." [31] In the absence of recognized party lines, the impression is nevertheless created in the student that Madison was generally understood to be quite close to the President.

[21] Ibid. 254–256. March 30, 1789.   [22] Ibid. 310. May 5, 1789.
[23] Ibid. 322–323. May 12, 1789. Washington also consulted on the same matter the Vice President, Jay, and Hamilton. See ibid. 319–321, and 321, note 83.
The day before he wrote to Madison on this subject, he had sent him confidential papers, possibly about New Madrid, and written: "As you are upon business which requires every information of the State of the Union and knowledge of our relative situation with G. Britain, I give you the perusal of them, . . ." Ibid., 321–322, and 321, note 84.
[24] Ibid. 369–370. August 5, 1789.   [25] Ibid. 374–375. August 9, 1789.
[26] Ibid. 393–394. August, 1789. This letter also asked Madison's advice on whether to consult the Senate about a couple of important matters. Ibid. 394.
[27] Ibid. 375, cited above.   [28] Ibid. 393, cited above.   [29] Ibid. 394.
[30] Ibid. 414–415. September 25 (?), 1789. See also his closing salutation, "I am your affectionate friend etc.," in the letter cited in note 20 above.
[31] Journal of William Maclay 94–95. Of course, the President also consulted others: See 30 Writings 311, note 67, 319–321, 368–369 (Senator Lee), 379 (Senator Butler), 413–414 (Secretary Hamilton and Acting Secretary Jay), 470–472 (James McHenry); 4 Diaries 14, 16–17.

WASHINGTON AND PROPOSED CONSTITUTIONAL AMENDMENTS. As the time approached for putting the new government into operation, Washington considered as Federalists "advocates for the Constitution" and as Antifederalists those "who wish to cause such great and premature amendments, as will render the government abortive."[32] In his First Inaugural Address he touched upon the question of constitutional amendments in general terms which tended to give the weight of his authority to support of the golden mean. He called the amending power an "occasional power" as contrasted with the "ordinary" objects of government. He said it was for Congress to decide "how far" its exercise was "rendered expedient" by "the nature of objections" to the "System" and "the degree of disquietude" which had given birth to them. He made no particular recommendations, but expressed confidence in Congress, adding:

For I assure myself that whilst you carefully avoid every alteration which might endanger the benefits of an United and effective Government, or which ought to await the future lessons of experience; a reverence for the characteristic rights of freemen, and a regard for the public harmony, will sufficiently influence your deliberations on the question how far the former can be more impregnably fortified, or the latter be safely and advantageously promoted.[33]

Some time possibly in May of 1789, the President wrote a letter to Representative Madison, who was on June 8 to make his speech on amendments in the House of Representatives, which clearly implies that Madison had submitted to him for comment his proposals of amendment:

Mr. Madison: As far as a momentary consideration has enabled me to judge, I see nothing exceptionable in the proposed amendments. Some of them, in my opinion, are importantly necessary, others, though in themselves (in my conception) not very essential, are necessary to quiet the fears of some respectable characters and well meaning Men. Upon the whole, therefore, not foreseeing any evil consequences that can result from their adoption, they have my wishes for a favourable reception in both houses.[34]

WASHINGTON ON WHY HE DID NOT LET THE TONNAGE BILL GO INTO EFFECT WITHOUT HIS SIGNATURE. To David Stuart the President wrote on July 26, 1789:

The opposition of the Senate to the discrimination in the Tonnage Bill, was so adverse to my ideas of justice and policy, that, I should have suffered

[32] 30 *Writings* 173–174. January 1, 1789.   [33] *Ibid.* 295.
[34] *Ibid.* 341–342, and 342, note 27. See also 1 *Annals* 440–468.

it to have passed into a Law without my signature, had I not been assured by some members of that body, that they were preparing another Bill which would answer the purpose more effectually without being liable to the objections, and to the consequences which they *feared* would have attended the discrimination which was proposed in the Tonnage Law.[35]

A WASHINGTON VETO WHICH DID NOT MATERIALIZE. In August of 1789 Washington asked Representative Madison:

Being clearly of opinion that there ought to be a difference in the wages of the members of the two branches of the Legislature would it be politic or prudent in the President when the Bill comes to him to send it back with his reasons for non-concurring? [36]

When the bill did come to him, however, he approved it, September 22, 1789, presumably on the ground that, while it provided the same pay for members of both houses prior to 1795, it also provided for an increase of pay for senators for that year, and left the question open for the period thereafter.[37] Had a veto materialized in this instance, it would presumably have been based upon grounds of policy rather than constitutional invalidity.[38]

THE QUESTION WHEN THE PERIOD ALLOWED BY THE CONSTITUTION TO THE PRESIDENT FOR CONSIDERATION OF A BILL BEGINS TO RUN. The Constitution in its veto clause provides:

If any Bill shall not be returned by the President within ten Days (Sundays excepted) after it shall have been presented to him, the Same shall be a Law, in like Manner as if he had signed it, unless the Congress by their Adjournment prevent its Return, in which Case it shall not be a Law.[39]

This language seems clearly to give the President ten days, not from final passage, but from actual presentation to him of the bill. That this was understood from the beginning seems to be indicated by a provision of the joint rules adopted by both houses in the first session of Congress for the enrollment, attestation, publication, and preservation of the acts of Congress. A joint standing committee should compare the enrolled with the engrossed bills, correct any errors, and report forthwith to the respective houses. Every bill should then be signed first by the Speaker and then by the President of the Senate.

[35] 30 *Writings* 363.   [36] *Ibid.* 394.   [37] 2 *Laws of the United States* 53-55.
[38] See Edward S. Corwin, *The President: Office and Powers* (2d ed., New York University Press, New York, 1941) 283-284.
[39] Article I, section 7.

After a bill shall thus have been signed in each House, it shall be presented, by the said committee, to the President of the United States for his approbation, it being first endorsed on the back of the roll, certifying in which House the same originated; which endorsement shall be signed by the secretary, or clerk, (as the case may be,) of the House in which the same did originate, and shall be entered on the journals of each House. The said committee shall report the day of presentation to the President, which time shall be also carefully entered on the journals of each House.[40]

THE TIME LIMIT ON THE FIRST REVENUE ACT. Madison, who had initiated the subject of import and tonnage duties,[41] moved to limit the time for the continuance of the bill for a duty on imports. "He imagined it might be considered by their constituents as incompatible with the spirit of the constitution, and dangerous to republican principles, to pass such a law unlimited in its duration." In justification of this position he called for safeguarding a constitutional prerogative of the democratic branch as against the Senate and even the President:

The constitution, . . . places the power in the House of originating money bills. The principal reason why the constitution had made this distinction was, because they were chosen by the People, and supposed to be best acquainted with their interests and ability. In order to make them more particularly acquainted with these objects, the democratic branch of the Legislature consisted of a greater number, and were chosen for a shorter period, so that they might revert more frequently to the mass of the People. Now, if a revenue law was made perpetual, however unequal its operation might be, it would be out of the power of this House to effect an alteration; for if the President chose to object to the measure, it would require two-thirds of both houses to carry it. Even if the House of Representatives were unanimous in their opinion that the law ought to be repealed, they would not be able to carry it, unless a great majority appeared in the Senate also.

Madison's motion received support from others in terms which were significant. Bland said the importance of the House depended upon its holding the purse-strings. Gerry spoke of the House as the "immediate representatives" of the people. Huntingdon looked with disfavor upon parting with their powers. Jackson thought the Senate might misunderstand the public voice. They were a permanent body, and might put what they considered the honor of the Government above the convenience of the people. White opposed what he called giving up to an already superior body the superior powers of the House relative to the revenue. The people, he thought, should be taxed only by representa-

[40] 1 *Annals* 58–59, 697–698.   [41] *Ibid.* 106–108. April 8, 1789.

tives chosen for that purpose; and the Senate were not an equal representation of the people. Tucker was against going on transferring powers until they became mere cyphers in the Government.

Opponents of Madison's idea were few but emphatic. Boudinot thus turned the constitutional argument against the Virginian:

> It was contended that the House were relinquishing their right to the purse-strings; what was their right? They can originate a money bill, but the Senate can alter and amend it; they can negative it altogether; the system of finance is under the mutual inspection and direction of both Houses. Then why should this branch attempt, unconstitutionally, to check the co-operating powers of the Senate?

Fisher Ames brushed aside the argument that the House was the democratic element in the Government. For what honest purpose should the people keep the purse-strings in their hands? He thought such talk carried fraud on its face. His concern was with safeguarding the public creditors. He insisted that public credit was not as safe under a despotic prince or a pure democracy as under our system. Under a pure democracy the whim and caprice of one body could dictate change. Both he and Boudinot pointed out that the money coming into the treasury could not be touched without an appropriation; though this did not keep Gerry from claiming that to collect money in the public coffers after the debt had been paid "would be such a temptation to the Executive to possess itself by force of the treasures of the nation, as he hoped would never be put in its way."

The House finally voted 41 to 8 to place a time limit upon the revenue act;[42] and the law as finally enacted carried such a limitation.[43] The debate shows a clear-cut division of opinion between proponents of aristocratic protection of creditor interests and exponents of popular control of taxation, with Madison on this occasion leading the latter to victory.

THE "LUMP-SUM" APPROPRIATIONS OF THE FIRST APPROPRIATION ACT. The first appropriation act enacted under the Constitution, approved September 29, 1789, provided simply

> That there be appropriated for the service of the present year, to be paid out of the moneys which arise, either from the requisitions heretofore made

[42] *Ibid.* 358–381. May 15 and 16, 1789.
[43] 2 *Laws of the United States* 2–5. Approved July 4, 1789. The limitation was contained in the sixth and last section of the act: "That this act shall continue and be in force until the first day of June, which shall be in the year of our Lord one thousand seven hundred and ninety-six, and from thence until the end of the next succeeding session of congress, which shall be held thereafter, and no longer."

upon the several states, or from the duties on impost and tonnage, the following sums, viz. A sum not exceeding two hundred and sixteen thousand dollars, for defraying the expenses of the civil list, under the late and present government; a sum not exceeding one hundred and thirty-seven thousand dollars, for defraying the expenses of the department of war; a sum not exceeding one hundred and ninety thousand dollars, for discharging the warrants issued by the late board of treasury, and remaining unsatisfied; and a sum not exceeding ninety-six thousand dollars, for paying the pensions to invalids.[44]

This was making "lump-sum" as distinguished from minutely itemized or "segregated" appropriations with a vengeance. Professor Corwin has pointed out that the act set a precedent against the applicability to the field of expenditure of the constitutional doctrine that, in order to avoid a transfer of its legislative power to the executive, Congress must lay down primary standards to guide executive discretion.[45] "No money shall be drawn from the Treasury, but in Consequence of Appropriations made by Law."[46] But this act, strengthened as it is as a precedent by having been passed at a time contemporaneous with the adoption of the Constitution,[47] indicates that Congress may, if it sees fit, merely provide maximal sums for broadly defined purposes.

CONGRESS IN ITS FIRST SESSION.[48] The constitutional history of the Presidency cannot be understood apart from the role of Congress in our governmental system. On January 1, 1789, Washington wrote to Lafayette that "federal sentiments seem to be growing with uncommon rapidity," and that he thought "the new Congress" would "not be inferior to any Assembly in the world."[49] On the whole, this prediction seems to have been fulfilled.

On March 29, before a quorum had been formed in either house, Madison wrote to Mr. Jefferson from New York:

It is not yet possible to ascertain precisely the complexion of the new Congress. A little time will be necessary to unveil it, and a little will probably suffice. With regard to the Constitution, it is pretty well decided that the

[44] *Ibid.* 73.
[45] Edward S. Corwin, *The President: Office and Powers* (2d ed., New York University Press, New York, 1941) 123–124. See James Hart, *An Introduction to Administrative Law with Selected Cases* (F. S. Crofts & Co., New York, 1940) 155–170.
[46] Constitution of the United States, Article I, section 9, § 7.
[47] *Cf.* 1 *Willoughby on the Constitution* (2d ed., Baker, Voorhis and Co., New York, 1929) §§ 28–29.
[48] See generally Henry von Hasseln, *The Work of the First Congress in 1789* (1946), ms. thesis for the M.A. degree at the University of Virginia, written under the present author.
[49] 30 *Writings* 185.

disaffected party in the Senate amounts to two or three members only; and that in the other House it does not exceed a very small minority, some of which will also be restrained by the federalism of the States from which they come. Notwithstanding this character of the Body, I hope and expect that some conciliatory sacrifices will be made, in order to extinguish opposition to the system, or at least break the force of it, by detaching the deluded opponents from their designing leaders.[50]

April 8 Madison reported to Edmund Randolph:

The subject of amendments has not yet been touched. From appearances there will be no great difficulty in obtaining reasonable ones. It will depend, however, entirely on the temper of the federalists, who predominate as much in both branches as could be wished. Even in this State [New York], notwithstanding the violence of its anti-federal symptoms, three of its six representatives at least will be zealous friends to the Constitution; and it is not improbable that a fourth will be of the same description.[51]

May 10 he again reported to Randolph that

No question has been made in this quarter or elsewhere, as far as I have learned, whether the General ought to have accepted the trust. On the contrary, opinions have been unanimous and decided that it was essential to the commencement of the Government, and a duty from which no private considerations could absolve him.[52]

Seventeen days later he wrote Mr. Jefferson:

The proceedings of the new Congress are, so far, marked with great moderation and liberality, and will disappoint the wishes and predictions of many who have opposed the Government. The spirit which characterizes the House of Representatives, in particular, is already extinguishing the honest fears which considered the system as dangerous to Republicanism.[53]

The last day of May he sent word to Randolph:

Our business here goes on very slowly, though in a spirit of moderation and accommodation which is so far flattering. . . . Scarcely a day passes without some striking evidence of the delays and perplexities springing merely from the want of precedents. Time will be a full remedy for this evil, and will, I am persuaded, evince a greater facility in legislating uniformly for all the States than has been supposed by some of the best friends of the Union.[54]

The first Congress was thus in a general sense federalist in complexion,

[50] 1 *Letters and Other Writings of James Madison* (published by order of Congress, R. Worthington, New York, 1884) 457–459.
[51] Ibid. 461–462.
[52] Ibid. 467–468.
[53] Ibid. 471, 473.
[54] Ibid. 473–474.

and accordingly in political harmony with the President.[55] If on the whole it did not generate as much heat in its first session as was generated in its second session and in later Congresses, this is probably to be attributed to the effect of the recent federalist victory in the ratification fight, the need of time for public opinion to crystallize with respect to policy and for parties to find their natural alignments and begin their organizational efforts, and the fact that the tasks of rounding out the organization were in these circumstances undertaken with more harmony than would be possible later and were for the most part not so well calculated to stir the deepest emotions as were the later issues of Hamilton's financial policies and our proper attitude towards England and France in the great struggle which began in 1793.[56]

The first task of the first session was to set the new machinery of government in motion. While in some cases it made mere temporary provisions,[57] it did such necessary things as to provide for administering the official oath to support the Constitution,[58] establish a revenue system,[59] and round out the structure of the central government by creating an administrative[60] and a judicial[61] system. This last it did upon a basis which has left a permanent imprint upon our constitutional order.

The second, but in every aspect equally important, task of the first session was to come to some decision with respect to demands for amendment of the new Constitution. This task also it performed in a manner which has stood the test of time. For on the one hand it avoided "premature" amendments which would have rendered the government "abortive,"[62] while on the other it proposed to the states a bill of rights calculated both to quiet the fears of the day and to provide safeguards which have become a cherished part of our political heritage.

The first session thus remains notable for its constructive achievements. In none of its major projects does Washington seem to have interfered. In none of them certainly did he assume an open leadership, except to define the golden mean with respect to the delicate question of

[55] See the section in the next following chapter entitled, "A Federalist Administration." On the personnel of the First Congress see especially Charles A. Beard, *The Economic Origins of Jeffersonian Democracy* (The Macmillan Co., New York, 1915) chap. 3.
[56] Cf. 8 *The Works of Alexander Hamilton* (Federal ed., in 12 vols., ed. by Henry Cabot Lodge, G. P. Putnam's Sons, New York and London, 1904) 425–429; Henry Cabot Lodge, *Alexander Hamilton* (American Statesmen series, Houghton, Mifflin and Co., Boston and New York, 1882) 45–46, 136–147, 160, 180, 185, 220, 223–224, 250–271, 281–282.
[57] See, for example, 2 *Laws of the United States* 53 (the post office), 72 (judicial processes), 74 (calling forth the militia).
[58] *Ibid.* 1–2.
[59] *Ibid.* 2, 7, 52.
[60] *Ibid.* 6, 32, 48.
[61] *Ibid.* 56, 72.
[62] 30 *Writings* 173. Washington to Knox. January 1, 1789.

proposed amendments. Congress, on the other hand, followed his advice in this respect and acted favorably upon such recommendations as he made by special messages on matters within his peculiar knowledge, interest, and responsibility.[63] His character, influence, and prestige, moreover, furnished a cement, if not strong legislative leadership. In the course of the excited discussion of a permanent seat for the government, this note was sounded by Vining in the House:

While we had a Washington, and his virtues, to cement and guard the Union, it might be safe; but when he should leave us, who will inherit his virtues, and possess his influence? Who would remain to embrace and draw to a centre, those hearts which the authority of his virtues alone kept in Union?[64]

Washington was from the first the chief asset of the Federalists, as he became in time the chief asset of the Federalist party.[65]

The later legislative leadership of Hamilton was merely foreshadowed by the adoption by the House of Representatives on September 21 of resolutions which recognized the "high importance" to the "national honor and prosperity" of "an adequate provision for the support of public credit," and "directed" the Secretary of the Treasury to prepare a "plan" for this purpose for presentation to the House at its next meeting. This was followed by an order directing the Secretary to apply to the state governors for statements of their public debts and other pertinent information for report at the next session.[66] Both actions were taken in conformity with the enumeration of the Secretary's duties in the act establishing the treasury department.[67]

[63] See preceding sections of this study, pp. 55 and 60.
[64] 1 *Annals* 870. September 3, 1789.
[65] 1 Homer Carey Hockett, *Constitutional History of the United States* (The Macmillan Co., New York, 1939) 259.
[66] 1 *Annals* 939.
[67] See 2 *Laws of the United States* 48 (chap. 12, sec. 2). Apparently without shame Joseph Barrell sought to profit by securing advance information on what Hamilton would recommend in his report to the second session of the First Congress. He wrote to General Webb that he had a sum in "indents," and as the General was intimate with Mr. Hamilton, "the man to whom we look for the resurrection of Public Credit," he asked him to find out Hamilton's ideas, and whether there was anything about them in his plan, and if anything, what. He could then judge whether to sell at the present price or purchase more. Joseph Barrell to Samuel Blachley Webb, Boston, October 8, 1789. 3 *Correspondence and Journals of Samuel Blachley Webb* (collected and edited by Worthington Chauncey Ford, New York, 1894; Wickersham Press, Lancaster, Pa.) 142. If General Webb asked Hamilton about the matter, what his reply was may be gathered from his response to a similar inquiry from Henry Lee, who at least had the grace to tell Hamilton not to comply if he thought the request "improper." Lee to Hamilton, Richmond, November 16, 1789. Hamilton answered that there might be no impropriety, but "you remember the saying with regard to Caesar's wife. I think the spirit of it applicable to every man concerned in the administration of the finance of

Likewise in conformity with this act was the action of the House in turning to the Secretary of the Treasury late in the session for a report on estimates for the first appropriation bill. As early as April 29 the House had appointed a committee to prepare and report an estimate of the supplies requisite for the current year and of the net produce of the impost.[68] On July 9 the House had ordered the report of this committee to lie on the table and be printed.[69] On July 24 a committee of ways and means had been appointed, with instructions to consider and report on the report of the earlier committee.[70] When, however, the treasury bill had become law on September 2,[71] and Hamilton's nomination to the secretaryship had been made and confirmed on September 11,[72] the House on September 17 ordered this committee of ways and means discharged from the business referred to it, referred such business to the Secretary of the Treasury, and ordered him to report to the House an estimate of the sums requisite to be appropriated during the current session toward defraying the expenses of the Civil List and of the War Department to the end of the year and for satisfying unpaid warrants drawn by the late Board of the Treasury.[73] Hamilton's report was received September 21 and referred to a committee of three.[74] Two days later the committee of the whole considered the bill making appropriations for the present year and made an amendment which the House accepted.[75] The first appropriation act was approved September 29,[76] the last day of the session.[77]

In the absence of strong executive leadership, how did Congress achieve the constructive results which have been mentioned?

The problem of leadership is a crucial one for all legislative assemblies. Such leadership may come from within or from without. The most likely source of effective leadership from without is the executive. In the English parliamentary system as we know it today, the leadership of the Cabinet is at once leadership from within and from without. It comes from within in the sense that the members of the Cabinet are members of Parliament, and from without in the sense that the Cabinet is, at the same time, the "efficient"[78] executive and administrative directorate.

---

a country. With respect to the conduct of such men, *suspicion* is ever eagle-eyed. And the most innocent things may be misinterpreted." Hamilton to Lee, New York, December 1, 1789. 5 *The Works of Alexander Hamilton* (John C. Hamilton, ed., Charles S. Francis & Co., New York, 1851) 445–447.

[68] 1 *Annals* 241, 303.
[69] *Ibid.* 645.
[70] *Ibid.* 696–697.
[71] 2 *Laws of the United States* 48–50.
[72] 1 *Annals* 80–81.
[73] *Ibid.* 929.
[74] *Ibid.* 939.
[75] *Ibid.* 947.
[76] 2 *Laws of the United States* 73.
[77] 1 *Annals* 96, 964.
[78] *Cf.* Walter Bagehot, *The English Constitution* (D. Appleton & Co., New York, 1906) 72, 80.

Under the separation of legislative and executive personnel required by our Constitution,[79] such executive leadership as is today allowed by Congress or forced upon it by the exigencies of party politics,[80] the multiplicity and complexity of its problems, and the demands of public opinion,[81] is necessarily leadership from without, and is in ordinary times made precarious by reason of this very fact. Under this separation of personnel, moreover, the immediate leadership of Congress has from the beginning had to be evolved from within.

The need of evolving this leadership from within was evident in the first session. Each house, as soon as it had a quorum, appointed a committee to prepare rules.[82] In both cases the rules provided for the previous question and for committees.[83] In the standing rules and orders of the House of Representatives, every bill was to be introduced by motion for leave or by order of the House on the report of a committee; and in either case a committee to prepare the same should be appointed.[84] It was also made a standing order of the day throughout the session for the House to resolve itself into a Committee of the Whole House on the State of the Union, when the rule limiting the times of speaking should not apply.[85] It was in Committee of the Whole that the full-dress debates of the House took place throughout the session. The committees of both houses were for the most part special or *ad hoc* committees; though the House soon provided a standing committee of elections.[86]

Under the bicameral system, moreover, the need developed at once for working out means of cooperation and compromise between two basically equal legislative chambers. This need led to the adoption of joint rules on the handling of bills [87] and to the institution of joint committees and of the conference.[88]

The problem of achieving constructive legislative results through the deliberative process was greatly simplified by special considerations which

[79] Article I, section 6, § 2.
[80] Henry Jones Ford, *The Rise and Growth of American Politics* (The Macmillan Co., New York, 1898) 356 *et passim.*
[81] Howard Lee McBain, *The Living Constitution* (The Macmillan Co., New York, 1929) 114 ff.
[82] The House had a quorum on April 1, and appointed such a committee the next day. 1 *Annals* 100–101. The Senate had a quorum on April 6, and appointed such a committee on the next day. *Ibid.* 16–18.
[83] *Ibid.* 20–21, 102–106.
[84] *Ibid.* 105. This rule continued: "In cases of a general nature, one day's notice, at least, shall be given of the motion to bring in a bill; and every such motion may be committed."
[85] *Ibid.* 105–106.
[86] *Ibid.* 126–128. April 13, 1789.   [87] *Ibid.* 26, 37, 58–59, 697–698.
[88] *Ibid.* 18–19, 33–34, 109, 306, 331–337, 808, 809, 948, etc.

in time ceased to prevail. In the first place, the legislative product, while in some instances of the highest importance, was small in quantity. Exclusive of the proposals of amendment, this product is contained within 76 pages of the *Laws of the United States.*

In the second place, the membership of both houses was exceedingly small as compared with that of today, and was never so small again. Rhode Island and North Carolina were not yet in the Union. The maximum legal size of the Senate was, therefore, only 22, and that of the House only 59.[89]

In the third place, the swing of the pendulum which had brought the Constitution into being was still in progress.[90] Exactly half the members of the Senate and eight of those in the House had been framers; and these men included "some of the most influential of the Convention members."[91] Madison himself was still in what may be called his Federalist period of thought, in important if not in all respects.[92] While the differences of outlook from which the divergencies between Federalists and Republicans later grew were already evident, these differences were as yet unorganized and remained merely those of individuals.[93] With party lines not yet clearly drawn, there was

[89] *Constitution of the United States,* Article I, section 2, § 3, and section 3, § 1. See 1 *Annals* 973 (January 13, 1790).

[90] Henry Jones Ford, *The Rise and Growth of American Politics* (The Macmillan Co., New York, 1898) 34–89. *Cf.* 3 Edward Channing, *A History of the United States* (The Macmillan Co., New York, 1937) 474–475, 481 ff. On the hypothesis of the "pendulum" see William Bennett Munro, "The Pendulum of Politics," 154 *Harper's Monthly Magazine* 718–725 (1926–1927).

[91] Charles C. Thach, *The Creation of the Presidency* (The Johns Hopkins Press, Baltimore, 1922) 141–142. Thach points out that, before the New York senators took their seats, there were 20 senators, half of whom had been framers, and thereafter there were 22 senators, half of whom had been framers. Hence the total number of framers in both houses was finally 19. See particularly Charles A. Beard, *The Economic Origins of Jeffersonian Democracy* (The Macmillan Co., New York, 1915) chap. 3 ("The Personnel of the First Administration").

[92] *Cf.* Sydney Howard Gay, *James Madison* (American Statesmen series, Houghton, Mifflin and Co., Boston and New York, 1898) 164 ff; Edward McNall Burns, *James Madison, Philosopher of the Constitution* (Rutgers University Press, New Brunswick, 1938) 12, 15–16, 19, 32, 37, 61–65, 72–73, 80, 90, 98 ff, 104 ff, 129 ff, 161, 165–166, 183–185, 200; Gaillard Hunt, *The Life of James Madison* (Doubleday, Page & Co., New York, 1902) 219–222, chap. 18 ("The Leader of the House"), chap. 22 ("Madison as a Partisan"), and especially 219–222, 337–338, *et passim* from p. 179; 9 *The Works of Alexander Hamilton* (Federal ed., ed. by Henry Cabot Lodge, G. P. Putnam's Sons, New York and London, 1904) 453–456.

[93] *Cf.* Henry Cabot Lodge, *George Washington* (American Statesmen series, Houghton, Mifflin and Co., Boston and New York, 1889) 61; Henry Cabot Lodge, *Alexander Hamilton* (American Statesmen series, Houghton, Mifflin and Co., Boston and New York, 1882) 136 ff, 153 ff; Arthur N. Holcombe, *The Political Parties of Today* (Harper & Bros., New York and London, 1924) 33–35, 41–46, 83; 1 John Bach McMaster, *A History of the People of the United States from the Revolution to the Civil War* (in 8 vols., D. Appleton & Co., New York, 1883) 567–568; Charles A. Beard, *The Economic Origins of Jeffersonian Democracy* (The Macmillan Co., New

enough community of thinking to get the legislative program through, without organized opposition or the need of the whip of party leadership, and under simple rules which gave much freedom to the individual member, produced genuine deliberation, and depended upon committees and the natural leadership of individuals to get business initiated and whipped into shape. In bringing up the question of a permanent seat of government, Scott told the House that this was a favorable moment to determine the matter:

We might be assured that at this time Congress possessed all their virtue and innocence; but it might be feared that would not be the case in future. Congress was now free from all factions, and as devoid as possible of the spirit of party and local views. It may happen that in a future day faction may compel Government to fix on some improper place, . . .[94]

In the fourth place, there were individual leaders whose talents and intellectual capacity furnished the ideas and the initiative to write into bills and into the proposed bill of rights concise expressions of mighty principles. Of Ellsworth in relation to the judiciary bill Maclay commented:

This vile bill is a child of his, and he defends it with the care of a parent, even with wrath and anger.[95]

Mr. Morris said he had followed Elsworth in everything; if it was wrong, he would blame Elsworth.[96]

Maclay also said the judiciary bill "was fabricated by a knot of lawyers."[97] Of Morris, in turn, he remarked: "His weight in our Senate is great on commercial subjects."[98] Perhaps the most conspicuous individual leader in the House was James Madison. Gay, in his very unsympathetic biography, remarks: "The direction of business seems, by common consent, to have been intrusted to Mr. Madison among the

---

York, 1915) 1–107, et passim; Charles A. Beard, *The American Party Battle* (The Macmillan Co., New York, 1929) 29 ff; Charles A. Beard, *An Economic Interpretation of the Constitution of the United States* (The Macmillan Co., New York, 1936) chap. 7 ("The Political Doctrines of the Members of the Convention").
[94] 1 Annals 816, 818. August 27, 1789. It may be noted that on May 14 Washington had written to Joseph Jones: "Your observations upon the necessity there is for good dispositions to prevail among the Gentlemen of Congress, are extremely just; and hitherto, everything seems to promise that the good effects which are expected from an accommodating and conciliating spirit in that body, will not be frustrated." 30 *Writings* 326. At that time, to be sure, the House was still engaged in its first major legislative debate, that on imposts and tonnage duties. 1 Annals 106–381 (April 8 to May 16).
[95] *Journal of William Maclay* 89. June 29, 1789.   [97] *Ibid.* 95. July 2, 1789.
[96] *Ibid.* 149. September 16, 1789.   [98] *Ibid.* 61. June 2, 1789.

many able men of that body." [99] It was Madison who took the initiative in the all-important matters of revenue [100] and constitutional amendments.[101] It was he who took up Boudinot's suggestion for creating the departments and first proposed that the heads of departments be removable by the President.[102] In the historic debate on the removal power he took a prominent part and finally lent the weight of his great influence and authority to the theory that the President had the implied power of removal by constitutional grant.[103] At other points of the proceedings his influence was exerted; [104] and it is evident that he had the full confidence of the President and was consulted by him even as he consulted the President on his proposals for amendment.[105]

The House initiated the import and tonnage [106] bills, the appropriation bill,[107] the bills creating the departments,[108] and the proposal of constitutional amendments.[109] Perhaps the most important things done by the Senate were to initiate and whip into shape the judiciary bill [110] and to prevent the House from following Mr. Madison in so fixing tonnage duties as to discriminate against England in favor of France.[111] There were other sharp differences between the two houses, as for example on conferring titles, having court writs run in the name of the

---

[99] Sydney Howard Gay, *James Madison* (American Statesmen series, Houghton, Mifflin and Co., Boston and New York, 1884) 136. See all of chapter 10, "The First Congress" (pp. 128–150).
[100] 1 *Annals* 106–107. April 8, 1789. Madison made this move just the day after rules of debate had been reported.
[101] *Ibid.* 440–441. June 8, 1789. [102] *Ibid.* 383–387. May 19, 1789.
[103] See especially *ibid.* 480–482, 514–521, 525, 527, 568–569, 600–608.
[104] See examples in this study and 1 *Annals passim*. Madison in first proposing import and tonnage duties advocated a discrimination with respect to the latter on the basis of whether the vessel were American, or one of a nation with whom we had formed treaties, or one of any other nation. 1 *Annals* 106–108. He was defeated, however, when the House voted to accede to the Senate's objections to tonnage discrimination in favor of France over England. *Ibid.* 632–633, 639–643. See also *Journal of William Maclay* 94–95, and Sydney Howard Gay, *James Madison* (American Statesmen series, Houghton, Mifflin and Co., Boston and New York, 1898) 134–136. Perhaps this was his most serious defeat, but it was primarily at the hands of the Senate.
[105] See the sections above entitled, "President Washington and Representative Madison in the first session" and "Washington and proposed constitutional amendments." 5 *The Writings of James Madison* (Gaillard Hunt ed., G. P. Putnam's Sons, New York and London, 1904) 339–425 gives the speeches of Mr. Madison in the first session, with footnote quotations from his letters on such important subjects as constitutional amendments, discriminatory tonnage duties, titles, the revenue system, departments, the removal question, the judiciary bill, the compensation bill, and the location of the seat of government.
[106] 1 *Annals* 106–107. Under the Constitution, of course, these bills were required to originate in the House. Article I, section 7, § 1.
[107] See references above, notes 68–77.   [108] 1 *Annals* 383 ff.   [109] *Ibid.* 440–441.
[110] *Ibid.* 18. This was started as early as April 7.
[111] See references above and *Journal of William Maclay* 87, 94; Gaillard Hunt, *The Life of James Madison* (Doubleday, Page & Co., New York, 1902) 172–174.

President, and recognizing the power of the President to remove the Secretary of the Treasury.[112] Legislative as well as executive sittings of the Senate were held with closed doors not only throughout this session but, with one exception, until the second session of the Third Congress.[113] To David Stuart Washington wrote:

Why they keep their doors shut when acting in a legislative capacity, I am unable to inform you; unless it is because they think there is too much speaking to the Gallery in the other House, and business thereby retarded.[114]

The Senate apparently was in a relative sense expected to be the representative of the few as well as of the states;[115] but it was still expected that the House would be the more important body, perhaps for this very reason. Madison favored paying senators more than representatives as necessary to get proper characters to fill the Senate,

as men of enterprise and genius will naturally prefer a seat in the House, considering it to be in a more conspicuous situation.[116]

In the House debates emphasis was placed by the precursors of Republicanism upon the need of protecting the position of that body as the popular branch of the government.[117] In the Senate William Maclay was indeed a sort of "original Jeffersonian Democrat,"[118] especially but not solely in opposing everything that tended toward the imitation of monarchy.[119]

The first session, indeed, despite its solid accomplishments, was not by any means a love feast of harmony and idealism. Besides the sharp differences between the two houses, the Senate was so divided on important issues that Vice President Adams had occasions to break ties by his casting vote.[120] The issue over discrimination in the tonnage duties showed a divergence of thinking which foreshadowed later party con-

---

[112] See references elsewhere.
[113] See 1 *Annals* 16.
[114] 30 *Writings* 363. July 26, 1789.
[115] *Cf.* 1 Max Farrand, *The Records of the Federal Convention of 1787* (rev. ed. in 4 vols., Yale University Press, New Haven, 1937) 408, 414, 421–423, 432, 437; Edward McNall Burns, *James Madison, Philosopher of the Constitution* (Rutgers University Press, New Brunswick, 1938) 72–73, 164–166; *The Federalist* (Hamilton ed., J. B. Lippincott & Co., Philadelphia, 1877) 434 ff (No. 57), 466 ff (Nos. 62–66).
[116] 1 *Annals* 679. July 16, 1789.
[117] See notably the debate on placing a time limit on the revenue measure. *Ibid.* 358–381.
[118] See *Journal of William Maclay* v ("Introduction" by Charles A. Beard), and *cf. ibid.* xvii ("Preface" by Edgar S. Maclay).
[119] See references under "Imitations of Monarchy" in chap. 2 above, pp. 28 ff.
[120] Vice President Adams broke ties on 29 occasions all told in the period of his incumbency (1789–1797). Henry Barrett Learned, "Casting Votes of the Vice-Presidents, 1789–1915," 20 *Amer. Hist. Rev.* 571–576 (1915). See also 1 George H. Haynes, *The Senate of the United States* (Houghton Mifflin Co., Boston, 1938) 231–240.

flict over the attitudes we should take toward England and France, respectively.[121] The hot fight over the permanent seat of government demonstrated a dangerous attachment to local and sectional interest and led to all sorts of out-of-doors bargaining and jockeying.[122] Discount as one must the suspicions of Maclay, what he called the tendency to form a "court party"[123] seems to have represented the loose combination of those who held views in favor of strong government and a strong executive. Maclay's journal presents enough evidence of what he called "caballing"[124] to make it clear that present-day politicians would have been at home.[125]

The reader of the House debates and of Maclay's journal is impressed by the fact that the written Constitution which had just been adopted was susceptible to adaptation in practice to various and divergent purposes.[126] The Constitution itself left it to Congress to round out the very structure of the government by establishing the administrative and judicial systems.[127] The way in which the first session exercised its admitted discretion in these respects had far-reaching effects upon our constitutional history. How different that history would have been if, on the one hand, inferior federal courts had not been created, or if, on the other hand, unqualified jurisdiction had been vested in the federal judiciary over all the classes of cases and controversies enumerated in Article III,[128] is an interesting subject for speculation.

In other respects the Constitution was silent, ambiguous, or at least not explicit. Thus it did not in terms authorize the judicial review which the now famous 25th section[129] of the judiciary act of 1789 calmly assumed.[130] Nor did it in terms authorize that Supreme Court review of state court decisions which were adverse to alleged federal authority or alleged federal rights, privileges, and immunities, by which the same section safeguarded "federal supremacy"[131] and gave the great Chief

[121] Sydney Howard Gay, *James Madison* (American Statesmen series, Houghton, Mifflin and Co., Boston and New York, 1898) 133–136. See especially 135.
[122] *Journal of William Maclay*, chap. 4. [124] *Ibid.* 111.
[123] *Ibid.* 119. [125] *Ibid.* 140.
[126] *Cf.* the statement of Mercer in the Philadelphia Convention: 2 Max Farrand, *The Records of the Federal Convention of 1787* (rev. ed. in 4 vols., Yale University Press, New Haven, 1937) 288–289.
[127] Article I, section 8, § 9; Article II, section 2, §§ 1 and 2; Article III, section 2, § 2.
[128] Charles Warren, "New Light on the History of the Federal Judiciary Act of 1789," 37 Harv. L. Rev. 49, 56, 62, 65–71, 76–77, 81–88, 109–110, 119–120, 123–127, 131–132 (1923–1924). See also 59, 108–109, 111–122, 125–131.
[129] 2 *Laws of the United States* 65–66.
[130] Caleb Perry Patterson, "The Supreme Court and the Constitution," 4 *Arnold Foundation Studies in Public Affairs* (Southern Methodist University, Dallas, Texas, 1936) No. 3 (pp. 19–20).
[131] 1 *Willoughby on the Constitution* (2d ed., Baker, Voorhis and Co., New York, 1929) chaps. 3–11.

Justice the means of protecting it in practice in his later historic decisions.[132]

With respect to one major subject which goes to the heart of the present study, Thach has well said:

... nothing is more vital than the relations of the executive head to the chief officers of the administrative departments, and the relations of the latter to the legislature. And yet the Constitution furnishes no final and authoritative decision of the question ... when the Constitution failed even to decide the fundamental question of whether the legislature or the chief executive was their master, it results that it was hardly possible to speak of the executive as completed.[133]

What Chief Justice Taft called "the legislative decision of 1789"[134] went far toward deciding that fundamental question by recognizing the removal power of the President in the face of constitutional silence upon the subject. At the time of this "decision" the federal courts had not been organized; and the Supreme Court was not in fact squarely faced with the issue of removal for one hundred and thirty-seven years afterward.[135] One is indeed startled to realize how different our central governmental structure would have been, had Congress in its first session decided this question in any one of three other ways.[136]

In general, more than one debate centered in no small measure around the effect of proposed action upon the balance of power as between the House, the Senate, and the Presidency.[137] The Constitution had established in broad outline the separation of powers and checks and balances; but it depended upon practice and interpretation to determine crucial details, not to mention the actual distribution of political influence. Since, moreover, in a shadowy sort of way the Presidency tended to symbolize monarchy, the Senate aristocracy, and the House popular government, more than one precedent was seen as making for or against the preponderance in the new government of one or the other of these tendencies.[138] The stakes seemed high, and the result was vigorous and illuminating debate in the grand manner.

[132] See Westel Woodbury Willoughby, *The American Constitutional System* (The Century Co., New York, 1919) chap. 3.
[133] Charles C. Thach, *The Creation of the Presidency* (The Johns Hopkins Press, Baltimore, 1922) 140–141.
[134] *Myers v. United States*, 272 U.S. 52, 163 (1926).
[135] *Ibid.*
[136] See Charles C. Thach, *The Creation of the Presidency* (The Johns Hopkins Press, Baltimore, 1922) chap. 6, "The Removal Debate."
[137] Note the debate on the removal power and on placing a time limit on the impost bill, as discussed elsewhere in this volume.
[138] *Cf.* Correa Moylan Walsh, *The Political Science of John Adams* (G. P. Putnam's Sons, New York and London, 1915), *passim*; 1 Max Farrand, *The Records of the*

WASHINGTON'S ESTIMATE OF THE POLITICAL PROSPECT AFTER ADJOURNMENT. In several letters written on October 13, 1789, a short time after the adjournment of the first session on September 29, Washington gave his estimate of the political prospect in optimistic terms. To the Comte de Rochambeau he wrote that

the political affairs of the United States are in so pleasing a train as to promise respectability to their government, and happiness to our Citizens. The opposition offered to the reform of our federal constitution has in a great measure subsided, and there is every reason to predict political harmony and individual happiness to the States and citizens of confederated America.[139]

To the Marquis de la Rouerie, *à propos* of monies due his officers from the United States, Washington followed words of regret by words of hope:

I can only express my regret that the political circumstances of the country have not heretofore capacitated a more punctual complyance with its engagements. But as there is a prospect that the finances of America will improve with the progression of its government, I can not but entertain a belief that the cause of the complaint will be removed and Confidence restored to our public Creditors. The measures to effect this desirable purpose must be proportioned to the means we possess; and altho' they may be slow, yet I trust they will be certain in their operation. I shall add to your satisfaction by informing you that the political affairs of the United States are in so pleasing a train as to promise respectability to our government and happiness to our Citizens.[140]

To Gouverneur Morris the President wrote privately:

It may not however be unpleasing to you to hear in one word that the national government is organized, and, as far as my information goes, to the satisfaction of all parties. The opposition to it is either no more, or hides its head. That it is hoped and expected it will take strong root, and that the non acceding States will very soon become Members of the Union. No doubt is entertained of North Carolina, nor would there be of Rhode Island had not the majority of that People bid adieu, long since to every principle of honor, common sense, and honesty. A material change however has taken place, it is

---

Federal Convention of 1787 (rev. ed. in 4 vols., Yale University Press, New Haven, 1937) 421–423, 424–425, 427–428; 3 *ibid.* 169; 1 *Annals* 106–108, 358–381, and at other points cited in this present study; J. Allen Smith, *The Spirit of American Government* (The Chautauqua Press, Chautauqua, The Macmillan Co., New York, 1907) 38, 130, 133–135, 137–140, 142, 145–150, 159, 161, 164–165, 187; *The Federalist* (Hamilton ed., J. B. Lippincott & Co., Philadelphia, 1877) 301 ff. (No. 39), 385–386, 400–402, 404–405, 434–440, 466–489, 503–504, 508–573.
[139] 30 *Writings* 437. See also Washington to Comte d'Estaing, October 13, 1789, *ibid.* 439; Washington to Lafayette, October 14, 1789, *ibid.* 448.
[140] *Ibid.* 437–438.

said, at the late election of representatives, and confident assurances are given from that circumstance of better dispositions in their Legislature at its next session, now about to be held.[141]

Then on December 27 Washington wrote to Jabez Bowen on the Rhode Island situation in terms which seem to have reflected the assurance of an established big power in relation to an isolated small power, if not to have carried the hint of a threat:

As it is possible the conduct of Rhode Island (if persevered in) may involve questions in Congress which will call for my Official decisions, it is not fit that I should express more than a wish, in reply to your letter, than that the Legislature at the coming Session will consider *well* before it again rejects the proposition for calling a Convention to decide on their accession to or rejection of the present Government. The adoption of it by No Carolina has left them *entirely* alone.[142]

ADMINISTRATIVE BILL-DRAFTING. It is of some interest to note a fact gleaned from the Washington *Diaries*. In December the President turned his attention to the problem of a national militia plan. He read European plans, a plan of Knox, and one by Steuben and "digested my thoughts" upon the subject. Then he put his ideas in writing

in order to send them to the Secretary for the Department of War, to be worked into the form of a Bill, with which to furnish the Committee of Congress which had been appointed to draught one.

Finally, he put his ideas on the subject in the form of a letter, which he sent to Knox.[143] Administrative planning of a legislative policy and at least contemplated embodiment of the plan into bill form thus began in the first year of operations under the Constitution.

[141] *Ibid.* 442–443. [142] *Ibid.* 485.
[143] 4 *Diaries* 59–60. December 18, 19, and 21, 1789. See also 1 *Annals* 714, 1082–1083.

Chapter 4

THE PRESIDENT AND THE SENATE [1]

TREATIES AND FOREIGN RELATIONS

WASHINGTON'S EARLY ASSUMPTION THAT THE PRESIDENT IS THE SOLE CHANNEL OF OFFICIAL INTERCOURSE WITH FOREIGN GOVERNMENTS. On September 29, 1789, the President sent a message to the two houses of Congress in which he informed them that the king of France had, by a letter "addressed to the President and Members of the General Congress of the United States of North America," announced the death of the Dauphin, and stated:

I shall take care to assure him of the sensibility with which the United States participate in the affliction which a loss so much to be regretted must have occasioned both to him and to them.[2]

Then on October 9 the President addressed a communication to "Our great and beloved Friend and Ally" in which he said the People of the United States condoled with him on the occasion, and assured his Majesty of "the unceasing gratitude and attachment of the United States." It appears significant that the President began this letter to the king with these words:

By the change which has taken place in the national government of the United States, the honor of receiving and answering your Majesty's letter of the 7th. of June, to "The President and Members of Congress" has devolved upon me.[3]

---

[1] The present writer wishes to express his indebtedness, in connection with this chapter, to George H. Haynes, *The Senate of the United States* (2 vols., Houghton Mifflin Co., Boston, 1938), and to refer the reader particularly to 1 *ibid.* chapter 2, and 2 *ibid.* chapters 12–14, 18–20. For the definitive study of the beginnings of the treaty making power in action see Ralston Hayden, *The Senate and Treaties, 1789–1817* (The Macmillan Co., New York, 1920), chapters 1 and 2 of which cut directly across parts of the first major topic of this chapter, "Treaties and Foreign Relations," and also carry forward to completion the history of topics herein considered only to the end of the calendar year, 1789.

[2] 30 *Writings* 420–421. See also 1 *Annals* 95, 963.

[3] 30 *Writings* 431–432.

When the message to Congress and the answer to the king are read together it is seen that the President preserved the forms which implied that he was now the sole channel of official intercourse with foreign governments. He told Congress that he would reply, and the king that he was now the one to receive and answer such communications.

WASHINGTON ON THE PRESIDENT AND FOREIGN NEGOTIATIONS. The first President had been in office less than a month when the Comte de Moustier "claimed the privilege of dealing directly with the President in diplomatic affairs."[4] Washington's reply was a polite but firm refusal. To what peculiar matters between the two nations did the Comte refer? We had the strictest ties of amity, by treaty. The United States were too remote to share in the local politics of Europe. Hence he must have referred to commercial affairs. Washington was little acquainted with such affairs. This would be enough to prevent him from "individually" negotiating on that subject. Much reciprocal advantage might result if the subject were intelligently handled; and he would not place, but be glad to remove any obstacles. He did not go in for "idle forms." Nor would he lose a major function of his office for an "imaginary dignity." But perhaps a young state should not depart altogether from established "rules of procedure" without "substantial cause." He preferred negotiation in writing and would himself use it as the mode, if obliged to negotiate. The established system, however, was for heads of departments to digest and prepare business. This system found its basis in utility, necessity, and reason; for it was impossible that the supreme magistrate could perform all business. In the commencement of the government he had to do many things personally. He would not allow a wall to be erected between himself and the diplomatic corps; nor was it beneath the dignity of the President of the United States occasionally to transact business with a foreign minister. But he would not then pretend to determine how the public would consider the establishment of a precedent of negotiation without any agency of a department head appointed for that purpose. Regard for the Comte and for France was expressed. He was asked to take this confidential letter as evidence of Washington's regret that he could not agree to the proposed mode of doing business. He added that he did not believe he "should be justified in deviating essentially from established forms."[5]

[4] *Ibid.* 333, note 10.
[5] *Ibid.* 333–335. Washington to Eléonor François Elie, Comte de Moustier. (Confidential.) May 25, 1789.

In this letter Washington set the precedent of considering the President's relation to foreign negotiation as analogous to that of a monarch of Europe rather than that of a foreign minister. He did not absolutely preclude the possibility of personal negotiation; and he of course assumed that the power of diplomatic intercourse was in principle his. But he established the system of negotiation through the agency of a foreign secretary as the normal practice in the new Government. On two important points his exact words may be quoted. He expressed his preference for written negotiation, which was so characteristic of the man, in these terms:

I have myself been induced to think, possibly from the habits of experience, that in general the best mode of conducting negotiations, the detail and progress of which might be liable to accidental mistakes or unintentional misrepresentations, is by writing. This mode, if I was obliged myself to negotiate with any one, I should still pursue.[6]

Of the relation of Chief Magistrate to department heads the President spoke as follows:

I have, however, been taught to believe, that there is, in most polished nations, a system established, with regard to the foreign as well as the other great Departments, which, from the utility, the necessity, and the reason of the thing, provides that business should be digested and prepared by the Heads of those departments.

The impossibility that one man should be able to perform all the great business of the State, I take to have been the reason for instituting the great Departments, and appointing officers therein, to assist the supreme Magistrate in discharging the duties of his trust.[7]

THE THEORY AND PRACTICE OF PRESIDENTIAL COMMUNICATION WITH THE SENATE. On May 25, 1789, the President of less than a month, in a special message, submitted to the Senate for "consideration and advice" certain Indian treaties which had been "negociated and signed" under orders of the late Congress. The treaties and pertinent papers were laid before the Senate, the message stated,

by the hands of General Knox under whose official superintendence the Business was transacted, and who will communicate to you information upon such points as may appear to require it.[8]

On June 11 another presidential message sent to the Senate a consular convention with France signed in 1784, altered under instructions of the late Congress, and as amended signed in November, 1788:

[6] *Ibid.* 334. [7] *Ibid.*
[8] *Ibid.* 332–333. For the report of Knox see 1 *Annals* 40–42.

I now lay before you the original, by the hands of Mr. Jay for your consideration and advice, the Papers relative to this Negociation are in his custody and he has my Orders to communicate to you whatever official Papers and information on the subject, he may possess and you may require.[9]

A message of June 15 announced that leave had been granted to Mr. Jefferson as minister to France, nominated Short to take charge in Mr. Jefferson's absence, and asked "your advice on the propriety of appointing him." [10]
Two days later Maclay recorded:

In now came Mr. Jay to give information respecting Mr. Short, who was nominated to supply the place of Mr. Jefferson at the court of France while Mr. Jefferson returned home. . . .[11]

The President wrote on August 2 to Senator Richard Henry Lee respecting some appointments, saying among other things:

As I am perfectly unacquainted with the Port of Yeocomico, and of the Characters living there, I would thank you for naming a fit person as a Collector for that district, on or before 1 Oclock tomorrow.[12]

Vice President Adams had early been concerned with the mode of communication by the President with the Senate. On May 7 Maclay wrote in his journal:

"There are three ways, gentlemen" (said our Vice President) "by which the President may communicate with us. One is personally. If he comes here, we must have a seat for him. In England it is called a *throne*. To be sure, it is behind that seat we must seek for shelter and protection. The second is by a minister of state. The third is by his chamberlain or one of his aides-decamp, I had almost said, but that is a military phrase. It may become a great constitutional question." [13]

Now on August 6 the Senate appointed a committee
to wait on the President of the United States, and confer with him on the mode of communication proper to be pursued between him and the Senate, in the formation of treaties, and making appointments to office.[14]

This committee had two conferences with the President, on August 8 and 10, respectively. In the first of these conferences the President said:

In all matters respecting Treaties, oral communications seem indispensably necessary; because in these a variety of matters are contained, all of which

---

[9] 30 *Writings* 346–347. For the fact see 1 *Annals* 46. See below (p. 100) for the Senate order that Jay appear before it in connection with this convention.
[10] 30 *Writings* 347. For the fact see 1 *Annals* 47.
[11] *Journal of William Maclay* 76. June 17, 1789. [13] *Journal of William Maclay* 20–21.
[12] 30 *Writings* 369. [14] 1 *Annals* 66.

not only require consideration, but some of them may undergo much discussion; to do which by written communications would be tedious without being satisfactory.

Since this would obviously not be the situation if the President kept in his own hands the sole function of negotiation and merely sought the consent of the Senate to his making a treaty of the completed draft, it is clear that Washington was thinking of the Senate as an advisory council in respect to instructions for negotiation as well as a body whose consent is a prerequisite of executive ratification. The only questions in his mind related to the procedures of oral communication:

> But it may be asked *where* are these oral communications to be made? If in the Senate Chamber, how are the President and Vice President to be arranged? The latter by the Constitution being ex-officio President of the Senate. Would the Vice President be disposed to give up the Chair? If not Ought the President of the United States to be placed in an awkward situation when there? These are matters which require previous consideration and adjustment for meetings in the Senate Chamber or elsewhere.[15]

He thought oral communications might be proper also for "discussing the propriety" of sending ministers abroad, fixing their grade,[16] and possibly other purposes; but for nominations he expressed at length a preference for written messages.[17]

The committee assured the President that the only object of the Senate was to be informed of his wishes, in which it would acquiesce. But he could plainly see that oral communication with respect also to nominations was what they wanted. One senator frankly said that his object in this was to get the Senate to vote *viva voce* on nominations, in place of the balloting system which Maclay had earlier helped put across. Finding all three senators against balloting, the President said nothing would sooner induce him to relinquish nominations by written messages than to accomplish this end. But he still so much preferred this method that he wrote to ask Madison for advice.[18]

The issue which had developed in the Senate over the *viva voce* vote versus the vote by ballot, in passing upon presidential nominations, is

---

[15] 30 *Writings* 373-374. August 8, 1789.
[16] For the view, however, that the *destination* and *grade* of foreign ministers are solely within the province of the President, and not subject to the negative of the Senate, see the opinion of Mr. Jefferson as Secretary of State, entitled, "Opinion on the question whether the Senate has the right to negative the grade of persons appointed by the Executive to fill Foreign Missions." April 24, 1790. 7 *The Writings of Thomas Jefferson* (Derby & Jackson, New York, 1859) 465-467.
[17] The President's analysis of this subject was definitive and predictive of practice from the beginning. For this reason it is set forth in full below, p. 122.
[18] 30 *Writings* 374-375. August 9, 1789.

revealed by Maclay's journal. When the President had nominated Short as *chargé d'affaires* in Mr. Jefferson's leave, Vice President Adams gave the Senate a discourse on forms and how they should give their advice and consent to nominations. Maclay took the position that it was like an election, and hence vote by ballot was clearly the spirit of the Constitution. Morris said this was beneath the dignity of the Senate. Maclay admitted it was the duty of every senator to disclose serious defects of nominees; but it was not to be expected that the President would nominate notoriously flagitious characters. Among his objections to open voting was one thus quaintly expressed:

I would not say, in European language, that there would be court favor and court resentments, but there would be about the President a kind of sunshine that people in general would be well pleased to enjoy the warmth of. Open voting against the nominations of the President would be the sure mode of losing this sunshine.[19]

Adams, as Maclay remembered to record the next day, had proposed that he rise in his chair and put the question in turn to each senator: do you advise and consent that Short be appointed *chargé d'affaires* at the court of France? Carroll thought a ballot was productive of caballing and bargaining. Ellsworth said it was suited for bashful men best, but the worst way for bad and unprincipled men. But Maclay was strongly of the belief that it was an antidote for caballing: no man could tell whether he was deceived in the bargain made or not. And at that time Maclay had his way: his motion for the ballot was carried by a vote of 11 to 7. He thought, however, that the losers showed uneasiness.[20] That he was right is indicated by the way in which the committee sought to use oral nominations as a means of reversing the decision.

In his second conference with the Senate committee the President took the position that since, in nominations and treaties, "the Senate is evidently a Council only to the President, however its concurrence may be to his Acts," it followed that "not only the *time* but the *place* and manner of consultation should be with the President." But since the place and manner might both vary with circumstances and presidential inclinations, he asked the Senate to accommodate its rules to the resulting uncertainty;

---

[19] *Journal of William Maclay* 76–78. Maclay also said: "A Senator, like another man, would have the interests of his friends to promote. The cause of a son or brother might be lodged in his hands. Will such a one, in such a case, wish openly to oppose the President's judgment?" It is interesting to note that while Maclay considered presidential influence as corruption, he seemed to think nepotism on the part of a senator commendable.

[20] *Ibid*. 78–79. See also pp. 79–80.

providing for the reception of either oral written propositions, and for giving their consent and advice in either the *presence* or *absence* of the President, leaving him free to use the mode and place that may be found most eligible and accordant with other business which may be before him at the time.

Some of his other observations on this occasion are worthy of remark. He thought the "indisposition or inclination" of the President might require that the Senate should be summoned to his house. He looked forward to the time when there would be an executive chamber, "where the Senate will generally attend the President." Different Presidents might have different inclinations or ideas on the manner of communication. Opinions of the President and Senate both might be changed by experience. The manner might vary with the kind of business:

On some occasions it may be most convenient that the President should attend the deliberations and decisions on his propositions; on others that he should not; or that he should not attend the whole of the time. In other cases again, as in Treaties of a complicated nature, it may happen that he will send his propositions in writing and consult the Senate in person after time shall have been allowed for consideration. Many other varieties may be suggested as to the *mode*, by practice.[21]

The committee reported to the Senate on August 20, and its report was accepted the next day, when it was

Resolved, that when nominations shall be made in writing by the President of the United States to the Senate, a future day shall be assigned, unless the Senate unanimously direct otherwise, for taking them into consideration; that when the President of the United States shall meet the Senate in the Senate Chamber, the President of the Senate shall have a chair on the floor, be considered as at the head of the Senate, and his chair shall be assigned to the President of the United States; that when the Senate shall be convened by the President of the United States to any other place, the President of the Senate and Senators shall attend at the place appointed. The Secretary of the Senate shall also attend to take the minutes of the Senate.

That all questions shall be put by the President of the Senate, either in the presence or absence of the President of the United States, and the Senators shall signify their assent or dissent by answering, *viva voce*, aye or no.[22]

Thus did the Senate not only carry out in full the suggestions of the President but reverse itself with respect to its method of taking a vote on nominations.

Maclay's rheumatism had led him to take a sick leave from July 20

[21] 30 *Writings* 377–379. August 10, 1789.   [22] 1 *Annals* 66–67.

to August 16.[23] Upon his return Izard, the chairman of the committee which had conferred with the President,[24] warned him that his balloting system would be reversed:

We have all been to dine with the great man. It's all disagreeable to him, and will be altered, etc.

Maclay was sure of his loss of character at court, as he called it, and reflected that in his ballot motion he had crossed the Rubicon, since it went to plucking up patronage by the roots. To undo this, he gathered, after talking with Izard, was a knot worthy of presidential interference. Influence, to Maclay, smacked too much of Walpole, and was neither more nor less than corruption.

Izard also told Maclay that the President had told the committee that he had consulted the members of the House, but not senators, as to his nominations. Senators, the President said, had an opportunity to give their advice and consent afterward.[25] This led Maclay to confide to his journal:

This small anecdote serves to divulge his [Washington's] conduct, or rather to fix my opinion of his conduct, for some time past, to wit, a courtship of and attention to the House of Representatives, that by their weight he may depress the Senate and exalt [his] prerogatives on the ruins. Mr. Izard was clearly of opinion that all the late measures flowed from the President. Mr. Madison, in his opinion, was seen in this business. The President showed great want of temper (as Izard said) when one of his nominations [that of Benjamin Fishbourn] was rejected. The President may, however, be considered as in a great measure passive in the business. The creatures that surround him would place a crown on his head, that they may have the handling of the jewels.[26]

When the Senate voted to abandon balloting, Maclay's colleague, Morris, said he hoped he would change his sentiments for *"his own sake."* Against the resolution went the vote of Maclay and only one other faint "No." "So the court party triumphs at large." [27]

The very day on which the Senate passed the resolution to accom-

[23] *Journal of William Maclay* 118–119.
[24] 1 *Annals* 66–67.
[25] See note 12 above, however, for Washington's request on August 2 that Senator Lee name a "fit person" for the collector at the port of Yeocomico, on the ground that he was himself "perfectly unacquainted" with the characters living there. This letter was in reply to one from Lee. See also the President's note to Senator Butler of South Carolina in 30 *Writings* 379. August 10, 1789. That letter seems *wholly* in response to an initiative taken by Butler.
[26] *Journal of William Maclay* 119–120. August 16, 1789. The first two brackets are those of the editor of Maclay's *Journal*.
[27] *Ibid.* 124–125. Maclay gives the date as August 21, 1789.

modate its rules to presidential discretion with respect to the place and manner of his dealing with it, the President sent the Senate a brief message announcing that he would meet the Senate in its chamber the next day to advise with them on the terms of the contemplated Indian treaties.[28] The two appearances which followed of the President in the Senate chamber were the beginning and the end of prior consultation in person, though not of prior consultation in writing.[29]

Some time in August Washington, in a confidential communication to Representative Madison, asked:

Should the sense of the Senate be taken on the propriety of sending public characters abroad, say, to England, Holland and Portugal;[30] and of a day for thanksgiving?

Would it be well to advise with them before the adjournment, on the expediency and justice of demanding a surrender of our posts?[31]

WASHINGTON'S FAMOUS EXPERIMENT IN PRIOR CONSULTATION OF THE SENATE IN PERSON WITH RESPECT TO A TREATY. It has been seen that Washington anticipated *oral* communication with the Senate in connection with the *negotiation* of treaties. Of historic significance is his first and last experiment with this method.

On August 20, 1789, the President approved the bill appropriating $20,000 for defraying the expenses of negotiating and treating with the Indian tribes.[32] The very next day Maclay recorded in his journal:

Notice was given just before we broke up that the President would be in the Senate chamber at half after eleven tomorrow to take the advice and consent of the Senate on some matters of consequence; but nothing communicated.[33]

This notice was given by a short message addressed to "Gentlemen of the Senate" and worded as follows:

The President of the United States will meet the Senate in the Senate Chamber at half past eleven o'clock tomorrow, to advise with them on the terms of the treaty to be negotiated with the Southern Indians.[34]

Of the scene which was enacted in the Senate chamber the next day no purely formal account can furnish those overtones which illumine

---

[28] 1 *Messages and Papers of the Presidents* 53. See also 1 *Annals* 67. August 21, 1789. This message does not appear in the Fitzpatrick edition of Washington's *Writings*.
[29] The incident is of such great importance as to call for treatment in full in the next following section.
[30] See note 16 above.
[31] 30 *Writings* 393-394.
[32] 2 *Laws of the United States* 34-35.
[33] *Journal of William Maclay* 125. August 21, 1789.
[34] 1 *Messages and Papers of the Presidents* 53. See also 1 *Annals* 67.

the reasons for its decisive character in hardening constitutional practice. For those overtones it is necessary to turn to the account which Senator Maclay set down in his journal.[35] His account reveals the prejudices of a plain and earnest republican who viewed with alarm what he considered the deliberate purpose of some to surround the Presidency with the trappings of monarchy and to fasten executive influence upon the new system of government in its very infancy.[36]

On Saturday, August 22, the Senate was on the coasting bill when, in Maclay's words,

The doorkeeper soon told us of the arrival of the President. The President was introduced, and took our Vice-President's chair. He rose and told us bluntly that he had called on us for our advice and consent to some propositions respecting the treaty to be held with the Southern Indians. Said he had brought General Knox with him, who was well acquainted with the business. He then turned to General Knox, who was seated on the left of the chair. General Knox handed him a paper, which he handed to the President of the Senate, who was seated on a chair on the floor to his right.

This paper was in effect a message to the Senate which sketched the background of the problem, referred to "the papers which have been laid before the Senate," and enumerated seven questions which were prefaced with this statement:

. . . As it is necessary that certain principles should be fixed previously to forming instructions to the Commissioners, the following questions arising out of the foregoing communications are stated by the President of the United States and the advice of the Senate requested thereon.[37]

Maclay continues:

Our Vice-President hurried over the paper. Carriages were driving past, and such a noise, I could tell it was something about "Indians," but was not master of one sentence of it. Seven heads, as we have since learned, were stated at the end of the paper which the Senate were to give their advice and consent to.

The President told us that a paper from an agent of the Cherokees was given to him just as he was coming to the Hall. He motioned to General Knox for it, and handed it to the President of the Senate. It was read. It complained hard of the unjust treatment of the people of North Carolina,

---

[35] The account of the incident given on the following pages is from *Journal of William Maclay* 125–130, except as otherwise indicated. An important *general* exception is mentioned in note 37 below.
[36] See *ibid*. "Introduction" by Charles A. Beard, and "Preface" by Edgar S. Maclay.
[37] 30 *Writings* 385–390. The quotations and summaries of the seven questions asked the Senate by the President which are given on the following pages are from this message. See also 1 *Annals* 67–77.

etc., their violation of treaties, etc. Our Vice-President now read off the first article, to which our advice and consent was requested. It referred back principally to some statements in the body of the writing which had been read.

The first question was worded as follows:

In the present state of affairs between North Carolina and the United States will it be proper to take any other measures for redressing the injuries of the Cherokees than those herein suggested?

The question was obviously meaningless without reference back to the body of the message. There it was stated that, "As the Cherokees reside principally within the Territory claimed by the North Carolina and as that State is not a Member of the present Union," it might be "doubted" whether the general government could do anything effective for the Cherokees, and it was suggested that the commissioners might be instructed to explain to the Cherokees the difficulties and to say the United States were not unmindful of the Treaty of Hopewell and would do them full justice as soon as these difficulties were removed.

Then, by Maclay's account,

Mr. Morris rose. Said the noise of the carriages had been so great that he really could not say that he had heard the body of the paper which had been read, and prayed that it might be read again. It was so [read]. It was no sooner read than our Vice-President immediately read the first head over again, and put the question: Do you advise and consent, etc.? There was a dead pause. Mr. Morris whispered me, "We will see who will venture to break silence first." Our Vice-President was proceeding, "As many as—"

I rose reluctantly, indeed, and, from the length of the pause, the hint given by Mr. Morris, and the proceeding of our Vice-President, it appeared to me that if I did not no other one would, and we should have these advices and consents ravished, in a degree, from us.

Mr. President: The paper which you have now read to us appears to have for its basis sundry treaties and public transactions between the Southern Indians and the United States and the States of Georgia, North Carolina, and South Carolina. The business is new to the Senate. It is of importance. It is our duty to inform ourselves as well as possible on the subject. I therefore call for the reading of the treaties and other documents alluded to in the paper before us.

I cast an eye at the President of the United States. I saw he wore an aspect of stern displeasure. General Knox turned up some of the acts of Congress and the protest of one Blount, agent for North Carolina. Mr. Lee rose and named a particular treaty which he wished read. The business labored with the Senate. There appeared an evident reluctance to proceed. The first article was about the Cherokees. It was hinted that the person just come from there might have more information. The President of the United States rose; said he had no objection to that article being postponed, and in the mean time he would see the messenger.

The second question implied knowledge of the course of action suggested in the message and was premised upon the assumption that that course would be followed:

Shall the Commissioners be instructed to pursue any other measures respecting the Chickasaws and Choctaws than those herein suggested?

The body of the paper stated that the distance of these tribes from the frontier settlements seemed to have prevented their involvement in similar difficulties with the Cherokees, and said the commissioners might be instructed to send them messages assuring them of our friendship and intention to extend a trade to them in conformity with the treaty of Hopewell, and be directed to report a plan for that purpose. While Maclay says this article was postponed, the *Annals* record that the second question was put and answered in the negative.[38] This meant that the Senate had no other suggestions to make in this regard. Perhaps it was the fact that the Chickasaws and Choctaws did not seem to constitute a serious problem that rendered it easy to advise letting it go at what the President suggested without any Southern senator's objecting.

Quite different were the questions asked in numbers 3–7 inclusive. These all related to the Creeks and hence involved the vital interest of Georgia. The third article asked a contingent question. If the commissioners found the treaties by which the Creeks had ceded land to Georgia ought to be considered valid, should they be instructed to insist upon a confirmation thereof? And if there was a refusal, should they be

instructed to inform the Creeks that the Arms of the Union shall be employed to compel them to acknowledge the validity of the said treaties and cessions?

Maclay continues:

... The third article more immediately concerned Georgia and the Creeks. Mr. Gunn, from Georgia, moved that this be postponed till Monday. He was seconded by Mr. Few. General Knox was asked when General Lincoln would be here on his way to Georgia. He answered *not till Saturday next*. The whole House seemed against Gunn and Few. I rose and said, when I considered the newness and importance of the subject, that one article had already been postponed; that General Lincoln, the first named

[38] 1 *Annals* 71. The accuracy of this statement is borne out by the fact that Maclay makes no reference to any action on the second question when the President again met with the Senate on Monday. Cf. *Journal of William Maclay* 126.

of the commissioners, would not be here for a week; the deep interest Georgia had in this affair—I could not think it improper that the Senators from that State should be indulged in a postponement until Monday; and more especially as I had not heard any inconvenience pointed out that could possibly flow from it.

The question was put and actually carried; but Elsworth immediately began a long discourse on the merits of the business. He was answered by Lee, who appealed to the Constitution with regard to the power of making war. Butler and Izard answered, and Mr. Morris at last informed the disputants that they were debating on a subject that was actually postponed. Mr. Adams denied, in the face of the House, that it had been postponed. This very trick has been played by him and his New England men more than once. The question was, however, put a second time and carried.

I had at an early stage of the business whispered Mr. Morris that I thought the best way to conduct the business was to have all the papers committed. My reasons were, that I saw no chance of a fair investigation of subjects while the President of the United States sat there, with his Secretary of War, to support his opinions and overawe the timid and neutral part of the Senate. Mr. Morris hastily rose and moved that the papers communicated to the Senate by the President of the United States should be referred to a committee of five, to report as soon as might be on them. He was seconded by Mr. Gunn. Several members grumbled some objections. Mr. Butler rose; made a lengthy speech against commitment; said we were acting as a council. No council ever committed anything. Committees were an improper mode of doing business; it threw business out of the hands of the many into the hands of the few, etc.

I rose and supported the mode of doing business by committees; that committees were used in all public deliberative bodies, etc. I thought I did the subject justice, but concluded the commitment can not be attended with any possible inconvenience. Some articles are already postponed until Monday. Whoever the committee are, if committed, they must make their report on Monday morning. I spoke through the whole in a low tone of voice. Peevishness itself, I think, could not have taken offense at anything I said.

As I sat down, the President of the United States started up in a violent fret. *"This defeats every purpose of my coming here,"* were the first words that he said. He then went on that he had brought his Secretary of War with him to give every necessary information; that the Secretary knew all about the business, and yet he was delayed and could not go on with the matter. He cooled, however, by degrees. Said he had no objection to putting off this matter until Monday, but declared he did not understand the matter of commitment. He might be delayed; he could not tell how long. He rose a second time, and said he had no objection to postponement until Monday at ten o'clock. By the looks of the Senate this seemed agreed to. A pause for some time ensued. We waited for him to withdraw. He did so with a discontented air. Had it been any other man than the man whom I wish to regard as the first character in the world, I would have said, with sullen dignity.

I can not now be mistaken. The President wishes to tread on the necks of the Senate. Commitment will bring the matter to discussion, at least in the committee, where he is not present. He wishes us to see with the eyes and hear with the ears of his Secretary only. The Secretary to advance the premises, the President to draw the conclusions, and to bear down our deliberations with his personal authority and presence. Form only will be left to us. This will not do with Americans. But let the matter work; it will soon cure itself.

Maclay

told Mr. Morris, on Saturday, that I would get a copy of the queries or articles to be answered to, and call on him, that we might make up our minds. He appointed this [Monday] morning, and I called accordingly. We talked and talked, but concluded nothing. I have several times called on him for a similar purpose, and thus always the matter has ended.

On Monday, August 24, as Maclay relates,

The Senate met. The President of the United States soon took his seat, and the business began. The President wore a different aspect from what he did Saturday. He was placid and serene, and manifested a spirit of accommodation; declared his consent that his questions should be amended.

The *Annals* reveal that on this day the Senate was wholly engaged in executive business, that the President was again accompanied by General Knox, and that the Senate answered the first question, which had been postponed over the week end, in the negative.[39] This meant that it agreed with the President that, since North Carolina was not in the Union, nothing more could be done with respect to the Cherokees than his message had proposed to do.

Maclay states that

A tedious debate took place on the third article. I was called upon by Mr. Lee, of Virginia, to state something respecting the treaty held by Pennsylvania. This brought me up. I did not speak long, but endeavored to be as pointed as possible. The third article consisted of two questions. The first I was for. I disliked the second, but both were carried.

This meant that if the commissioners found the treaties valid, they should insist upon confirmation and in case of refusal threaten compulsion of arms.

The fourth question asked, if the commissioners found the United

[39] 1 *Annals* 71. Maclay does not mention this point.

States could not justly urge confirmation of the treaties, whether they should do their best to obtain a cession of the Oconee lands; and if so, whether they should, if necessary, offer the Creeks four enumerated conditions: (a) a compensation in money or goods up to [blank] dollars to be paid by Georgia "or in failure thereof by the United States"; (b) a *free* port on the Altamaha or St. Mary's Rivers or any other place mutually agreed to by Georgia and the Creeks; (c) distribution of pecuniary considerations and military distinctions among influential chiefs "on their taking oaths of allegiance to the United States"; (d) a "solemn guarantee by the United States to the Creeks of their remaining territory and to maintain the same if necessary by a line of military Posts."

According to Maclay,

The fourth article consisted of sundry questions. I moved pointedly for a division. Got it. Voted for the first and opposed the second part. A long debate ensued, which was likely to end only in words. I moved to have the words "in failure thereof by the United States" struck out, and although Elsworth, Wyngate, and Dalton had spoken on the same side with me, yet I was not seconded. My colleague had in private declared himself of my opinion also. It was an engagement that the United States would pay the stipulated purchase money for Georgia in case Georgia did not. The arguments I used on this subject were so plain I need not set them down. Yet a shame-facedness, or I know not what, flowing from the presence of the President, kept everybody silent.

The next clause was for a free port on the Altamaha or Saint Mary's River. This produced some debate, and the President proposed "secure" port in place of "free" port. Agreed to. Now followed something of giving the Indians commissions on their taking the oaths to Government. It was a silly affair, but it was carried without any debate.

Maclay makes no mention of the fourth and last condition or concession to be offered the Creeks if it became necessary to persuade them to cede the Oconee lands; but the *Annals* state that the fourth question was "wholly answered in the affirmative."[40] This meant that the President's propositions, as amended at his suggestion, were so far accepted.

The fifth question involved a major decision of policy:

But if all offers should fail to induce the Creeks to make desired cessions to Georgia shall the Commissioners make it an Ultimatum?

The sixth question stated an alternative to the fifth. If the cession should not be made an ultimatum, should the commissioners make a

[40] *Ibid.* 72.

treaty to include the disputed lands within the limits assigned to the Creeks? and if not, should a temporary boundary be fixed at the Oconee line and the other parts of the treaty be concluded? and if so, should the free port and the pecuniary and honorary considerations be granted? and should the treaty of Hopewell be the basis in other respects of such a treaty with the Creeks?

According to Maclay,

Now followed a clause whether the cession of lands should be made an ultimatum with the Creeks. There was an alternative in case should this be negatived; but, strange to tell, the Senate negatived both, when it was plain only one should have been so. A boundary was named by the following clause which the commissioners were to adhere to. Money and honorary commissions were to be given to the Indians. The old treaties with the Creeks, Chocktaws, and Chickasaws were made the basis of future treaty, though none of them were read to us nor a single principle of them explained (but it was late).

Maclay appears to have got lost in the complications of questions five and six. That the Senate did not take contradictory actions appears from the account in the *Annals*. The Senate gave a negative answer to the fifth question and to the first part of the sixth, but divided the sixth and gave an affirmative answer to other parts of the sixth.[41] This meant that it took the perfectly consistent position that the cession by the Creeks to Georgia should not be made an ultimatum, and that the commissioners should not make a treaty *to assign* the disputed lands to the Creeks, but that they should make a treaty along the lines indicated on the basis of a *temporary* boundary at the Oconee line.

The seventh question was:

Shall the sum of 20,000 Dollars appropriated to Indian expenses and treaties be wholly applied if necessary to a treaty with the Creeks? If not what proportion?

Maclay concludes:

The twenty thousand dollars applied to this treaty, if necessary. This closed the business. The President of the United States withdrew, and the Senate adjourned.

The *Annals* say that all the money was to be used for this purpose, at the discretion of the President, and that he was also to fill in the blank amount mentioned in the first condition of the fourth question as the amount to be paid to the Creeks, if necessary, for a cession of the lands, by Georgia or "in failure thereof by the United States."[42]

[41] *Ibid.*   [42] *Ibid.*

94 THE AMERICAN PRESIDENCY IN ACTION

These details have been given not for their own sake but because they are necessary to analysis of the significance of this apparently unique [43] incident in American history. It is important to recognize, however, that its uniqueness did not consist in prior consultation of the Senate with respect to treaties yet to be negotiated, but in making such prior consultation *in person*. On several occasions in the next three years the President consulted the Senate in advance *by written message*.[44] It is getting ahead of the story, but may be mentioned in passing, that prior consultation *in writing* did not break down until it came to drafting the instructions of Jay for the making of his famous treaty. The delicacy of our relations with Great Britain at that time caused the President to play his cards close to his chest and thus to set the historic precedent by which the President has come to consult the Senate as a body only after the draft of a treaty has been negotiated, and hence both to take unto himself the creative initiative in treaty making and foreign policy generally and to emphasize the arm's length relation between himself and the Senate in respect to a function in which the two thirds rule makes cooperation so urgent.[45]

The importance of the precedent established by Washington's experiment with prior consultation *in person* is no less great because it was negative in character. As international relations became more complex and at times far more delicate, personal consultation would probably have broken down for the same reason that prior consultation in writing broke down; so the precedent of 1789 hardly matches that of 1794. Yet the fact remains that a practice which Washington seems clearly to have expected would be established as a matter of course was still-born on the very threshold of our constitutional experience; and the abandonment of the method was a first step in the abandonment of prior consultation in

---

[43] *Cf.* Edward S. Corwin, *The President: Office and Powers* (2d ed., New York University Press, New York, 1941) 232.

[44] See messages of February 9, 1790, 1 *Messages and Papers of the Presidents* 64–65; August 4, 1790, *ibid.* 68–69; August 11, 1790, *ibid.* 71–72; January 19, 1791, *ibid.* 81 ff; March 7, 1792, *ibid.* 110 ff; March 8, 1792, *ibid.* 115. See also Edward S. Corwin, *The President: Office and Powers* (2d ed., New York University Press, New York, 1941) 232–233.

[45] Edward S. Corwin, *The Constitution and World Organization* (Princeton University Press, Princeton, 1944) chap. 3, especially pp. 33–34, 36; Edward S. Corwin, *The President: Office and Powers* (2d ed., New York University Press, New York, 1941), 232–235. President Polk revived, in connection with the Oregon question, the practice of prior consultation in writing: 5 *Messages and Papers of the Presidents* 2299–2300. But see *United States v. Curtiss-Wright Export Corp.*, 299 U.S. 304, 319 (1936). It is to be especially noted that prior consultation by informal conferences with the Senate Committee on Foreign Relations or a subcommittee thereof is quite a different thing. See Kenneth Colegrove, *The American Senate and World Peace* (The Vanguard Press, New York, 1944) 27–31.

any form as the normal practice, and hence in reducing the term "advice" in the constitutional phrase "advice and consent" to a formalism as meaningless or as unreal as it now is in the enacting clause of English statutes.[46]

What the President was doing, it should be noted, was formulating the instructions of the commissioners and asking the Senate's "advice and consent" to these instructions. A reading of the message which he brought with him to the Senate shows that it was a succinct but carefully worded summary of the situation and a definition of the problem involved in drafting the instructions. There were alternatives, but only

[46] The enacting clause of acts of parliament may be reproduced from an act of 1921: "Be it enacted by the King's Most Excellent Majesty, *by and with the advice and consent* of the Lords Spiritual and Temporal, and Commons, in this present Parliament assembled, and by the authority of the same, as follows:—" (Italics supplied). *Public General Acts*—11 & 12 *Geo. V* (1921) 1. Maitland has pointed out that the form had crystallized by the time of Henry VII in much its present wording, "assent" or "advice and assent" being used where "advice and consent" now appears, and "by" where "by and with" now appears. F. W. Maitland, *The Constitutional History of England* (Cambridge University Press, Cambridge, 1920) 184 ff. In 1920 Maitland stated that the wording of the enacting clause has for 200 years been what it is today. *Ibid.* 381. In this form, then, it was known to the framers of the Constitution in 1787. See 1 *Annals* 556. Did they not copy this formula in drafting the clauses on treaty making and appointments? While there is admittedly contemporaneous evidence which indicates it was expected that the President should or would seek the *advice* of the Senate in the *making* of treaties as well as its *consent* to ratification of the completed treaty draft, as the very incident under discussion shows, nevertheless, quite aside from any question of the "intent of the framers," but rather with respect to the question whether the President acted *unconstitutionally* when he gave up prior consultation in person and then prior consultation in writing, three observations may be made: (1) After granting that the actual legislative process in the mother country did not in 1789 include the King as a mere ceremonial formality, as it now clearly does, one may still note that the reduction of the "advice" of the Senate in treaty-making to formalism but represents a process by which a wide divergence often develops between legal formulas and actual practice—a process which must have been understood by the framers, and which incidentally is illustrated in the present legislative process in the mother country. (2) The very fact that the framers copied a legal formula in these clauses tends to diminish the pertinence of taking the language used as the attempt to define and enact as *mandatory* a *precise* procedure. (3) Since the President *nominates*, the "advice" of the Senate, as distinguished from its "consent," in relation to the *appointment* of officers, necessarily has little or no *legal* meaning; hence, it seems clear that in *this* clause the framers used "by and with the advice and consent" as a bit of legal formalism which would have had the same legal significance if the word "advice" had been omitted. It will be remembered that Washington, in his conversations with the Senate committee, did not assume that Senate "advice" on his nominees was required, and preferred from the first to make nominations in writing for the Senate to take or leave; though it should be added that in his message on the Fishbourn rejection he did propose that in case of doubt the Senate would do well to ask his reasons for the nomination. This did imply something of the council-to-the-President idea; but he implied that it was purely optional when he admitted the Senate did not have to explain its reasons for rejection any more than he had to explain his reasons for nomination. See below, this chapter, and Edward S. Corwin, *The President: Office and Powers* (2d ed., New York University Press, New York, 1941) 68–70, 345 (note 16), 346 (note 18).

such as might be contained in any notes from which instructions were to be drafted.

The President had a practical reason for wishing to avoid long delay,[47] and, being a military man,[48] seems to have felt out of place in the atmosphere of a deliberative body. So he nearly lost his temper on Saturday, though he had himself in hand by Monday. On Saturday all the questions were postponed except the second, which was answered as the President obviously desired. On Monday the President probably got just what he wanted. In so far as the Senate exercised discretion, it did so in a choice between alternatives which the President himself had framed. The net result was thus highly satisfactory from his point of view.

Why then was the experiment not repeated? The initiative for a repetition rested with the President, to be sure; but he would almost certainly be influenced by the Senate's reaction as well as his own; and one senses that neither party felt comfortable in such a situation. Experience apparently showed that the President's observations shortly before on why nominations should be sent by written messages were in no small part applicable in spirit also in the consideration of instructions for treaty negotiators. Indeed, the symbolic story has persisted to this day that as Washington left the Senate chamber "he said he would be damned if he ever went there again" or "*swore* he would never go to the Senate again." [49]

[47] This reason was given in the body of his message. It appeared that South Carolina and Georgia had agreed to meet the Creeks "the 15th. of September ensuing. As it is with great difficulty the Indians are collected together at certain seasons of the year it is important that the above occasion should be embraced if possible on the part of the present Government to form a Treaty with the Creeks." See also the President's letter to Lincoln on August 11, while the bill for the appropriation was still before the House. 30 *Writings* 379–380. The President had also hurried in his nominations for commissioners, sending one name on August 20, the day he approved the bill, and the other two the next day. 1 *Annals* 65–67.

[48] Cf. Henry Jones Ford, *The Rise and Growth of American Politics* (The Macmillan Co., New York, 1898) 100–101, 103–104, 131, 133.

[49] Edward S. Corwin, *The President: Office and Powers* (2d ed., New York University Press, New York, 1941) 412, cites this story but thinks Maclay's journal appears to disprove its authenticity. He traces the story to an account of a Cabinet meeting of November 10, 1824, in Monroe's Administration, which is given by John Quincy Adams. The tale was there recounted by Mr. Crawford in both forms in which it is summarized in the text above. Crawford said Washington "at an early period of his Administration" had "gone to the Senate with a project of a treaty to be negotiated, and been present at their deliberations upon it. They debated it and proposed alterations, so that when Washington left the Senate-chamber he said he would be damned if he ever went there again. And ever since that time treaties have been negotiated by the Executive *before* submitting them to the consideration of the Senate." President Monroe said he had gone into the Senate about eighteen months after the first organization of the government in 1789, and had then heard that "something like this had occurred." "Crawford then repeated the story, varying the words, so as to say that Washington *swore* he would never go to the Senate again." 6 *Memoirs of John Quincy Adams* (J. B. Lippincott & Co., Philadelphia, 1876) 427.

The instructions to the commissioners,[50] while far more detailed than the questions submitted to the Senate, seem to have conformed quite closely to the votes on the part of the Senate with respect to those questions. These instructions were to be "the governing principles of your conduct" and to be regarded as secret; but it was added:

But many circumstances may arise, which may render some degree of modification necessary. In every event, however, you will please to remember, that the Government of the United States are determined, that their administration of Indian affairs shall be directed entirely by the great principles of justice and humanity.

A final question which arises from this incident is this: If the Senate had voted to "make it an Ultimatum" under the circumstances indicated, and the President had so instructed the commissioners, what bearing would this have had upon the express power of Congress to declare war?[51] Indeed, the commissioners were to be—and were—"instructed to inform the Creeks that the Arms of the Union shall be employed to compell them to acknowledge the validity of the said treaties and cessions," if the commissioners found them valid and the Creeks refused to confirm them. However, it never came to that; for while the commissioners found the alleged cessions valid, Alexander McGillivray, though protesting peace, refused to negotiate at all.

WASHINGTON ON THE IMPLICATIONS OF THE CONCEPTION OF THE SENATE AS AN ADVISORY COUNCIL IN FOREIGN RELATIONS. On July 14, 1789, President Washington wrote to the Acting Secretary for Foreign Affairs, John Jay, that he could not form a decided opinion on a paper from Jay without a view of the transactions with the Spanish minister. He wished also to know "whether, if the negotiations are renewed, it can be made to appear from anything that that Gentleman has said, as the result of an advance towards it from him, in his official character?" Unless this were the case, and prima facie the reverse,

[50] These are given in full in 1 *American State Papers, Indian Affairs* (Gales and Seaton, Washington, 1832) 65–68. See also the fragment in 30 *Writings* 392. For the report of the commissioners after their failure with the Creeks, see 1 *American State Papers, Indian Affairs* (Gales and Seaton, Washington, 1832) 68 ff. It may be noted that the instructions were issued thus:
"Geo. Washington.
"By command of the president of the United States:
"H. Knox."

[51] *Cf.* the Pacificus-Helvidius debate cited in note 61 below. Note that Lee seems to have raised this issue in the Senate discussion of the President's propositions. See Maclay's account above. On the other hand, see 7 John Bassett Moore, *A Digest of International Law* (Government Printing Office, Washington, 1906) 340–341.

will it not convey to him and his court an idea that a change of sentiment has taken place in the governing powers of this country? Will it be expedient and proper for the President (at this moment) to encourage such an idea? at any rate without previously advising with the Senate? [52]

It would seem that this question was asked on the assumption, which Washington seems originally to have entertained, that the Senate was his advisory council on foreign policy generally because its consent was necessary to the making of the treaties in which foreign policy at major points crystallizes. His question seems to have meant, whether a change of policy, even on renewing negotiations, ought to be made on the responsibility of the President alone, without the advice of the Senate. The President, to be sure, was the organ of intercourse with foreign nations; but did he not need the advice and consent of the Senate to his expression of what the policy of the United States was? [53]

Some time in August Washington asked Madison in a confidential communication:

Should the sense of the Senate be taken on the propriety of sending public characters abroad, say, to England, Holland and Portugal; . . . [54]

Would it be well to advise with them before the adjournment on the expediency and justice of demanding a surrender of our Posts? [55]

In the *Washington Papers* "at the end of 1789" there is a document in his own hand headed "Queries" which an editorial note suggests was "probably submitted either to Madison or to Jefferson": [56]

1st. If there should be a Majority, or a large minority, in the Senate for continuing the negotiations (maugre the difficulty with respect to the navigation of the Mississippi) from an opinion that the terms, *upon the whole*, ought to be acceded to; will the President stand justified under the notification of Mr. Gardoqui's leave of absence, and intended departure by the first opportunity, for letting him do this without submitting the matter in some form or another to the Senate? notwithstanding it is the opinion of the President that the claim of the U.S. to this Navigation ought not to be weakened by any negotiation whatsoever.

2d. Is there not something in the expression of the answer of Mr. Jay to Mr. Gardoqui that may be construed into a relaxation on this point, when the present derangements are done away, and we shall be in a condition to renew the Negotiations under the new Governt.

---

[52] 30 *Writings* 355.
[53] See Edward S. Corwin, *The President: Office and Powers* (2d ed., New York University Press, New York, 1941) 208-209.
[54] See, however, Mr. Jefferson's opinion on whether the Senate had the right to "negative the grade," cited above in note 16.
[55] 30 *Writings* 394.   [56] *Ibid.* 486, note 78.

THE PRESIDENT AND THE SENATE 99

3d. Would it be improper, besides withholding or qualifying the expression above alluded to, to convey verbally (a memorandum of which to be taken) but delicately to Mr. Gardoqui that from the very nature of things, and our peculiar situation we never can loose sight of the use of that Navigation however it might be restrained, and that by a just and liberal policy both Countries might derive reciprocal advantages?

He had better, in my opinion, return with our ideas to this effect, delicately and tenderly expressed, than with any hope or expectation of our yielding the navigation of a River which is so tenaciously contended for by a large part of the Union, and the relinquishment of which, or the fear of which, founded on appearances, would occasion, certainly, the separation of the Western territory.[57]

This document is important in that it seems to express the dilemma in which the view that the Senate was an advisory council in the conduct of diplomacy had placed Washington. With Gardoqui[58] about to leave under the possible impression from Jay that we might relax our demand for nagivation of the Mississippi,[59] and with the Senate not to meet until perhaps after he had departed, would the President not be forced to choose between diplomatic ineffectiveness on a point involving the vital economic interest of the West and the very integrity of the nation, and assuming on his own initiative and responsibility to make his position, and hence necessarily that of the United States,[60] clear?

The "queries" do not make explicit whether the emphasis on the "tenderness" of the proposed statement to the Spanish representative resulted in part from the fear that any statement so vigorous as to set in motion forces that might lead to war, might, *at least* unless the Senate approved or were known to be in favor, be an infringement of the power

[57] Ibid. 486–487.
[58] Don Diego de Gardoqui, *encargado de negocios* from Spain to the United States since 1785. George Pellew, *John Jay* (American Statesmen series, Houghton, Mifflin and Co., Boston and New York, 1890) 232. See *ibid.* 232–236; 4 *Diaries* 17.
[59] For the diplomatic background of this document see Gaillard Hunt, *The Life of James Madison* (Doubleday, Page & Co., New York, 1902) chap. 7 ("The Mississippi Question") and p. 154; 3 Edward Channing, *A History of the United States* (The Macmillan Co., New York, 1937) 489–491; the citation in the preceding note; John Holladay Latané, *A History of American Foreign Policy* (Doubleday, Page & Co., Garden City, 1927) 26–36, 43–46, 54–57; Thomas A. Bailey, *A Diplomatic History of the American People* (3d ed., F. S. Crofts & Co., New York, 1946) 23–24, 32, 44–50, 68–69; 1 *The American Secretaries of State and Their Diplomacy* (Samuel Flagg Bemis, ed., Alfred A. Knopf, New York, 1927) 28, 145–152, 197–199, 243–250; 2 *ibid.* 37–58, 120–129, 221–227; Frank Monaghan, *John Jay* (The Bobbs-Merrill Co., New York & Indianapolis, 1935) 255–261. On the Nootka incident see Thomas A. Bailey's book, cited above in this note, pp. 54–55.
[60] See note 16 above and Jefferson to Morris, August 16, 1793, 4 *The Writings of Thomas Jefferson* (Washington ed., Derby & Jackson, New York, 1859) 47; Jefferson to Genet: November 22, 1793, *ibid.* 84–85; December 9, 1793, *ibid.* 90–92; December 31, 1793, *ibid.* 99–100.

of Congress to declare war.[61] The twentieth century reader will realize that such a narrow view of presidential diplomacy would have made Woodrow Wilson guilty of an infringement of the war power when he warned Germany that the United States would hold her to a "strict accountability."

In any event, the dilemma suggested by these "queries" illustrates the practical necessity for creative presidential diplomacy *without* the necessity of obtaining at *every* juncture the "advice and consent" of the Senate by *prior* consultation, whether in person or in writing.

ATTENDANCE OF JAY AS ACTING SECRETARY OF FOREIGN AFFAIRS AT MEETINGS OF THE SENATE. It has already been noted that the President on May 25, 1789, sent a message with Indian treaties and pertinent papers to the Senate "by the hands of General Knox," with the statement that Knox would give the Senate requisite information.[62] Maclay's entry would seem to indicate that Knox on this occasion merely acted as a glorified messenger:

A message was announced from the President by General Knox. . . . and the General Knox advanced and laid the papers—being very bulky—on the table. . . .[63]

Mention has also been made of a message of June 11, covering a consular convention with France, signed in November, 1788, which the President submitted to the Senate "by the hands of Mr. Jay," with the statement that the latter had "my Orders" to give the Senate needed information.[64] The sequel has become historic. On July 21 the Senate

Ordered, That the Secretary of Foreign Affairs attend the Senate tomorrow, and bring with him such papers as are requisite to give full information relative to the consular convention between France and the United States.[65]

Accordingly, on July 22, 1789,

The Senate were today mostly engaged in executive business. The Secretary of Foreign Affairs attended, agreeably to order, and made the necessary explanations; . . .[66]

---

[61] *Cf.* the Pacificus-Helvidius debate of 1793: 1 *Letters and Other Writings of James Madison* (published by order of Congress, R. Worthington, New York, 1884) 607–654; 4 *The Works of Alexander Hamilton* (Federal Edition, ed. by Henry Cabot Lodge, G. P. Putnam's Sons, New York and London, 1904) 432–489; Edward S. Corwin, *The President's Control of Foreign Relations* (Princeton University Press, Princeton, 1917) 7–32.
[62] 30 *Writings* 332–333.
[63] *Journal of William Maclay* 48.
[64] 30 *Writings* 346–347. See for the fact 1 *Annals* 46.
[65] 1 *Annals* 52.
[66] *Ibid.*

The Senate then passed a resolution as follows:

Whereas, a convention referred this day to the Senate bears reference to a convention pending between the Most Christian King and the United States, previous to the adoption of our present Constitution,

Resolved, That the Secretary of Foreign Affairs, under the former Congress be requested to peruse the said convention, and to give his opinion how far he conceives the faith of the United States to be engaged, either by former agreed stipulations, or negotiations entered into by our Minister at the court of Versailles, to ratify, in its present sense or form, the convention now referred to the Senate.[67]

Five days later the Secretary of Foreign Affairs "reported his opinion upon the consular convention between France and the United States, as follows: . . ." There follows in the *Annals* a written report of some length signed by John Jay.[68] The record thus shows the Acting Secretary attending a meeting of the Senate on July 22 in response to its "order" of the day before and making the necessary explanations on the business before this executive session.[69]

In the message to the Senate, dated June 15, which nominated Short as *chargé* at the Court of France, the President stated:

There are in the Office for Foreign Affairs papers which will acquaint you with his character, and which Mr. Jay has my directions to lay before you at such time as you may think proper to assign.[70]

Maclay has already been given as authority that two days later Jay came in to give information about Short.[71]

The *Annals* contain records which indicate that the President used Knox as his agent to deliver written messages to both houses of Congress. Thus on August 7 an item in the Senate proceedings was "A message

---

[67] *Ibid.* 52–53.
[68] *Ibid.* 53–55. July 27, 1789. See 5 John Bassett Moore, *A Digest of International Law* (Government Printing Office, Washington, 1906) 184–185.
[69] This appearance of Jay in the Senate and the one described immediately below, as well as the provision of law noted in chapter 7 below, by which the Secretary of the Treasury should make report and give information on matters referred to him by either house or appertaining to his office, "in person or in writing, (as he may be required,)," furnish precedents for the constitutionality of having cabinet members sit and speak in Congress. Such a plan has often been advocated, and was expressly provided for in the Constitution of the Confederate States of America. Henry Steele Commager, *Documents of American History* (2d ed., F. S. Crofts & Co., New York, 1940) 378. The present writer is strongly of opinion, however, that such a plan would be a dangerous venture. See James Hart, *The Ordinance Making Powers of the President* (The Johns Hopkins Press, Baltimore, 1925) 295–296, 302; Harold J. Laski, *The American Presidency* (George Allen & Unwin, Ltd., London, 1940) lecture 2, especially pp. 104–117.
[70] 1 *Messages and Papers of the Presidents* 50. See for the fact 1 *Annals* 47 (June 16).
[71] *Journal of William Maclay* 76. May 17, 1789.

from the President of the United States, by General Knox."[72] On the same message the House proceedings are more specific:

The following message was received from the President of the United States, by General Knox, who delivered therewith sundry statements and papers relating to the same.[73]

A similar record appears for August 10.[74]

In this connection may be noted what Maclay wrote in his journal for August 20. Mr. Lear had for two days past been "introduced quite up to the Vice-President's table to deliver messages." Since the *Annals* record messages of the 18th and 20th presenting nominations to office,[75] it may be that the President regularly used a private secretary to deliver messages of that sort. On the 20th Izard objected to Lear's being received as indicated above. Maclay had understood that the "'head of a department'" should be admitted to the table "if he came to deliver a message," but that a private secretary should be received only at the bar. He grumbled in his journal that the Clerk of the House was received only at the bar, though he was in his opinion "a more respectable character than any domestic of the President."[76]

THE FIRST USE BY A PRESIDENT OF A PRIVATE AGENT IN DIPLOMACY. On October 13, 1789, after the adjournment of the Senate, President Washington wrote to Gouverneur Morris a letter in which he said it was important to both countries that the treaty of peace with Great Britain should be observed and performed with perfect and mutual good faith, and that a treaty of commerce should be concluded on principles of reciprocal advantage, and that accordingly

I wish to be ascertained of the Sentiments and Intentions of the Court of London on these interesting Subjects.

The President continued:

It appears to me most expedient to have these Inquiries made informally, by a private Agent; and understanding that you will soon be in London, I desire you in that Capacity, and on the Authority and Credit of this Letter, to converse with His Britannic Majesty's Ministers on these Points, vizt: whether there be any and what Objections to now performing those Articles in the Treaty, which remain to be performed on his Part; and whether they incline to a Treaty of Commerce with the United States on any and what Terms.

This communication, Washington went on, ought "regularly" to have been made to Morris by the Secretary of State, but that office was not

[72] 1 *Annals* 59. [74] *Ibid.* 62, 715. [76] *Journal of William Maclay* 123–124.
[73] *Ibid.* 710. [75] *Ibid.* 65–66.

filled, and his desire of avoiding delays induced him to make it under his own hand. He concluded:

It is my wish to promote Harmony and mutual Satisfaction between the two Countries, and it would give me great pleasure to find that the Result of your Agency in the Business now communicated to you, will conduce to that End.[77]

Another letter of the same date told Morris that the former letter would give him the "credence necessary to enable you to do the business, which it commits to your management," and proceeded to give him his instructions, which were carefully and succinctly worded. Here it needs only to be remarked that Washington reminded Morris that in the late session of Congress a very respectable number of both houses inclined to a discrimination of duties unfavorable to Britain, which would have taken place but for conciliatory considerations and the probability that the late change in our government and circumstances would lead to more satisfactory arrangements, and that the privilege of trade with the British West Indies was regarded here as of the highest importance, so that he should be careful not to countenance any idea of dispensing with it in a treaty; instructed him to get their views on the latter point, since it was not expedient to commence negotiations without first having good reasons to expect their satisfactory termination; and authorized him to remark that their omitting to send a minister here when we had sent one to London had not made an agreeable impression in this country, and to ask their future conduct on similar occasions. "It is in my opinion very important," the President declared, "that we avoid errors in our system of policy respecting Great Britain."[78]

[77] 30 *Writings* 439–440. Knox approved the idea of a private agent and mentioned Bancroft. Hamilton approved but mentioned Morris. Madison preferred to await Mr. Jefferson, and thought with Jay that while Morris was talented, his judgment was questionable. Madison said also that the move might commit the President to Morris for the post of minister in France or England, and Morris might negotiate with this in mind. 4 *Diaries* 16–17. See Memorandum dated December, 1789, in 5 *The Writings of James Madison* (Gaillard Hunt, ed., G. P. Putnam's Sons, New York and London, 1904) 433–434.

[78] 30 *Writings* 440–442. See also the private letter, Washington to Morris, of the same date: *ibid.* 442–445.

It may be noted that on February 14, 1791, the President informed the Senate of what he had done: "Conceiving that in the possible event of a refusal of justice on the part of Great Britain we should stand less committed should it be made to a private rather than to a public person, I employed Mr. Gouverneur Morris, who was on the spot, and without giving him any definite character, to enter informally into the conferences before mentioned. For your more particular information I lay before you the instructions I gave him and those parts of his communications wherein the British ministers appear either in conversation or by letter. . . .

. . . .

"Their views being thus sufficiently ascertained, I have directed Mr. Morris to discontinue his communications with them." 1 *Messages and Papers of the Presidents* 88. See also 31 *Writings* 214–215; 2 *Annals* 1801. *Cf.* 2 *Annals* 2015.

Thus was inaugurated the first of a long line of instances in which Presidents have used private agents in the conduct of diplomacy.[79]

THE QUESTION WHETHER INDIAN TREATIES SHOULD BE RATIFIED. In September, 1789, the Senate resolved that the President "be advised to execute and enjoin the observance of the treaty" concluded at Fort Harmar in the preceding January between Governor St. Clair of the Western Territory and the sachems and warriors of named Indian nations.[80]

Shortly thereafter the Senate received a message from the President asking that body to clarify its intention:

It is said to be the general understanding and practice of nations, as a check on the mistakes and indiscretions of ministers or commissioners, not to consider any treaty negotiated and signed by such officers as final and conclusive until ratified by the sovereign or government from whom they derive their powers.

This practice had been adopted by the United States in treating with European nations, and the President was inclined to think it advisable to observe it in treating with the Indians:

for though such treaties, being on their part made by their chiefs or rulers, need not be ratified by them, yet, being formed on our part by the agency of subordinate officers, it seems to be both prudent and reasonable that their acts should not be binding on the nation until approved and ratified by the Government.

He thought this point "should be well considered and settled, so that our national proceedings in this respect may become uniform and be directed by fixed and stable principles."

The treaties in question had raised two questions in his mind on which "I request your opinion and advice." These were (1) "whether those treaties were to be considered as perfected and consequently as obligatory without being ratified;" and if not, (2) whether they ought to be ratified.

In advising him "to execute and enjoin an observance of" these treaties the Senate "doubtless intended to be clear and explicit," but without further explanation he feared he would misunderstand their meaning,

for if by my *executing* that treaty you mean that I should make it (in a more particular and immediate manner than it now is) the act of Govern-

---

[79] Henry Merritt Wriston, *Executive Agents in American Foreign Relations* (The Johns Hopkins Press, Baltimore, 1929) 368–371 *et passim*.
[80] 1 Annals 79–80. September 8, 1789.

ment, then it follows that I am to ratify it. If you mean by my *executing it* that I am to see that it be carried into effect and operation, then I am led to conclude either that you consider it as being perfect and obligatory in its present state, and therefore to be executed and observed, or that you consider it as to derive its completion and obligation from the silent approbation and ratification which my proclamation may be construed to imply.

He was inclined to take the latter as their intention, but it was certainly best for all doubts to be removed. He concluded by asking early consideration so that he might know their sentiments before the departure of the Governor of the Western Territory.[81]

The Senate ordered this message committed;[82] and the next day the committee reported that Indian treaties had never been ratified, that therefore formal ratification of this treaty was not expedient or necessary, and that the Senate resolution authorized the President to enjoin a due observance thereof. The signature of Indian treaties had ever been considered as a full completion thereof.[83]

For this proposed resolution, however, the Senate passed as a substitute one which resolved, "That the Senate do advise and consent that the President of the United States ratify" the said treaty.[84]

The language here employed may be compared with that which had been used in July with reference to the French consular convention:

Resolved, unanimously, That the Senate do consent to the said convention, and advise the President of the United States to ratify the same.[85]

THE HOUSE AND TREATIES. In a message of August 7, 1789, the President said:

If it should be the judgment of Congress that it would be most expedient to terminate all differences in the Southern district, and to lay the foundation for future confidence by an amicable treaty with the Indian tribes in that quarter, I think proper to suggest the consideration of the expediency of instituting a temporary commission for that purpose, to consist of three persons, whose authority should expire with the occasion.[86]

The House ordered this message with accompanying papers committed to a committee of the whole.[87] With gallery doors shut, such committee resolved that an act ought to pass for the necessary expenses attending any such negotiations or the appointment of commissioners.

[81] 30 *Writings* 406–408. September 17, 1789. See also 1 *Annals* 40–42, 83–84.
[82] 1 *Annals* 83–84.
[83] *Ibid.* 84–85. September 18, 1789.
[84] *Ibid.* 87. September 22, 1789.
[85] *Ibid.* 55. July 29, 1789.
[86] 30 *Writings* 372. See also 1 *Annals* 59–60.
[87] 1 *Annals* 711. August 7, 1789.

The House then ordered a committee to prepare a bill or bills,[88] and again resolved itself into a committee of the whole to consider the bill so reported. This bill directed that commissioners, not exceeding three, should be appointed and allowed compensation.

At this point Sedgwick touched off a debate on the House and treaties which anticipated some of the issues of the great debate several years later on the execution of the Jay treaty.[89] He

> moved to strike out that part of the clause restraining the number of commissioners to three. He thought it a dangerous doctrine to be established, that the House had any authority to interfere in the management of treaties. . . . If the power here assumed was not given by that instrument [the Constitution], he would ask gentlemen where they meant to stop. Will not the recognition of such a principle in practice, tend to determine that the powers of this branch extended to all cases incident to legislative authority, notwithstanding the restrictory clauses of the *magna charta*? Those with respect to treaties may be construed to allude to treaties of commerce only; that, as they have the privilege of declaring war, they have a natural right to inquire into the principles and reasons upon which their declarations are founded. This, it may be supposed, cannot be exercised without having some connexion with the other branch of the Government in forming treaties. In this way, the House may usurp a power destructive of the balance of the three branches, and which the people never intended they should exercise.
>
> . . . How far . . . treaties would be obligatory if they contravened an existing law, might be a matter of doubt. He knew the executive authority in England possessed the power of destroying a legislative act by the terms of a treaty;[90] but whether the President had a similar power was questioned by some gentlemen of great information; yet no one ever doubted but the President, by and with the advice and consent of the Senate, could employ what and as many negotiators as he pleased. . . .

Stone replied that the President and Senate might appoint commissioners and empower them to negotiate without consulting the House; but the House had a right to give an opinion on the subject, either before or after the treaty was ratified. It might grant the money on what terms it judged proper. To keep up a good understanding the President had suggested to the House consideration of the expediency of a temporary commission of three.

[88] *Ibid.* 714. August 8, 1789.
[89] See 5 *ibid.* 394, 426–785, 821, 940–1298.
[90] See D. L. Keir and F. H. Lawson, *Cases in Constitutional Law* (The Clarendon Press, Oxford, 1928) 298–303, 310–312, especially 299, note 1, and 302, quotation from the *Federalist. Cf.* A. V. Dicey, *Introduction to the Study of the Law of the Constitution* (8th ed., Macmillan & Co., Ltd., London, 1920) 61–62.

Page insisted the House had a right to say what money should be expended in this way. They could say whether they would grant any or not; otherwise, the President and Senate might do as they pleased in the matter and call upon the House in all cases to defray their expense. He

remarked that the clause in the constitution gave . . . the power of making treaties, but it did not say all treaties. He therefore hoped the House would reserve the power of declaring what treaties were necessary, by making provision accordingly.

Tucker said the power of appointment was unquestionably vested in the President and Senate, "but it was inactive unless the offices were first established by law." So he concluded the Legislature had the power to establish the office of commissioners and determine the number. The President's message had called upon the House to consider the expediency of making a treaty with the Southern Indians and of instituting a board of commissioners for that purpose. What then had the House to do with providing money until the first point was determined? He thought it "indispensably necessary" for Congress to institute the office before appointments could be made; otherwise, the President and Senate might create as well as fill offices, and run the Union into inconvenient if not ruinous expenses. If these commissioners were not instituted by law, they might be considered as part of the treaty-making power, so that two thirds of the Senate would be necessary to their appointment; but if "we" say there shall be three commissioners, the President would be able to make the appointments with the consent of a majority of the Senate. That the President had nominated Short as *chargé* in the leave of absence of Mr. Jefferson, he thought, was not inconsistent with his view:

The Executive in this case did not create the office, for the time of Mr. Jefferson's appointment had not expired; the minister only solicited leave of absence, and it is a constitutional power in the President to fill up offices during the recess of the Senate; . . .[91]

Smith sought to refute Tucker. The President and Senate might carry their treaty-making power into effect as they deemed meet. Suppose it was absolutely necessary during the next recess of Congress to send an envoy to the Dey of Algiers; would it be proper to delay so necessary a business until this House could be convened? He thought Page's dis-

---

[91] This statement represented a tenable argument except in its last clause; but clearly, since the President sought the consent of the Senate in the case of Short, the incident had no relation to the constitutional provision respecting filling vacancies *in the recess of the Senate*.

tinction between treaties of commerce and of peace, that the President and Senate might form the one and not the other, could not be warranted "on any pretense whatsoever." At this point Page

said, that he conceived the House had a concurrent jurisdiction in the formation of treaties, by the exercise of their constitutional powers, necessary to give them efficacy.

Smith had never heard of this idea before. If the House could limit the President to three commissioners, and more should be found necessary, he could not appoint them without infringing the powers of the House.

Sumter said that if the sum was so limited as to enable the President barely to pay for a treaty conducted by three commissioners, there could be no danger in the precedent.

Baldwin did not think the temporary institution of three commissioners anything like the establishment of an office.

When a vote was taken, Sedgwick's motion to strike out passed in the affirmative.[92] The bill as finally enacted did not specify the number of commissioners.[93]

In this brief and inadequate debate there were thrown up several important questions of constitutional law. By express reference or logical implication these included : (1) whether a treaty later in time superseded an earlier statute; (2) whether a statute later in time superseded an earlier treaty;[94] (3) what was the relation of the power to *negotiate* treaties to the power of the purse;[95] (4) whether a diplomatic appointment could be made until the office had been created by law, or whether

---

[92] 1 *Annals* 716–724. August 11, 1789.

[93] The consideration of this bill lasted through August 12, and the bill was sent to the Senate August 13. See *ibid.* 724–730. For the bill as finally enacted see 2 *Laws of the United States* 34–35. Approved August 20, 1789.

In discussing a motion of Jackson made at the same time Madison observed: "By the constitution, the President has the power of employing these troops [those already raised] in the protection of those parts [of the frontiers from the depredations of the hostile Indians] which he thinks require them most. . . .

". . . nor can it be proper to give an indefinite power to the Executive to raise troops." 1 *Annals* 724. But compare Jackson's proposed clause in *ibid.* 723–724 with some later statutes on the same subject.

[94] See 1 *Willoughby on the Constitution* (2d ed., Baker, Voorhis and Co., New York, 1929) chap. 35 and § 321; 5 John Bassett Moore, *A Digest of International Law* (Government Printing Office, Washington, 1906) §§ 776–777. This work will hereinafter be cited as *Moore's Digest*. See also Edward S. Corwin, *The President: Office and Powers* (2d ed., New York University Press, New York, 1941) 243, 401; 5 Green Haywood Hackworth, *Digest of International Law* (Government Printing Office, Washington, 1943) § 489. This work will hereinafter be cited as *Hackworth's Digest*.

[95] *Cf.* 5 *Moore's Digest* § 759; 5 *Hackworth's Digest* 28–30, 198–199, in their bearing on whether the House has to make a special appropriation in advance for every negotiation which is to be undertaken. Presumably this problem was avoided for the most part by lump sum appropriations for defraying the expenses of foreign intercourse. See 2 *Laws of the United States* 111, 310–311, 328, 365, 527, 561.

on the other hand diplomatic offices existed by virtue of the law of nations, so that appointments could be made to them without prior legislation;[96] (5) whether the two thirds rule with respect to treaties applied to every vote taken in the Senate in connection with treaties or only to the final vote on "advice and consent" to ratification of the completed treaty;[97] (6) what was the relation of the power to make treaties to such legislative powers of Congress as that of regulating foreign commerce;[98] (7) whether the House of Representatives had a concurrent jurisdiction with respect to treaties in so far as their execution called for appropriations or for other implementing legislation.[99]

This is not the place to explore these constitutional issues either in terms of constitutional history or present-day constitutional law. For present purposes it suffices to stress two points: (1) that such critical issues emerged, albeit tentatively, in the very first session of Congress; and (2) that a written constitution which left such questions in a position in which they were debatable by reasonable men cannot in any factual sense be said to have predetermined, except in broad outlines, the interrelations which were to develop between the several organs of the general government.

WASHINGTON TO THE EMPEROR OF MOROCCO. December 1, 1789, the President wrote to the Emperor of Morocco to give our own peaceful revolution as an excuse for his not getting the regular marks of attention. We regretted, he said, that we could not comply with the terms for removing the hostile disposition of the regencies of Tunis and Tripoli; we had no mines of gold or silver, nor as yet riches from agriculture and commerce. But there was reason to think we would be gradually useful to our friends. The Emperor's favors had made a deep impression

[96] See Madison to President Monroe, May 6, 1822, 3 *Letters and Other Writings of James Madison* (published by order of Congress, R. Worthington, New York, 1884) 268; President Monroe to Madison, May 10, 1822, 6 *The Writings of James Monroe* (Hamilton ed., G. P. Putnam's Sons, New York and London, 1898) 285–286; Edward S. Corwin, *The President: Office and Powers* (2d ed., New York University Press, New York, 1941) 65–66, 343.
[97] See 2 George H. Haynes, *The Senate of the United States* (Houghton Mifflin Co., Boston, 1938) 664–665. See generally *ibid.* chap. 12 ("The Senate's Part in Treaty Making and Foreign Relations") and chap. 18 ("The President and the Senate: Accord and Discord").
[98] See the debates on the Jay treaty cited in note 89 above; 5 *Moore's Digest* §§ 735–736; 5 *Hackworth's Digest* §§ 462–463, 486–488.
[99] See debates on the Jay treaty cited in note 89 above; 5 *Moore's Digest* §§ 758–759; 5 *Hackworth's Digest* 198–199; Edward S. Corwin, *The President: Office and Powers* (2d ed., New York University Press, New York, 1941) 205–206, 402; John Austin Stevens, *Albert Gallatin* (American Statesmen series, Houghton, Mifflin and Co., Boston, 1884) 100–125.

on the United States. The President assured his Majesty that, "while I remain at the Head of this Nation, I shall not cease to promote every Measure that may conduce" to mutual friendship and harmony, and informed him that the Congress would assemble in the course of the winter,

and I shall take Care that Nothing be omitted that may be necessary to cause the Correspondence, between our Countries, to be maintained and conducted in a Manner agreeable to your Majesty, and satisfactory to all the Parties concerned in it.[100]

It appears that in this communication the President committed himself to the policy of continuing the payment of tribute to the piratical Emperor.[101] Did he all but commit the nation also, in the eyes of the Emperor? If the President is the sole voice of the nation in foreign relations, is it not both required and allowable for foreign countries to take his voice as that of the nation?[102] They may indeed be bound to know that under our Constitution the President may not ratify a "treaty" until he has secured the consent of the Senate.[103] But may they consider that a treaty negotiated by a plenipotentiary within his instructions is of high moral force?[104] Short of treaties, moreover, there are executive agree-

---

[100] 30 *Writings* 434-436.
This communication was apparently drafted by Jay. On December 1 the President read the Moroccan papers and sent them to Jay to prepare answers. 4 *Diaries* 56.
[101] See John Holladay Latané, *A History of American Foreign Policy* (Doubleday, Page & Co., Garden City, 1927) 58-59, 123; Thomas A. Bailey, *A Diplomatic History of the American People* (3d ed., F. S. Crofts & Co., New York, 1946) 51-52, 91-93; 1 *The American Secretaries of State and Their Diplomacy* (Samuel Flagg Bemis, ed., Alfred A. Knopf, New York, 1927) 265-271; 2 *ibid.* 8, 89-92, 125-126.
[102] "He [the President] being the only channel of communication between this country and foreign nations, it is from him alone that foreign nations or their agents are to learn what is or has has [sic] been the will of the nation, and whatever he communicates as such, they have a right and are bound to consider as the expression of the Nation, and no foreign agent can be allowed to question it, to interpose between him and any other branch of government, under the pretext of either's transgressing their functions, nor to make himself the umpire and final judge between them. I am, therefore, Sir, not authorized to enter into any discussions with you on the meaning of our Constitution in any part of it, or to prove to you that it has ascribed to him alone the admission or interdiction of foreign agents. I inform you of the fact by authority from the President." Secretary of State Jefferson to Mr. Genet, November 22, 1793. 4 *The Writings of Thomas Jefferson* (Washington ed., Derby & Jackson, New York, 1859) 84-85. *Cf.* Westel Woodbury Willoughby, *The Fundamental Concepts of Public Law* (The Macmillan Co., New York, 1924) 312-315; Quincy Wright, "The United States and International Agreements," 38 *Amer. J. of Int. Law* 341-355 (1944); Edwin Borchard, "Shall the Executive Agreement Replace the Treaty?" 38 *ibid.* 637-643 (1944). See also 8 *Hackworth's Digest* (General Index) 239, under "President of U.S.," references to "Foreign relations, conduct of."
[103] *Cf.* Westel Woodbury Willoughby, *The Fundamental Concepts of Public Law* (The Macmillan Co., New York, 1924) 312-315; 5 *Hackworth's Digest* 25-74, especially 56-57.
[104] *Cf.* 5 *Moore's Digest* §§ 743-745, 747-750; 5 *Hackworth's Digest* 56-57.

ments [105] and diplomatic commitments. How far may they take these to involve the word of the nation? Now suppose that an executive agreement is made *ultra vires,* or that a diplomatic commitment or indeed a ratified treaty cannot constitutionally be fulfilled except by the consent of another organ of Government.[106] Are other nations entitled to regard our failure to go through with any such commitments as a moral or legal breach of faith? This much is generally admitted: that it would be a breach of faith under the *law of nations* for Congress in its *constitutional discretion* to refuse to make an appropriation or enact any other legislation called for by a treaty.[107] How this dualism has worked out in constitutional practice is an important topic.

WASHINGTON TO THE CHIEFS AND WARRIORS OF THE CHOCTAW NATION. In this communication, dated December 17, 1789, the President said he had sent Major Doughty, one of our warriors, to convince them that the United States would remember the treaty of Hopewell, and enjoined them to guard and protect him and show him the places at which trading posts should be established, and to support such posts when established. Further injunctions were: to listen to what the Major should say in the name of the United States, "for he will speak only truth," to regard the United States as their firm and best support, to keep friendship with the Chickasaws, and to reject the advice of bad men who might attempt to poison their minds with suspicions against the United States.[108]

NOMINATIONS AND APPOINTMENTS

WASHINGTON ON APPOINTMENTS IN A REPUBLIC. On March 21, 1789, Washington wrote to a correspondent:

I have no conception of a more delicate task, than that, which is imposed by the Constitution on the Executive. It is the nature of Republicans, who are nearly in a state of equality, to be extremely jealous as to the disposal of all honorary or lucrative appointments. Perfectly convinced I am, that, if injudicious or unpopular measures should be taken by the Executive under the New Government with regard to appointments, the Government itself would be in the utmost danger of being utterly subverted by those measures. So

---

[105] See Wallace McClure, *International Executive Agreements* (Columbia University Press, New York, 1941), and review thereof by Edwin Borchard in 42 *Col. L. Rev.* (1942) 887; 5 Moore's Digest §§ 752–756; 5 Hackworth's Digest 390–433.
[106] See citations in note 99 above. [108] 30 *Writings* 479–480.
[107] See citations in note 99 above.

necessary is it, at this crisis, to conciliate the good will of the People: and so impossible is it, in my judgment, to build the edifice of public happiness, but upon their affections.[109]

WASHINGTON AND NOMINATIONS: HIS FORMULATION OF GENERAL PRINCIPLES. Office seekers did not wait for Washington's election to make known their desires, but wrote to him well in anticipation of that event. To such a solicitation he replied at least as early as June 8, 1788.[110] As early as January 1, 1789, he found "it would take more time than I could well spare" to notice all the applications for office.[111] By March 21,

Scarcely a day passes in which applications of one kind or another do not arrive. . . . I have found the number of answers, which I have been necessitated to give in my own hand, an almost insupportable burden to me.

What is more significant is his statement:

Insomuch, that had I not early adopted some general principles, I should before this time have been wholly occupied in this business.

At that time he summarized his general principles as follows:
   (1) to enter office without any engagements.
   (2) not to be influenced by motives of amity or blood.
   (3) to take into account three principal factors:
     (a) fitness.
     (b) comparative claims "from the former merits and sufferings in service."
     (c) equal distribution among the states.

He had been led to these principles, he said, by "a due concern for my own reputation not less decisively than a sacred regard to the interest of the community." "My errors," he added, "shall be such as result from the head, and not from the heart."[112]

In various replies he amplified these general principles and added to them. He spoke of "due regard" to "fitness," "the pretensions of different candidates," and, "so far as is proper," "political considerations."[113] He early came to see the importance of

[109] *Ibid.* 240.
[110] 29 *Writings* 508–509. Washington to Samuel Hanson. Washington said in part: ". . . I was not a little concerned at an application for employment under a Government which does not yet exist, and with the Administration of which (in case it should be adopted and carried into execution) it is *much more* than possible I may never be concerned." Yet he tried not to offend Hanson. Apparently Hanson applied again later. See Washington to Hanson, January 10, 1789: 30 *Writings* 177–178.
[111] 30 *Writings* 174. Washington to Henry Emanuel Lutterloh.
[112] *Ibid.* 237–241. Washington to Samuel Vaughan.
[113] *Ibid.* 225. Washington to Benjamin Harrison. March 9, 1789.

the equal distribution of those appointments (so far as that matter might be conveniently arranged) among Inhabitants of the various States of the Union.[114]

When the occasion arose, he expressed himself as follows on another aspect of the matter:

the difficulty which I fear might occur in conferring important offices upon persons, however meritorious they may really be, who have resided but a little while, and are consequently but little known in America. A single disgust excited in a particular State on this account, might, perhaps, raise a flame of opposition that could not easily, if ever, be extinguished.[115]

He had objection to displacing one man merely to make room for another:

For it appears to me, it will be a most unpleasant thing to turn out of office one man, against whom there is no charge of misconduct, merely to make room for another, however conspicuous his integrity and abilities may be.[116]

Washington thus emphasized the importance of past services as a proper consideration:

... several of the candidates, who have already come forward, have claims to the public attention and gratitude, which cannot be set aside without a palpable act of injustice. Some of them are men of unquestionable talents, who have *wasted* the flower of their lives, in the civil or military service of their country: men who have materially injured their properties, and excluded themselves from obtaining a subsistence for their families by the professions they were accustomed to pursue. There are some, I may add, who have shed their blood and deserved all a grateful Country has to bestow. Nor are they, in my judgment, incapable of reflecting lustre on the most dignified stations.[117]

Shortly after taking office he wrote to an office seeker that he should have

the consolation of reflecting that I entered upon my duty without the restriction of a single engagement, and, if I know myself, under no partial influences.[118]

Washington's resolution not to be motivated by ties of blood was put to a test when Bushrod Washington asked to be made district attorney. He replied that Bushrod could not doubt his wishes to see him get any job in the new government to which he was competent, but added that

[114] *Ibid.* 236. Washington to Gustavus Scott. March 21, 1789.
[115] *Ibid.* 239. Washington to Samuel Vaughan, with respect to his son.
[116] *Ibid.* 242. Washington to Edward Stevens. March 21, 1789.
[117] *Ibid.* 239-240. Washington to Samuel Vaughan.
[118] *Ibid.* 316. Washington to William Heath. May 9, 1789.

however deserving he might be of the one suggested, his standing at the bar would not justify his uncle's making him district attorney over some of the oldest and most esteemed General Court lawyers who desired the job. The President continued:

> My political conduct in nominations, even if I was uninfluenced by principle, must be exceedingly circumspect and proof against just criticism, for the eyes of Argus are upon me, and no slip will pass unnoticed that can be improved into a supposed partiality for friends or relatives.[119]

Washington's principle of not disturbing "actual occupancy"[120] was applied when in August of 1789 he wrote to Wilson Miles Cary that the man he had recommended to fill an office in the customs could not consistently be appointed, for under the law there was only one office at Hampton, and by the general rule prescribed to himself for nominations, that office was filled by the former naval officer there. He emphasized that failure to appoint Cary's man was from no want of faith in his recommendation but from justice and impartiality which the public demanded and from which he hoped he should never intentionally depart.[121]

Washington made it a rule, even after he took office, to make no commitments until the particular office had been created by law and indeed until it became necessary to make a nomination. In August of 1789 he wrote:

> ... without considering myself at liberty to give either encouragement or discouragement to the wishes of Gentlemen who have offered themselves as Candidates for offices, I have invariably avoided giving any sentiment or opinion; for the purpose of reserving myself unembarrassed with promises until all the Candidates are known and the occasion, when decision shall become necessary on my part.[122]

In September he wrote in a similar vein to Edmund Randolph with respect to the candidacy of a Mr. Powell:

> ... I can only repeat to you what I say to all others upon similar occasions, that is, I leave myself entirely free until the office is established and the moment shall arrive when the nomination is to be made, then, under my best information and a full view of all circumstances I shall endeavor to the best of my judgment to combine justice to individuals with the public good making the latter my primary object.[123]

[119] Ibid. 366. July 27, 1789.
[120] Ibid. 225. Washington to Benjamin Harrison.
[121] Ibid. 377. August 10, 1789.
[122] Ibid. 383. Washington to Cyrus Griffin. August 20, 1789.
[123] Ibid. 397-398. September 8, 1789.

Though Washington was doubtless sincere in adopting his high principles of appointment, the terms in which he replied to office seekers varied. Thus to an early request from Henry Emanuel Lutterloh he rejoined that he "invariably" mentioned "the impropriety of bringing such things before me." [124] But to Benjamin Lincoln he wrote:

But without deviating from that line of proceeding which I had chalked out for myself, . . . you need not doubt my inclinations are very sincere and very strong to serve you, if I can do it, consistently with my duty to the public. This I say, because I have known you in public life; for I do not intend to be swayed, in the disposal of places, by motives arising from the ties of friendship or blood.

He added that he could not then tell what offices would be created or "what pretensions may be urged in favor of different candidates." [125]

Likewise to Francis Hopkinson:

Be assured then, that my inclinations to serve you are sincere and strong, not because I have a friendship for you (for friendship ought not to have anything to do with the matter) but because I think you capable of serving the public well.

Again he added that he was making no engagements for the sake of his own reputation and the interest of the community.[126]

Doubtless he considered a copying job a special case when on March 15, 1789, he wrote to his sister, Elizabeth Washington Lewis, to offer it to her son, with life in the family. He said he was glad to give him a preference, but desired an early reply because he would have many solicitations.[127]

Similarly in July he decided to offer "a place in my family" to Mr. Thomas Nelson, son of his "old friend and acquaintance," General Nelson. He thought this was Nelson's only chance for a job, since most clerkships, he presumed, would by law or custom go to the principals. There were few he would take into his family without any personal knowledge or good information; but in this case he did so "at all hazards." [128] In writing to Nelson himself, he gave the compensation as $660 plus board, lodging, and washing, and described the duties as follows:

The duties that will be required of you, are, generally, to assist in writing, receiving and entertaining company, and in the discharge of such other mat-

[124] *Ibid.* 174. January 1, 1789. At such an early date applications were especially embarrassing to Washington, of course. [126] *Ibid.* 228. March 13, 1789.
[125] *Ibid.* 226. March 11, 1789. [127] *Ibid.* 228–229. March 15, 1789.
[128] *Ibid.* 365. Washington to David Stuart. July 26, 1789.

ters as it is not convenient or practicable for the President to attend to in person.[129]

When George Abbott Hall, state collector of customs at Charleston, wanted to be the same under the United States, he had the support of seven South Carolinians, including Edward and John Rutledge. The President acknowledged Hall's application and all these recommendations, saying to John Rutledge:

At this time it would, perhaps, be improper for me to say any thing more on the subject, than that it will be peculiarly agreeable to me, if upon a general view of the business, I shall be able to make the discharge of my duty to the Public, comport with the inclinations of so many respectable members of the community as have interested themselves in favor of the Candidate in question.[130]

In reply to two letters from General Comfort Sage, the President said "my not having received any immediate application from you, expressive of your readiness to fill the office," and not "any unfavorable representations respecting your reputation," had been the cause of not nominating him for surveyor of the Port of Middletown. The appointee's wishes had been "made known to me *in season*" and his character represented as such as would "undoubtedly secure," in a person who had thus declared himself ready to accept, proper execution of the duties. His "only object was to have the public business put into a train of being performed with certainty." To Sage, disappointed because unappointed, Washington added that he hoped he would do him the justice to believe he had been far from designing to do anything "disagreeable or prejudicial to you."[131]

To an applicant whose conduct and walk of life had for many years been unknown to the President, he wrote to advise that he "obtain the most ample testimony of your sobriety, Industry, &c. from the wellknown and respectable characters of your City."[132] "Personal applications to me," he declared to another, would be of no use.[133] All *he* required, he told the mother of another, was the name of the applicant and testimonials on his "abilities, integrity and fitness."[134]

Shortly after he took office Washington declared:

It will undoubtedly often happen that there will be several candidates for the same office whose pretensions, abilities and integrity may be nearly equal,

[129] *Ibid.* 367. July 27, 1789.
[130] *Ibid.* 309–310, 311, note 67.
[131] *Ibid.* 382. August 18, 1789.
[132] *Ibid.* 270. Washington to William Milnor. April 5, 1789.
[133] *Ibid.* 329. Washington to James Kelso. May 21, 1789.
[134] *Ibid.* 328. Washington to Mary Wooster, with respect to her son. May 21, 1789.

and who will come forward so equally supported in every respect as almost to require the aid of supernatural intuition to fix upon the right. . . .

He added that he was determined to nominate the most deserving and those who would perform their tasks to the interest and credit of the United States "if such characters could be found by my exploring every avenue of information respecting their merits and pretensions that it is in my power to obtain." [135]

To James Madison the President wrote in September of "my solicitude for drawing the first characters of the Union into the Judiciary." [136] When he offered a Supreme Court appointment to Robert Hanson Harrison, he said that "the administration of justice is the strongest cement of good Government" and hence "the first organization of the federal judiciary is essential to the happiness of our Country, and to the stability of our political system." He added:

Under this impression it has been the invariable object of my anxious solicitude to select the fittest characters to expound the Laws and dispense justice.[137]

In carrying out this purpose the President had difficulties similar to those of his successors in office. In August he wrote to Madison:

What can I do with A———— L———— he has applied to be nominated one of the Associate Judges; but I cannot bring my mind to adopt the request. The opinion entertained of him by those with whom I am most conversant is unpropitious and yet few men have received more marks of public favor and confidence than he has. These contradictions are embarrassing.[138]

In the same letter he asked Madison if he did not nominate Colonel Carrington for the western judgeship, "can you think of any other that would suit him, of new creation; by this I mean, which has not an actual occupant or one who, from similarity of Office may have better pretensions to it." [139] Again, he wrote to Madison that Mr. Pendleton

---

[135] *Ibid.* 313–314. Washington to James Bowdoin. May 9, 1789.
[136] *Ibid.* 414. September 25 (?), 1789. He said that this solicitude, plus a desire "to silence the clamours, or more properly, *soften* the disappointment of smaller characters," had almost determined him to nominate Mr. Blair and Colonel Pendleton Associate and District Judges, trusting to their acceptance. Ex-President Taft's quotation from Mr. Evarts that "Some we appointed and more we disappointed" seems to have been true from the beginning. William Howard Taft, *Our Chief Magistrate and His Powers* (Columbia University Press, New York, 1925) 55.
[137] 30 *Writings* 417. September 28, 1789.
[138] *Ibid.* 393–394. August, 1789. The editor's note says the reference was to Arthur Lee. *Ibid.* 393, note 9.
[139] *Ibid.* 393. This question was preceded by another which suggests that the President was careful to consider *amour propre*: "Would it do *now* that Mr. Barton has declined the Judges Seat (Western Territory) to nominate Col Carrington for that Office?"

might *see* or it might be *explained* to him why he was nominated as District Judge rather than to the Supreme Bench, though there was no objection to the latter if his health was competent and his mental faculties unimpaired by age. He could hardly serve under the present form of the Act, but might be able to execute the duties of district judge.[140] In asking Pendleton to serve, the President made the proposed explanation. He said he and other friends thought the Supreme Bench, with the "fatigue of Circuit Courts," would be too much for his infirm health, but nominated him to the district court of Virginia, which would entail not much greater personal exertion than the duties of his present station. He gave as his reason that he believed it "necessary to avail our Country of your abilities and the influence of your example."[141]

The Attorney General would be an officer with whom the President would naturally come in frequent personal contact. The human side of Washington's motivation in naming Edmund Randolph to this post was revealed in a letter to Madison:

Mr. Randolph, in this character, I would prefer to any person I am acquainted with of not superior abilities, from habits of intimacy with him.[142]

Washington was particularly anxious to get outstanding men for the federal bench. He made John Jay Chief Justice,[143] and wrote John Rutledge that his anxious solicitude to select first characters for the judiciary had overruled the opinions of some of Rutledge's friends that he would not accept a seat on the Supreme Court.[144] He also thought the judiciary should be filled with men who were tried as well as qualified:

From the promising abilities and good character I have heard of Mr. Robert Smith, I entertain a very favorable opinion of his merits; but, as in the Person of a Judge, the World will look for a character and reputation founded on service and experience, I cannot conceive that the appointment of so young and inexperienced a man as Mr. Smith would be considered as a judicious choice by the community in general, though it might meet the approbation

---

Other illustrations of this care are given above. The present letter added, in deference to the principle of distribution among the States: "As Virga. has given and may furnish characters for important offices probably it would be better to exclude her also on this occasion."
140 *Ibid.* 414–415. September 25 (?), 1789. The President added: "His acceptance of the first would depend in great measure, I presume, upon the light in which the District Judges are considered, that is, whether superior in rank to any State Judges."
141 *Ibid.* 419–420. Washington to Edmund Pendleton. September 28, 1789.
142 *Ibid.* 414–415. September 25 (?), 1789.
143 "It is with singular pleasure that I address you as Chief Justice of the Supreme Court of the United States." Washington to Jay, October 10, 1789. *Ibid.* 428. Note the title. The Supreme Court now prefers "Chief Justice of the United States."
144 *Ibid.* 421–422. September 29, 1789. Rutledge accepted: see *ibid.* 465 (Washington to Edward Rutledge, his brother).

of those who have had the best opportunity of becoming acquainted with his talents. In such important appointments as the Judiciary, much confidence is necessary, and this will not be given fully to an untried man.[145]

When Robert Hanson Harrison returned his commission as judge of the Supreme Court, Washington was so anxious to have him accept that, expressing the hope that the circuit duty of members of that Court would be abolished, he sent him the commission once again, though he added that he would be satisfied with Harrison's decision.[146]

The President was so disturbed by rumors that some in Virginia had wondered that Chancellor George Wythe had been *"overlooked"* that he wrote to Edmund Randolph in confidence to ask him to inform Wythe of his principles in the business, if it could be done in a delicate manner, and also to see that it was not "altogether unknown" why he had appointed Cyrus Griffin as District Judge for Virginia, in case the propriety of the appointment were questioned. "I have prejudices against none," he wrote, "nor partialities which shall bias me in favor of any one."[147]

The Griffin appointment was one about which Washington seems to have been sensitive. He explained his reasons to Randolph[148] and to Joseph Jones, who had applied for the position after the President had directed Griffin's commission to be made out. One reason had been that the latter's appointment as temporary Indian commissioner had unexpectedly vacated his position on the council of Virginia, with the result that he was now not only out of office but in want of the emoluments of one. In every nomination, he said, he had tried to make fitness of character the primary object;

If with this the peculiar necessities of the Candidates could be combined, it has been, with me, an additional inducement to the appointment.

[145] Washington to General Otho Holland Williams, November 22, 1789, *ibid*. 461. Of Robert Smith Washington also wrote to McHenry: ". . . the age and inexperience of the latter is in my opinion an insuperable objection. For however good the qualifications or promising the talents of Mr. Smith may be, it will be expected that the important offices of the General Government, and more especially those of the Judges should be filled by men who have been tried and proved." *Ibid*. 471–472. For the same reason the President wrote William Fitzhugh that Paca certainly stood prior to Thomas, whom Fitzhugh had recommended for district judge for Maryland. *Ibid*. 484–485.
[146] *Ibid*. 466–467. Washington took this course on the suggestion of McHenry. *Ibid*. 470. Harrison, however, persisted in his refusal to serve, and James Iredell of North Carolina was given the position. *Ibid*. 467, note 37. It is to be noted that on November 27, 1789, Hamilton wrote Colonel Harrison asking him in highly complimentary terms to reconsider. 5 *The Works of Alexander Hamilton* (John C. Hamilton, ed., Charles S. Francis & Co., New York, 1851) 446. This was two days after the President had asked him to reconsider.
[147] 30 *Writings* 472–474. November 30, 1789. Randolph reported that he had had a satisfactory talk with Wythe about the matter. *Ibid*. 474, note 51.
[148] *Ibid*. 473.

Another factor had been the certainty that Griffin would accept; for Colonel Pendleton's declination had been received too late for previous inquiry and consultation before the day for the session of the District Court; and Washington did not want to hazard making a second choice in uncertainty of acceptance.[149]

Though in the beginning relatively few federal offices were created, it must be remembered that Washington had to fill them all at an early date in order to put the government into full operation. Most of these offices were created on or after July 31;[150] and the session adjourned September 29.[151] Accordingly nominations were sent to the Senate in batches.[152] In his hurry to get the task finished in time[153] and his desire to secure outstanding men, Washington was forced to nominate many men without previously consulting them.[154]

In consequence, declinations became an embarrassment. Edmund Pendleton declined the district judgeship for Virginia,[155] Thomas Johnson that for Maryland,[156] and Thomas Pinckney that for South Carolina.[157] Harrison twice returned his commission as a member of the Supreme Court.[158] John Marshall, who had solicited the appointment as attorney for the district of Virginia, found that circumstances prevented his acceptance.[159] It is not surprising, therefore, to find the President, after reporting in confidence to James McHenry that he had sent Harrison his commission a second time, and had received a declination from Johnson and no word of Richard Potts, the Attorney, and Nathaniel Ramsey, the Marshal, for the Maryland district, going on to say:

Thus circumstanced with respect to Maryland, I am unwilling to make a new appointment of Judge for that District until I can have an assurance, or at least a strong presumption, that the person appointed will accept; for it is to me an unpleasant thing to have Commissions of so important a nature returned; and it will, in fact, have a tendency to bring the government into discredit.

So he asked McHenry to find out, by a mode left to his discretion, if Alexander Contee Hanson, just appointed Chancellor of the State, would accept:

[149] *Ibid.* 468–469. November 10, 1789.
[150] On that date the act to regulate the collection of duties was approved. Prior to that time only four statutes had been approved, the fourth of which had established the Department of Foreign Affairs and created the offices of Secretary and chief clerk thereof. See 2 *Laws of the United States* 1–31.
[151] 1 *Annals* 96, 964.   [152] See *ibid.* 56, 65, 80, 89, 93.   [153] See 30 *Writings* 382.
[154] See *ibid.* 417, 418–419, 419–420, 421–422, 424–425, 446–447, 457–458, 465, 466–467, 468. Even after the adjournment of the Senate time was pressing. See *ibid.* 469, 471.
[155] *Ibid.* 469; 1 *Annals* 89.
[156] 30 *Writings* 470.
[157] *Ibid.* 465.
[158] *Ibid.* 466–467, and note 37 on latter page.
[159] *Ibid.* 463.

It is a delicate matter and will not bear any thing like a direct application if there is the least doubt of a refusal.

If Hanson did not wish the job, then the President asked McHenry to give him information on William Paca. Paca was finally appointed;[160] but what Washington said of him in this confidential letter suggests that his appointments were made not without an eye to the sound Federalist principles of the persons concerned:

Mr. Paca has been mentioned for that appointment, and altho' his sentiments have not been altogether in favor of the General Government, and a little adverse on the score of Paper emissions etc. I do not know but his appointment on some other accounts might be a proper thing.[161]

It may be noted that on October 12 Lear wrote to the postmaster of Providence, Rhode Island, in reply to an inquiry, that the President

never interferes in the appointment of any Officers whose appointment does not by Law come under his immediate cognizance. Mr. Osgood must act as he pleases in the appointment of his deputies.[162]

When Governor Huntington wrote to recommend Comfort Sage to supply the place of Mr. Miller as surveyor of the Port of Middletown, Connecticut, provided the latter should resign, the reply was that, since there had been no intimation from Miller of an intention to resign, the President could not at present with propriety take any further notice of the application on behalf of General Sage than to acknowledge receipt of it.[163]

The reader may judge for himself whether the President was doing what he disclaimed doing when, in offering Mr. Jefferson appointment as Secretary of State, he wrote:

Unwilling as I am to interfere in the direction of your choice of Assistants, I shall only take the liberty of observing to you that, from warm recommendations which I have received in behalf of Roger Alden, Esqr., Assistant Secretary to the late Congress, I have placed all the Papers thereunto belonging under his care. Those Papers which more properly appertain to the Office of Foreign-Affairs are under the Superintendence of Mr. Jay, who has been so obliging as to continue his good-offices, and they are in the immediate charge of Mr. Remson.[164]

Finally, Washington wrote to Edward Rutledge on November 23:

I . . . am very happy to learn, that the appointments under the general Government have given so much satisfaction in your part of the Union.

[160] Ibid. 484.
[161] Ibid. 470–472. November 30, 1789.
[162] Ibid. 436, note 88.
[163] Ibid. 482.
[164] Ibid. 447. October 13, 1789.

122   THE AMERICAN PRESIDENCY IN ACTION

Added to the consciousness of having brought forward such Characters only to fill the several Offices of the United States, as from my own knowledge, or the strictest enquiries I conceived would do justice to the public, and honor to themselves, I have the happiness to find, so far as my information extends, that they are highly acceptable to the good people of this Country.[165]

Though Washington had probably heard expressions of approval mainly if not exclusively from Federalist-minded men of prominence, and though he probably would have discounted the opinions of others, it must have given him a sense of relief to think his appointments had on the whole been satisfactory. For as early as March 21 he had written to Edward Stevens:

Altho' I can easily conceive that the general principles on which nominations ought in good policy and equity to be made may be easily ascertained still I cannot possibly form a conception of a more delicate and arduous task, than particular application of those principles to practice.[166]

WASHINGTON ON WHY NOMINATIONS SHOULD BE MADE BY WRITTEN MESSAGES RATHER THAN ORALLY. At his first conference with the Senate committee on the mode of communication between the President and the Senate, the President gave his reasons for preferring to make nominations in writing rather than in person. His analysis is so clear and

[165] Ibid. 464–465. In the letter to Edmund Randolph of November 30, 1789, cited above, in which the President showed some uneasiness over not having offered a judicial appointment to George Wythe, and over having offered one to Cyrus Griffin, he stated: "For having in every appointment endeavored, as far as my own knowledge of Characters extended, or information could be obtained, to select the fittest and most acceptable Persons; and having reason to believe that the appointments which have been made heretofore have given very general satisfaction . . ." Ibid. 473–474.
  As late as December 12, 1789, the President wrote Robert Morris that he was inclined to believe a Mr. Hamilton was qualified for the office he solicited, but stuck to the self-prescribed rule already mentioned, which, in order to preserve his freedom of choice in all nominations, forbade any engagement whatever until the nomination had been made. Ibid. 476–477.
[166] Ibid. 241. See a communication dated September 25, 1789, from Washington to Secretary of the Treasury Hamilton, who had been commissioned September 11, sending a list of selected candidates from a great variety of applicants for suitable offices and asking him and Mr. Jay to take the further trouble of running them over to find if one was "under *all circumstances*" more eligible than Mr. O. for the Post Office. He asked an opinion by 11 o'clock. An editorial note says Mr. O. was Samuel Osgood. Washington informed Hamilton at the same time of his *"present* intention" of nominating "Mr. Jefferson for Secretary of State and Mr. Edmd. Randolph as Attorney Genl." Ibid. 413–414, and note 45. September 25, 1789.
  See also a letter from John Jay to Charles Pettit, dated July 14, 1789, in which the Acting Secretary explained that harmony between department heads and between a department head and his subordinates made it "improper" for him to *recommend* Pettit to the President for appointment in any *other* department. 3 *The Correspondence and Public Papers of John Jay* (Henry P. Johnson, ed., G. P. Putnam's Sons, New York and London, 1891) 372–373.

cogent that it seems to express the logic of the practice of all[167] Presidents in following this method:

With respect to Nominations

My present Ideas are that as they point to a single object unconnected in its nature with any other object, they had best be made by written messages. In this case the Acts of the President, and the Acts of the Senate will stand upon clear, distinct and responsible ground.

Independent of this consideration, it could be no pleasing thing I conceive, for the President, on the one hand to be present and hear the propriety of his nominations questioned; nor for the Senate on the other hand to be under the smallest restraint from his presence from the fullest and freest inquiry into the Character of the Person nominated. The President in a situation like this would be reduced to one of two things: either to be a silent witness of the decision by Ballot, if there are objections to the nomination; or in justification thereof (if he should think it right) to support it by argument. Neither of which might be agreeable: and the latter improper; for as the President has a right to nominate without assigning his reasons, so has the Senate a right to dissent without giving theirs.[168]

THE CASE OF BENJAMIN FISHBOURN: THE FIRST EXAMPLE OF "SENATORIAL COURTESY"? Haynes finds that in the First Congress the Senate rejected only one of the President's nominations to office.[169] In response, the President sent the Senate a written message, which began as follows:

Gentlemen of the Senate: My nomination of *Benjamin Fishbourn* for the place of Naval Officer of the Port of Savannah not having met your concurrence, I now nominate Lachlan McIntosh for that place. Whatever may have been the reasons which induced your dissent, I am persuaded they were such as you deemed sufficient. Permit me to submit to your consideration,

---

[167] President Harding in what Haynes calls "an unprecedented procedure" presented his Cabinet nominations to the Senate in person. 1 George H. Haynes, *The Senate of the United States* (Houghton Mifflin Co., Boston, 1938) 206, note 2.

[168] 30 *Writings* 374. August 8, 1789.

[169] 1 George H. Haynes, *The Senate of the United States* (Houghton Mifflin Co., Boston, 1938) 54, 56–57. August 3, 1789, "The Senate entered on executive business. The President communicated to them a list of about one hundred appointments as collectors, naval officers, and surveyors. The Senate advised and consented to about one-half the list; the rest lay till to-morrow." 1 *Annals* 56. August 4, "The Senate again entered on executive business, and advised and confirmed all the remainder of the list of appointments presented yesterday, one excepted." *Ibid.* 57. August 7, the message on the Fishbourn rejection which is considered in the text below, and which is dated August 6, was laid before the Senate. *Ibid.* 60–61. On the same day the Senate did advise and consent to the appointment of Lachlan McIntosh for naval officer at Savannah, nominated in place of Fishbourn in the same presidential message. *Ibid.* 62. August 10, "On motion to commit the message from the President of the United States relative to the nomination of Mr. Fishbourn: It was postponed until a committee, appointed on the 6th of August to wait on the President of the United States, should report." *Ibid.* 62. The committee appointed on August 6 was the one to confer with the President on the mode of communication between him and the Senate. *Ibid.* 66.

whether on occasions, where the propriety of nominations appear questionable to you, it would not be expedient to communicate that circumstance to me and thereby avail yourselves of the information which led me to make them, and which I would with pleasure lay before you. Probably my reasons for nominating Mr. Fishbourn may tend to shew that such a mode of proceeding in such cases might be useful. I will therefore detail them.

This the President proceeded to do at some length. He referred to the man's "irreproachable" conduct as an officer "in actual service"—"chiefly under my own Eye." He said the offices he had been given in Georgia showed confidence in him. He mentioned "private letters of recommendation" and "oral testimonials in his favor" "from several of the most respectable characters in that State." But since the latter had been secondary considerations with him, he did not think it necessary to communicate them.[170]

On the assumption that the Senate should be thought of as an advisory council to the President in the matter of nominations, the mode of procedure suggested by the President appeared sound. The reason it did not take hold was probably that the relations of the President and the Senate soon developed into arm's length dealings between two independent organs, one representing the Executive and the other representing a branch of the Legislature,[171] albeit one vested with certain checks upon the Executive.

Several eminent writers[172] cite the Fishbourn case in terms which make it an example of what is now called "senatorial courtesy." None of these substantiates the statement with any contemporaneous evidence. The only one of them who cites any authority at all for the statement is Haynes in his notable work on the Senate. He cites only Benton's *Abridgment*, which in a note calls this

a strong instance of the deference of the Senate to the Senators of the State interested in the nomination, Col. Fishbourn having been rejected simply because the Georgia Senators preferred another.[173]

---

[170] 30 *Writings* 370-371. August 6, 1789. See also 1 *Annals* 60-61. Fishbourn had apparently applied for office as early as September 20, 1788. 30 *Writings* 170-171. Washington to Benjamin Fishbourn. December 23, 1788.
[171] Cf. Edward S. Corwin, *The Constitution and World Organization* (Princeton University Press, Princeton, 1944) 32 ff.
[172] Henry Jones Ford, *The Rise and Growth of American Politics* (The Macmillan Co., New York, 1898) 260; Edward S. Corwin, *The President: Office and Powers* (2d ed., New York University Press, New York, 1941) 69, 345-346; 1 George H. Haynes, *The Senate of the United States* (Houghton Mifflin Co., Boston, 1938) 54, 56-57; 2 *ibid.* 736-737. The present writer is indebted to all three authors in many ways. The notable works of Corwin and of Haynes, in particular chapter 2 of the latter, on "Setting Senate Precedents in the First Congress," cut across the present study at many points.
[173] 1 *Abridgment of the Debates of Congress, from 1789 to 1856, by the Author of the Thirty Years' View* (D. Appleton & Co., New York, 1857) 17, note.

Benton, who was born in 1782, is in no sense a contemporaneous source, and he cites none in his note; but he was in a position to pick up a traditional story of the reasons for the rejection which may well have been true. There was clearly some special reason for senatorial rejection of Fishbourn's name alone. From Washington's letter to Fishbourn digested in a footnote below [174] it would appear that Fishbourn thought charges of which Washington was unaware had been brought against him in the Senate. The present writer knows of no evidence on the subject which is definitive.

The Fishbourn message amounted to calling the Senate down in rather sharp terms. When Maclay returned from his leave of absence Izard reported to him that "the President showed great want of temper . . . when one of his nominations was rejected." [175]

THE "HAPPENING" OF A VACANCY. The Constitution provides that

The President shall have Power to fill up all Vacancies that may happen during the Recess of the Senate, by granting Commissions which shall expire at the End of the next Session.[176]

Professor Corwin has pointed out that usage, supported by Opinions of Attorneys General, has established that for a vacancy to "happen" during a recess it is not necessary that it "happen to take place," "first occur," or "originate," but merely that it "happen to exist," in such recess.[177]

It may be of some interest to note that Washington assumed that, when a party declined during a recess the commission to an office to which he had been nominated by the President and appointed by and with the advice and consent of the Senate without previously consulting him, a vacancy had occurred which he might fill by a recess appointment. Thus he first appointed Thomas Pinckney District Judge for South Carolina; [178] but when Pinckney declined,[179] he wrote to William

---

[174] After the rejection, Fishbourn wrote to the President, and received a reply from William Jackson by direction of the President, in which it was said that when the latter had nominated Fishbourn, "he was ignorant of any charge existing against you, and, not having, since that time, had any other exhibit of the facts which were alledged in the Senate than what is stated in the certificates which have been published by you, he does not consider himself competent to give any opinion on the subject." 30 *Writings* 412. September 25, 1789.

[175] *Journal of William Maclay* 119.   [176] Article II, section 2, § 3.

[177] Edward S. Corwin, *The President: Office and Powers* (2d ed., New York University Press, New York, 1941) 75–76, 349, note 33. See especially the able opinion of Attorney General William Wirt, October 22, 1823, 1 *Official Opinions of the Attorneys General of the United States* (Benjamin F. Hall, compiler, Robert Farnham, publisher, Washington, 1852) 631.

[178] 1 *Annals* 89, 93.   [179] See 30 *Writings* 465.

Drayton that, the office "having become vacant," he had appointed him and enclosed a commission to the end of the next session of the Senate.[180] Again, in explaining to Joseph Jones why he had not appointed him District Judge for Virginia, he spoke of Colonel Pendleton's declination of the position as a resignation.[181] Still again, when Thomas Johnson[182] refused his commission as District Judge for Maryland, Washington wrote James McHenry confidentially that he was unwilling, after Johnson's resignation, to make a new appointment until he had assurance or a strong presumption of an acceptance.[183] Later he wrote William Fitzhugh that, Johnson having declined, he had appointed Paca.[184] This presidential assumption is not subject to exception. The problem which caused early doubts[185] was whether the President might fill vacancies which had actually *occurred* while the Senate was *in session*.

POLITICS AND APPOINTMENTS

POOR DAVY HARRIS. Maclay tried to sponsor one David Harris for a federal job in Baltimore. He took the matter up with his colleague, Morris, who was guarded on the subject, and did not offer to help, but suggested that Maclay send Harris's petition to the President. Maclay, however, had been asked by Harris to put the request into the hands of Colonel Humphreys, secretary to the President, and determined to do so. He went to the President's and gave it to Humphreys, whom he thought cold. His hopes of success were not high: "I am an ill courtier. The part I have taken in the Senate has marked me as no courtier, and I fear will mark poor Davy as a man not to be brought forward."[186]

Such was the case. Maclay later recorded that Davy Harris had lost his nomination.[187]

POLITICAL SUPPORT FOR A CANDIDATE. Oliver Wolcott, Jr., was Comptroller of Public Accounts of Connecticut in 1788–1789.[188] When the

[180] *Ibid.* 457–458. November 18, 1789.
[181] *Ibid.* 468–469. See also 1 *Annals* 89, 93.
[182] See 1 *Annals* 89, 93.
[183] 30 *Writings* 470–472. November 30, 1789.
[184] *Ibid.* 484–485. December 24, 1789.
[185] See, for example, Madison to Jefferson, January 10, 1801, 2 *Letters and Other Writings of James Madison* (published by order of Congress, R. Worthington, New York, 1884) 170.
[186] *Journal of William Maclay* 72–73, 87–88. June 12, 27, 1789.
[187] *Ibid.* 124–125. August 21, 1789.
[188] 1 George Gibbs, *Memoirs of the Administrations of Washington and John Adams* (edited from the papers of Oliver Wolcott, William van Norden, Printer, New York, 1846) 17.

Department of the Treasury was being organized, Representative[189] Jeremiah Wadsworth from that state advised him to apply to the President for a Treasury post, "referring him to the Senate and House of Representatives, where tell him if he finds a single objection you will withdraw your application." He recommended the application because "every body applies" and because he would probably succeed since Connecticut had no other applicant for national office.[190] Three days later Wolcott wrote his application, in which he said:

The gentlemen who represent the State of Connecticut, in the Senate and House of Representatives, are best acquainted with the degree of merit on which I venture to found this application. If they do not concur in a proper recommendation, I cannot hope and do not wish to succeed.[191]

When he heard he was to be appointed Auditor instead of Comptroller, he was prepared to decline, but accepted when the appointment had been made.[192] Gibbs states it as a fact, presumably founded on the evidence quoted above, that Wolcott's application was "seconded by the Connecticut delegation." [193]

UNASHAMED WIRE-PULLING. On January 2, 1789, James Seagrove wrote from Savannah to General Samuel Blachley Webb:

. . . it behooves us all to look round and try what we can get. I am advised by all my friends this way to offer for the Collectorship of the Impost for

[189] 1 *Annals* 99.
[190] 1 George Gibbs, *Memoirs of the Administrations of Washington and John Adams* (edited from the papers of Oliver Wolcott, William van Norden, Printer, New York, 1846) 19. August 12, 1789.
[191] *Ibid.* 20.
[192] *Ibid.* 20–23.
[193] *Ibid.* 18. Other letters of interest in this volume are one from Wolcott to his father, Oliver Wolcott, Senior, December 2, 1789, on the general financial outlook of the general government and his opinion that the efforts to establish that government were "an experiment of doubtful success" (*ibid.* 24–25); John Trumbull to Wolcott, December 9, 1789, on the President's New England tour (*ibid.* 26); Wolcott to his father, December 21, 1789, on "the Southern gentlemen . . . growing more federal," though he presumed it would appear that a great portion of the taxes would come from the states north of the Potomac, and on his accumulated business and his opinion that affairs had not been left in proper condition by the late board of the Treasury (*ibid.* 26); a report from Wolcott to Secretary Hamilton, November 29, 1789, on terms of settlement to liquidate the old requisition system (*ibid.* 29–31); Oliver Wolcott, Senior, to Oliver Wolcott, Junior, December 23, 1789, on the prospects for the Union and the rate of interest on the public debt (*ibid.* 33–34). Of the late presidential tour Trumbull reported: "I see the President has returned all fragrant with the odour of incense. It must have given him satisfaction to find that the hearts of the people are united in his favour; but the blunt and acknowledged adulation of our addresses must often have wounded his feelings. We have gone through all the popish grades of worship, at least up to the *Hyperdoulia*. This tour has answered a good political purpose, and in a great measure stilled those who were clamoring about the wages of Congress and the salaries of officers."

Georgia—and have little doubt of being Nominated by our Senators to Congress—But this alone will not do. It will also be necessary to have as many friends as possible in the Senate. I shall therefore make no apology, but at once ask your aid in this Business with your friends— . . . Write me as soon as you can, and send me a list of all the Senators in the New England & Middle States; . . .[194]

Then on February 22 Seagrove wrote again to "Dear Sam":

do my dear fellow Canvis for me among the Senators— . . . There will be four Candidates for that office from Georgia—so that it must be determined by a Vote of the Senate—the Bearer Colo. Few will nominate me with the others. Our other Senator [James Gunn] I expect on [no?] Friendship from; I despise the Man as altogether unworthy of the appointment he has—and as I warmly opposed him in hope of getting in Genl Wayne—I know he will wish to disappoint me. His Man will be a Wretch who now fills the Office of Collectorship at this place—his Name is Ruben Wilkinson—he is from our back Woods low and illiterate as possible, but served our Honorable Senator Gunn in geting him Votes at the election, by which he is bound to him. Majr. Wm. Pierce & Majr. John Habersham are also for it—a beast a sot Villain and Drunkard—a Wm. Gibbons Senr. brings up the rear. I have wrote all my friends that I can think of to remember me. . . . If I could visit York for a few Months and bustle about among my old acquaintances I think I should stand a good chance. In case I loose the Collector's Office there is other appointments under the New Governt. which may answer. I hope you have some object in view for yourself—now is the time my dear fellow for you to fix.[195]

Seagrove's language suggests that he may have thought appointments were made by the Senate rather than by nomination of the President and appointment by him by and with the advice and consent of the Senate. Editorial notes say that on August 3 Seagrove's name was sent to the Senate for Collector of Customs at St. Mary's, and that it was confirmed on the 5th; and that Habersham was appointed Collector of Customs at Savannah.[196]

ROMANCE AND OFFICE SEEKING. From New York General Webb himself wrote on June 7, 1789, to Miss Hogeboom:

[194] 3 *Correspondence and Journals of Samuel Blachley Webb* (collected and edited by Worthington Chauncey Ford, New York, 1894; Wickersham Press, Lancaster, Pa.) 120-121. This letter and the next are quoted by 2 George H. Haynes, *The Senate of the United States* (Houghton Mifflin Co., Boston, 1938) 736.
[195] 3 *Correspondence and Journals of Samuel Blachley Webb* (collected and edited by Worthington Chauncey Ford, New York, 1894; Wickersham Press, Lancaster, Pa.) 123-124.
[196] *Ibid.* 121, 123.

The appointments under the New Government are to be made by my old Patron General Washington, and I am a candidate for an office that will be permanent and honorable, and have the assurances of friendship from our President; but at the same time there are many others on the list.—My wish is an office that may enable me to reside in this State & at present I have the most flattering expectations—To accomplish this business all my friends advise my being on the Spot,—and they have convinced me of the propriety of their advice . . . . it was in Idea, to give me an appointment which would oblige me to go to Europe, and was it not for my friendship for you, it is probable it might have been agreeable to me, but as the matter now stands it cannot meet my wishes,—nor will I hear of it. . . .[197]

To the same lady he wrote again on September 6:

My expectations of an Office is in the Judiciary line, . . . Indeed my dear Girl I am extremely anxious, and believe me when I declare it is more on your account, than my own. . . . I have been obliged to decline one or two proposals from the President, and have been apprehensive, that he was displeas'd,—but in an interview I had with him yesterday evening, my fears on that had [sic] are done away.—All I can say is, that if I am disappointed, it will not be owing to a want of disposition in the President to serve me, or from any misconduct of my own. To time I must leave the event, and shall endeavor to keep a contented mind, happen what may. . . .[198]

On September 27, however, he had to report to Miss Hogeboom:

I am sorry to tell you, my dear friend, that I have failed in the appointment which I expected. It was determined yesterday. The President sent for me and fully convinced me of the necessity he was under of giveing it to my friend Colo. Smith, Son-in-law to the Vice-President,—at the same time giveing me the most flattering assureances of his disposition to serve me, on some future occasion should any thing offer which would be acceptable. I was obliged to acquiess with a good grace, tho: I confess to you my disappointment was great, and yet was it not for my Love and esteem for you, I should not care anything for it,—An idea was again conveyed to me of going abroad, when I was obliged to tell the President, candidly, that no appointment of that kind could meet my wishes.[199]

THE VICE PRESIDENT ON WASHINGTON'S EXERCISE OF THE POWER TO MAKE NOMINATIONS. On August 30, 1789, Vice President Adams wrote to Silvanus Bourn:

I must caution you, my dear Sir, against having any dependence on my influence or that of any other person. No man, I believe, has influence with

[197] Ibid. 133–134.   [198] Ibid. 139.   [199] Ibid. 141.

the President. He seeks information from all quarters, and judges more independently than any man I ever knew. It is of so much importance to the public that he should preserve this superiority, that I hope I shall never see the time that any man will have influence with him beyond the powers of reason and argument.[200]

PRESIDENT WASHINGTON'S INVITATIONS TO SENATOR MACLAY. The symbolic character of Washington is so overpowering, and his letters so expressive of high motives, that it is well to point out anything which even shows the possibility of his having acted from political motives. In this connection may be mentioned the timing of Washington's invitations to Senator Maclay to the theater and to dinner, respectively. The first invitation was on Monday, May 11,[201] in the midst of the fight over a title for the President, and when on Saturday Maclay had denounced such "bombastic nonsense." [202] The second invitation was for Thursday, August 27,[203] and was made on the preceding Monday, after Maclay had on Saturday been the chief cause of the President's displeasure in his famous attempt to seek in person the advice and consent of the Senate to instructions for the Indian commissioners.[204] Was such timing accidental or deliberate? and if deliberate, from what motive? [205]

When on August 21 the other Senator from Pennsylvania, Robert Morris, said in the Senate that "he hoped his colleague would change his sentiments" on the *viva voce* vote on presidential nominations "for *his own sake*," Maclay confided to his journal:

> The words *for his own sake* were not without a meaning. I have never been at the table of the President or the Vice-President, or [been] taken the least notice of, for a considerable time, by the diplomatic corps or the people of *ton* in the city. But I care not a fig for it. . . .[206]

The President's invitation to dinner came along six days later; but it may be that social pressure was practised in New York in 1789 as it has been practised in Washington in later times, and as, indeed, it is practised everywhere upon those who are at once socially ambitious and so

---

[200] 9 *The Works of John Adams* (Charles Francis Adams, ed., Little, Brown and Co., Boston, 1854) 561.
[201] *Journal of William Maclay* 28–30.
[202] *Ibid.* 25–28.   [203] *Ibid.* 134–135.   [204] *Ibid.* 125–130.
[205] Little weight can, of course, be given to Maclay's reaction to the invitation: "I really was surprised at the invitation. It will be my duty to go; however, I will make no inferences whatever. I am convinced all the dinners he can now give or ever could will make no difference in my conduct. . . ." *Ibid.* 130. Maclay was full of suspicions.
[206] *Ibid.* 124–125.

spineless as to have to keep up with the right people. Maclay was neither.[207]

A FEDERALIST ADMINISTRATION. Nothing can be said, with reference to 1789, of the President's role as party leader, for there were no avowed and organized parties. When in the course of a short time such parties emerged, Hamilton became and remained until his death the leader of the Federalists,[208] and Mr. Jefferson became the leader of the Republicans. Washington sought to rally all friends of the Constitution and to stand above party. The difficulties of John Adams as President arose in no small degree from the fact that Hamilton and not he was the recognized leader of the Federalists, even those in his cabinet.[209] Mr. Jefferson was thus the first President who was also the recognized leader of the majority party.[210]

Yet Washington's Administration was from the beginning, as it became more definitely and clearly so in his second term,[211] as parties began to take on definite form, a Federalist Administration. Mr. Beard has shown the superficiality of the view that there was no continuity between the Federalist and Anti-Federalist alignment over ratification of the Constitution and the Federalist and Republican alignment which emerged in clear form before Washington retired to Mount Vernon.[212] The same considerations, in no small degree economic, which made men sympathetic or antagonistic toward the proposed Constitution, made them take opposing views with respect to its construction, the organization of the government, and the development of federal policies.

In 1795 President Washington wrote to the Acting Secretary of State:

I shall not, whilst I have the honor to administer the government, bring

[207] Three days after being in the President's theater party Maclay used his best ridicule against titles in the Senate. *Ibid.* 32–36. On September 1, five days after he dined at the President's, Maclay's vote was turning the tide in favor of the lowest salaries, though the next day pain kept him away. *Ibid.* 141. It was on September 26 that Maclay stood up against Adams and Ellsworth in an argument on whether the President was immune to judicial process. *Ibid.* 163.
[208] See Henry Cabot Lodge, *Alexander Hamilton* (American Statesmen series, Houghton, Mifflin and Co., Boston and New York, 1882) 136. But see also *ibid.* 278–279.
[209] W. E. Binkley, *The Powers of the President* (Doubleday, Doran & Co., Garden City, 1937) 43–46; Charles Francis Adams, "The Life of John Adams," 1 *The Works of John Adams* (Charles Francis Adams, ed., Little, Brown and Co., Boston, 1856) chap. 10 ("The Presidency"). See also 8 *ibid.* (1853) 541–675; 9 *ibid.* (1854) 3–101.
[210] W. E. Binkley, *The Powers of the President* (Doubleday, Doran & Co., Garden City, 1937) 50. The present writer owes a general debt to this book.
[211] *Cf.* Edward S. Corwin, *The President: Office and Powers* (2d ed., New York University Press, New York, 1941) 80–81; Robert C. Brooks, *Political Parties and Electoral Problems* (Harper & Bros., New York and London, 1923) 50–51.
[212] Charles A. Beard, *The Economic Origins of Jeffersonian Democracy* (The Macmillan Co., New York, 1915) chap. 3 ("The Personnel of the First Administration").

a man into any office, of consequence knowingly, whose political tenets are adverse to the measures which the *general* government are pursuing; for this, in my opinion, would be a sort of political Suicide; that it wd. embarrass its movements is most certain.[213]

In the first year of the government there was naturally no occasion for the President to make such a statement. His only criterion at that time was the attitudes men had shown in the fight over ratification; and his appointment of Paca indicates he did not at the outset apply that criterion with absolute rigor.[214] Nevertheless, as Mr. Beard has pointed out:

The government that began with the inauguration of Washington, on April 30, 1789, was therefore no non-partisan government chosen without regard to the constitutional conflict which had just closed.[215]

He states that of the 39 men who had signed the Constitution, 26 became members of Congress or received appointment under the new government;[216] and that of the 55 men who had at one time or another sat in the Philadelphia Convention,[217] 30 went into the new government in one capacity or another.[218] It is unnecessary here to reproduce Mr. Beard's list of Washington appointments or his personnel analysis of Congress; but they point to the fact that in all branches of the new government the Administration was predominantly Federalist in complexion, in that sense of Federalist which had a basic continuity with the future as well as with the past. Washington of course never publicly spoke of himself in partisan terms,[219] and that for three reasons. In the first place, his aversion to parties as dangerous to his conservative principles inhibited him from the avowed admission of their existence.[220] In the second place, he considered his assumption of a partisan attitude inconsistent with his roles as chief of state and national hero. In the third place, he deliberately sought to use these roles to forestall the

[213] 34 *Writings* 315. September 27, 1795. Private letter.
[214] See 30 *Writings* 471, 484, and comment in the preceding section (p. 112) entitled, "Washington and nominations: his formulation of general principles."
[215] Charles A. Beard, *The Economic Origins of Jeffersonian Democracy* (The Macmillan Co., New York, 1915) 106–107.
[216] *Ibid.* 104.
[217] See Fred Rodell, *Fifty-Five Men* (The Telegraph Press, New York and Harrisburg, 1936) 275–277; 3 Max Farrand, ed., *The Records of the Federal Convention of 1787* (2d ed. in 4 vols., Yale University Press, New Haven, 1937) Appendix B.
[218] Charles A. Beard, *The Economic Origins of Jeffersonian Democracy* (The Macmillan Co., New York, 1915) 105.
[219] But see references in chapter 1 above, and in Charles A. Beard, *The Economic Origins of Jeffersonian Democracy* (The Macmillan Co., New York, 1915) 87–89, to Washington's interest in and quiet efforts in behalf of securing the choice in 1788 of Federalists rather than Anti-Federalists.
[220] *Cf.* his Farewell Address: [First Draft], 35 *Writings* 51, 55–56; *ibid.* 214, 223–229.

emergence of parties or at least to soften their intensity.[221] Realistically considered, however, Washington and his Administration must from the very beginning be described as Federalist. That he transcended Federalism as no other Federalist did was but a part of his unique position in American history.[222] Even as late as October 1, 1792, when Mr. Jefferson had determined to retire from office, and in the very conversation in which the President took up the differences between him and Hamilton, he records that he told the President, who was still undecided whether to retire at the end of his first term:

As to himself, his presence was important; that he was the only man in the United States who possessed the confidence of the whole; that government was founded in opinion and confidence, and that the longer he remained, the stronger would become the habits of the people in submitting to the government, and in thinking it a thing to be maintained; that there was no other person who would be thought anything more than the head of a party.[223]

[221] *Cf.* his reasons for accepting the Presidency, as quoted in chap. 1 above, and his efforts to keep Jefferson and Hamilton working together in the cabinet despite their growing differences, as ably analyzed in Leonard D. White, "Public Administration Under the Federalists" (1944) 24 *Boston U. Law Rev.* 144, 156–172, especially 165–172.
[222] See in chapter 1 above the section (p. 1) entitled, "Washington's unique position."
[223] The *Anas:* 9 *The Writings of Thomas Jefferson* (Derby & Jackson, New York, 1859) 121. See *ibid.* 120–123.

Chapter 5

THE PRESIDENT
AS ADMINISTRATIVE CHIEF

. .

SOME EARLY ACTS OF WASHINGTON AS ADMINISTRATIVE CHIEF. As an administrator Washington made the final decisions, but only after exercising his best judgment in the light of the views of advisors.[1] As early as May 5, 1789, he thanked Alexander Hamilton for his "friendly communications" and asked "that you will permit me to entreat a continuation of them as occasion may arise. The manner chosen for doing it, is most agreeable to me."[2] He kept Jay and Knox as Acting Secretaries held over from the Confederation until the bills for the establishment of the great departments had been enacted by Congress.[3] To the latter, as "The Acting Secretary at War," he sent papers relative to a treaty with the Cherokees, saying he understood matters of this kind had been considered as belonging to his department "to examine and report thereon," and asked Knox for a "summary report" on the enclosed papers and similar ones in the latter's hands "as soon as may be."[4] This communication, written on the fifth day after his inauguration, showed the methodical dispatch with which Washington sought the mastery of executive business.

On May 29 the President wrote to Governor Walton of Georgia:

The unhappy situation of affairs between the State of Georgia and the Creeks will soon be a subject of deliberation, and I am persuaded will

---

[1] See Leonard D. White, "Public Administration Under the Federalists," in (1944) 24 *Boston U. L. Rev.* 144–186, especially 145–156. The present writer has also had the benefit of discussing Washington as an administrator with Mr. Louis Brownlow. See also 4 *The Writings of Thomas Jefferson* (Washington ed., Derby & Jackson, New York, 1859) 415–417, and 5 *ibid.* 93–94.
[2] 30 *Writings* 311, note 67.
[3] See Jared Sparks, *The Life of George Washington* (Tappan and Dennet, Boston, 1844) 410; George Pellew, *John Jay* (American Statesmen series, Houghton, Mifflin and Co., Boston and New York, 1890) 262; Jay Caesar Guggenheimer, "The Development of the Executive Departments, 1775–1789," *Essays in the Constitutional History of the United States in the Formative Period, 1775–1789* (J. Franklin Jameson, ed., Houghton, Mifflin and Co., 1889) 154, 165–166.
[4] 30 *Writings* 313. May 9, 1789.

THE PRESIDENT AS ADMINISTRATIVE CHIEF 135

receive all that dispatch that the nature of the case may require, and the circumstances of the Government admit.[5]

The expression, "a subject of deliberation," carried implications of Washington's habits of mind which may almost be said to foreshadow the later emergence of the institutional beginnings of the cabinet.

In the period, June 4–8, the President read and made extracts of the letters of our minister to France, Mr. Jefferson, to Secretary Jay. "This was the beginning," says an editorial note, "of a practice which Washington continued, more or less throughout his presidency."[6] Here was a striking aspect of his methodical administrative method.

By June 8 Washington had become sufficiently adjusted to his new position to undertake a comprehensive survey of the administrative business of the United States as it stood at that time. That he should conceive such a survey to be his administrative responsibility was characteristic. His method of procedure was to address identical letters to the Acting Secretary for Foreign Affairs, the Acting Secretary at War, and the Board of the Treasury, and a similar letter to the Acting Postmaster General.[7] In the "present unsettled state of the Executive Departments," he said, it was not "expedient to call upon you for information officially," but "informal communications" would not be "improper or unprofitable." He was less occupied than he would be hereafter, and hence desired to obtain "an acquaintance with the real situation of the several great Departments, at the period of my acceding to the administration of the general Government." Accordingly, he asked of each "in writing" such a "clear account" of his department "as may be sufficient (without overburdening or confusing the mind which has very many objects to claim its attention at the same instant) to impress me with a full, precise, and distinct *general idea* of the affairs of the United States, so far as they are comprehended in, or connected with that Department." He added that his reason for this "notification" was that he was now at leisure to inspect such papers and documents as might be necessary to be acted upon hereafter or that would give him insight into the business and duties of that department.[8] An editorial note says that none of the replies is in the Washington papers, but that there are what appear to be Washington's notes on such replies.[9] Two notable features of this circular communication are Washington's preference for basing his judgment upon written reports and the clear conception he had of the presidential function of over-all administrative management.

The thoroughness with which the President examined the replies is

[5] Ibid. 337–338.
[6] Ibid. 343, note 29.
[7] Ibid. 344, note 30.
[8] Ibid. 343–344.
[9] Ibid. 344, note 30.

indicated by his follow-up letters to the Acting Postmaster General. On July 3 he wrote that officer that he had inspected the papers sent by him; but, though the Post Office had on the whole been profitable since 1782, "I should wish to know the causes of the decrease from that source" between 1785, when there had been a profit, and 1789, when there had been a loss. "I must, therefore, request you to send me, *in detail,* the receipts and expenditures of the Post Office" for 1784 and 1788. The returns from the several post offices for these years, he continued, would show which were productive; and the accounts of the General Post Office for these years would show the cause of the difference between receipts and expenditures. If the cause lay in the resolves of Congress, he conceived it must have been either by the increased cost of stages as compared with riders or by directing mail to be carried to parts where the cost exceeded the produce. But he presumed the documents now requested would fully explain the matter.[10]

The President was still not satisfied. On July 17 he again wrote the Acting Postmaster General to say he had received the Post Office Acts in detail for 1784 and 1788. "But there still remains one point on which I would wish to have further information." It was not shown by any documents sent to him whether the annual profit "has been lodged in the Treasury of the United States, or appropriated to the use of the Post Office Department." He would "thank you for early and satisfactory information on this head."[11]

When Congress resolved that for the time being the President be requested to transmit copies of its Acts to the several state executives, the President sent a circular to the governors enclosing an Act, but cautiously saved a precedent with respect to executive communication with the state executives in these words:

> . . . As Congress have not yet established any Department through which communications can be officially made from the General Government to the Executives of the several States, . . .[12]

On June 15 the President sent a message to the Senate announcing that he had granted a leave of absence to Mr. Jefferson as minister to France, nominating William Short to take charge in Mr. Jefferson's absence, and asking "your advice on the propriety of appointing him."[13]

[10] *Ibid.* 352–353.   [11] *Ibid.* 356.   [12] *Ibid.* 344–345. June 8, 1789.
[13] *Ibid.* 347, note 35. See for the fact 1 *Annals* 47 (June 16–18, 1789).
  For the text of the message see 1 *Messages and Papers of the Presidents* 50. The President said Mr. Jefferson's application was for "permission to return home for a few months" and "it appearing to me proper to comply with his request." He added that Jay had his "directions" to lay before the Senate at its convenience papers in the Office of Foreign Affairs "which will acquaint you with his [Short's] character."

THE PRESIDENT AS ADMINISTRATIVE CHIEF

It will be noted that the President assumed authority to grant a leave of absence to a minister. This alarmed Senator Maclay:

The message about Mr. Short touches a matter that may be drawn into a precedent. . . . The leave for return, etc., is not laid before the Senate. Granting this power to be solely with the President, the power of dismissing ambassadors seems to follow, and some of the courtiers in the Senate fairly admit it. I chose to give the matter a different turn, and delivered my opinion: That our concurring in the appointment of Mr. Short fully implied the consent of the return of Mr. Jefferson; that if we chose to prevent the return of Mr. Jefferson, it was only to negative the nomination of Mr. Short or any other one to fill his place. . . .[14]

To Leonard de Neufville the President wrote:

As all public accounts and matters of a pecuniary nature will come properly under the inspection of the Treasury Department of the United States, I shall, when that department is organized and established, have those papers laid before the Secretary thereof, and so far as my official agency may be necessary in the business it will meet with no delay.[15]

When Representative James Jackson of Georgia sent some letters to the President, Lear wrote him that the President had directed him to inform Jackson

that he is now engaged in obtaining from the Secretary of the War and every other channel such information relative to the situation of Indian affairs as will enable him to form a just opinion thereon.[16]

On August 2, the President wrote to Senator Richard Henry Lee:

The extreme hurry in which I have been for several days, to compare the merits and pretensions of the several applicants for appointments under the Revenue in order that the nominations might speedily follow the passing of the Collection Bill . . .[17]

He had actually signed the collection bill on July 31,[18] and he sent in a complete list of nominations the day after writing the letter quoted.[19]

---

[14] *Journal of William Maclay* 79–80.
    It is to be observed that Jay had not felt at liberty to grant this leave of absence: ". . . The reasons assigned for your wishing to make a short visit to America are in my opinion sufficient to justify you in asking leave, and myself in granting it; but, my dear sir, there is no Congress sitting, nor have any of their servants authority to interfere. As soon as the President shall be in office I will, without delay, communicate your letters to him, and urge the business with all the despatch in my power. To this I shall be prompted not only by official duty, but by that personal esteem and regard with which I am, dear sir, . . ." Jay to Jefferson, March 9, 1789. 3 *The Correspondence and Public Papers of John Jay* (Henry P. Johnston, ed., G. P. Putnam's Sons, New York and London, 1891) 366.
[15] 30 *Writings* 350. June 29, 1789.
[16] *Ibid.* 358. July 22, 1789.
[17] *Ibid.* 368. See 1 *Annals* 17.
[18] 2 *Laws of the United States* 7–31.
[19] 30 *Writings* 368, note 69.

The dates show that Washington was prompt to put into motion the revenue system created by Congress.

On August 11, while the bill was still pending for commissioners to attend a treaty with the Southern Indians, Washington wrote Benjamin Lincoln to inform him he wanted him as one of the commissioners. He asked, however, that this intimation be kept to himself, as it was not certain commissioners would be appointed, and if so, other circumstances might render its concealment proper.[20]

Another leave of absence was granted when Lear wrote to John Taylor Gilman, one of the commissioners for settling the accounts of the United States with the individual States, saying that the President had directed that he be granted leave of absence for three weeks. This was on August 12.[21] On September 28 the President wrote to Gilman:

. . . I should be very unwilling that a temporary illness should deprive a man of his office unless the public good rendered a new appointment absolutely necessary. . . .

Since, therefore, General Irwin (Irvine) had informed him that "the presence of the whole Board will not be absolutely necessary 'till some final settlement of Accounts is about to take place," he would delay making any new appointment in the hope of Gilman's recovery.[22] On December 14, however, Lear wrote Gilman that he had been directed by the President to notify him that he had been informed by the other commissioners that business was retarded and soon would be at a stand without his presence, and that his attendance could not be well delayed beyond the first or certainly the middle of January without injury to the public. The President wished Gilman to give him immediate information, so that another person might be appointed "and the public business not be unnecessarily retarded."[23]

In the administrative transition from the Confederation, the President was compelled to ask other officers to hold over. To the three wardens of the Port of New York he wrote that the time had arrived for the United States to provide for "keeping up the proper supplies for the Light Houses in different Ports," but since the Treasury Department was not yet organized so as to do so, he had to ask them still to "continue the superintendence of the Light House in this Port, keeping an exact account of the expenses." These would be reimbursed by the Treasurer of the United States as soon as one was appointed. "He will also be authorized to take the management of the business into his hands and make the necessary contracts accordingly."[24]

[20] Ibid. 379–380.
[21] Ibid. 380.
[22] Ibid. 417–418.
[23] Ibid. 418, note 58.
[24] Ibid. 381–382. August 18, 1789.

THE PRESIDENT AS ADMINISTRATIVE CHIEF

A similar problem was how to get money under an appropriation from impost and tonnage duties before the Treasury Department was organized. The President wrote to the Secretary of War, relative to such an appropriation for the expense of treating with the Indians:

I have therefore to request that you will use your exertions to obtain the necessary means for carrying the intention of Congress into effect. As soon as the Treasury Department shall be organized, Warrants will issue for the monies according to Law.[25]

In another case Congress had directed a survey which required ascertaining certain points in Canada, but had made no provision for the expenses of the survey. Since the consent of Lord Dorchester was necessary, the President informed the Secretary of War that he had "seen fit to direct" Acting Secretary Jay to send a special messenger to secure such consent. "I hereby direct you," he continued, to advance to the messenger employed by Jay, out of money appropriated to Indian Affairs and located in the bank of New York subject to your order, the sum of $350 for the expense of his mission "and to be accounted for by him on his return," "which sum shall be replaced in your hands as soon as provision is made" for carrying the survey into effect.[26] The President was thus assuming authority to direct that one department head advance the money for an expenditure by another for which Congress had not yet made an appropriation.

Indeed, on the day before the President had written Knox that this survey was of too great importance to the United States to await the organization of the Treasury Department and had directed him to advance to the surveyor $1,125 out of money for treaty negotiations with the Southern Indians, the sum to be replaced as soon as provision could be made to defray the expenses of the survey.[27]

The President early began his practice of asking department heads for opinions. On September 17 Lear, by direction of the President, sent Knox a letter from Governor George Clinton and asked an opinion on "the expediency of his making an official or other communication of the information contained therein to the Congress. . ."[28] Already in August a confidential communication to Representative Madison had illustrated his characteristic technique of submitting written questions to his advisers in anticipation of getting their oral advice.[29]

There is one important document of 1789 which the President issued in his capacity of Commander in Chief. On October 6 he wrote to in-

[25] *Ibid.* 391. August 26, 1789.
[26] *Ibid.* 394–395. September 5, 1789.
[27] *Ibid.* 395, note 12. September 4, 1789.
[28] *Ibid.* 408, note 35.
[29] *Ibid.* 393–394.

form Governor Arthur St. Clair of the Western Territory that Congress had authorized the President to call forth the militia of the states to protect the frontiers against the Indians, and to give him his instructions. Washington stated his policy of peace on reasonable terms, and called for information about the attitude of the Wabash and Illinois tribes and the means of preserving peace with them. St. Clair was to inform the Indians of the desire of the United States that hostilities cease as a prelude to a treaty; but if they continued hostilities or meditated incursions against the frontiers of Virginia or Pennsylvania or our troops or posts, and there was no time to inform the President and receive further orders,

then you are hereby authorized and empowered in my name to call on the lieutenants of the nearest counties of Virginia and Pennsylvania for such detachments of militia as you may judge proper, not exceeding, however, one thousand from Virginia and five hundred from Pennsylvania.

The President said he had directed letters to the two governors on the act of Congress and "these conditional directions" to St. Clair, so that there might be no obstructions. The said militia was to act in conjunction with federal troops for such defensive or offensive operations

as you and the commanding officer of the troops conjointly shall judge necessary for the public service and the protection of the inhabitants and the posts.

The President outlined the terms of actual militia service.[30] He made it clear that war with the Wabash ought to be avoided by all means consistent with the security of the frontier inhabitants and of the troops and with "the national dignity." In the existing "indiscriminate hostilities," he said, it was extremely hard if not impossible to say a war without further measures would be just on the part of the United States. But he added that if, after manifesting clearly to the Indians the disposition of the General Government for peace and the extension of a just protection to the said Indians, they should continue their incursions, "the United States will be constrained to punish them with severity." Washington concluded by directing St. Clair to proceed as soon as possible with safety to execute the orders of the late Congress as to the inhabitants of the Mississippi River villages,[31] who should as soon as possible "possess the lands to which they are entitled by some known and fixed principles;" by informing him that he had ordered copies of the Fort

---

[30] The act of Congress had prescribed: "and that their pay and subsistence, while in service, be the same as the pay and subsistence of the troops abovementioned." 2 *Laws of the United States* 74.
[31] He mentioned specifically St. Vincennes and Kaskaskia.

Hamar treaty to be printed and forwarded to him, together with the ratification and his proclamation enjoining its observance; and by recommending earnestly an early and pointed attention to the obtaining of precise knowledge of the waters emptying into the Ohio on the northwest and into Lakes Erie and Michigan, the length of the portages between, and the nature of the ground.[32]

The Constitution had empowered Congress to *provide for* calling forth the militia to execute the laws of the Union, suppress insurrections and repel invasions.[33] Congress in its first session had so provided to the extent of enacting:

That, for the purpose of protecting the inhabitants of the frontiers of the United States from the hostile incursions of the Indians, the president is hereby authorized to call into service, from time to time, such part of the militia of the states, respectively, as he may judge necessary for the purpose aforesaid; . . .[34]

Congress had, in short, provided for calling forth the militia, for that aspect of the third of the constitutional purposes which it had specified, by leaving the matter to the judgment and discretion of the Commander in Chief and Chief Executive.[35] Then he in his turn had *formally redelegated* a *limited* part of his delegated discretion to his agent on the spot, as the practical circumstances of the situation necessitated. His letter to Governor St. Clair also makes clear that, in the case of the Indians, congressional delegation to him of discretion with respect to calling forth the militia was in effect delegation of the determination of peace or war.

Just before Washington set out for his New England tour he wrote an official letter to Secretary of the Treasury Hamilton which reveals how his official expenses were handled. He said $2005 was necessary to take up notes given for money advanced for "the household of the President of the United States" before the organization of the Treasury Department. This plus the $2000 already advanced by the Secretary for taking up notes would complete the payment of all monies advanced for the use of the President previous to Hamilton's coming into office. $1000 and a draft on Boston for $500 would also be wanting for the President; and in his absence Mr. Robert Lewis would draw from the Secretary such money as might be wanting "for the use of the Household" during his journey.[36]

---

[32] 30 *Writings* 429-431. On the legal and administrative relation between the President and the Governor of the Western territory see 2 *Laws of the United States* 33 for an act which had been approved August 7, 1789.
[33] Article I, section 8, § 15. [35] Cf. *Martin v. Mott*, 12 Wheat. 19, 28-32 (1827).
[34] 2 *Laws of the United States* 74. [36] 30 *Writings* 445-446. October 13, 1789.

In the Washington Papers "at the end of 1789" there is a "Plan of American Finance" in Washington's handwriting which an editorial note says "may or may not have been submitted to Hamilton."[37]

Another indication of Washington's methodical administrative practice is indicated by an editorial note in his *Writings*:

> On December 8, or thereabouts, Washington wrote out a memorandum of extracts from the report of the Commissioners appointed to treat with the Southern Indians, and extracts of the letters from sundry persons in Kentucky and other parts of the western country, for the purpose of clarifying the Indian situation in his mind. . . .[38]

When dispatches from the President to Governor Beverley Randolph under date of October 3 did not reach the latter until the last day of November, Washington considered the matter of some importance not only in itself but also in relation to "the general regulation of the post Office." He wrote to ask the Governor to help him investigate the cause, why the letters were retained, and whether it was due to inattention of any postmaster or to a worse cause. "An investigation and discovery of this matter may prevent future offences of the like nature." Washington had inquired of the New York postmaster whether the letters had been detained in his office, and asked the Governor to look at the stamp to help him check up on that official's alibi.[39]

A letter to the Secretary of the Treasury on December 17 shows Washington in the role of administrative and diplomatic planner. He said he was uncertain of the condition and even of the Office in which the accounts of our disbursements for the subsistence of prisoners of war remained; and since negotiations might take place (whenever the Union was completed) in which an accurate understanding of these accounts would become necessary, he suggested to Hamilton the expediency of some immediate attention to them. Though much property would doubtless be lost to the United States for want of vouchers and negligence on our part, yet he had always thought that even so there was a very considerable balance in our favor. His present wish was to have the subject so far investigated as to avoid committing ourselves by bringing forward accounts which had better continue dormant. If there were no such danger, then it was desirable that the business be placed in a state to enable us to speak from a general knowledge of the facts and in a proper tone, in case the demand of the American posts should draw

[37] *Ibid.* 454-455, and note 17 on latter page. The document is editorially dated October (?) 1789.
[38] *Ibid.* 476, note 53. The note says this document covers 18 folio pages.
[39] *Ibid.* 477-478. December 14, 1789.

THE PRESIDENT AS ADMINISTRATIVE CHIEF 143

pecuniary subjects into discussion. He believed lists of property carried away by the British when they evacuated the posts occupied during the late war were lodged in the Office of Foreign Affairs.[40]

This letter suggests another characteristic of Washington as an administrator which is further illustrated by several other incidents recorded in this study. That is his concern for the careful custody and systematic use of official papers.[41] This archival sense is one of the first marks of a good administrator.[42]

Some of the administrative activities of the President in the last two months of the calendar year are recorded in the *Diaries*. November 16 the President had to dinner the commissioners who had failed to commit the Creeks to a treaty.[43] Five days later he received their report, which he read through and expressed the intention of reading more carefully again.[44] The next day, a Sunday, he had a long talk with the commissioners.[45] The next Wednesday he called on Jay and Knox "on business."[46] On December 1 he read the Moroccan papers and sent them to Jay to draft answers.[47] On December 8 he finished making extracts of the report of the Indian commissioners and of many other papers on Indian and Western affairs.[48] On the 15th he called on Knox and gave him "the heads" of many letters to write to people in the West, mainly on Indian affairs.[49] On the 18th he read and digested his thoughts on European plans and the plans of Knox and Steuben for a national militia.[50] The next day he put his ideas on the militia subject in writing to send to Knox for throwing into the form of a bill for the congressional committee appointed to draft such a bill.[51] Two days later he put his ideas on that subject in the form of a letter, which he sent to Knox.[52] Two days after that he sent Knox despatches from Virginia on frontier conditions and Indian "depredations" and asked his attendance the next day to talk the matter over.[53] Knox came, and after a full talk the President instructed him on the answers.[54]

[40] Ibid. 478–479.   [41] Cf. 1 *Writings* xlii–xliii.
[42] Cf. "The Role of Records in Administration," *Staff Information Circulars*, No. 11 (The National Archives, Washington, July, 1941). This circular consists of three papers read before the Federal Records Conference in Washington, January 29, 1941: Ernst Posner, "The Role of Records in German Administration"; Helen L. Chatfield, "The Role of Records in the Administration of the Federal Government of the United States"; Edna B. Poeppel, "The Role of Records in American Business Administration." See also Helen L. Chatfield, "The Role of the Archivist in Public Administration" (The National Archives, May, 1942); Ernst Posner, "Public Records Under Military Occupation" (The National Archives, MPD 43–13, May, 1943); "Publications of the National Archives" (The National Archives, Publication No. 46–13, April, 1946).
[43] 4 *Diaries* 52–53.   [46] Ibid. 55.   [49] Ibid. 58.   [52] Ibid.
[44] Ibid. 53–54.   [47] Ibid. 56.   [50] Ibid. 59.   [53] Ibid. 60–61.
[45] Ibid. 54.   [48] Ibid. 57.   [51] Ibid. 60.   [54] Ibid. 61.

Chapter 6

MISCELLANEOUS CONSTITUTIONAL QUESTIONS RAISED IN HOUSE DEBATE

. .

CONSTITUTIONAL ASPECTS OF THE COMPENSATION OF THE PRESIDENT. In his First Inaugural Washington had renounced "every pecuniary compensation" and all "personal emoluments" and requested that estimates be confined to his "actual expenditures."[1] The Congress had already requested the proprietor of the house lately occupied by the President of Congress to put it and its furniture in proper condition for the residence and use of the President, and otherwise at the expense of the United States to provide for his temporary accommodation.[2]

On July 13 the House received the report of its committee on the compensation of the President, Vice President, and members of Senate and House. This report appears to have provided $20,000 plus certain additional allowances for the President and $5,000 for the Vice President.[3] White asked in what style the President was expected to live. "He observed there was provision for the expenses of a house, furniture, secretaries, clerks, càrriages and horses. Perhaps the sum proposed might be too much or too little." Page noted that President Washington had refused compensation, but said the Constitution required compensation, so it was their duty to provide it.

A constitutional issue was now injected into the discussion:

Mr. Lawrence did not know, whether the sum proposed was enough for the President or not; but according to the terms of the constitution, it ought to be granted as one sum, because he is to receive no other emolument whatever from the United States, or either of them. Now, if it is declared he shall receive twenty thousand dollars, and, exclusive of that sum, we make him an allowance for furniture, horses, carriages, &c., such an allowance is an emolument beyond the compensation contemplated in the constitution; but

---

[1] 30 *Writings* 295–296. [3] See *ibid.* 662.
[2] 1 *Annals* 19–20, 149–150. April 15, 1789.

144

I have no objection to blend these sums together, declaring the whole to be the compensation contemplated by the constitution.

He went on to raise another constitutional objection in these words:

Besides, if we establish salaries for his secretaries and clerks, we establish them officers of the Government; this will be improper, because it infringes his right to employ a confidential person in the management of those concerns, for which the constitution has made him responsible.

So he moved to strike out "all that related to horses, carriages, furniture, &c."

Sherman liked a net sum as a way of avoiding accounts to be settled by the President with the United States, and

Mr. Sedgwick considered this a constitutional question, and therefore thought it deserved serious investigation. The provision made in the report, for paying the expenses of enumerated articles, does not leave the President in the situation intended by the constitution, which was, that he should be independent of the Legislature, during his continuance in office; that he should have a compensation for his services, not to be increased or diminished during that period; but there is nothing that will prevent us from making further allowances, provided that the twenty thousand dollars is all that is given as a compensation. By this construction, one of the most salutary clauses of the constitution will be rendered nugatory. From these considerations, he was led to believe that the report was founded on unconstitutional principles.

Baldwin, however,

did not think the constitution was infringed; it was intended that the compensation should not be increased or diminished, during the President's continuance in office. Now it might be as well fixed, by making the allowance in part money, and part furniture, &c. as by declaring a precise sum; it will still be a stated compensation.

Tucker wanted to strike out all the items except furniture and plate and rent for the house. The first two of these ought always to be furnished by Government, for if every new President had to buy them, it might put him to great inconvenience unless he were paid a year's salary in advance. Besides, when he retired, they would not sell for half the cost.

Madison

did not think the report interfered with either the spirit or letter of the constitution, and therefore was opposed to any alteration, especially with respect to the property of a fixed nature. He was sure, if the furniture and plate, and house rent, could be allowed, some of the other articles might also.

Horses and carriages, said Madison, would cost money and sell for little after four years, to the loss of the President. Besides, the House had already undertaken to defray such expenses and had so set a precedent for their enumeration.

White argued that it would be better if a certain sum was assigned for the expenses; but as it now stood, there was no certainty in it. One President might circumscribe it to a quarter of what another would; so the compensation would not be fixed. In so saying he seems to have forgotten that the constitutional provision in question referred only to the period for which the President should have been elected.[4] He was prepared to pay the salary in advance for the first year, to allow the President to take care of extra expenses.

Livermore said: give the President a fixed compensation equal to his usefulness, but do not direct so much to one use, so much to another. It could not be called a compensation when direction was given on how it should be expended. Anyway, why direct him in the style in which he should live? Let him have his salary to spend as he thought proper.

Stone, too, thought the provision of these items would be declaring this to be the house, the horses, and the carriages the President should use. If he did not like them and would not have them, was it intended to impeach him as guilty of a breach of law? No; for no part of the Constitution allowed them to dictate to him on this head. Let the President rather than Congress set his style of living; and if he chose economy, they should not prevent him.

Vining, on the other hand, thought the House had the right to show what they expected of the President, who, as representative of the nation, ought to have a proper degree of dignity attached to his office. He wanted neither splendor nor penury. Nor did he have any constitutional scruples; for the Constitution appeared to be silent, and if so, the House could interfere. How could they agree to provide plate and furniture, but hesitate on clerks and a secretary? Were not the latter as necessary as the former?

Lawrence's motion to strike out passed in the affirmative; and then Page moved to raise the proposed $20,000 to $30,000.

Smith wanted to know if the House would saddle the President with the expense amounting, he understood, to near $10,000, which had already been incurred under the resolution of April 15, for furniture and putting the house in order. He thought the House inconsistent in

[4] "The President shall, at stated Times, receive for his Services, a Compensation, which shall neither be encreased nor diminished during the Period for which he shall have been elected, and he shall not receive within that Period, any other Emolument from the United States, or any of them." Article II, section 1, § 7.

ordering these things for the President and then refusing to let them be applied to his use.

Sherman disagreed. That expense was to be paid by the United States, and the furniture would be their property, to do what they pleased with. There was no inconsistency, since the former vote had been only for the temporary accommodation of the President.

Benson said the business had been properly conducted. It was not contemplated to throw the furniture or any other expense on the President. He presumed the property belonged to the United States, but they would sell to the President such part as he chose to purchase. Nor was the President confined to the house. He might give it up and take another.

Page's motion to strike out $20,000 and insert $30,000 was divided, and the first part carried, while the second part lost. It was then moved to strike out the words secretary and clerks. This motion was put and carried after the following quoted exchange:

Mr. Madison thought the Executive Magistrate ought not to have the power of creating offices; yet if he appointed his secretary and clerks, and they were recognized, either with respect to salary or official acts, they became officers of the Government.

Mr. Benson did not think it necessary to recognize any such officers; they were to be esteemed the mere instruments of the President, and not as sharing in the administration.[5]

Three days later the House resumed consideration of the subject, and Livermore moved to fill the blank with $18,000. But Fitzsimons said he had voted to strike out $20,000 in order so to *increase* the sum as to include the expense, all of which had now been erased.

In view of the heavy initial expenses of a President, which would bear especially hard upon him or his family, if, for example, he were but three months in office, Tucker proposed $26,000 for the first year and $16,000 for every other year, with $10,000 to be paid in advance and the rest quarterly.

In the further discussion of the proper amount, Baldwin said "it must be left to experiment," and indicated that the committee had split the difference between the low estimate of $15,000 and the high estimate of $25,000. Page's motion for $30,000 was voted down; but his motion for $25,000 carried by 30 to 17.[6]

The House then turned to discussion of interesting questions relating to the compensation of the Vice President and of senators and representatives which cannot be gone into here. But a bill was prepared by a

[5] 1 *Annals* 657–662. July 13, 1789.   [6] *Ibid.* 668–671. July 16, 1789.

select committee to provide for the compensation of the President and Vice President, and just before it was ordered engrossed,

on motion of Mr. Smith, of South Carolina, a clause was added to the bill, by which the President is to have the use of the furniture and other effects now in his possession, belonging to the United States.[7]

The next day the bill was passed and sent to the Senate.[8] As approved by the President, it provided for the President $25,000, "with the use of the furniture and other effects, now in his possession, belonging to the United States," in the exact language of the Smith amendment.[9]

Two days after its approval by the President, Maclay recorded in his journal:

The Appropriation bill was taken up. And now Colonel Schuyler brought forward an account of eight thousand dollars expended by Mr. Osgood in repairing and furnishing at the house which the President lives in. This was a great surprise to me, although a vote had originated in the House of Representatives for furnishing the house, yet I considered that allowance for all this had been made in the President's salary. I was, however, taken so unwell that I had to come home.[10]

It thus appears that at the last minute the House added again to the presidential salary the use of the furniture and other effects, and that the use of the house was included in the other effects. It is to be noted also that the salary plus the use of such effects was voted in the law "in full compensation for their[11] respective services, to commence with the time of their entering on the duties of their offices respectively, and to continue so long as they shall remain in office, and to be paid quarterly, out of the treasury of the United States." If no change of salary and no additional emoluments were later voted to the President during "the period for which he shall have been elected,"[12] then it would seem that the provision was pretty clearly constitutional. It is also evident that the question of the amount was closely tied up with the "style of living" of the Chief Magistrate.[13]

Fear of Executive Power: Proposed Amendments to Article II.

On August 18, 1789, when the House of Representatives had under

[7] *Ibid.* 684, 701. August 3, 1789.   [8] *Ibid.* 701. August 4, 1789.
[9] 2 *Laws of the United States* 56. Approved September 24, 1789.
[10] *Journal of William Maclay* 162–163. September 26, 1789.
[11] The plural, "their," was used because the provision applied to the Vice President as well as the President.
[12] Constitution, Article II, section 1, § 7.
[13] See above, chapter 2, the section (p. 11) entitled, "The question of an appropriate 'style of living' and 'line of conduct' for the President."

consideration the subject of amendments to the Constitution, Tucker moved to refer certain propositions of amendment to the Committee of the Whole. Three of these would have made in Article II changes of far-reaching implications for the future of the Presidency. The first of these would have provided:

Nor shall any person be capable of holding the office of President of the United States more than eight years in any term of twelve years.

The second was to change the words, "be commander in chief," to "have power to direct (agreeable to law) the operations" of the army and navy and of the militia when called into active federal service. The third offered this additional clause:

He shall also have power to suspend from his office, for a time not exceeding twelve months, any officer whom he shall have reason to think unfit to be entrusted with the duties thereof; and Congress may, by law, provide for the absolute removal of officers found to be unfit for the trust reposed in them.

The motion to refer was, however, turned down by the House.[14]

On these three proposals only a word of comment is here necessary. The first would have made it impossible for a President to stand for reelection for a third consecutive term, and is thus part of the history of an issue which has been agitated from the time of the Philadelphia Convention to the present day. The second should be read in connection with an express decision of the Philadelphia Convention by which it had deliberately changed the wording of one of the enumerated powers of Congress from "make war" to "declare war." This change had been moved by Madison and Gerry so as to leave "to the Executive the power to repel sudden attacks." It is significant, however, that

On the remark of Mr. King that *"make"* war might be understood to "conduct" it which was an Executive function, Mr. Elseworth gave up his objection . . .[15]

The amendment now advocated by Tucker would have immeasurably weakened the position of the Commander in Chief by expressly making his direction of military operations subordinate to the legislative dictates of Congress. The result could only have proved detrimental, and might have proved disastrous.

[14] 1 *Annals* 790–792.
[15] 2 Max Farrand, *The Records of the Federal Convention of 1787* (rev. ed. in 4 vols., Yale University Press, New Haven, 1937) 313, 318–320; Clarence Arthur Berdahl, *War Powers of the Executive in the United States* (University of Illinois, Urbana, 1921) 61. *Cf.* James Hart, *The Ordinance Making Powers of the President* (The Johns Hopkins Press, Baltimore, 1925) 238–250.

Tucker's third proposal would have expressly provided for the legislative-grant theory of the removal power, and thus, in the view of the present writer as well as of James Madison, have seriously endangered the position of the President as "the" Executive in the sense in which Congress is "the" Legislature and the hierarchy of courts "the" Judiciary in terms of the separation of powers.[16]

CONSTITUTIONAL ISSUES RELATING TO THE EXECUTIVE RAISED IN THE DEBATE ON THE SEAT OF THE GOVERNMENT. Nothing excited the first session of the First Congress so much as the debate over where the permanent seat of the government should be. No law was enacted, because the Senate decided to postpone the question just before adjournment.[17] But the bill which the House passed and sent to the Senate[18] authorized commissioners appointed by the President under his direction to purchase land and erect buildings for the permanent seat at the most eligible situation on the banks of the Susquehanna in the State of Pennsylvania, and provided that meanwhile the seat should continue in the city of New York.

The issue aroused so much heat that it is not surprising that Southerners like Madison from Virginia and Tucker from South Carolina[19] seized upon alleged constitutional objections to bolster arguments of policy and to protect sectional interest.

In Committee of the Whole Tucker objected to giving discretionary power to the President and commissioners appointed by him which no body of men but the Legislature should exercise. The proposal would give them authority to fix the permanent seat on any part of a line five or six hundred miles in extent. "Were we sent here to give such powers to any men?" Congress should fix the spot and not leave it to any one, no matter how eminent his station, to say where they should assemble to legislate. There might be danger in the precedent. So he moved that the commissioners report to Congress, and not the President, for execution at a future session. His motion lost by a vote of 21 for and 29 against;[20] but he had raised for the first time the issue of the delegation of legislative authority to the President.[21]

[16] See chapter 7 below.
[17] 1 Annals 95; Journal of William Maclay 164–165. September 28, 1789.
[18] Journal of William Maclay 145 ff; 1 Annals 945–946. September 22, 1789. For the House debate see 1 Annals 816–822, 867–921, 929–933, 939–945, 955–962, especially 915–920.
[19] See 1 Annals 99. [20] Ibid. 909, 913–914. September 5, 1789.
[21] See James Hart, The Ordinance Making Powers of the President (The Johns Hopkins Press, Baltimore, 1925), and the extensive literature on the subject of delegated legislation.

Madison objected to the enactment of a *law* providing for continuation of the temporary seat in New York, on the ground that it would attempt to give the President a power over the adjournment of Congress which the Constitution expressly denied him. The clause which forbids either house during the session of Congress to adjourn to any other place without the consent of the other [22] implies, he argued, that the two houses by concurrence could adjourn to any other place which they thought proper. In the veto clause, a question of adjournment is expressly excepted.[23] Any attempt, therefore, to adjourn by law would be unconstitutional. He could not subscribe to the doctrine that the seat of government might be a place different from that where the Congress sat, and might be established by law, while the Legislature might remove elsewhere. Could Congress have a seat of government over which they were empowered to exercise exclusive legislation and yet reside two or three hundred miles from it?

Sherman, however, pointed out that, while the power of adjournment is independent of the President as to time [24] and place, it was proper to declare by law where the seat of government should be, so that officers who were called upon to be present at the seat of government might know where to repair. He admitted that Congress could adjourn to some other place.

There was further discussion. Lawrence recalled that the Virginian had voted for Wilmington and Philadelphia [25] as the temporary seat without voicing any constitutional scruples. He also observed that the judiciary act declared the Supreme Court should be held at the seat of government. How should the judges discover where the seat of government was, unless it was declared? Madison explained his former votes in favor of Wilmington and Philadelphia on the ground that, "when an objectionable clause is under consideration, it becomes proper for its opponents to agree to everything they conceive to be an amendment, in order that if the proposition passes, it may pass in the least imperfect form." Lawrence, however, clinched the refutation of Madison's trumped-up argument by pointing out that it applied equally to a permanent and a temporary seat. When the vote was taken, Madison's motion to strike out this provision was defeated, 23 voting for and 29 against.[26]

[22] Article I, section 5, § 4.
[23] Article I, section 7, § 3.
[24] But see Article II, section 3. This power has never been exercised. See William Howard Taft, *Our Chief Magistrate and His Powers* (Columbia University Press, New York, 1925) 48.
[25] See 1 Annals 918–919.
[26] *Ibid.* 940–945. September 21, 1789. *Cf.* remarks of Carroll just before the final vote on the bill: *ibid.* 945–946.

Chapter 7

THE ESTABLISHMENT OF THE GREAT DEPARTMENTS [1]

. .
.

THREE "ORGANIC" ACTS OF CONGRESS

THREE "ORGANIC" ACTS OF THE FIRST SESSION. The term "organic act"[2] is a useful one to designate a legislative enactment which, in its *substance,* is of a constitutional character in the British sense of the term constitution, but which, in its *form,* is not part of the written, rigid[3] Constitution in the American sense, but an ordinary statute enacted and hence repealable at any time by the legislature. Of four[4] such organic acts passed by the first session of Congress, three are highly pertinent to this study. These are the acts which created the three great departments of Foreign Affairs, of War, and of the Treasury.[5]

The Constitution had created the Presidency, but had by clear implication left the creation of the great departments to Congress. For it had twice referred to such departments,[6] and had delegated to Congress the powers to create offices[7] and to make all laws necessary and proper to carry into execution not only its own enumerated powers but all powers vested in the central government or any department or officer thereof.[8]

---

[1] See generally Lloyd Milton Short, *The Development of National Administrative Organization in the United States* (The Johns Hopkins Press, Baltimore, 1923) chap. 2 ("Administrative Organization: 1775–1789") and chap. 3 ("Foundations of Administrative Organization: 1789–1800").
[2] Joseph Barthélemy et Paul Duez, *Traité de droit constitutionnel* (Nouvelle édition, Libraire Dalloz, Paris, 1933) 29, 35.
[3] This term, *rigid* constitutions, is of course used in the sense in which it is used by Bryce in contrast with *flexible* constitutions. See 1 James Bryce, *The American Commonwealth* (The Macmillan Co., New York, 1910 ed., 1912) 360–364; and James Bryce, "Flexible and Rigid Constitutions," in 1 *Studies in History and Jurisprudence* (Oxford University Press, New York, H. Frowde, London, 1901) 124–213.
[4] The fourth, not pertinent here, was the Judiciary Act of 1789. 2 *Laws of the United States* 56 ff.
[5] *Ibid.* 6, 32, 48.
[6] Article II, section 2, §§ 1 and 2.
[7] Article II, section 2, § 2.
[8] Article I, section 8, § 18.

THE QUESTION OF A HOME DEPARTMENT

THE QUESTION WHETHER A HOME DEPARTMENT SHOULD BE CREATED. When the question of the creation of departments was first brought forward, Vining favored the creation of a Home Department, but on Livermore's objection that home affairs might be blended with the others withdrew his motion for the time being.[9] Over two months later he renewed his proposal in Committee of the Whole. His resolution called for a Home Department to be headed by a Secretary, with a long list of duties, some of which were those of a glorified chief clerk, while others were

to see to the execution of the laws of the union; . . . to report to the President plans for the protection and improvement of manufactures, agriculture, and commerce; . . . to report what post roads shall be established; . . . to issue patents . . .

Finally, the Secretary was,

in general, to do and attend to all such matters and things as he may be directed to do by the President.

To this proposal various objections were offered. Benson said there could be no necessity for an officer to see to the execution of the laws of the United States when a judiciary was instituted with adequate powers. White questioned whether a separate department was needed for all or any of these duties. So why incur the expense of a great department? Huntington

thought the Secretary of Foreign Affairs was not so much overcharged with business but that he might attend to the major part of the duties mentioned in the resolution.

Vining defended his resolution. He had waited until the great Executive departments had been established, but none of these had embraced the duties he had enumerated. He

conceived that the President ought to be relieved from the inferior duties of his station, by officers assigned to attend to them under his inspection; he could then, with a mind free and unembarrassed with the minutiæ of business, attend to the operations of the whole machine.

Had he been using the administrative vocabulary of today, he would have said the President's position was properly one of over-all administrative management. He thought most of these duties

[9] 1 *Annals* 383, 385–386. May 19, 1789.

foreign to either of those officers; and that they could not be performed with advantage any other way than by an officer appointed specially for the purpose.

In the language of today, Vining believed in departmentalization along functional lines. He did not think the expense a "solid objection" in view of the information the office would furnish. He favored a "confidential officer" for this purpose. Curiously enough, he disclaimed any personal motives and the desire to serve any particular man.

Sedgwick thought the office unnecessary and stressed the need for the strictest economy. Gerry said the people would suspect the creation of sinecures and the intent of establishing monarchy

by raising round the Executive a phalanx of such men as must be inclined to favor those of whom they hold their places.

Vining asked why these essential duties would be more expensive this way than any other; but his resolution "lost by a considerable majority."

When the Committee rose, Sedgwick, as he had indicated he would do, moved that a committee be appointed to bring in a bill to change the name of the Department of Foreign Affairs, to give the principal officer in that department the custody of the records and seal of the United States, and to make other provisions needed in the premises. His motion passed in the negative.[10]

The next Monday, however, the matter was taken care of when, in connection with action on the report of the committee on joint rules for the enrollment, attestation, publication, and preservation of the acts of Congress, the House resolved that a committee ought to be appointed to prepare a bill or bills to provide, "without the establishment of a new department," for several duties which Vining had listed.[11] The upshot was an act approved September 15, which changed the name of the Department of Foreign Affairs to Department of State, and that of the Secretary of Foreign Affairs to Secretary of State, and provided for the first of what are now called the "home functions" of that department.[12]

[10] *Ibid.* 692–695. July 23, 1789.   [11] *Ibid.* 697–698. July 27, 1789.
[12] 2 *Laws of the United States* 51–52. From Chesterfield, Va., Mr. Jefferson wrote the President: "When I contemplate the extent of that office, embracing as it does the principal mass of domestic administration, together with the foreign, I cannot be insensible of my inequality to it . . . but it is not for an individual to chuse his post. you are to marshal us as may best be for the public good: . . ." He referred of course to the office of Secretary of State. If the President wished him to return to New York, "my chief comfort will be to work under your eye, my only shelter the authority of your name, and the wisdom of measures to be dictated by you, and implicitly executed

THE GREAT DEBATE ON THE TENURE OF OFFICE

THE FOUR CONSTITUTIONAL THEORIES WHICH EMERGED IN THE RE-
MOVAL DEBATE. No sooner had Boudinot proposed the creation of
departments than Madison raised a question which precipitated one of
the most notable debates of congressional history by moving resolutions
which said of the heads of departments that they were "to be removable
by the President." [13] In the extended House debate which followed there
emerged four distinct theories of the removal power under the Constitution.[14] First, what may be called *the impeachment theory* held that,
since the Constitution provides for the removal of all civil [15] officers
upon impeachment by the House and conviction by the Senate, it follows from the maxim of legal construction, *expressio unius est exclusio
alterius*, that the framers intended that this should be the sole and exclusive method by which such officers should be removed. Secondly,

---

by me. . . ." 30 *Writings* 447, note 7. December 15, 1789. From Georgetown, Md.,
Madison wrote the President on January 4, 1790, that he had been sorry to find Mr.
Jefferson "so little biased" in favor of the domestic aspects, "but was glad that his
difficulties seemed to result chiefly from what I take to be an erroneous view of the
kind and quantity of business annexed to that which constituted the foreign department. He apprehends that it will far exceed the latter which has of itself no terrors to
him. On the other hand it was supposed, and I believe truly that the domestic part
will be very trifling, and for that reason improper to be made a distinct department.
After all if the whole business can be executed by one man, Mr. Jefferson must be
equal to it; If not he will be relieved by a necessary division of it. All whom I have
heard speak on the subject are remarkably solicitous for his acceptance, and I flatter
myself that they will not in the final event be disappointed." *Ibid.* 448, note 7. See
Leonard D. White, "Public Administration Under the Federalists," in (1944) 24
Boston U. L. Rev. 144, 156–172.
[13] 1 *Annals* 383–385. May 19, 1789.
[14] See Charles C. Thach, *The Creation of the Presidency, 1775–1789* (The Johns
Hopkins Press, Baltimore, 1922) 144; Edward S. Corwin, *The President's Removal
Power under the Constitution* (National Municipal League Monograph Series, National
Municipal League, New York, 1927) 12. The present writer wishes to express his
great debt to these two studies, upon which his analysis of the "legislative decision of
1789" has been founded. Since both works are so frequently quoted or otherwise used
below, it will be convenient *hereinafter to designate them in citations by abbreviated
titles.* Since no other work of Thach is cited in this volume, his monograph will be
cited simply as *Thach.* In line with the policy, expressed in a prefatory note, of
simplifying citations, the usual *op. cit.* will be omitted as unnecessary. Since, however,
other works of Corwin are cited throughout this volume, this brochure of his will be
cited as Corwin's *Removal Power.* The brochure itself is out of print, and hence may
be unavailable to the reader. It may, therefore, be noted that, while all citations are
from the brochure, most of it had been published in Edward S. Corwin, "Tenure of
Office and the Removal Power under the Constitution," 27 *Col. L. Rev.* 353–399
(1927), and it is reprinted in full in 4 *Selected Essays on Constitutional Law* (published under the auspices of the Assoc. of Amer. Law Schools, Douglas B. Maggs,
general editor, The Foundation Press, Inc., Chicago, 1938) 1467–1518.
[15] Military officers are not liable to impeachment, by an inference which results from
the statement in the Constitution that all civil officers are so liable. Article II, section 4.

what may be called *the President-and-Senate theory* held that, since the power to remove from office is but an incident of the power to appoint to office, and since the Constitution vests the latter power in the President by and with the advice and consent of the Senate,[16] it follows that the framers implied that the power of removal of non-judicial [17] officers is also vested in the President by and with the advice and consent of the Senate. Thirdly, what may be called *the legislative-grant theory* held that, in delegating to Congress the powers of creating offices and of making all laws which should be necessary and proper for carrying into execution the powers vested in it or in the central government or any department or officer thereof, the framers impliedly vested in Congress the power to determine by law the tenure as well as the duties and compensation of the non-judicial officers it created, and hence the power to provide such mode of removing them as it might see fit. Fourthly, what may be called *the constitutional-grant theory,* held that, from the constitutional clauses which vest in the President the executive power,[18] the power of appointment,[19] and the duty to take care that the laws be faithfully executed,[20] it is to be implied that the framers intended to vest in him alone the power of administrative direction of all non-judicial civil officers, and hence [21] the power to remove them at his pleasure as a necessary means of making this power of administrative direction effective.

It will be pointed out later that, in point of fact, some of those who held the legislative-grant theory thought it was not only expedient but almost a constitutional duty to vest the power of removal in the President; while that theory may be, and was, held by some who thought that, *in the absence of legislation,* one of the other major theories would prevail.[22] Meanwhile, however, this fourfold classification of theories will serve as a useful oversimplification.

MADISON'S SUMMARY OF THE FOUR THEORIES. To Edmund Randolph Madison wrote on June 21:

[16] Article II, section 2, § 2.
[17] The Constitution of course specifies that federal constitutional judges shall hold office during good behavior. Article III, section 1.
[18] The opening sentence of Article II.
[19] Article II, section 2, § 2.
[20] Article II, section 3.
[21] Thach has done a good service in noting that the constitutional-grant men emphasized removal as a sanction of the power of direction rather than the power of direction as an accidental consequence of the power of removal. *Thach* 158–159. *Cf.* Edward S. Corwin, *The President: Office and Powers* (2d. ed., New York University Press, New York, 1941) 81 ff.
[22] As will be pointed out below in the section (p. 201) entitled, "Analysis of the House decision," it has been Corwin's major contribution to the analysis of this decision to point out this last-mentioned fact.

THE ESTABLISHMENT OF THE GREAT DEPARTMENTS

The Constitution has omitted to declare expressly by what authority removals from office are to be made. Out of this silence, four constructive doctrines have arisen: 1. That the power of removal may be disposed of by the Legislative discretion. To this it is objected that the Legislature might then confer it on themselves, or even on the House of Representatives, which could not possibly have been intended by the Constitution. 2. That the power of removal can only be exercised in the mode of impeachment. To this the objection is that it would make officers of every description hold their places during good behavior, which could have still less been intended. 3. That the power of removal is incident to the power of appointment. To this the objections are that it would require the constant session of the Senate; that it extends the mixture of Legislative and Executive power; that it destroys the responsibility of the President, by enabling a subordinate Executive officer to intrench himself behind a party in the Senate, and destroys the utility of the Senate in their Legislative and Judicial characters, by involving them too much in the heats and cabals inseparable from questions of a personal nature; in fine, that it transfers the trust in fact from the President, who, being at all times impeachable, as well as every fourth year eligible by the people at large, may be deemed the most responsible member of the Government, to the Senate; which, from the nature of the institution, is and was meant, after the Judiciary, and in some respects without that exception, to be the most irresponsible branch of the Government. 4. That the Executive power being in general terms vested in the President, all power of an executive nature not particularly taken away must belong to that department; that the power of appointment only being expressly taken away, the power of removal, so far as it is of an Executive nature, must be reserved. In support of this construction it is urged that exceptions to general positions are to be taken strictly, and that the axiom relating to the separation of the Legislative and Executive functions ought to be favored. To this are objected the principle on which the 3d construction is founded, and the danger of creating too much influence in the Executive Magistrate.

The last opinion has prevailed, but is subject to various modifications, by the power of the Legislature to limit the duration of laws creating offices, or the duration of the appointments for filling them [sic!], and by the power over the salaries and appropriations. In truth, the Legislative power is of such a nature that it scarcely can be restrained, either by the Constitution or by itself; and if the federal Government should lose its proper equilibrium within itself, I am persuaded that the effect will proceed from the encroachments of the Legislative department. If the possibility of encroachments on the part of the Executive or the Senate were to be compared, I should pronounce the danger to lie rather in the latter than the former. The mixture of Legislative, Executive, and Judiciary authorities, lodged in that body, justifies such an inference; at the same time, I am fully in the opinion that the numerous and immediate representatives of the people composing the other House will decidedly predominate in the Government.[23]

THE IMPEACHMENT THEORY. It will bring out the variety of lights in which the position of the President in the new central government was viewed in 1789 to quote some of the considerations which were advanced in the House for and against these four theories and generally for and against removal by the President alone. No attempt will be made in this and the next three sections to assess the extent to which particular quoted passages represent fully the views of the speakers or of others.

The impeachment theory was advanced at the very outset of the debate by Smith of South Carolina.[24] Though he received only negligible support,[25] Smith defended his position vigorously throughout. His thesis was that, as no other mode of removal was directed by the Constitution, only this mode was contemplated.[26] He further maintained that no other mode was necessary. For what causes other than impeachable offenses should a man be removed? Sickness or ignorance? Presidential nomination and senatorial approval provided against the appointment of ignorant officers. They could not be removed for causes which subsisted before they took office. Their ignorance must therefore arise after their appointment. But this was an unlikely case. Under the Constitution, a suspected man would have a fair trial before an impartial tribunal instead of being the abject slave of the President. The President might be misinformed by envious men around him, and the removed officer would have his reputation blasted and his "property"[27] in his office sacrificed.

[23] 1 *Letters and Other Writings of James Madison* (published by order of Congress, R. Worthington, New York, 1884) 477-479.
[24] 1 *Annals* 383, 387.
[25] The only members who voiced support were Huntington (*ibid.* 477) and to an extent Jackson and Page, who seemed to waver between the impeachment and President-and-Senate theories. *Ibid.* 389, 505-509, 539-541, 570-576, 603-604. At one point Madison said he believed only one other besides Page held the impeachment theory. *Ibid.* 605.
[26] *Ibid.* 475.
[27] Smith's view of tenure during good behavior, and subject only to impeachment, was grounded upon his conception that an office holder had a *property* right in his office. Thus he said: "As the matter stands in the constitution, he knows, if he is suspected of doing any thing wrong, he shall have a fair trial, and the whole of his transactions be developed by an impartial tribunal." But under presidential removal, ". . . his reputation is blasted, his property sacrificed. I say his property is sacrificed, because I consider his office as his property. He is stripped of this, and left exposed to the malevolence of the world, contrary to the principles of the constitution, and contrary to the principles of all free Governments, which are, that no man shall be despoiled of his property, but by a fair and impartial trial." *Ibid.* 476. Again he said: ". . . yet the doctrine of gentlemen will enable the President, or the President with the advice of the Senate, to inflict the punishment without trial, when the constitution requires it to be done on impeachment and conviction." *Ibid.* 489. Still again: "An honorable gentleman has said, he did not see how this case could be brought before a court of

To the argument that it was absurd that *inferior* officers should be removable only on impeachment, he replied that under the Constitution these officers could be established on such terms as the Legislature judged proper; but that neither the appointment nor the removal of department heads could be otherwise performed than was directed in the Constitution. He admitted, however, that Congress could fix the term of a superior office, and that a superior officer might be suspended pending trial and conviction.[28] He declared that an indolent person would neglect[29] his duty and for that cause he presumed he might be impeached. If the Constitution did not extend to insanity or disability by reason of sickness, then let the law declare him removed until his recovery. But gentlemen's arguments went to prove the Constitution authorized removal for this reason. Why, the same arguments would apply if the President and Vice President became delirious; but he thought they could not constitutionally be removed for such a cause.[30]

---

justice in order to obtain their decision. That gentleman is no stranger to a just and venerable law maxim. Wherever a man has a right, he has a remedy; if he suffers a wrong, he can have a redress; he would be entitled to damages for being deprived of his property in his office." *Ibid.* 530. This position did not, however, go unchallenged. Thus Hartley declared: "The gentleman further contends, that every man has a property in his office, and ought not to be removed but for criminal conduct; he ought not to be removed for inability. I hope this doctrine will never be admitted in this country.... If he has an estate in his office, his right must be purchased, and a practice like what obtains in England will be adopted here; we shall be unable to dismiss an officer without allowing him a pension for the interest he is deprived of. Such a doctrine may suit a nation, which is strong in proportion to the number of dependents upon the crown, but will be very pernicious in a republic like ours.... never let it be said that he has an estate in his office when he is found unfit to perform his duties." *Ibid.* 499. Similarly Livermore: "I do not admit that any man has an estate in his office. I conceive all officers to be appointed during pleasure, except where the constitution stipulates for a different tenure, unless indeed the law should create the office, or officer, for a term of years." *Ibid.* 565. Boudinot put the matter in a nutshell: "If it be said that this is an injury to the individual, I confess that it is possible that it may be so. But ought we not in the first place to consult the public good? But on mature consideration, I do not apprehend any very great injury will result to the individual from this practice; because, when he accepts of the office, he knows the tenure by which he is to hold it, and ought to be prepared against every contingency." *Ibid.* 550. Referring to presidential removal of department heads on the one hand and tenure during good behavior of judges on the other hand, Fisher Ames declared: "But the removability of the one class, or the immovability of the other, is founded on the same principle, the security of the people against the abuse of power. Does any gentleman imagine that an officer is entitled to his office as to an estate? Or does the Legislature establish them for the convenience of an individual? For my part, I conceive it intended to carry into effect the purposes for which the constitution was intended." *Ibid.* 492–493. Compare Stone's rather thoroughly watered down conception of public office as a contract. *Ibid.* 590. See James Hart, *An Introduction to Administrative Law with Selected Cases* (F. S. Crofts & Co., New York, 1940) 20–21.

[28] 1 *Annals* 391–392, 475–477.
[29] *Ibid.* 489. But see the Constitution, Article II, section 1, § 6.
[30] 1 *Annals* 489.

Smith's principle of construction was turned against him: the provision that judges should hold during good behavior implied that no other officers should so hold.[31] His answer was that this provision was to distinguish the tenure of judges from the fixed terms of Representatives, Senators, and the President, and that the tenure during good behavior for life which was specially provided for judges was not the same as tenure during good behavior for the term which Congress might prescribe in establishing non-judicial offices.[32]

In refutation of Smith's reasoning Madison said he would lament such a "fatal error" in the Constitution, but rather regarded impeachment as a "supplemental security."[33] Boudinot said impeachment was punishment for crimes and not "intended as the ordinary means of re-arranging the departments."[34] He added that tenure during good behavior would destroy presidential responsibility, and that if the Secretary of Foreign Affairs had a paralytic stroke, *salus populi* would demand his dismission.[35] Hartley declared: "If offices are to be held during good behavior, it is easy to foresee that we shall have as many factions as heads of departments." The result, he thought, would be corruption in one of the great departments of government which might destroy the balance without which the constitution would fall amidst the ruins.[36]

The only alternative of the impeachment theory was that a power of removal resided somewhere in the government.[37] If the latter conclusion had not been reached, the effect upon the Presidency must have been profound. The thoughtful view of Thach may be quoted:

> There is no evidence that the House realized the full importance of this action. To have declared the magistracy permanent except for the right of removal by impeachment would necessarily have made the department heads the real executive. An incoming President would have found in office men whose position, so far as he was concerned, was assured. They would have ideas of their own and connections of their own. Since he could not control them, they would very naturally act in accordance with these ideas in carrying out their duties. On the other hand, Congress would have been forced to use the weapon of impeachment as a means of political control. It is extremely probable that very soon some more easily worked system of control would have been evolved, with the result that responsibility would have been to the legislature. This, of course, would have meant some sort of ministerial government. The refusal of the House to accept the argument that the only way under the Constitution to get rid of a minister was a legislative process

[31] *Ibid.* 390–391.
[32] *Ibid.* 527–528.
[33] *Ibid.* 387.
[34] *Ibid.* 390.
[35] *Ibid.* 488.
[36] *Ibid.* 499.
[37] Thach 145. For full citation see note 14 above. Cf. 1 *Annals* 390–391, 560.

THE ESTABLISHMENT OF THE GREAT DEPARTMENTS

in which the lower House would take the initiative was, consciously or not, a refusal to establish ministerial government, with all that this entailed.[38]

Would this result have been altered if Congress, following Smith's admissions, had given department heads one year terms, and authorized the President to dismiss at pleasure all inferior executive officers and to suspend department heads pending their trial?

THE PRESIDENT-AND-SENATE THEORY. Bland precipitated action on this theory when he moved to add to the words "to be removable by the President" the words "by and with the advice and consent of the Senate."[39] His motion was lost,[40] but the discussion showed a sharp divergence of opinion concerning the place of the Senate in the constitutional system.

In advocating the President-and-Senate doctrine, White insisted the Senate was an executive body when performing its constitutional executive functions. He continued:

Every question respecting treaties or public officers must go through their hands. Why shall we make the President responsible for what goes through other hands? He is not solely responsible agreeably to the constitution, for the conduct of the officers he nominates, and the Senate appoints; why then talk of a greater degree of responsibility than is known to the constitution?[41]

Gerry thought *permanency* was expected in the Magistracy, and hence the Senate was combined in the appointment to office; but that if the President alone removed, he could destroy all that had been done.[42] Livermore insisted the power to *make* implies the power to *unmake*.[43] Gerry rose again to argue that the President could carry out his faithful execution duty by suspending an officer in a recess of the Senate. He continued:

It is said, that if the Senate should have this power, the Government would contain a two-headed monster; but it appears to me, that if it consists in blending the power of making treaties and appointing officers, as executive powers, with their legislative powers, the Senate is already a two-headed monster; if it is a two-headed monster, let us preserve it a consistent one; for surely it will be a very inconsistent monster, while it has the power of appointing, if you deprive it of the power of removing.[44]

Page denied that the Senate was a dangerous and aristocratic body, and affirmed:

[38] *Thach* 145.
[39] 1 *Annals* 388–389, 396–397.
[40] *Ibid.* 398.
[41] *Ibid.* 398.
[42] *Ibid.* 491; *Thach* 148.
[43] 1 *Annals* 497.
[44] *Ibid.* 524.

The principles laid down in the constitution clearly evince that the Senate ought not only to have a voice in the framing of laws, but ought also to see to their execution.[45]

Jackson made this argument:

It is admitted [sic], that in cases of ambassadors and public ministers, it would be improper to recall them without the concurrence of the Senate; because the Senate are combined with the President, and strongly too, in the objects of their negotiations. How then can gentlemen discriminate?[46]

Stone declared:

I should be extremely unhappy if I could believe that the association of the powers of the President and Senate is so monstrous as some gentlemen conceive. . . . in all the great business of the executive department, in everything serious and affecting the Government, there is not only a temporary association, but a continued one. The first and most interesting communication of these powers is of a continued duration. The appointing officers is but a temporary connexion; but in making treaties, in which all our concerns are at stake, the connexion is durable. Is not the same information necessary for two thirds of the Senate, as for the President, as they are to advise him in the negotiation, and concur with him in the ratification? And how can this necessary information be obtained, but by a connexion with the Executive Magistrate? . . .

. . . It is laid down in the constitution that the President shall nominate, and the Senate approve; we are bound, then, to carry this balance throughout all the subjects to which it relates.[47]

Such views were, however, held by only a minority of the House;[48]

[45] *Ibid.* 540. Compare the statement of Stone: "The executive business of this officer [the Secretary of Foreign Affairs] is under the superintendence and management of the Senate, as well as the President. Treaties with foreign nations must be conducted by the advice of the Senate, and concluded with their consent. Hence results a necessity in that body's having a concern in the choice and dismissal of the Secretary of Foreign Affairs. I do not see any other sure or safe bottom on which the question can be determined." *Ibid.* 589. Earlier in the same speech Stone thus dismissed the Madisonian appeal to the separation of powers: "A separation of the powers of Government, between the legislative, executive, and judicial branches, is considered as the proper ground for our opinion, and a principle which we must admit. Are we to get it brought into the constitution? For I apprehend there is no such principle as a separation of those powers brought into the constitution at present, but to the degree which an examination will appear to exist. Is there any express declaration, that it is a principle of the constitution to keep the legislative and executive powers distinct? No. Has the constitution in practice kept them separate? No. Whence is this idea drawn? That it is a principle in this constitution, that the powers of Government should be kept separate? No sure ground is afforded for it in the constitution itself. It is found in the celebrated writers on government; and, in general, I conceive the principle to be a good one. But if no such principle is declared in the constitution, and that instrument has adopted exceptions, I think we ought to follow those exceptions, step by step, in every case to which they bear relation." *Ibid.* 587.
[46] *Ibid.* 577.   [47] *Ibid.* 586.   [48] Thach 150.

THE ESTABLISHMENT OF THE GREAT DEPARTMENTS 163

and their refutation was undertaken by various members of the majority. Madison went to the heart of the matter:

> Again, is there no danger that an officer, when he is appointed by the concurrence of the Senate, and has friends in that body, may choose rather to risk his establishment on the favor of that branch, than rest it upon the discharge of his duties to the satisfaction of the executive branch, which is constitutionally authorized to inspect and control his conduct? And if it should happen that the officers connect themselves with the Senate, they may mutually support each other, and for want of efficacy reduce the power of the President to a mere vapor; in which case, his responsibility will be annihilated, and the expectation of it unjust. The high executive officers, joined in cabal with the Senate, would be the foundation of discord, and end in an assumption of the executive power, only to be removed by a revolution in the Government. . . .[49]

Vining said White's principle that he who appoints must remove "may be a good one, but it is not a general one." He thought the "best principle" was that "he who is responsible for the officer, ought to have the power of removing him." He then went on to say that on White's own principle it might be contended that the President should have the power of removal:

> because it is he who appoints. The constitution says, he shall nominate, and, under certain qualifications, appoint. The Senate do not appoint; their judgment only is required to acquiesce in the President's nomination. . . .

The power of removal, he contended,

> cannot be within the legislative power of the Senate, because it is of an adverse nature; it cannot be within the executive power of the Senate, because they possess none but what is expressly granted by the constitution.[50]

Boudinot thus developed the working and implications of the President-and-Senate theory:

> If the President complains to the Senate of the misconduct of an officer, and desires their advice and consent to the removal, what are the Senate to do? Most certainly they will inquire if the complaint is well founded. To do this, they must call the officer before them to answer. Who, then, are the parties? The supreme Executive officer against his assistant; and the Senate are to sit as judges to determine whether sufficient cause of removal exists. Does not this set the Senate over the head of the President? But suppose they shall

---

[49] 1 *Annals* 480. *Thach* 150 points out that Madison's remarks indicated in effect fear of approximating "ministerial responsibility to the upper chamber," and that this would have resulted "almost inevitably."

[50] 1 *Annals* 482–484.

decide in favor of the officer, what a situation is the President then in, surrounded by officers with whom, by his situation, he is compelled to act, but in whom he can have no confidence, . . .

A still "more solid objection," he continued, was that if the Senate refused to concur in a removal, and the House later impeached the officer, the Senate would have pre-judged the case.[51] On the same side of the issue Ames stated:

If the President is inclined to shelter himself behind the Senate, with respect to having continued an improper person in office, we lose the responsibility, which is our greatest security; the blame among so many will be lost.[52]

Hartley asserted:

The President is the representative of the people in a near and equal manner; he is the guardian of his country. The Senate are the representatives of the State Legislatures; but they are very unequal in their representation.[53]

Clymer saw that the location of administrative direction was at stake:

The Executive must act by others; but you reduce him to a mere shadow, when you control both the power of appointment and removal; if you take away the latter power, he ought to resign the power of superintending and directing the executive parts of the Government into the hands of the Senate at once, and then we become a dangerous aristocracy, or shall be more destitute of energy than any Government on earth.[54]

Benson denied the present application of the general rule that removal was an incident of appointment:

If the President and Senate are to be considered as one body, deliberating together on the business of appointments, every individual of which participates equal powers, the reasoning that has been urged will hold good. But I take it for granted that they are two distinct bodies, and can only give a simple affirmative or negative. No member of the Senate has power to offer an original proposition. In short, the moment we depart from this simple idea, that the provision in the constitution is intended for any other purpose but to prevent the President from introducing improper persons into office, we shall find it difficult to form any certain principle upon which they ought to act; and our opinions and deliberations will be discordant and distracted.

To those who said a presidential power of suspension would be sufficient he replied that it was inconsistent to give this constructive power, and in the same breath to object to giving the power of removal by construction.[55] Vining thus denied that senatorial consent in removals was analogous to such consent in appointments:

[51] Ibid. 487.   [52] Ibid. 495.   [53] Ibid. 500.   [54] Ibid. 509.   [55] Ibid. 526.

It has been asked, if the same properties are not requisite in removing a man from office as to appoint him? I apprehend a difference in the degree of information necessary. A man's ability may be known to many persons, they may entertain even a good opinion of his integrity; but no man, without a superintending power, can bring this fidelity to the test. The President will have every opportunity to discover the real talents and honesty of the officer; the Senate will have none but from common fame. How then are their properties equal?[56]

The same idea was later repeated by Goodhue.[57] Senatorial participation, in the view of Ames,

creates a permanent connexion; it will nurse faction; it will promote intrigue to obtain protectors and to shelter tools. Sir, it is infusing poison into the constitution; . . . it is tempting the Senate with forbidden fruit; it ought not to be possible for a branch of the Legislature even to hope for a share of the executive power; for they may be tempted to increase it, by a hope to share in the exercise of it.[58]

Of the rejection by the House majority of this theory Thach has said:

The final action taken by the House can thus be interpreted in no other sense than to mean that, so far as was possible, the majority wished to give an unmistakable quietus to the idea, not unnatural in itself, and certainly held by some, that the two clauses allowing senatorial participation in executive matters constituted the Senate a permanent executive council, or, in fact, that it was an executive council at all. There was equally, as Madison's remarks showed, a keen apprehension of creating an approximation to ministerial responsibility to the upper chamber, a result which would follow almost inevitably from allowing the Senate to control removals.[59]

THE LEGISLATIVE-GRANT THEORY. The House majority wanted the President to have the power of removal, but differed among themselves over whether Congress should grant him the power or should merely recognize that he had it impliedly from the Constitution.[60] Madison, who shifted from the legislative-grant to the constitutional-grant theory in the course of the debate,[61] said at the outset:

Congress may establish offices by law; therefore, most certainly, it is in the discretion of the Legislature to say upon what terms the office shall be held, either during good behavior or during pleasure.[62]

Lawrence put it thus:

The constitution had certainly intended that Congress should define the tenure of office, or it would never have declared the Judges should continue

[56] *Ibid.* 532.
[57] *Ibid.* 555.
[58] *Ibid.* 563.
[59] Thach 150.
[60] *Ibid.*
[61] *Ibid.* 151; Corwin's *Removal Power* 13.
[62] 1 *Annals* 389.

during good behavior. This constitutional provision in their favor was to render them independent of the Legislature, which it was not supposed would be the case if nothing on this head had been declared.

Accordingly, the silence of the Constitution made it depend upon the will of the Legislature how the foreign affairs department

should be constituted and established by law, and the conditions upon which he shall enjoy the office. We can say he shall hold it for three years from his appointment, or during good behavior; and we may declare unfitness and incapacity causes of removal, and make the President alone judge of this case. We may authorize the President to remove him for any cause he thinks proper. . . . Gentlemen admit, that we have a right to limit the duration of the office. What is authorizing the removal by the President but limiting it?

The only remaining question was one of expediency, which he thought called for vesting the power in the President.[63]

Perhaps the leading advocate of the legislative-grant theory was Sedgwick, who said:

I do conceive, Mr. Speaker, that this officer will be the mere creature of the law; . . . now, this officer being the creature of the law, we may declare that he shall be removed for incapacity, and if so declared, the removal will be according to law.[64]

Madison now said that under the constitutional-grant theory a legislative declaration could do no harm, while if the Constitution was silent, it was probably submitted to legislative discretion.[65] On the merits, he strongly favored the presidential power; "it is not to be presumed that a vicious or bad character will be selected" by the suffrage of three, and soon six, millions of people;

If the Government of any country on the face of the earth was ever effectually guarded against the election of ambitious or designing characters to the first office of the State, I think it may with truth be said to be the case under the constitution of the United States. . . .

It is evidently the intention of the constitution that the first Magistrate should be responsible for the executive department; so far therefore as we do not make the officers who are to aid him in the duties of that department responsible to him, he is not responsible to his country. . . .[66]

Lawrence spoke again to the main point:

[63] Ibid. 392-393.   [64] Ibid. 478-479.
[65] Ibid. 482. By this time, however, he was advocating the constitutional-grant theory, saying that he had examined the constitution more closely and had his "doubts whether we are not absolutely tied down to the construction declared in the bill." Ibid. 480-481.
[66] Ibid. 479-480.

This is a case omitted, or it is not.[67] If it is omitted, and the power is necessary and essential to the Government and to the great interests of the United States, who are to make the provision and supply the defect? Certainly the Legislature is the proper body. It is declared they shall establish offices by law. The establishment of an office implies everything relative to its formation, constitution, and termination; consequently, the Congress are authorized to declare their judgment on each of these points.

The way to supply the defect was to place the power in the President:

In the constitution, the heads of departments are considered as the mere assistants of the President, in the performance of his executive duties. He has the superintendence, the control, and the inspection of their conduct; he has an intimate connexion with them; they must receive from him his orders and directions; they must answer his inquiries in writing when he requires it. . . .

It appears to me, that the power can be safely lodged here. But it has been said by some gentlemen, that if it is lodged here, it will be subject to abuse; that there may be a change of officers, and a complete revolution throughout the whole executive department, upon the election of every President. I admit this may be the case, and contend that it should be the case, if the President thinks it necessary. I contend that every President ought to have those men about him in whom he can place the most confidence, provided the Senate approve his choice. But we are not from thence to infer, that changes will be made in a wanton manner, and from capricious motives;

for because of the senatorial check on the appointment of their successors, "it may be fairly presumed, that changes will be made on principles of policy and propriety only." [68]

Sedgwick again explained his position in these words:

The power of creating offices is given to the Legislature. Under this general grant, the Legislature have it under their supreme decision to determine the whole organization, to affix the tenure, and declare the control. This right of determining arises, not from express words, but by natural construction. So the Legislature may determine that an office may be held three, five, or seven years; to be removable by the President, the President and Senate, or the Legislature, or any other person whom they might introduce into office, merely for that particular purpose. This appears to me to be the true construction; and unless something decisive is shown from the constitution, I shall favor this opinion.

On grounds of expediency Sedgwick, like Lawrence, was strongly in favor of presidential removals:

[67] On *casus omissus* in statutory interpretation, see Earl T. Crawford, *The Construction of Statutes* (Thomas Law Book Co., St. Louis, 1940) § 169.
[68] 1 *Annals* 503–504.

... all the duties detailed in the bill are, by the constitution, pertaining to the department of the Executive Magistrate. ... If expediency is at all to be considered, gentlemen will perceive that this man is as much an instrument in the hands of the President, as the pen is the instrument of the Secretary in corresponding with foreign courts.[69]

Lee stressed the necessary and proper clause as the basis of the legislative-grant theory:

It has been said by my colleague, (Mr. White) that the constitution does not vest the power of making this declaration by law. I disagree with him; because the constitution vests in Congress power to make all laws necessary and proper to carry into execution the powers vested by the constitution in the Government of the United States, or in any department or officer thereof. Now, he admits that the constitution vests the power of removal, by necessary implication, in the Government of the United States. Have not Congress, therefore, the power of making what laws they think proper to carry into execution the powers vested by the constitution in the Government of the United States?

He went on to say that, since the framers provided for the separation of powers, it was "our bounden duty to imitate their great example, and to support the separation which they have formed. The Legislature has the power to create and establish offices; but it is their duty so to modify them as to make them conform to the general spirit of the constitution." This meant vesting the executive power of removal in the President.[70] Sylvester also mentioned the necessary and proper clause and the power to create offices:

Having then the power to create offices, and discharging from office, they have a right to delegate the exercise of it to whom they please. And to whom can this be more properly entrusted than to the President of the United States?[71]

THE CONSTITUTIONAL-GRANT THEORY. After Madison definitely embraced the constitutional-grant theory, he thus expressed the scope and limits of the legislative power in relation to offices:

If there is any point in which the separation of the legislative and executive powers ought to be maintained with greater caution, it is that which relates to officers and offices. The powers relative to offices are partly legislative and partly executive. The Legislature creates the office, defines the powers, limits its duration,[72] and annexes a compensation. This done, the legislative power

[69] Ibid. 541–542.   [70] Ibid. 545–546.   [71] Ibid. 583–584.
[72] That by this expression Madison meant the *duration* of the *office itself*, not the *term* of the *officer*, is made reasonably clear by the discussion below of the meaning of tenure at the pleasure of the President as understood by Madison. Yet Madison

THE ESTABLISHMENT OF THE GREAT DEPARTMENTS

ceases. They ought to have nothing to do with designating the man to fill the office. That I conceive to be of an executive nature. Although it be qualified in the constitution, I would not extend or strain that qualification beyond the limits precisely fixed for it. We ought always to consider the constitution with an eye to the principles upon which it was founded. In this point of view, we shall readily conclude that if the Legislature determines the powers, the honors, and emoluments of an office, we should be insecure if they were to designate the officer also. The nature of things restrains and confines the legislative and executive authorities in this respect; and hence it is that the constitution stipulates for the independence of each branch of the Government.

Let it be understood that the Legislature is to have some influence both in appointing and removing officers, and I venture to say the people of America will justly fear a system of sinecures. . . .[73]

At the very outset of the lengthy debate,

Mr. Vining said, there were no negative words in the constitution to preclude the President from the exercise of this power; but there was a strong presumption that he was invested with it; because it was declared, that all executive powers should be vested in him, except in cases where it is otherwise qualified; . . .[74]

Ames put the constitutional-grant theory in a nutshell:

The constitution places all executive power in the hands of the President, and could he personally execute all the laws, there would be no occasion for establishing auxiliaries; but the circumscribed powers of human nature in one man, demand the aid of others. . . . He must have assistants. But in order that he may be responsible to his country, he must have a choice in selecting his assistants, a control over them, with power to remove them when he finds the qualifications which induced their appointment cease to exist. . . .

The executive powers are delegated to the President, with a view to have a responsible officer to superintend, control, inspect, and check the officers necessarily employed in administering the laws. The only bond between him and those he employs, is the confidence he has in their integrity and talents; when that confidence ceases, the principal ought to have power to remove those whom he can no longer trust with safety. . . .[75]

Boudinot contributed this pertinent remark:

Is it not made expressly the duty of the Secretary of Foreign Affairs to obey such orders as shall be given him by the President? And would you keep in

---

himself did not at every point of the argument consistently maintain his stand. See his expression marked [sic], in the quotation cited in note 23 above, and notes 163 and 181 below. Perhaps this enforces his view that the legislative power has "an elastic and Protean character."

[73] 1 *Annals* 604–605.   [74] *Ibid.* 388.   [75] *Ibid.* 492–493.

office a man who should refuse or neglect to do the duties assigned him? Is not the President responsible for the administration?[76]

Ames, in a later speech, thus interpreted the opening sentence of Article II as a grant of power:

It is declared that the executive power shall be vested in the President. Under these terms all the powers properly belonging to the executive department of the Government are given, and such only taken away as are expressly excepted. If the constitution had stopped here, and the duties had not been defined, either the President had had no powers at all, or he would acquire from the general expression all the powers properly belonging to the executive department.[77]

That Madison's general approach was still that which he had expressed in the Philadelphia Convention, is suggested by remarks he let fall in proposing amendments to the Constitution:

In our Government it is, perhaps, less necessary to guard against the abuse in the executive department than any other; because it is not the stronger branch of the system, but the weaker: . . . the legislative . . . is the most powerful, and most likely to be abused, because it is under the least control. . . .[78]

Vining expressed similar sentiments:

There have been few Governments overthrown by the independence of the Executive. What are the consequences of clipping its wings? Anarchy and confusion, and a struggle between the Legislative and Executive, in which the latter is generally sacrificed on the altar of despotism. Thus, I conceive, the liberty of the people to be involved in our decision. If by legislative encroachment we weaken the executive arm, we render it incapable of performing the functions assigned it by the constitution, and subject it to become an easy prey to the other branches of the Government.[79]

On the other hand, there were those in the House who viewed with alarm any extension of executive power. Bland complained:

A new President might, by turning out the great officers, bring about a change of the ministry, and throw the affairs of the Union into disorder; would not this, in fact, make the President a monarch, and give him absolute power over all the great departments of Government? It signifies nothing that the Senate have a check over the appointment, because he can remove, and tire out the good disposition of the Senate.[80]

[76] *Ibid.* 549.   [77] *Ibid.* 561.
[78] *Ibid.* 454. Compare his language in the Philadelphia Convention of 1787: 1 Max Farrand, *The Records of the Federal Convention of 1787* (rev. ed. in 4 vols., Yale University Press, New Haven, 1937) 35, 99–100, 421–423.
[79] 1 *Annals* 592.   [80] *Ibid.* 397.

THE ESTABLISHMENT OF THE GREAT DEPARTMENTS

Smith of South Carolina warned:

Perhaps gentlemen are so much dazzled with the splendor of the virtues of the present President, as not to be able to see into futurity.[81]

Huntington thus dismissed the conception of responsibility:

But if we have a vicious President, who inclines to abuse this power, which God forbid, his responsibility will stand us in little stead.[82]

White flatly denied that the opening sentence of Article II was a grant of general executive power:

I differ also with my colleague in the principle that he has laid down, that this is in its nature an executive power. The constitution . . . enumerates under each department the powers it may exercise. . . . The executive power is vested in the President; but the executive powers so vested, are those enumerated in the constitution. . . . My ideas of the legislative and executive powers are precisely the same. . . .[83]

Smith denied that the power of removal was executive in nature. He took it that the Constitution had distributed the powers of Government on the same principles as most of the states; and on examining the constitutions of most of them, he did not find that any gave this power to the governor, though some of them gave him the power to suspend. He continued:

Can gentlemen see the danger on one side only? Suppose the President averse to a just and honorable war which Congress has embarked in, can he not countenance the Secretary of War . . . in the waste of public stores, and misapplication of the supplies. Nay, cannot he dragoon your officer into a compliance with his designs, by threatening him with a removal by which his reputation and property would be destroyed? If the officer were established on a better tenure, . . . He would be a barrier to your Executive officer, and save the State from ruin.[84]

Gerry argued that presidential removal

subverts the clause which gives the Senate the sole power of trying impeachments, because the President may remove the officer in order to screen him from the effects of their judgment on an impeachment.[85]

Livermore objected that the constitutional-grant theory asserted in effect that

it takes the whole power of the President and Senate to create an officer, but half the power can uncreate him. Surely a law passed by the whole Legislature cannot be repealed by one branch of it; . . .

He also objected that the President

[81] Ibid. 475.   [82] Ibid. 477–478.   [83] Ibid. 485.   [84] Ibid. 490.   [85] Ibid. 491.

may ruin him on bare suspicion. Nay, a new President may turn him out on mere caprice, or in order to make room for a favorite.[86]

Jackson said bluntly that

This may hold good in Europe, where monarchs claim their powers *jure divino*, but it never can be admitted in America, under a constitution delegating only enumerated powers. It requires more than a mere *ipse dixit* to demonstrate that any power is in its nature executive, and consequently given to the President of the United States by the present constitution; but if this power is incident to the executive branch of Government, it does not follow that it vests it in the President alone, because he does not possess all executive powers.

He thus predicted the consequences:

Are we, then, to have all the officers the mere creatures of the President? This thirst of power will introduce a treasury bench into the House, and we shall have ministers obtrude upon us to govern and direct the measures of the Legislature, and to support the influence of their master. And shall we establish a different influence between the people and the President? I suppose these circumstances must take place, because they have taken place in other countries. The executive power falls to the ground in England, if it cannot be supported by the Parliament; therefore a high game of corruption is played, and a majority secured to the ministry by the introduction of placemen and pensioners.

To the argument that the Secretary of Foreign Affairs might be seized with a fit of lunacy, Jackson replied that there was no way to get rid of a mad President, a mad Congress, or mad judges. He continued his dire predictions:

Let it be remembered, that the constitution gives the President the command of the military. If you give him complete power over the man with the strong box, he will have the liberties of America under his thumb. . . . Then, says he, I have got the army; let me have but the money, and I will establish my throne upon the ruins of your visionary republic. . . . Behold the baleful influence of the royal prerogatives when officers hold their commissions during the pleasure of the crown![87]

Page, too, asserted "that this clause of the bill contains in it the seeds of royal prerogative"; and in defiance to the Federalist emphasis upon "the energy of the Government,"[88] he declared:

---

[86] *Ibid.* 497. [87] *Ibid.* 505–507.
[88] *Ibid.* 509. See 1 Max Farrand, *The Records of the Federal Convention of 1787* (Yale University Press, New Haven, 1937) 282–293; *The Federalist*, No. 70 (Hamilton ed., J. B. Lippincott & Co., Philadelphia, 1880) 522; Lynton K. Caldwell, *The Administrative Theories of Hamilton and Jefferson* (University of Chicago Press, Chicago, 1944) 23–30.

THE ESTABLISHMENT OF THE GREAT DEPARTMENTS

Every thing which has been said in favor of energy in the Executive, may go to the destruction of freedom, and establish despotism. This very energy, so much talked of, has led many patriots to the Bastile, to the block, and to the halter.[89]

Gerry resumed his objections:

Little then will it answer to say we can impeach the President, when he can easily cover all his crimes by an application of the revenue to those who are to try him. . . .

But if we give the President the power to remove, . . . you virtually give him a considerable power over the appointment, independent of the Senate; for if the Senate should reject his first nomination, which will probably be his favorite, he must continue to nominate until the Senate concur; then immediately after the recess of the Senate, he may remove the officer, and introduce his own creature, as he has this power expressly by the constitution. The influence created by this circumstance, would prevent his removal from an office which he held by a temporary appointment from his patron.[90]

Smith claimed that the deduction of the power of removal from the opening sentence of Article II

proves too much, and therefore proves nothing; because it implies that powers which are expressly given by the constitution, would have been in the President without the express grant. I ask the gentlemen, if the constitution had been silent with respect to his exercising the power of granting reprieves and pardons,[91] whether the President would have that authority? I apprehend it is in some degree an executive power.

He went on to argue a negative intent of the framers from their silence:

If the convention who framed the constitution meant that he should have the power of removal, the propriety of inserting it must have occurred to them, . . . As it must have occurred to them, and they have omitted it, I take it for granted they never intended to give it to him.[92]

White said deduction of the removal power from "the general nature of executive power" was a doctrine "not to be learned in American Governments"; that in Virginia, "all the great officers are appointed by the General Assembly"; that if the doctrine

is to be supported by examples, it must be by those brought from beyond the Atlantic; we must also look there for rules to circumscribe the latitude of this principle, if indeed it can be limited.

[89] 1 *Annals* 509.   [90] *Ibid.* 522–523.
[91] Smith of course referred to the fact that the pardoning power was a prerogative of the King (Crown). 1 Sir William Blackstone, *Commentaries on the Laws of England* (in 2 vols., W. E. Dean, New York, 1851) Book I, 201.
[92] 1 *Annals* 530.

He then proceeded to apply to the removal power a doctrine which has an honored place, with respect to *emergency* powers, in Anglo-American political tradition:

> It would be better for the President to extend his powers on some extraordinary occasions, even where he is not strictly justified by the constitution, than the Legislature should grant an improper power to be exercised at all times. I believe there is not an Executive power but which goes sometimes beyond the strict letter of the law. But a partial evil is easier sustained than a general one. I will relate an example. In Virginia, when the operations of the war required the exertions of the Chief Magistrate beyond the authority of the law, our late Governor, Nelson, whose name must be dear to every friend to liberty, was obliged to issue his warrants, and impress supplies for the army, though it was well known he exceeded his authority. His warrants were executed, his country was benefited by this resolute measure, and he himself afterwards indemnified by the Legislature. This corresponds with practice under every limited Government. And although I do not wish to encourage acts of this kind, I say it would be better for the Executive to assume the exercise of such a power on extraordinary occasions than for us to delegate to him authority to exercise an extraordinary power on all occasions.[93]

Page followed up his attack upon the Federalist conception of "energy" with an attack upon the Federalist conception of "responsibility":[94]

> ... great stress was laid upon increasing the President's responsibility. I think it had more weight with some gentlemen than it deserved; for, instead of increasing his responsibility, I think it diminishes it—because I hold it an incontrovertible maxim, that the more power you give him, the more his responsibility is lessened. By making the heads of all the departments dependent upon the President, you enable him to swallow up all the powers of Government; you increase his influence, and every one will be studious to please him alone.

Page went on to make a telling point in these words:

> Now, what necessity, let me ask gentlemen, was there for a constitutional provision to enable the President to obtain their advice if it was understood that all such officers were to be the mere creatures of the President, dependent

---

[93] *Ibid.* 534, 537. On the act of indemnity in preference to prior delegation of *emergency* powers, see A. V. Dicey, *Introduction to the Study of the Law of the Constitution* (8th ed., Macmillan & Co., London, 1920) 47–48, 228–233, 408–409; James Hart, "The Emergency Ordinance: A Note on Executive Power," 23 *Columbia Law Review* 528–535 (1923).

[94] For the Federalist (Hamiltonian) conception of "responsibility" see Lynton K. Caldwell, *The Administrative Theories of Hamilton and Jefferson* (University of Chicago Press, Chicago, 1944) 28–30.

THE ESTABLISHMENT OF THE GREAT DEPARTMENTS 175

upon his will alone? Would not such a situation compel them to do every thing he directed?

He continued:

By this grant of power you secure the President against impeachment; you fence him round with a set of dependent officers, through whom alone it is probable you could come at the evidence of the President's guilt, in order to obtain his conviction on impeachment.

Page also looked to the Senate rather than the President to protect the rights of the states:

> Some gentlemen contend that the Senate are a dangerous and aristocratic body; but I contend that they are a safe and salutary branch of the Government, representing the republican Legislatures of the individual States, and intended to preserve the sovereignty and independence of the State Governments, which they are more likely to do than the President, who is elected by the people at large. A popular President, influenced by the sentiments of his electors, may be induced to believe that it would be best for the general interest that those Governments were destroyed; but as long as we have that body independent of him, and secured in their authority, we may safely defy such impotent attempts; they will watch his conduct, and prevent the exercise of despotic power.[95]

Jackson argued that the department heads were constitutional executive officers:

I appeal to the good sense of the committee to determine, whether these officers are not established by the constitution as heads of departments. How then can they be merely instruments of the President, to conform implicitly to his will? for I deny the principle that they are mere creatures of the law. They have constitutional rights which they may exercise.

The President, Jackson thought,

is constitutionally armed with high and dangerous powers, which, if left unchecked and unrestrained, might be productive of dangerous consequences. But to extend those powers would increase the danger to an alarming degree; if you grant him the power of removing whom he pleases from office, you will give him a complete control over the whole Treasury Department. Having got the sword, give him the purse, with the army and navy, and what is there left for him to require? With the command of the strong box, he would be able to raise up a legion of officers who would support his measures, secure his election, and thus perpetuate his political existence. . . . We already hear the sounding title of highness and most honorable trumpeted in our ears, which, ten years since, would have exalted a man to a station as high as Haman's gibbet.[96]

[95] 1 *Annals* 539–540.   [96] *Ibid.* 551–553.

To the conclusion that it was the President who appointed, rather than the President and the Senate, Gerry replied:

If we observe the enacting style of the statutes of Great Britain, we shall find pretty nearly the same words as those used in the constitution, with respect to appointments—Be it enacted by the King's Most Excellent Majesty, by and with the advice and consent of Parliament. Here it might be said that the King enacts all laws; but I believe the truth of this fact will be disputed in that country. I believe no one will pretend to say that the King is the three branches of Parliament; and, unless my colleagues will do all this, I never can admit that the President in himself has the power of appointment.

To the argument from presidential "responsibility" Gerry responded:

But it is said, the President is responsible for the conduct of this officer. I wish to know what this responsibility is. . . . Suppose, in the case of the Secretary of the Treasury, there should be a defalcation of the public revenue; is he to make good the loss? . . . The constitution shows the contrary by the provision made for impeachment; and this I take to be one of the strongest arguments against the President having the power of removing one of the principal officers of Government—that he is to bear his own responsibility.

The suggestion that the President was the particular representative of the people Gerry met with a query:

Is the creature of the deputy of a deputy nearer to the people than the creature of their deputy? Would that gentleman consider the issue of his wife's maid nearer akin to him than the issue of his wife?[97]

The refutation by Smith of South Carolina of the view of the opening sentence of Article II as a grant of power deserves quotation:

What powers are executive, or incidental to the executive department, will depend upon the nature of the Government; because some powers are vested in the Executive of a monarchy that are not in an aristocracy, and in the Executive of an aristocracy that are unknown in a democracy. The legislatures of republics appoint to office; this power is exercised by the Executives of monarchies. . . . Can the President establish corporations?[98] Can he prevent citizens from going out of the country?[99] He cannot. Yet these powers are exercised, as executive powers, by the King of Great Britain. . . . From this I am led to believe that the gentleman may be wrong, when he considers the power of removal as an executive power, and incidental to the prerogative

[97] *Ibid.* 556–557.
[98] Smith of course referred to the prerogative power of the King (Crown) to establish corporations. 1 Sir William Blackstone, *Commentaries on the Laws of England* (in 2 vols., W. E. Dean, New York, 1851) Book I, 393–394.
[99] Smith of course referred to the prerogative power of the King (Crown) to issue the writ, *ne exeat regnum. Ibid.* 198–199.

of the President. For my part, I conceive the President is to exercise all executive powers granted in the constitution, . . .[100]

After repeating that the "doctrine of energy in Government . . . is the true doctrine of tyrants," Page asserted flatly:

The liberty and security of our fellow-citizens is our great object, and not the prompt execution of the laws.[101]

Stone sought to refute the construction of the opening sentence of Article II by a *reductio ad absurdum:*

Now, if the position, that all executive power vests in the President, is true and solid, the extension of it can never run into absurdity. If gentlemen determine executive powers by implication, however dangerous the ground may be, we must go through; the Congress must have all legislative power; . . . This House appoints its own officers; but in every case, the President has the power of removal; because the power is incidental to the Executive. How are we to get rid of this absurdity? Besides, if all executive power is vested in the President, what right has this House to prescribe him rules to interfere in forming executive offices? The Executive can better form them for itself. . . . The gentleman from Virginia says, we may limit the duration of this officer. But why do this? The executive powers are continual. Why are we to suspend their operation? . . . If the present office is wholly executive, the House has no right to meddle in the business.[102]

When Carroll proposed to place a time limit on the act to establish the Department of Foreign Affairs,

Mr. Stone expressed himself in favor of the motion in order that the House might preserve their due share of the Government. If the officer became expensive, and was so much under the control of the President, he would never consent to the repeal of a law which thus extended his influence.

When Boudinot pointed out the House could limit the Secretary's salary or "determine" it altogether, Stone said:

[100] 1 *Annals* 566–567.
[101] *Ibid.* 572. Page also said: "But I am astonished at the arguments of gentlemen, who contend, that granting this authority to the President, is the best security to public liberty. . . . and being persuaded . . . that the heaped-up powers on the Chief Magistrate especially as the bill proposes, does not render him more responsible; but, on the contrary, by increasing his importance, and multiplying his dependents, directly tends to diminish his responsibility, and secure him, if not against suspicion, at least against charges of delinquency. . . . But, sir, I wish, . . . to get rid of an expression . . . which must serve to break down the spirit of our officers of state, and make them crouch before the President, as the heads of such departments at Constantinople now do before the Grand Seignior. . . . Strike out the clause, sir, and you leave your officers responsible to the President, but not abject tools to him. . . ." *Ibid.* 570–571.
[102] *Ibid.* 588–589.

If you make this law permanent, and give permanent salaries, . . . the House will have no control over this department, unless two thirds of both Houses acquiesce in the repeal.[103]

MADISON ON THE OPENING SENTENCE OF ARTICLE II AS A GRANT OF POWER—"THE EXECUTIVE POWER"—TO THE PRESIDENT. The student of our constitutional history cannot fail to be impressed by the fact that the theory that the opening sentence of Article II of the Constitution[104] is a grant of "the" executive power was expressed by Madison, Jefferson[105] and Hamilton.[106] Of their historic pronouncements the first in time was that of Madison in the removal debate of 1789. Though at first he tended to support his motion for the clause, "to be removable by the President," on the legislative-grant theory, he soon had this to say:

I have, since the subject was last before the House, examined the constitution with attention, and I acknowledge that it does not perfectly correspond with the ideas I entertained of it from the first glance. . . .

By a strict examination of the constitution, on what appears to be its true principles, and considering the great departments of the Government in the relation which they have to each other, I have my doubts whether we are not absolutely tied down to the construction declared in the bill. . . .[107]

After then expounding the constitutional-grant theory, he added:

If this is the true construction of this instrument, the clause in the bill is nothing more than explanatory of the meaning of the constitution, and therefore not liable to any particular objection on that account. If the constitution is silent, and it is a power the Legislature have a right to confer, it will appear to the world, if we strike out the clause, as if we doubted the propriety of vesting it in the President of the United States. I therefore think it best to retain it in the bill.[108]

Later, however, he repudiated the legislative-grant theory,[109] and finally supported motions avowedly intended so to modify the bill as to

[103] *Ibid.* 599-600.
[104] "The Executive Power shall be vested in a President of the United States of America." Article II, section 1, § 1.
[105] See Secretary Jefferson's written opinion to President Washington of April 24, 1790, entitled, "Opinion on the question whether the Senate has the right to negative the grade of persons appointed by the Executive to fill Foreign Missions," in 7 *The Writings of Thomas Jefferson* (Washington ed., Derby & Jackson, New York, 1859) 465-467.
[106] See the first of the famous "Pacificus" papers of Hamilton, in 4 *Works of Alexander Hamilton* (Federal Edition, ed. by Henry Cabot Lodge, G. P. Putnam's Sons, New York and London, 1904) 432 ff.
[107] 1 Annals 480-481.
[108] *Ibid.* 482.
[109] *Ibid.* 515. Apparently his objection to it arose from the realization that Congress might not see fit to delegate the power to the President alone. See section below (p. 201) entitled, "Analysis of the House decision."

THE ESTABLISHMENT OF THE GREAT DEPARTMENTS 179

imply the constitutional-grant rather than the legislative-grant theory.[110] His prestige then and since as an expounder of the Constitution he had helped to frame, together with the use of that prestige by Chief Justice Taft in the case of *Myers* v. *United States*,[111] justifies quotation of his view that the opening sentence of Article II is a general grant of power. After citing the opening sentences of the first three Articles of the Constitution, he added significantly:

I suppose it will be readily admitted, that so far as the constitution has separated the powers of these great departments, it would be improper to combine them together; and so far as it has left any particular department in the entire possession of the powers incident to that department, I conceive we ought not to qualify them further than they are qualified by the constitution. . . .[112]

This did not point out, though the speaker may have had in mind, the difference in the wording of Articles I and II,[113] upon which Hamilton later in 1793 laid explicit stress.[114] From this point Madison plunged into his main argument:

[110] *Ibid.* 600–608. It is specifically recorded that Madison seconded the first of Benson's motions and expressly favored the second. He probably seconded the latter also.
[111] 272 U.S. 52 (1926).
[112] 1 *Annals* 481.
[113] The opening sentences of Articles I and II are as follows, with italics supplied by the present writer: "All legislative Powers *herein granted* shall be vested in a Congress of the United States, which shall consist of a Senate and House of Representatives." Article I, section 1. "*The* Executive Power shall be vested in a President of the United States of America. . . ." Article II, section 1, § 1. Thach quotes the notes of John Adams on the speech in the Senate in which Ellsworth stated that what was granted in Article II was not the executive powers thereinafter enumerated, but "the executive power." *Thach* 155. Thach points out that the objection which the opposition brought against this interpretation of the sentence was not "fairly met," but thinks "it might have been." *Ibid.* 165. The present writer would take the Madison-Jefferson-Hamilton interpretation of the opening sentence of Article II to mean that it is a *grant* of *the* executive power; that is, of all powers which are, theoretically or historically, clearly "executive" in nature, which are relevant to national authority under our federal system, which are not expressly limited in the thereinafter enumerated powers of the President, and which are otherwise consistent with the letter and spirit of the Constitution.
[114] In the first of the "Pacificus" papers cited above in note 106. Corwin uses the Pacificus-Helvidius debate to cast doubt upon Hamilton's having by 1793 given up the view he had expressed in the *Federalist* that removals would require the consent of the Senate, and upon Madison's retention in 1793 of the view that the opening sentence of Article II was a grant of "the" executive power to the President. The present writer offers brief quotations which speak for themselves:
"With these exceptions, the *executive power* of the United States is completely lodged in the President. This mode of construing the Constitution has indeed been recognized by Congress in formal acts, upon full consideration and debate; of which the power of removal from office is an important instance. . . ."—*Pacificus.* 7 *The Works of Alexander Hamilton* (ed. by J. C. Hamilton, Charles S. Francis & Co., New York, 1851) 81.
"It may be proper, however, to take notice of the power of removal from office, which appears to have been adjudged to the president by the laws establishing the executive departments, and which the writer ["Pacificus"] has pressed into his service. To justify any favorable inference from this case, it must be shown that the powers of war and

The constitution affirms, that the executive power shall be vested in the President. Are there exceptions to this proposition? Yes, there are. The constitution says, that in appointing to office, the Senate shall be associated with the President, unless in the case of inferior officers, when the law shall otherwise direct. Have we a right to extend this exception? I believe not. If the constitution has invested all executive powers in the President, I venture to assert that the Legislature has no right to diminish or modify his executive authority.

Madison then proceeded to make the application to the question of removal:

The question now resolves itself into this, Is the power of displacing, an executive power? I conceive that if any power whatsoever is in its nature executive, it is the power of appointing, overseeing, and controlling those who execute the laws. If the constitution had not qualified the power of the President in appointing to office, by associating the Senate with him in that business, would it not be clear that he would have the right, by virtue of his executive power, to make such appointment? Should we be authorized, in defiance of that clause in the constitution,—"The executive power shall be vested in a President," to unite the Senate with the President in the appointment to office? I conceive not. If it is admitted that we should not be authorized to do this, I think it may be disputed whether we have a right to associate them in removing persons from office, the one power being as much of an executive nature as the other; and the first only is authorized by being excepted out of the general rule established by the constitution, in these words, "the executive power shall be vested in the President." [115]

MADISON'S HISTORIC DEFENSE OF THE CONSTITUTIONAL-GRANT THEORY. At a later point in the debate, Madison elaborated his defense of the constitutional-grant theory of the removal power in language which has become a classic. After noting that "several constructions have been put upon the constitution relative to the point in question," he proceeded to refute the legislative-grant theory:

... The gentleman from Connecticut (Mr. Sherman) has advanced a doctrine which was not touched upon before. He seems to think (if I under-

---

treaties are of a kindred nature to the power of removal, or at least are equally within a grant of executive power. Nothing of this sort has been attempted, nor probably will be attempted. Nothing can, in truth, be clearer, than that no analogy, or shade of analogy, can be traced between a power in the supreme officer, responsible for the faithful execution of the laws, to displace a subaltern officer employed in the execution of the laws; and a power to make treaties, and to declare war, such as these have been found to be in their nature, their operation, and their consequences."—Helvidius. 1 *Letters and Other Writings of James Madison* (published by order of Congress, R. Worthington, New York, 1884) 619. Now read Corwin's *Removal Power* 24–26 and see what is left of his reasoning.
[115] 1 *Annals* 481–482.

stand him rightly) that the power of displacing from office is subject to legislative discretion; because it having a right to create, it may limit or modify as it thinks proper. I shall not say but at first view this doctrine may seem to have some plausibility. But when I consider, that the constitution clearly intended to maintain a marked distinction between the legislative, executive, and judicial powers of Government; and when I consider, that if the Legislature has a power, such as contended for, they may subject and transfer at discretion powers from one department of our Government to another; they may, on that principle, exclude the President altogether from exercising any authority in the removal of officers; they may give it to the Senate alone, or the President and Senate combined; they may vest it in the whole Congress; or they may reserve it to be exercised by this House. When I consider the consequences of this doctrine, and compare them with the true principles of the constitution, I own that I cannot subscribe to it.

He next devoted a paragraph to refutation of the impeachment theory:

Another doctrine, which has found very respectable friends, has been particularly advocated by the gentleman from South Carolina, (Mr. Smith). It is this: when an officer is appointed by the President and Senate, he can only be displaced for malfeasance in his office by his impeachment. I think this would give a stability to the executive department, so far as it may be described by the heads of departments, which is more incompatible with the genius of republican Government in general, and this constitution in particular, than any doctrine which has yet been proposed. The danger to liberty, the danger of mal-administration, has not yet been found to lie so much in the facility of introducing improper persons into office, as in the difficulty of displacing those who are unworthy of the public trust. If it is said, that an officer once appointed shall not be displaced without the formality required by impeachment, I shall be glad to know what security we have for the faithful administration of the Government. Every individual, in the legal chain which extends from the highest to the lowest link of the Executive Magistracy, would find a security in his situation which would relax his fidelity and promptitude in the discharge of his duty.

Then he proceeded to demolish the President-and-Senate theory:

The doctrine, however, which seems to stand most in opposition to the principles I contend for, is, that the power to annul an appointment is, in the nature of things, incidental to the power which makes the appointment. I agree that if nothing more was said in the constitution than that the President, by and with the advice and consent of the Senate, should appoint to office, there would be great force in saying that the power of removal resulted by a natural implication from the power of appointing. But there is another part of the constitution, no less explicit than the one on which the gentleman's doctrine is founded; it is that part which declares that the executive power shall be vested in a President of the United States. The association of the Senate with the President in exercising that particular function, is an exception to this general rule; and exceptions to general rules, I conceive, are ever to be taken strictly. But there is another part of the constitution which inclines, in my judgment, to favor the construction I put upon it: The President is required to take care that the laws be faithfully executed. If the duty to see that the laws be faithfully executed be required at the hands of the Chief Magistrate, it would seem that it was generally intended that he should have the species of power which is necessary to accomplish that end. Now, if the officer when once appointed is not to depend upon the President for his official existence, but upon a distinct body, (for where there are two negatives required, either can prevent the removal,) I confess I do not see how the President can take care that the laws be faithfully executed. It is true, by a circuitous operation, he may obtain an impeachment, and even without this it is possible he may obtain the concurrence of the Senate for the purpose of displacing an officer; but would this give that species of control to the Executive Magistrate which seems to be required by the constitution? I own, if my opinion was not contrary to that entertained by what I suppose to be the minority on this question, I should be doubtful of being mistaken, when I discovered how inconsistent that construction would make the constitution with itself. I can hardly bring myself to imagine the wisdom of the convention who framed the constitution contemplated such incongruity.

After next extolling the separation of powers, and saying that if any blending occurred, it was "in order to admit a partial qualification, in order more effectually to guard against an entire consolidation," and that the Constitution [116] should be expounded "so as to blend them as little as possible," he stated:

> Every thing relative to the merits of the question as distinguished from a constitutional question, seems to turn on the danger of such a power vested in the President alone.

Madison then weighed the relative dangers of removal by the President on the one hand and of the President and Senate on the other. His

---

[116] Madison understood the Constitution to embody the separation of powers by implication. He said at this point: "I think, therefore, when we review the several parts of this constitution, when it says that the legislative powers shall be vested in a Congress of the United States under certain exceptions, and the executive power vested in the President with certain exceptions, we must suppose they were intended to be kept separate in all cases in which they are not blended, and ought, consequently, to expound the constitution so as to blend them as little as possible." *Ibid.* 517. This is often expressed by saying that, while the Constitution has no "distributing clause" like those of some state constitutions, the separation of powers is to be inferred, under the maxim, *expressio unius est exclusio alterius*, from a reading together of the opening sentences of Articles I, II, and III, respectively. Frank J. Goodnow, *The Principles of the Administrative Law of the United States* (G. P. Putnam's Sons, New York and London, The Knickerbocker Press, 1905), 31–32.

earlier general statement of the position of the President under our constitutional system is at this point pertinent:

> When we consider that the First Magistrate is to be appointed at present by the suffrages of three millions of people, and in all human probability in a few years' time by double that number, it is not to be presumed that a vicious or bad character will be selected. . . . With all the infirmities incident to a popular election, corrected by the particular mode of conducting it, as directed under the present system, I think we may fairly calculate that the instances will be very rare in which an unworthy man will receive that mark of the public confidence which is required to designate the President of the United States. Where the people are disposed to give so great an elevation to one of their fellow-citizens, I own that I am not afraid to place my confidence in him, especially when I know he is impeachable for any crime or misdemeanor before the Senate, at all times; and that, at all events, he is impeachable before the community at large every four years, and liable to be displaced if his conduct shall have given umbrage during the time he has been in office. Under these circumstances, although the trust is a high one, and in some degree, perhaps, a dangerous one, I am not sure but it will be safer here than placed where some gentlemen suppose it ought to be.
>
> It is evidently the intention of the constitution, that the first Magistrate should be responsible for the executive department; so far therefore as we do not make the officers who are to aid him in the duties of that department responsible to him, he is not responsible to his country. . . .[117]

So now, after discounting the dangers of presidential power, Madison continued:

> . . . Vest this power in the Senate jointly with the President, and you abolish at once that great principle of unity and responsibility in the executive department, which was intended for the security of liberty and the public good. If the President should possess alone the power of removal from office, those who are employed in the execution of the law will be in their proper situation, and the chain of dependence be preserved; the lowest officers, the middle grade, and the highest, will depend, as they ought, on the President, and the President on the community. The chain of dependence therefore terminates in the supreme body, namely, in the people, who will possess, besides, in aid of their original power, the decisive engine of impeachment. Take the other supposition; that the power should be vested in the Senate, on the principle that the power to displace is necessarily connected with the power to appoint. It is declared by the constitution, that we may by law vest the appointment of inferior officers in the heads of departments; the power of removal being incidental, as stated by some gentlemen. Where does this terminate? If you begin with the subordinate officers, they

[117] 1 *Annals* 479–480.

are dependent on their superior, he on the next superior, and he on—whom? On the Senate, a permanent body, a body, by its particular mode of election, in reality existing forever; a body possessing that proportion of aristocratic power which the constitution no doubt thought wise to be established in the system, but which some have strongly excepted against. And let me ask gentlemen, is there equal security in this case as in the other? Shall we trust the Senate, responsible to individual Legislatures, rather than the person who is responsible to the whole community? It is true, the Senate do not hold their offices for life, like aristocracies recorded in the historic page; yet the fact is, they will not possess that responsibility for the exercise of Executive powers which would render it safe for us to vest such powers in them. But what an aspect will this give to the Executive? Instead of keeping the departments of government distinct, you make an executive out of one branch of the Legislature; you make the Executive a two-headed monster, to use the expression of the gentleman from New Hampshire, (Mr. Livermore,) you destroy the great principle of responsibility, and perhaps have the creature divided in its will, defeating the very purposes for which a unity in the Executive was instituted. These objections do not lie against such an arrangement as the bill establishes. I conceive the President is sufficiently accountable to the community; and if this power is vested in him, it will be vested where its nature requires it should be vested; if any thing in its nature is executive, it must be that power which is employed in superintending and seeing that the laws are faithfully executed. The laws cannot be executed but by officers appointed for that purpose; therefore, those who are over such officers naturally possess the executive power. If any other doctrine be admitted, what is the consequence? You may set the Senate at the head of the executive department, or you may require that the officers hold their places during the pleasure of this branch of the Legislature, if you cannot go so far as to say we shall appoint them; and by this means, you link together two branches of the Government which the preservation of liberty requires to be constantly separated.[118]

MACLAY ON THE SENATE DEBATE ON THE REMOVAL POWER.[119] As early as June 18 Maclay was recording in his journal that "some of the courtiers in the Senate fairly admit" that the power of dismissing ambassadors belonged to the President. The matter was already being "agitated with great warmth in the House of Representatives" with respect to the Secretary of Foreign Affairs. Maclay thought it "easy to see what the court opinion will be" in the Senate:

Indeed, I entertain no doubt but that many people are aiming with all their force to establish a splendid court with all the pomp of majesty. Alas!

[118] *Ibid.* 515–519.
[119] Cf. 3 *Works of John Adams* (Charles Francis Adams, ed., Little and Brown, Boston, 1851) 408–412. See the comment in *Thach* 155, 157.

poor Washington, if you are taken in this snare! How will the gold become dim! How will the fine gold become changed! How will your glory fade! [120]

Madison's House leadership in favor of the President's power of removal excited Maclay's suspicions. He said Madison was charged with courting the French through Mr. Jefferson, by his stand for discriminatory duties, but that he thought him more likely guilty of another charge:

. . . his urging the doctrine of taking away the right of removals of officers from the Senate in order to pay his court to the President, whom, I am told, he already affects to govern. Time will, however, throw light on both these subjects. . . .[121]

On July 9 Maclay got copies of the three bills for the great departments and recorded his reactions. He thought the bills "calculated on a scale of great expense." He objected to "the lessening of the power of the Senate" by "taking away from them any vote in the removal of officers." He also complained of what he was pleased to consider "placing the President above business and beyond the power of responsibility, putting into the hands of his officers the duties required of him by the Constitution."[122] Apparently Maclay saw in the policy of these bills another imitation of monarchy:

But for the House of Representatives, by a side-wind, to exalt the President above the Constitution, and depress the Senate below it, is—but I will leave it without name. They know the veneration entertained for General Washington, and believe the people will be ready to join in the cry against the Senate, in his favor, when they endeavor to make him a party. They think they have fast hold of us, and that we dare not refuse our assent to these bills, and so several of them have not failed to declare.

Indeed, he did not see any need for this legislation at all:

Nor do I see the necessity of having made this business a subject of legislation. The point of view in which it has presented itself to me was that the President should signify to the Senate his desire of appointing a Minister of Foreign Affairs, and nominate the man. And so of the other necessary departments. If the Senate agreed to the necessity of the office and the men, they would concur; if not, they would negative, etc. The House would get the business before them when salaries came to be appointed, and could thus give their opinion by providing for the officers or not.[123]

[120] *Journal of William Maclay* 80.
[121] *Ibid.* 94–95.
[122] Contrast Washington to Comte de Moustier. May 25, 1789. 30 *Writings* 333–335.
[123] *Journal of William Maclay* 101.

In so saying he of course ignored the importance of a systematic organization of administration and the implications of the constitutional provision that offices should be established by law.[124]

On July 14 the Senate took up the Foreign Affairs bill. Maclay spoke against the first clause, that there should be an executive department, on the ground he had committed to his journal. He thus developed one of his arguments:

There are a number of such bills, and may be many more, tending to direct the most minute particle of the President's conduct. If he is to be directed, how he shall do everything, it follows he must do nothing without direction. To what purpose, then, is the executive power lodged with the President, if he can do nothing without a law directing the mode, manner, and, of course, the thing to be done. May not the two Houses of Congress, on this principle, pass a law depriving him of all powers? You will say it will not get his approbation. But two thirds of both Houses will make it a law without him, and the Constitution is undone at once.

Not only was this line of argument out of character for Maclay, whose constant fear was monarchical exaltation of the President; but the argument was patently absurd when directed against a bill which made it the duty of the Secretary of Foreign Affairs to do what the President ordered him to do.[125] Needless to say, the first clause was carried.

Then came consideration of the removal clause; and Maclay was the first to rise. He repeated objections which had been urged in the House. In his opinion the Constitution never contemplated any other mode of removal except after impeachment. But if tenure during pleasure were constitutional, then the consent of the Senate was required. Under the Constitution the Senate was the "great check" or the "balance" of the government. By these checks the stability of government was placed in their hands.

He expressed still another objection to the clause. The chief clerk, appointed by the Secretary without the consent of the Senate, would upon the removal of the Secretary become the principal, and might remain so during the presidency, since the Senate could not force the President to nominate a new Secretary. This, said Maclay, was a direct stroke at the power of the Senate. So he moved to strike the whole clause.

Langdon wanted to strike out only the part of the clause relating to the President's removal power. Ellsworth stated the position which Benson and Madison had elaborated in the House; but Maclay thought he carefully avoided impeachment. He

[124] Article II, section 2, § 2.   [125] 2 *Laws of the United States* 6.

THE ESTABLISHMENT OF THE GREAT DEPARTMENTS 187

absolutely used the following expressions with regard to the President: *"It is a sacrilege to touch a hair of his head, and we may as well lay the President's head on the block and strike it off with one blow."* [126]

The debate lasted into the next two days. Carroll spoke on "the want of power in the President, and a desire of increasing it. *The king can do no wrong.*" The ministers were the ones to answer for anything improper. "How strangely this man has changed!" cried Maclay in his journal. Ellsworth also lamented the want of power in the President, and asked, did we *ever quarrel* with the power of the Crown? He answered his own question in the negative: our quarrel had been with the power of parliament. "We must extend the executive arm." [127]

There was much maneuvering to get the Senate to vote away its negative on presidential removals. Maclay confided to his journal: "I have seen more caballing and meeting of members in knots this day than I ever observed before. . . . It seems as if a court party was forming; indeed, I believe it was formed long ago." And again, on the next day of the removal debate: "It was all huddling away in small parties. Our Vice-President was very busy indeed; running to every one." In discussion on this day Paterson, after he got warmed up, "flew over to England; extolled its Government; wished, in the most unequivocal language, that our President had the same powers." Presently "Dalton rose and said a number of things in the most hesitating manner. It was his recantation; [he] had just now altered his mind." Then: "But now recantation was in fashion. Mr. Bassett recanted, too, though he said he had prepared himself on the other side." And "everybody believed that John Adams was the great converter." While Maclay was up, Adams treated him from the Chair with "studied inattention." Senator Grayson of Virginia, however, made this dire prediction:

"The matter predicted by Mr. Henry is now coming to pass: consolidation is the object of the new Government, and the first attempt will be to destroy the Senate, as they are the representatives of the State Legislatures."

The vote on Maclay's motion to strike out the removal clause was a dramatic one:

---

[126] Maclay adds: "He [Ellsworth] had sore eyes, and had a green silk over them. On pronouncing the last of the two sentences, he paused, put his handkerchief to his face, and either shed tears or affected to do so."

[127] Maclay attributes to Ellsworth this metaphorical statement of the constitutional-grant theory: "'I buy a square acre of land. I buy the trees, water, and everything belonging to it. The executive power belongs to the President. The removing of officers is a tree on this acre. The power of removing is, therefore, his. It is in him. It is nowhere else. Thus we are under the necessity of ascertaining by implication where the power is.'"

After all the arguments were ended and the question taken the Senate was ten to ten, and the Vice President with joy cried out, "It is not a vote!" without giving himself time to declare the division of the House and give his vote in order.

Maclay confided to his journal:

What avowed and repeated attempts have I seen to place the President above the powers stipulated for him by the Constitution.

He was most surprised at Paterson, who had been described to him as a staunch Revolution man and genuine Whig.[128]

Two days later (July 18) those who were against the bill asked for the yeas and nays in the same form as originally voted, with the casting vote of the Vice President. Butler had been for striking out, but was now absent. So Ellsworth withdrew to preserve the tie.

Lee made a motion that the officer should be responsible. It was opposed by Maclay on the ground that it would be cruel to make him responsible for measures in which he could have no free agency, because the bill made him an abject creature of the President. He thought they would, therefore, have to trust to *respondeat superior*. Maclay recorded that Lee's motion "was lost, of course." Of this vote Thach has remarked:

Again an opportunity for ministerial government was offered, and again rejected, "of course." [129]

Maclay could not see what Langdon aimed at in moving to strike out "to be appointed by the said principal officer." One presumes that Langdon wanted to leave the appointment in the President and Senate. When, however, Dr. Johnson "complained of the approbation of the President in the last part of the clause as reflecting on the Senate, to whom the Constitution had given the power of approving," Maclay made a speech in which he said that while the clause called the chief clerk an inferior officer, "he will be the man who will do the business." Calling him an inferior officer paved the way for his appointment by the department head. Of course he would take care of the office records, even if the principal should be removed. Why, then, this clause?

Clearly to put it into the power of a President, if so minded, to exercise this office without the advice or consent of the Senate as to the affair. The consent of the President at the end of the clause points out this clearly. This is a kind of a consent unwarranted by the Constitution. The President removes the principal—the clerk pleases him well, being a man of his approbation. The

[128] *Journal of William Maclay* 106–114.   [129] Thach 157.

Senate can not force him to a nomination, and the business may proceed during his presidency. . . . The design is but ill concealed. . . .

Paterson and Morris did not seem averse to striking out the latter part of the clause; but Morris acquitted the House in general of any design against the Senate. Maclay

. . . rose and said I thought nothing on this subject which I would not avow. The House of Representatives had debated four days on a direct clause for vesting the President with this power; and, after having carried it with an open face, they dropped and threw out the clause, and have produced the same thing, cloaked and modified in a different manner by a side-wind. I liked, for my part, plain dealing, and there was something that bore a very different aspect in this business.[130]

There Maclay leaves the matter;[131] but while the *Annals* record that the Senate passed the bill on this day,[132] the provision under discussion, which presumably was for presidential approbation of appointment by the principal officer of the chief clerk, does not appear in the act as approved by the President.[133] It was probably struck out by the Senate, with the House yielding on the point.[134]

THACH ON THE SIGNIFICANCE OF THE SENATE'S ACTION ON THE REMOVAL QUESTION. Of the Senate's acceptance of the House position on this vital issue Thach has remarked:

There can, then, be no question that the matter of removal was voted upon by the Senate with a full knowledge of what it signified in all its aspects. The issue was crystal clear, and the majority of former Convention members were found voting for the bill as it stood, the division being Read, Bassett, Ellsworth, Strong, Paterson, and Morris against Butler, Langdon, Johnson and Few. The significance of the vote is the greater when it is remembered that instances where a political body voluntarily deprives itself of power are very few in all the history of government.[135]

THE STATUTORY RESULT. The net result of the removal debate was the incorporation in *all three* bills of what was, *mutatis mutandis*, an identical provision. This may be given in the form in which it appears in the act creating the Treasury Department:

---

[130] *Journal of William Maclay* 116–118.
[131] This was July 18. On July 20 Maclay obtained sick leave, and the next entry in his journal is for August 16. *Journal of William Maclay* 118–119. The three bills establishing the Departments of Foreign Affairs, War, and Treasury were approved July 27, August 7, and September 2, respectively. See below (p. 216) Maclay's account of Senate action on removal of the Secretary of the Treasury.
[132] 1 *Annals* 51.
[133] 2 *Laws of the United States* 7.
[134] Cf. 1 *Annals* 685 and 701–702.
[135] Thach 157–158.

That whenever the secretary shall be removed from office by the president of the United States, or in any other case of vacancy in the office of secretary, the assistant shall, during the vacancy, have the charge and custody of the records, books, and papers, appertaining to the said office.[136]

THE QUESTION OF THE SCOPE OF THE PRESIDENT'S POWER OF REMOVAL UNDER THE "LEGISLATIVE DECISION OF 1789." The issue over the removal power was threshed out in connection with the Secretary of Foreign Affairs,[137] and the conclusion then applied to the other two secretaries.[138] By that conclusion the department heads were given no fixed terms, on the understanding that they held office at the pleasure of the President.

While the Treasury bill was under consideration, Madison raised the question of the tenure of the comptroller.[139] What is pertinent here is the remarks made by him and others with respect to the *scope* of the "decision" which had just been made on the question of tenure. Madison, in opening the subject, remarked that in his view the duties of this officer partook of a judicial quality, and therefore the Legislature might establish the office on a footing to answer its purpose.[140] Stone said the comptroller was an *inferior* officer, and hence his appointment might be vested in the President; but

according to the determination which had already taken place, it did not necessarily follow that he should have the power of dismissal.[141]

Sedgwick, who had been a legislative-grant man, said he thought the office of comptroller bore a "strong affinity" to the executive branch, and added these significant words:

He also conceived that a majority of the House had decided that all officers concerned in executive business should depend upon the will of the President for their continuance in office; and with good reason, for they were the eyes and arms of the principal Magistrate, the instruments of execution.[142]

Benson, arch exponent of the constitutional-grant theory,

did not like the object of the motion, because it was, in some measure, setting afloat the question which had already been carried.

He wished there might be some certainty in knowing what was the tenure of officers; he thought they were well fixed now, if nothing more was done

---

[136] 2 *Laws of the United States* 50. Cf. *ibid.* 7 (Foreign Affairs) and 32–33 (War).
[137] 1 *Annals* 383–399, 412, 473–608, 614.
[138] *Ibid.* 399–412, 615–631, 635–639, 643.
[139] *Ibid.* 635–639. June 29 and 30, 1789. See also below (p. 197), the section of this study entitled, "The tenure of the comptroller."
[140] 1 *Annals* 635–636.   [141] *Ibid.* 637.   [142] *Ibid.* 637–638.

with the question. The judges hold theirs during good behavior, as established by the constitution; all others, during pleasure. He was afraid the present motion would lead to a different construction from the one lately adopted; by devices of this kind, he apprehended the Legislature might overthrow the executive power; he would therefore vote against it, if it were not withdrawn.[143]

Madison further defended his position, but let his motion lie over, and withdrew it the next day.[144]

In this connection mention may be made of various other offices created at the first session, all of which were left by statutory provision or silence to be filled by the President and Senate, except as is otherwise herein indicated. An act to regulate the collection of duties provided for naval officers, collectors, and surveyors, and prescribed their duties, without any reference to their tenure.[145] When the Treasury Department was later established, the Secretary had as one of his duties "to superintend the collection of the revenue." [146]

The act to provide for the government of the western territory stated that the governor should now report to the President rather than the old Congress, and that all officers set up under the Northwest Ordinance should now be appointed by the President by and with the advice and consent of the Senate. It further provided:

. . . and in all cases where the United States in congress assembled, might, by the said ordinance, revoke any commission or remove from any office, the president is hereby declared to have the same powers of revocation and removal.

That in case of the death, removal, resignation, or necessary absence, of the governor of the said territory, the secretary thereof shall be, and he is hereby authorized and required to execute all the powers, and perform all the duties of the governor, during the vacancy occasioned by the removal, resignation, or necessary absence, of the said governor.

Since the Northwest Ordinance gave the judges tenure during good behavior, this act of 1789 carried that provision over.[147] The tenure of territorial judges, however, is even more clearly a special case than the tenure of the comptroller. In other respects the act of 1789 was presumably meant to follow the pattern of the Benson amendment.

[143] *Ibid.* 638.
[144] *Ibid.* 638–639.
[145] 2 *Laws of the United States* 7–31. Approved July 31, 1789.
[146] *Ibid.* 48.
[147] *Ibid.* 33. Approved August 7, 1789. For the provision of the Northwest Ordinance on judges, see 1 Stat. L. 51, note. The point is emphasized in Corwin's *Removal Power* 33.

The Department of Justice was not created until eighty-one years later;[148] but the judiciary act of 1789 provided, in its very last sentence, as follows:

> ... And there shall also be appointed a meet person, learned in the law, to act as attorney general for the United States, who shall be sworn, or affirmed, to a *faithful execution of his office;* whose duty it shall be to prosecute and conduct all suits in the supreme court, in which the United States shall be concerned, and to give his advice and opinion upon questions of law, when required by the President of the United States, or when requested by the heads of any of the departments, touching any matters that may concern their departments, and shall receive such compensation for his services as shall, by law, be provided.[149]

This act also created the offices of district attorneys[150] and marshals, and prescribed their duties. While it made no reference to the tenure or removal of the Attorney General and the district attorneys, it expressly enacted

> That a marshal shall be appointed, in and for each district, for the term of four years, but shall be removable from office at pleasure.[151]

It may reasonably be inferred that the Attorney General and the district attorneys, as well as the surveyors and collectors, and presumably the naval officers,[152] were understood to hold at pleasure; and that the removability of marshals was specified, lest it be inferred that they could be removed only upon impeachment within their terms as specified by law. The expression, "shall be removable," though it sounds like an expression of the legislative-grant theory, is hardly to be so taken, in view of what had gone before.

It may be added that the marshal of each district could appoint deputies, who should be removable at pleasure by the district judge or the circuit court.[153] Here Congress seems to have been regulating the

---

[148] 16 Stat. L. 162–165 (June 22, 1870).
[149] 2 *Laws of the United States* 71. Approved September 24, 1789.
[150] *Ibid.* 71.   [151] *Ibid.* 66.
[152] It is presumed that, by virtue of Article II of the Constitution and the legislative decision of 1789, the powers of the old Congress under Articles 2 and 13 of the articles of war of October 3, 1787 [4 *Journals of The American Congress: From 1774 to 1788* (in 4 vols., Way and Gideon, Washington, 1823) 649–651] as carried over by section 4 of an act approved September 29, 1789 (2 *Laws of the United States* 74), passed to the President of the United States.
[153] 2 *Laws of the United States* 66. Collectors also could appoint deputies. *Ibid.* 17. The Supreme Court and the District Courts were empowered to appoint clerks for their respective courts, the clerk of each district being made clerk also of the Circuit Court in such district; and the said clerks were to give bond. *Ibid.* 59. Here Congress was clearly vesting the appointment of inferior officers in the courts of law; but no reference was made to the tenure of court clerks.

THE ESTABLISHMENT OF THE GREAT DEPARTMENTS

tenure of inferior officers whose appointment was not vested in the President.

Another act made temporary provision for the postal system inherited from the Confederation. Its pertinent language is as follows:

> That there shall be appointed a post master general; his powers and salary, and the compensation to the assistant or clerks and deputies which he shall appoint, and the regulations of the post office, shall be the same as they last were under the resolutions and ordinances of the late congress. The post master general shall be subject to the direction of the president of the United States in performing the duties of his office, and in forming contracts for the transportation of the mail.[154]

There was no reference to removal; but there was express reference to presidential administrative direction. As Thach has emphasized, the evidence of the removal debate demonstrates

> the erroneousness of the commonly accepted explanation that the presidential control over administration is an accidental result of the possession of the power of removal. The exact reverse is the true explanation. The power of removal was rather derived from the general executive power of administrative control. The latter power has not been an extra-constitutional growth. It was the conscious creation of the men who made the Constitution. The President has possessed it as a constitutional power from the beginning of government under the Constitution.[155]

Finally, as will be noted in detail in a later section, all three department heads were authorized to appoint a chief clerk or assistant and other clerks.[156]

In the discussion recorded above, Benson interpreted the legislative decision of 1789 as meaning that all officers except judges held during

---

[154] *Ibid.* 53. Approved September 22, 1789.

[155] Thach 158–159. Corwin points out that President Jackson expressed precisely the same view in connection with his removal of Duane. Edward S. Corwin, *The President: Office and Powers* (2d ed., New York University Press, New York, 1941) 81 ff. Cf. the reference on p. 88 to Jackson's Protest as the *first* and *last* prior statement in one place of the ideas of the Taft opinion in the *Myers Case* with the arguments of "Mr. Madison and his associates" as reported in this study.

[156] See below, section entitled, "Statutory duties of the subordinate officers in the first three departments." The President and Senate were authorized to fill vacancies in the board of commissioners for the settlement of accounts between the United States and individual states; and this board was empowered to appoint clerks. 2 *Laws of the United States* 32. Were these clerks "officers"? Cf. Frank J. Goodnow, *The Principles of the Administrative Law of the United States* (G. P. Putnam's Sons, New York and London, The Knickerbocker Press, 1905) 222–225. See also 2 *Laws of the United States* 21, 26–27, for customs inspectors, measurers, weighers, and gaugers, and *ibid.* 36, 46–47, for "persons" appointed to ascertain the tonnage of vessels.

Res. No. 4 provided *retroactively* that John White, late a commissioner to settle the accounts between the United States and three named states, and his two named clerks, "be considered as in office until the fourth day of February" preceding. *Ibid.* 76.

pleasure, and Sedgwick that all executive officers held at the will of the President. Most of the officers provided for by the first session were to be appointed by the President and Senate, and under this interpretation held at the pleasure of the President.

Did Sedgwick mean literally that, in the absence of legislation, the same applied to inferior officers appointed by department heads? As long as the President could control departments heads, the question was of no great practical importance.

It seems clear that some 23 members of the House, at least, believed that Congress had the power to regulate the tenure of inferior officers.[157] Congress vested the appointment of clerks of court in the courts of law without mentioning their tenure, and empowered the courts to remove deputy marshals appointed by the marshals.[158]

THE MEANING OF TENURE DURING PLEASURE AS ESTABLISHED BY THE "LEGISLATIVE DECISION OF 1789." We are today so familiar with the legislative fixing of terms of years for the tenure of executive officers that we are apt to miss the meaning of tenure during pleasure as understood by the House majority of 1789. Madison's motion with respect to the comptroller was that he should hold office during a term of [blank] years, unless sooner removed by the President.[159] It is highly significant that he described this proposal as a "modification"[160] which was justifiable on the special ground that the prime function of the comptroller was neither executive nor judicial but partook of both, and that his suggestion was repudiated as reopening the decision on tenure which had just been made.[161] Logically, this can mean only that tenure during pleasure did not mean tenure subject to removal at pleasure during a

[157] Two men expressly so held: Smith of South Carolina (1 Annals 476–477, 529, 569), and Sherman (ibid. 511). If the same conclusion was logically necessary for the 18 legislative-grant men, and for Vining, Ames, and Boudinot, the total is 23, which is only 5 short of a majority of the 54 men considered. White (ibid. 486) and Livermore (ibid. 565) seem, on the other hand, to have meant that, from the principle that the mode of removal follows from that of appointment, the President could remove inferior officers whose appointment was vested in him by law. Note the comments of Vining (ibid. 483), Lawrence (ibid. 501), and Madison (ibid. 519, 569). Doubtful are Page (ibid. 573) and Baldwin (ibid. 579), though perhaps the latter should be the 24th man in favor of the congressional regulation of the tenure of inferior officers. There may, of course, have been others. See section below, entitled, "Analysis of the House decision." In this analysis and similar ones below, the present writer claims neither exhaustiveness nor conclusiveness.

[158] See above, this section, text and note 153. In authorizing marshals and collectors to appoint deputies Congress seems to have been following an ancient practice. See Mechem on Public Officers (Callaghan and Co., Chicago, 1890) 370–374. See also Dismuke v. United States, 297 U.S. 167 (1936).

[159] 1 Annals 636.   [160] Ibid.

[161] See the next preceding (p. 190) and next following (p. 197) sections of this study.

THE ESTABLISHMENT OF THE GREAT DEPARTMENTS

fixed term, but tenure for as long a time as the President saw fit.[162]

For those who held that the legislature could regulate the tenure even of superior officers this conclusion was a matter of policy; but for Madison it was a matter of constitutional law. It is true that at one point in the debate he said the House should know, when it created the office, whether removal was to be by the President or the President and Senate, so as to decide whether to create it for an indefinite or a precise time, and that he also stated in broad terms his defense of his proposal for giving the comptroller a fixed term.[163] At the very end of the debate, however, when Carroll wanted to place a time limit on the act, and Gerry suggested limiting the appointment of the officer to a term of years, Madison said the former proposal would abridge the power of the President, and the latter still more so.[164]

Madison appears never to have departed from this view; and what he meant by it is brought out by his reaction to the tenure of office act of 1820,[165] by which various executive officers were given four-year terms. On December 10, 1820, he wrote from Montpelier to Mr. Jefferson:

The law terminating appointments at periods of four years is pregnant with mischiefs such as you describe. It overlooks the important distinction between repealing or modifying the office and displacing the officer. The former is legislative, the latter an Executive function; and even the former, if done with a view of re-establishing the office and letting in a new appointment, would be an indirect violation of the theory and policy of the Constitution. If the principle of the late statute be a sound one, nothing is necessary but to limit appointments held during pleasure to a single year, or the next meeting of Congress, in order to make the pleasure of the Senate a tenure of office, instead of that of the President alone. If the error be not soon corrected, the task will be very difficult; for it is of a nature to take a deep root.[166]

Later in the same month Madison wrote to the same effect to President Monroe:

Is not the law vacating periodically the described offices an enroachment on the Constitutional attributes of the Executive? The creation of the office

[162] See *Thach* 148, on the idea of some of the members of the House in the removal debate that the "magistracy" was "a permanent body." See also below, this chapter, p. 226, section entitled, "The question whether the Secretary of the Treasury should be authorized to report plans." Tenure at pleasure would indeed be permanent tenure unless and until the President should remove the officer.
[163] 1 *Annals* 568, with which compare *ibid*. 394, and the next following section of this study, p. 197. See also his language in the letter to Randolph cited in note 23 above.
[164] 1 *Annals* 599–600.
[165] 5 Stat. L. 582. Approved May 15, 1820. See Corwin's *Removal Power* 20.
[166] 3 *Letters and Other Writings of James Madison* (published by order of Congress, R. Worthington, New York, 1884) 196.

is a legislative act; the appointment of the officer, the joint act of the President and Senate; the tenure of the office, (the judiciary excepted,) is the pleasure of the President alone; so decided at the commencement of the Government, so acted on since, and so expressed in the commission.

Once the appointment had been made, he said, the Senate and House had no power relating to it unless in the event of an impeachment or unless they abolished the office, "by which the officer indirectly loses his place," and which would be a "virtual infringement" of the separation of powers if done "merely to get rid of the tenant" and re-establish the office with a new one. He had never read the debates on the law of 1820, nor looked for "precedents which may have countenanced it." But he suspected these were confined to the Territories and had their origin in the ordinance of the old Congress, "in whom all powers of Government were confounded."[167] Later, he wrote to Mr. Jefferson that if there were any precedent in the "Congressional code," it "must have blindly followed the territorial examples."[168]

In 1834 Madison wrote to John M. Patton a confidential letter in which, after discussing the controversy on removals in the Jackson Administration, he added:

The legislative power is of an elastic and Protean character, but too imperfectly susceptible of definitions and landmarks. In its application to tenures of office, a law passed a few years ago, declaring a large class of offices vacant at the end of every four years, and, of course, to be filled by new appointments. Was not this as much a removal as if made individually and in detail? . . .[169]

With respect to precedents for the law of 1820, the legislation of 1789, in merely establishing the post office on a temporary basis, cannot be said to have limited the term of the postmaster general;[170] in continuing

[167] *Ibid.* 200. December 28, 1820.
[168] *Ibid.* 202. January 7, 1821.
[169] 4 *ibid.* 343. March 24, 1834.
[170] See 2 *Laws of the United States* 53. Was there anything inconsistent with tenure at the pleasure of the President in the following quotations from the records of the old Congress? "The Congress then proceeded to the election of a post-master general for one year, and until another is appointed by a future Congress, when Benjamin Franklin, esq. was unanimously chosen." July 26, 1775. 1 *Journals of The American Congress: From 1774 to 1788* (Way and Gideon, Washington, 1823) 124. "*Resolved*, That Richard Bache be appointed post-master general in the room of Dr. Franklin, who is absent." November 7, 1776. *Ibid.* 540. See *ibid.* 556; 3 *ibid.* 716. The old Congress had established offices, made appointments to them, issued administrative directives to the officers, and possessed a power of removal. See *Articles of Confederation*, Art. 9: "The United States in Congress assembled, shall have authority . . . to appoint such other committees and civil officers as may be necessary for managing the general affairs of the United States, under their direction; . . ." 3 *ibid.* 589. Note that its power of removal was *implied* from its power of appointment, or its powers of appointment and direction.

THE ESTABLISHMENT OF THE GREAT DEPARTMENTS   197

the Northwest Ordinance [171] in force except as respected appointment and removal, by inference continued not only tenure during good behavior of the judges but the three-year term of the governor; and in fixing the terms of United States marshals, set an explicit precedent for the later act. No other case has been noted in which it fixed the term of office; [172] but specification of the term of the governor and of marshals was the sort of thing Madison later deplored as setting a bad precedent. The policy has, however, been continued since 1820, and long-standing practice has now overruled Madison on the point.[173]

THE TENURE OF THE COMPTROLLER. Mention has already been made of Madison's motion relating to the comptroller.[174] He observed that the Committee of the Whole had gone through the Treasury bill without making any provision on the tenure of that officer:

It will be necessary, said he, to consider the nature of this office, to enable us to come to a right decision on the subject; in analyzing its properties, we shall easily discover that they are not purely of an executive nature. It seems to me that they partake of a judiciary quality as well as executive; perhaps the latter obtains in the greatest degree. The principal duty seems to be deciding upon the lawfulness and justice of the claims and accounts subsisting between the United States and particular citizens: this partakes strongly of the judicial character, and there may be strong reasons why an officer of this kind should not hold his office at the pleasure of the executive branch of the Government. I am inclined to think that we ought to consider him something in the light of an arbitrator between the public and individuals, and that he ought to hold his office by such a tenure as will make him responsible to the public generally; then again it may be thought, on the other side, that some persons ought to be authorized on behalf of the indi-

[171] 4 *Journals of the American Congress: From 1774 to 1788* (Way and Gideon, Washington, 1823) 752.
[172] See the next preceding section of this study (p. 194). The commissioners to treat with the Southern Indians were indeed temporary officers appointed for a specific purpose.
[173] See Corwin's *Removal Power* 16-17, 20 (especially note 39), 56-58. Indeed, the question arises whether a majority of the House in 1789 believed that Congress *might* fix the terms of officers. This view was unequivocally expressed by Jackson (1 *Annals* 391), Smith of South Carolina (*ibid.* 391, 392, 528), Lawrence (*ibid.* 392, 501), Livermore (*ibid.* 565), Gerry (*ibid.* 600), and Sedgwick (*ibid.* 541-542, 605). Two members referred to the point without clear commitment: Sylvester (*ibid.* 584), and Stone (*ibid.* 589). If all 18 legislative-grant men (including Sylvester, Lawrence, and Sedgwick, above), plus Vining, Ames, Boudinot, and Sherman, must logically have so held, as Jackson, Smith, Livermore, and Gerry expressly did, the total is 26, which is but 2 short of a majority of the 54 men considered. There may have been others who held the same view. See section below (p. 201) entitled, "Analysis of the House decision."
[174] 1 *Annals* 635-639. See also the two next preceding sections of this study, starting on p. 190 and p. 194, respectively.

vidual, with the usual liberty of referring to a third person, in case of disagreement, which may throw some embarrassment in the way of the first idea.

Madison then made this significant assertion:

Whatever, Mr. Chairman, may be my opinion with respect to the tenure by which an executive officer may hold his office according to the meaning of the constitution, I am very well satisfied, that a modification by the Legislature may take place in such as partake of the judicial qualities, and that the legislative power is sufficient to establish this office on such a footing as to answer the purpose for which it is prescribed.

One might have expected him to move tenure during good behavior for the comptroller; but what he actually moved was, that this officer should hold his office during [blank] years, unless sooner removed by the President. He went on to explain that this would make him dependent upon the Government in several different ways.[175] But this would necessitate making him impartial with respect to the individual. What Madison actually proposed, however, was not to make the comptroller impartial, but to give the aggrieved individual a right to petition the Supreme Court for redress, and thus recourse to an independent tribunal. He said provisions of this kind existed in two states.[176]

Stone misunderstood Madison as saying the officer would be reappointed rather than reappointable at the end of his term, and objected that that amounted to tenure during good behavior. Nor did he think it necessary to consider the comptroller as a judge and give an express appeal from his decision to the Supreme Court, since every man would have such a remedy at common law.[177]

Smith of South Carolina, consistently with his general position, approved the idea of a fixed term, but

thought during that time he ought to be independent of the Executive, in order that he might not be influenced by that branch of the government in his decisions.[178]

Sedgwick asked if the effect would not be tenure during good behavior; but Madison interrupted to explain he had been misapprehended. Sedgwick then objected:

[175] In Madison's own words: "by this means the Comptroller would be dependent upon the President, because he can be removed by him; he will be dependent upon the Senate, because they must consent to his election for every term of years; and he will be dependent upon this House, through the means of impeachment, and the power we shall reserve over his salary; by which means we shall effectually secure the dependence of this officer upon the Government." 1 Annals 636.
[176] Ibid. 635–636.
[177] Ibid. 637.   [178] Ibid.

THE ESTABLISHMENT OF THE GREAT DEPARTMENTS

... he did not see that the proposition came up to the intention he [Madison] had expressed; so far from making him independent, as a judge ought to be, it subjected him to more subordination than any other officer.[179]

The comments which fell from the lips of Sedgwick and Benson on the scope of the decision which the House had already made on tenure, have already been quoted.[180] Madison replied that he did not seek a decision further than gentlemen were prepared:

> When I was up before, said he, I endeavored to show that the nature of this office differed from the others upon which the House had decided; and, consequently, that a modification might take place, without interfering with the former distinction; so that it cannot be said that we depart from the spirit of the constitution.
> Several arguments were adduced to show the Executive Magistrate had constitutionally a right to remove subordinate officers at pleasure. Among others it was urged, with some force, that these officers were merely to assist him in the performance of duties, which, from the nature of man, he could not execute without them, although he had an unquestionable right to do them if he were able; but I question very much whether he can or ought to have any interference in the settling and adjusting the legal claims of individuals against the United States. The necessary examination and decision in such cases partake too much of the judicial capacity to be blended with the executive. I do not say the office is either executive or judicial; I think it rather distinct from both, though it partakes of each, and therefore some modification, accommodated to those circumstances, ought to take place. I would, therefore, make the officer responsible to every part of the Government.
> Surely the Legislature have the right to limit the salary of an officer; if they have this, and the power of establishing offices at discretion, it can never be said that, by limiting the tenure of an office, we devise schemes for the overthrow of the executive department.
> If gentlemen will consult the true spirit and scope of the constitution, they will perhaps find my propositions not so obnoxious as some seem to think.[181]

He was willing to let his motion lie over, however; and it is recorded that the next day he withdrew it.[182]

Madison's suggestion thus met with no response and led to no results; and this fact in itself sharpens the decisiveness of the legislative decision of 1789. On the other hand, the reasoning which Madison employed on this occasion furnishes both an anticipation and high authority for

---

[179] *Ibid.* Sedgwick thought duties of the Comptroller which he enumerated were executive, and hence wanted him dependent upon the President. *Ibid.* 637–638.
[180] See the next to the last preceding section (p. 190) of this study.
[181] 1 *Annals* 638–639. Note the carelessly broad language of the next to the last paragraph and see notes 23 and 163 above.
[182] *Ibid.* 639.

certain much later developments of our constitutional history.[183] The importance of Madison's remarks for limitation of the scope of the legislative decision of 1789 on the basis of the character of the functions of the office was pointed out by Corwin in 1927.[184] When Madison, who had argued for the constitutional-grant theory on the basis of the separation of powers, was ready to maintain that the prime function of the comptroller was neither executive nor judicial, though it partook of both, he logically implied that the doctrine of the separation of powers was an oversimplification of the governmental process which did not express an exhaustive and clear-cut classification of all governmental functions. Madison further thought that the power of Congress to create offices authorized it to regulate the tenure of an officer vested with such hybrid powers. The fact that his proposal went no further than to fix a term of years for the comptroller was but a conclusion from premises which would logically have justified the fixing of tenure during good behavior, or subject to removal by the President only for cause. Still further, Madison advanced the idea that the function of settling claims between individuals and the government was so far judicial in quality as to call for resort to judicial review and to make presidential interference in the settlement of particular claims unwarranted. Suffice it to say here that Madison thus laid the bases in 1789 for the general line of argument by which a hundred and forty-six years later the Supreme Court, after having upheld the legislative decision of 1789,[185] decided that the President's power of removal was conditional upon the power of Congress to specify the sole causes of such removal in connection with the members of quasi-judicial commissions.[186] Even Chief Justice Taft, while he thought the President should have power to remove a member of such a commission if on the whole he did not think that he exercised his function in a wise manner, admitted that the President could not properly interfere, for example, with a quasi-judicial decision made in a particular instance after notice and hearing.[187]

[183] These developments were specifically the statutory prescription in 1921 of the special tenure of the Comptroller General of the United States, and the statutory limitation of presidential removal, with respect to the members of certain federal regulatory commissions, to removal for certain specific causes. The latter limitation was upheld, in the *Humphrey Case*, cited below in note 186, with respect to members of the Federal Trade Commission.
[184] Corwin's *Removal Power* vii–viii, 17–21. This study was published after the *Myers Case* of 1926 and before the *Humphrey Case* of 1935, for citations of which see notes 185 and 186 below.
[185] *Myers v. United States*, 272 U.S. 52 (1926).
[186] *Humphrey's Executor v. United States*, 295 U.S. 602 (1935). See James Hart, *Tenure of Office Under the Constitution* (The Johns Hopkins Press, Baltimore, 1930); Corwin's *Removal Power* viii *et passim*.
[187] *Myers v. United States*, 272 U.S. 52, 135 (1926).

ANALYSIS OF THE HOUSE DECISION. In analyzing this historic decision, the legislative history of the bills in the House may first be summarized. Madison's original clause on the removal of department heads was, "to be removable by the President." [188] The bill to establish the Department of Foreign Affairs was first taken up. Bland's motion to add, "by and with the advice and consent of the Senate," was "put and lost"; [189] and then it was voted "by a considerable majority" to adopt Madison's wording.[190] A motion by White, seconded by Page, to strike out this clause was defeated, 20 yeas against 34 nays.[191] Thereupon Benson carried out his intention, announced before the latter vote was taken,[192] of making two motions aimed at so amending the language of the bill as to make it express a legislative declaration of the constitutional-grant theory. The first motion was to insert a clause containing the words, "whenever the said principal officer shall be removed from office by the President of the United States, or in any other case of vacancy." The vote was taken on this motion with the knowledge that if it passed, Benson would make his second motion. When his first motion passed, he proceeded according to plan to move to strike out the words, "to be removable by the President." His plan and purpose he explained at the outset in this language:

... If we declare in the bill that the officer shall be removable by the President, it has the appearance of conferring the power upon him. Now, I think this improper; because it would be admitting the House to be possessed of an authority which would destroy those checks and balances which are cautiously introduced into the constitution, to prevent the amalgamation of the legislative and executive powers. For this reason I shall take the liberty of submitting an alteration, or change in the manner of expression, so that the law may be nothing more than a declaration of our sentiments upon the meaning of a constitutional grant of power to the President. . . .[193]

Madison, saying that Benson's wording expressed to his mind the meaning of the Constitution, seconded and supported his move. Benson's first motion was carried, 30 to 18, and his second motion was carried, 31 to 19.[194] The bill to establish the Department of Foreign Affairs was then sent to the Senate by a vote of 29 to 22.[195] On the bill to establish the Department of War, the vote in favor of Benson's alteration was 24 to 22.[196] The same alteration went into the bill to create the Department of the Treasury, by what vote is unknown.[197]

[188] 1 *Annals* 385.
[189] *Ibid.* 397–398.
[190] *Ibid.* 399.
[191] *Ibid.* 473–474, 599.
[192] *Ibid.* 525–527.
[193] *Ibid.* 525.
[194] *Ibid.* 600–608.
[195] *Ibid.* 614.
[196] *Ibid.* 615.
[197] See *ibid.* 385, 412, and *Journal of William Maclay* 101, 133.

Thus a majority of the House wrote into the bill language which was proposed for the express purpose of giving implied recognition of the constitutional-grant theory. In his opinion in *Myers* v. *United States*[198] Chief Justice Taft treated the "legislative decision of 1789" as if it had in *substance*, as it certainly had in *form*, represented a clean-cut victory for the views of "Mr. Madison and his associates" of the constitutional-grant school of thought. Thach also concludes:

The question of the relation of the President to the heads of the departments was settled with as much finality as a legislative interpretation could, thereby eliminating all possibility of a political control of the executive officers by the legislature either as a whole or through either of its houses.[199]

Nevertheless, if by a constitutional-grant victory is meant that that theory was held by a majority of the House, analysis of the vote by Thach and Corwin, and of the views expressed by members on the floor by Corwin, shows that there was no such victory.[200]

Vote analysis is facilitated by the fact that the yeas and nays are recorded in the *Annals* on the two Benson motions for amendment and the vote on final passage of the Foreign Affairs bill as so amended.[201]

In the House 53 members voted on one or more of the three motions, and 28 members spoke on the issues involved, though one of these, Bland, did not vote on any of these three motions. Analysis of the House vote involves classifying members by the way they voted as checked with the way they spoke.

Those who favored a legislative recognition of the constitutional power of the President alone to remove would be expected to vote for both Benson motions and for final passage of the bill. Of these there were 13. Those who favored a legislative delegation to the President alone of the power of removal would be expected to vote for the first Benson motion, against the second Benson motion, and for final passage. Of these there were 12. These two groups together made 25 members in favor of the President alone having this power. It may be guessed that these 25 in large measure coincided with the 24 who favored the Benson alteration of the War Department bill, and the unknown number who

---

[198] 272 U.S. 52 (1926).
[199] Thach 143.
[200] *Ibid.* 153–155, and Corwin's *Removal Power* 12, note 22, and generally 12–23. The "victory" is undermined by the facts: (1) that a majority did not favor the resulting recognition of a constitutional power of removal in the President alone, and (2) that such recognition was not in itself logically inconsistent with the belief in an ultimate congressional power to control tenure, and hence did not include a determination on that question one way or the other. These facts are ably enforced in Corwin's *Removal Power*.
[201] 1 *Annals* 603, 608, 614.

voted for the same alteration of the Treasury bill. Of these 25, the 12 legislative-grant men seem to have constituted what may be called the *core* of that school, all of whom wanted the President to have the removal power.

Those who opposed any sort of provision in the bill in favor of the President, because they were for removal by the President and Senate or by impeachment only, or because they objected on principle to legislative interference in the matter, would be expected to vote against both Benson motions and against final passage. Of these there were 16.

Of the 12 remaining members who voted on one or more of the three motions, those who voted against the second Benson motion would be expected to be legislative-grant men. Of these there were 7, though it should be added that of these 7 there were 3 who voted against final passage and 1 who did not vote on final passage.

Of the remaining 5 members, 1 (Baldwin) who voted for both Benson motions but did not vote on final passage may be called a constitutional-grant man; 1 (Huger) who did not vote on the Benson motions but voted for final passage may be classed simply as for removal by the President alone; 2 (Jackson and Stone) who did not vote on the Benson motions but voted against final passage may be classed as against removal by the President alone; and 1 (Leonard) who voted for both Benson motions but against final passage may be classed as a constitutional-grant man.

Classification by vote analysis alone thus yields these totals: for the President, 35; against the President, 18; constitutional-grant men, 15; legislative-grant men, 19. The odd man is not classed as favoring constitutional or legislative grant, but merely as for the President. The lineup for and against the President is in totals nearly the same as that on the original or White-Page motion to strike out.

This vote analysis needs to be checked with what was said by members. This task is difficult, and is undertaken with diffidence; for every time the present writer examines the debate he notes new facts or takes new views. Only 27 of the 53 men who have been considered spoke on the problem at all.[202] Several speakers who favored the President admitted the arguments were not conclusive either way.[203] No doubt for this reason, two men shifted their positions during the debate.[204] Per-

---

[202] Twenty-eight spoke, but Bland did not vote on any of the 3 motions which form the basis of the above vote analysis.

[203] See, for example, 1 *Annals* 532 (Vining), 542 (Sedgwick), 560 (Ames), 583–584 (Sylvester), 608 (Hartley).

[204] Madison and Sylvester. For Madison, see above, this chapter. For Sylvester, see 1 *Annals* 393, 583–585.

haps for the same reason, some seem to have wavered between two theories,[205] or not to have been entirely clear or self-consistent,[206] at least as their remarks are reported.[207] Some did not speak on all aspects of the problem, and hence now defy *complete* classification.

The last point becomes of supreme importance when it is remembered that a major contribution of Corwin to this subject was his pointing out the fallacy of the assumption that every member fell simply into one of the four pigeonholes represented by the four major theories. In particular, he showed that the legislative-grant theory did not necessarily or (for some members) actually stand in a mutually exclusive relationship with the constitutional-grant (or the President-and-Senate) theory. For it was possible to hold, and was indeed by some held, that, *in the absence of legislation,* the President alone (or the President and Senate)[208] was constitutionally empowered to remove, but that this power was *conditional* upon the power of Congress in creating offices and under the necessary and proper clause to regulate tenure of office.[209] Men with such views *may or may not* have *voted* as legislative-grant men; for they may have wanted to regulate the matter or they may have preferred to support the constitutional inference which in their view would obtain in the absence of legislation. For those who gave silent votes it is impossible to determine which view they took. For those who spoke it is in some cases impossible to draw a clear-cut conclusion.

In this situation it becomes necessary to explain the shifts made in the classification by votes on account of the remarks of the individuals who are shifted. Though Madison shifted his position during the debate, he voted and became a leading exponent of the constitutional-grant theory, and hence is still so classed. Tucker remains a legislative-grant man, but one who feared delegation of the removal power to the President.[210] Bland becomes the fifty-fourth man, as he favored removal by the President and Senate, but did not vote on any of the three motions under consideration. Boudinot is shifted from the legislative-grant to the constitutional-grant column, since his explanation of his vote leaves him a constitutional-grant man who *may* have believed in the ultimate power

[205] Notably Page (1 *Annals* 509, 540, 573, 603) and Jackson (*ibid.* 389, 576).
[206] Some instances of ambiguity, doubt, and inconsistency are mentioned below. A detailed examination would probably show other instances.
[207] See 1 *Annals* 952–955 for severe criticism by members of the way in which their remarks on the floor had been reported.
[208] See below for comment on Corwin's interpretation of Sherman's remarks.
[209] Corwin's *Removal Power* 9, 15–16, 18–21, 56–57.
[210] Tucker explained his position in 1 *Annals* 607–608.

of legislative control.²¹¹ Vining remains in the constitutional-grant column, though he admitted the ultimate legislative power of control.²¹² Ames also remains a constitutional-grant man, though in speaking he supported his argument by falling back upon legislative control as an alternative.²¹³ Sumter remains against presidential removal, on what precise grounds his remarks did not make clear.²¹⁴ Sedgwick and Lee remain legislative-grant men who nevertheless gave quasi-constitutional arguments for making the grant to the President.²¹⁵ Sherman remains against the President, but is not classed as a legislative-grant man despite some of his language.²¹⁶

Corwin lists Sylvester as belonging to the "congressional" (legislative-control) party, and then proceeds to treat him as a constitutional-grant man who believed in the ultimate power of legislative control.²¹⁷ Sylvester first took the President-and-Senate position,²¹⁸ but later changed his mind. He then stated that both appointment and removal were constitutional executive powers of the President except as the Constitution qualified the former. Yet he went on to say that Congress might vest removal in whom it pleased, and that Congress should make the decision and enable the President "to exercise the duties vested in him."²¹⁹ This trend of his thought plus his legislative-grant vote may mean that he was not entirely convinced with his own constitutional-grant argument. Hence, he is kept in the legislative-grant column.

Of the 28 men who spoke, 16 favored removal by the President alone, and 12 opposed it. Fifty-four men spoke and/or voted on at least one of the three motions.²²⁰ After making the above-mentioned shifts, the net

---

²¹¹ Boudinot's explanation of his vote may be found in *ibid*. 606. The present writer regards it as somewhat ambiguous on the point in issue, especially when read in connection with some of his earlier remarks in *ibid*. 547 and 550. For while on p. 547 he said Congress could "modify" the principles of the Constitution, but that the principle of presidential removal was to be found in the Constitution and hence would "serve as a line to direct the modification by Congress," on p. 550 he said, "I do not mean, that if it was not vested in him by the constitution, it would be proper for Congress to confer it." The present writer does not regard this as a contradiction. Apparently Boudinot thought it was all right for Congress to provide under the necessary and proper clause for removal by the President, but that this was not so much an exercise of free discretion as the implementation of a principle already implied by the Constitution. In short, his position was even more clearly than that of Sedgwick and Lee one that called, on constitutional grounds, for removal by the President alone. See also *ibid*. 390, 486, 488.
²¹² *Ibid*. 388, 398, 482, 531, 532, 595, 608.   ²¹⁴ *Ibid*. 558, 573, 614.
²¹³ *Ibid*. 492, 494, 560, 562, 564.   ²¹⁵ See below.
²¹⁶ See below, however, for the last-minute concession that Sherman should be classed as a believer in ultimate legislative control.
²¹⁷ Corwin's *Removal Power* 12 (note 22), 15.
²¹⁸ 1 *Annals*, 393.   ²¹⁹ *Ibid*. 582–585.
²²⁰ Fifty-three men voted on at least one of the three motions, while Bland spoke but voted on none of them.

result is as follows: for the President, 34;[221] against the President, 20;[222] constitutional-grant men, 16;[223] legislative-grant men, 18,[224] of whom 1 feared delegation of the power to the President;[225] for the President for unknown reasons, 1.[226] The line-up of 34 for the President and 20 against him was in totals exactly the same as that on the original or White-Page motion to strike out.

Following the lead of Corwin, one finds that at least 3 of the 16 constitutional-grant men clearly or arguably believed in the ultimate power of legislative control.[227] This makes 21 in favor of this view, which is 7 short of a majority of the 54 who participated. Since 6 constitutional-grant men voted silently,[228] and 4 of them did not express themselves on this point,[229] it is possible that some of these 10 would have supported ultimate legislative control. There were only 3 constitutional-grant men, however—Madison,[230] Benson,[231] and Moore[232]—who may reasonably be said to have positively declared that the constitutional power of removal is *illimitable*. This means that only these 3 men positively affirmed the position taken by Chief Justice Taft in the *Myers Case*.[233] As 3 out of 16 out of 54, they were, in truth, in Corwin's apt phrase, "a fraction of a fraction."[234]

The position that Congress had ultimate power of control was *tenable* by President-and-Senate men also. Corwin tries to recruit Sherman for this purpose;[235] and it will be shown below that doubts should probably be resolved in favor of this view. Bland proposed to insert in the bill, "by and with the advice and consent of the Senate," though at a time before the distinction between a legislative construction and a legislative delegation had been sharpened. He seems to have intended a legislative construction, but must be classed as doubtful.[236] The other President-and-Senate men who spoke seem, with some possible exceptions, to have argued against legislative delegation, though they may have taken this

---

[221] This number is reduced by 1 because of Tucker.
[222] This number is increased by 2 because of Tucker and Bland.
[223] This number is increased by 1 by the shift into this column of Boudinot.
[224] This number is decreased by 1 by the shift mentioned in the preceding note.
[225] That is, Tucker.   [226] That is, Huger.
[227] That is, clearly Vining and Ames, and arguably Boudinot.
[228] That is, Brown, Burke, Griffin, Muhlenberg, Sinnickson, and Leonard.
[229] That is, Baldwin, Clymer, Goodhue, and Scott.
[230] 1 *Annals* 514, 515, 569, 600, 601, 604–605.
[231] *Ibid.* 388, 397, 525, 600–601, especially 525, lines 18–32.
[232] *Ibid.* 606. The inclusion of Moore in this group is an inference which interprets his remarks in the light of his straight constitutional-grant vote.
[233] 272 U.S. 52, 164, 176 (1926). See, however, James Hart, *Tenure of Office Under the Constitution* (The Johns Hopkins Press, Baltimore, 1930) chap v.
[234] Corwin's *Removal Power* 13–14.   [235] *Ibid.* 15 (including note 30), 21.
[236] See 1 *Annals* 388–389, 394, 396–397.

THE ESTABLISHMENT OF THE GREAT DEPARTMENTS 207

position because they knew that a majority favored the President, whom they strongly opposed.[237] The survey in the note below leaves only 4 opponents of the President as seriously doubtful. It has been seen that the views of 10 constitutional-grant men are, on this point, unknown. The total number of doubtful men is thus 14. If only half of these favored legislative control, they would make up a majority for that view. But a demonstrable conclusion seems impossible.

It is worth pointing out that if *all* the 10 doubtful constitutional-grant men were on the side of the Chief Justice, he would have only 13 out of 54; while if 7 of the 10 were on the other side, they would make a majority of 28 out of 54.

The present writer is accordingly unable to affirm or deny the correctness of the conclusion that a majority favored the ultimate power of Congress to regulate tenure. While he does not deny the possibility or even the probability of such a conclusion's being correct, he does not see how its correctness can be positively demonstrated.

Corwin remarks:

> If, then, the question is, what significance the majority of congress [the House?] attributed to the bill in its final form as a reading of the constitution, the answer must be that at least they did not regard it as settling the question against the senate in such a sense that congress could not again unsettle it in the senate's favor.[238]

This ingenious conclusion is probably true. Its acceptance requires only the assumptions: (1) that, though most of those who accepted the theory of legislative control favored vesting the power in the President, at least two of them so strongly that they almost said the logic of the Constitution called for such a solution, nevertheless they must all have admitted, in the last analysis, that Congress had discretion to vest this power in the President and Senate; and (2) that the President-and-Senate men would have gone along (or expected their successors in some future Congress to go along) with a bill which undertook to *vest*

---

[237] In this connection, the 12 opponents of the President who spoke may be considered together. The following stated expressly that Congress could not give the President the power to remove the Secretary of Foreign Affairs: Jackson (*ibid.* 391); White (*ibid.* 533, 536, 537); Smith of South Carolina (*ibid.* 528, 567–568); Gerry (*ibid.* 491, 521, 522, 523, 524, 558, 596, 598, 606, but cf. 557); Livermore (*ibid.* 498, 566, but cf. 496); Huntington (*ibid.* 477); Stone (*ibid.* 586–590); Page (*ibid.* 399, 509, 539, 570, but cf. 571, which seems inconsistent or else garbled in reporting). Sherman (see below) and Sumter (*ibid.* 614) remain doubtful; and Tucker has already been counted as a legislative-grant man. Bland is classed as doubtful in the text above. The only seriously doubtful men are thus Page, Sherman, Sumter, and Bland. If all of them were classed as for ultimate legislative control, the total would be only 25, and 3 recruits would be needed from the constitutional-grant men whose views on the point are unknown.

[238] Corwin's *Removal Power* 16. See also *ibid.* 19–22.

the power in the President and Senate, much as the legislative-grant men went along with a bill which *recognized* a *constitutional* power of removal in the President. This hypothetical coalition of divergent views, however, is but analogous to the actual coalition of divergent views which finally accepted the constitutional-grant language in the three bills. Both coalitions have the common weakness that neither represents demonstrated agreement upon the same theory on the part of any 28 of the 54 men considered. Corwin's coalition merely proves what his demolition of the Chief Justice's coalition proves: that the decision of the House fixed neither an unambiguous nor an irreversible precedent for the future. Since, however, nothing succeeds like success, the Chief Justice's coalition has this historic advantage over Corwin's, that it did enact the constitutional-grant language in all three bills and thus establish the constitutional-grant theory as the working theory of our constitutional system, unless and until later changed by valid congressional action. The effect of this fact upon the course of our constitutional history was undeniably profound.

The constitutional-grant bloc was, on any count, less than a third of the total. How, then, did it put across in the bill language which supported its theory? The answer lies in the parliamentary strategy of Benson.[239] Of the 30 members who voted for his first motion, 15 have been classed as constitutional-grant men and 15 as legislative-grant men. Of the 31 who voted for his second motion, 15 have been listed as constitutional-grant men, and 16 have been listed as against removal by the President. Of the 29 who voted for final passage of the bill, 14 have been listed as constitutional-grant men, 14 have been listed as legislative-grant men, and 1 has been listed as for the President. In a word, the constitutional-grant men voted for all three motions, and were joined in turn on the first Benson motion *and* final passage by the core of the legislative-grant men, and on the second Benson motion by those who opposed removal by the President alone. The principal alignment in the last analysis was between those who favored and those who opposed removal by the President alone. For after voting against the second Benson motion the core of legislative-grant men went along with the constitutional-grant men on final passage.

Why did Madison shift from the legislative-grant to the constitutional-grant theory? The hypothesis is advanced that when he first embraced the legislative-grant view he visualized simply a statutory provision for *presidential* removal, but that when Sherman had seemed to state the legislative-grant theory in terms of *full* legislative discretion as to *who*

[239] See *Thach* 153–155.

might be given the power, Madison concluded that it was more in harmony with the general spirit of the Constitution as well as sound policy to base the President's power upon the solid rock of the Constitution. What other explanation is there for his otherwise remarkable statement that Sherman's theory had not been before advanced? [240]

If this hypothesis be accepted, it suggests that the line was not sharp in Madison's mind between sound constitutional theory and sound public policy. One explanation may be that Madison, the representative of 1789, had been Madison, the framer, only two years before, and was now dealing with a subject which the framers had obviously left to dubious inference. A more general explanation, however, is the obvious one. The fact is noted by Corwin that what Madison himself called the *argumentum ab inconvenientibus* [241] was prominent in the debate,[242] as it regularly is in congressional debates on constitutional issues. By the orthodox rule of construction, such arguments are supposed to be given no weight; but *Corpus Juris* says that consequences, while not to be taken into account when the legislative intention is plain from the language, may be considered when such intention is but "inadequately or vaguely expressed." [243] We have the authority of Mr. Justice Holmes for the conclusion that views of public policy rather than logic determine great constitutional decisions even of the courts.[244] Is it not generally true that a man's choice between *debatable* constitutional positions is, *and ought to be,* determined by the fact that the position chosen rather than the alternative seems to be the better means to nonlegal ends which seem paramount? [245] Mr. Jefferson, indeed, once stated in a legal opinion

[240] See 1 *Annals* 515.
[241] Madison to Samuel Johnston, June 21, 1789. 5 *The Writings of James Madison* (Hunt ed., G. P. Putnam's Sons, New York and London, 1904) 410.
[242] Corwin's *Removal Power* 13. Corwin's reference is to the constitutional-grant arguments, but does not the same apply to other arguments also?
[243] 59 *Corpus Juris* (William Mack and Donald J. Kiser, eds., The American Law Book Co., New York, Butterworth & Co., London, 1932) "Statutes," § 574. The legislative intent is also to be derived from the act as a whole. *Ibid.* § 594. On the other hand, in connection with the relation of the opening sentence of Article II of the Constitution to the clause authorizing the President to require the opinion in writing of the principal officer in each of the executive departments, *ibid.* § 596, which deals with conflicting clauses, says that general and particular clauses should be harmonized, if possible, but that a particular clause overrides a general one with which it is in conflict, except where the "statute as a whole" makes it clear that this would defeat the intent of the legislature. See section below (p. 239) entitled, "An Interpretation of the Administrative Legislation of the First Session in Terms of Its Underlying Administrative Theory."
[244] Oliver Wendell Holmes, "The Path of the Law," *Collected Legal Papers* (Harcourt, Brace and Co., New York, 1921) 180–184.
[245] *Cf.* James Hart, *Tenure of Office Under the Constitution* (The Johns Hopkins Press, Baltimore, 1930). *Cf.* William Draper Lewis, *Interpreting the Constitution* (The Michie Co., Charlottesville, Va., 1937) 48–50.

that the *argumentum ab inconvenienti* is one of the great foundations of the law.[246] The argument is questionable, therefore, by which Corwin discounts on this score the reasoning of most of the constitutional-grant men as based upon expediency.[247]

The case of Vining supports Corwin's refutation of the interpretation of the decision by Chief Justice Taft.[248] Vining voted as a straight constitutional-grant man. On the floor, he supported this view, but also used language which seemed to fall back upon the legislative-grant theory as an alternative.[249] He also explained his vote by saying he "acquiesced" in the second Benson motion because he was satisfied the Constitution vested the power in the President and thought the clause more apt to obtain the acquiescence of the Senate as a legislative construction than as a positive relinquishment of power that body might otherwise think itself in some degree entitled to.[250] Clearly Vining cannot be said to have given a contemporaneous construction[251] to the effect that the President is vested by the Constitution with an *illimitable* power of removal *even* of the Secretary of Foreign Affairs.

On the other hand, Corwin fails to point out some significant remarks of Sedgwick and Lee. The former was a leading spokesman of the legislative-grant school, and he so voted. At one point, however, he said:

> It appears to me that such a body [the Senate] is more likely to misuse this power than the man whom the united voice of America calls to the Presidential chair. As the nature of the Government requires the power of removal, I think it is to be exercised in this way by a hand capable of exerting it with effect, and *the power must be conferred upon the President by* [in accordance with?] *the constitution, as the executive officer of the Government.*[252]

If this statement be thought ambiguous, one may quote Sedgwick's remarks on the Benson motions:

> If I understand the subject rightly, there seem to be two opinions dividing the majority of this House. Some of these gentlemen seem to suppose that, by the constitution, and by implication and certain deduction from the principles of the constitution, the power vests in the President. Others think it

---

[246] 5 *Writings of Thomas Jefferson* (Washington ed., Derby & Jackson, New York, 1859) 370–371.
[247] See note 242 above, and Madison's comment in defense in 1 *Annals* 601.
[248] Corwin's *Removal Power* 12 (note 22), 15, 16 (note 31).
[249] 1 *Annals* 388, 531–532, 595.
[250] *Ibid.* 608.
[251] See Jacobus tenBroek, "Use by the United States Supreme Court of Extrinsic Aids in Constitutional Construction," 27 *Calif. L. Rev.* 157, 171, 174–179 (1939).
[252] 1 *Annals* 479. Cf. *ibid.* 479, 542–543, 565, 605–606. Italics are supplied by the present writer.

is a matter of legislative determination, *and that they must give it to the President on the principles of the constitution.* . . .[253]

Did this not mean that the spirit, if not the law, of the Constitution called for the vesting of the power to remove at least the Secretary of Foreign Affairs in the President alone? It is quite true that at another point Sedgwick said that

The power of creating offices is given to the Legislature. Under this general grant, the Legislature have it under their supreme decision to determine the whole organization, to affix the tenure, and declare the control. . . . So the Legislature may determine that an office may be held three, five, or seven years; to be removable by the President, the President and Senate, or the Legislature, or any other person whom they might introduce into office, merely for that particular purpose.[254]

This statement is not consistent with the two previously quoted. Though it, rather than they, may represent Sedgwick's strictly legal view, can it not be said that, in the instant case, at least, he favored vesting the power in the President not only as a matter of policy but as practically called for by the logic of the Constitution? Such a view must have gone far in reconciling Sedgwick in voting for final passage of the bill. Does it not work, at least in some degree, in at least a moral or quasi-legal sense, against using Sedgwick to support the claim that Congress may properly vest the removal of the Secretary of State in the President by and with the advice and consent of the Senate?

Lee thought, at least at first, that the Secretary of Foreign Affairs was an inferior officer.[255] Even so, he said it was the duty of the Legislature to modify offices to make them conform to the general spirit of the Constitution.[256] The views of Ames, Vining, Sylvester, and Boudinot also suggest that they would have thought that, in the assumption by Congress of legislative control, it would be contrary to the "spirit" of the Constitution to vest the removal of the Secretary of Foreign Affairs, at least, anywhere but in the President. There are thus in all at least 6 men to whom this consideration is pertinent, and to them *may* belong some other constitutional and legislative-grant men whose precise views are unknown. Corwin has thus somewhat overworked his case against the Chief Justice.

Nor does the present writer interpret Sherman's remarks precisely as Corwin does and as Madison apparently did. Corwin holds that Sherman thought the President and Senate could remove in the absence

[253] *Ibid.* 602. Italics are supplied by the present writer.
[254] *Ibid.* 541–542.   [255] *Ibid.* 386.   [256] *Ibid.* 545–546.

of legislation, but that Congress had the ultimate power to regulate the matter,[257] though he admits that at one point Sherman expressed "doubt" on the latter question. The present writer, however, finds Sherman himself either self-contradictory or more readily made consistent on the theory that he rejected ultimate legislative control.[258] Yet in Corwin's favor are Madison's contemporaneous understanding of Sherman's remarks and the fact that in the Philadelphia Convention Sherman had advocated legislative supremacy.[259] It is believed that it is fairer to concede this President-and-Senate man to the column of those who believed in ultimate legislative control; but this concession does not materially alter the general picture.

Thach has pointed out that in both houses together there were 19 framers, of whom only 2 out of 8 in the House and 4 out of 11 in the Senate opposed removal by the President.[260] Thus 13 of the 19 framers

[257] Corwin's *Removal Power* 15 (text and note 30), 21.
[258] In 1 *Annals* 510–511 Sherman considered it an "established principle" that the power which appoints may also remove. Then he said that if the Secretary was an inferior officer, Congress "may vest the appointment in the President alone, and the removal will be in him of consequence. But if this reasoning be not admitted, we can by no means vest the appointment, or removal either, in the Chief Magistrate alone. As the officer is the mere creature of the Legislature, we may form it under such regulations as we please, . . ." Now this last statement seems in flat contradiction with the one immediately preceding, unless it be assumed that the language was garbled in reporting, and that the last statement referred back to the alternative assumption that the Secretary was an inferior officer, and expressed ultimate legislative control for such officers. It is worth noting that this last statement was explained in words which rather seem to have impressed Madison with the startling potentialities of the legislative-grant position. Sherman continued: "We may say he shall hold his office during good behavior, or that he shall be annually elected. We may say he shall be displaced for neglect of duty, and point out how he shall be convicted of it; without calling upon the President or Senate." In *ibid.* 559 he said: "Some gentlemen suppose, if the President has not the power by the constitution, we ought to vest it in him by law. For my part, I very much doubt if we have the power to do this." This is consistent with the interpretation suggested above and inconsistent with the idea that the Secretary was a mere creature of the law. But at a later point (*ibid.* 599) Sherman said: "If gentlemen will consent to make a general law, declaring the proper mode of removal, I think we should acquire a greater degree of unanimity, which, on this occasion, must be better than carrying the question against a large minority." This was inconsistent with the preceding "doubt," and may be explicable as a mere gesture to defeat Benson's parliamentary strategy. On the interpretation here suggested, Sherman thought removal followed appointment, but that, while Congress might regulate the tenure of inferior officers, it could not vest the removal of superior officers in the President alone. On Corwin's interpretation, Sherman believed in ultimate legislative control when he uttered one sentence, despite the fact that his preceding sentence had declared that Congress could not vest removal of a superior officer in the President alone. The present writer readily admits, however, that his own interpretation is strained, and yields to Corwin's position for reasons stated in the text.
[259] 1 Max Farrand, *The Records of the Federal Convention of 1787* (rev. ed. in 4 vols., Yale University Press, New Haven, 1937) 68.
[260] *Thach* 141–142, 157–159. The present writer has varied Thach's figures to include Senator King, of New York, who was not present for the first crucial votes (*ibid.* 142, note 1), but who, as noted below, voted for removal by the President in the final showdown on the *Treasury* bill.

were in favor of removal by the President, though of the 6 of these who were members of the House, 3 have been listed as legislative-grant men.

No effort is made to classify the individual senators with reference to the four main theories or their attitudes to the ultimate power of legislative control.[261] Even for the House, the classification made is not offered as conclusive; and while *more* men may have believed in the *ultimate* power of legislative control in the cases of the Secretary of War and especially of the Treasury, than in the case of the Secretary of Foreign Affairs, it is evident that the *voting* lines held pretty firm in the one case and at least sufficiently firm in the other.

SUMMARY OF GENERAL CONCLUSIONS ON THE "LEGISLATIVE DECISION OF 1789." Concerning this historic decision certain of the general conclusions which the above analysis has produced may be thus summarized:

(1) Made as it was by the very first session of Congress under the Constitution, which contained a dozen and a half framers, this decision has necessarily been the starting point of all serious discussion of the issues involved.

(2) So far as the legislative product is concerned, it supports the constitutional-grant theory, *though not necessarily against the theory of ultimate legislative control.*

(3) When to this fact is added the great prestige of Madison, it is not surprising that the decision has been taken, by those like Chief Justice Taft who approach it with strong convictions in favor of the President, to support also the idea that the President's power of removal is illimitable.

(4) Only a trifling minority of the House supported the impeachment theory.

(5) A clear minority of the House favored removal by the President and Senate.

(6) A clear *majority* of the House favored removal by the President alone.

(7) A clear minority of less than a third of the House favored the constitutional-grant theory either as the exclusive constitutional mode of

[261] Ellsworth seems clearly to have been a constitutional-grant man, while Maclay seems to have been an impeachment man who yet insisted on the President-and-Senate theory as the alternative. See above (p. 184), section entitled, "Maclay on the Senate debate on the removal power." For the rest, see Maclay, and 3 *The Works of John Adams* (Charles Francis Adams, ed., Little and Brown, Boston, 1851) 408–412, which was used by Thach.

removing superior officers or as the construction which should prevail in the absence of legislation.

(8) Only a trifling minority of 3 members of the House can be said to have *expressly* taken the position enunciated by Chief Justice Taft in the *Myers Case*, that the constitutional power of the President is illimitable; though there may have been others who actually held this view.

(9) Whether those in the House who viewed tenure of office as *per se* a matter for legislative determination, plus those who viewed it as a matter which the legislature might control if it saw fit, constituted a majority, the present writer is not prepared to deny or affirm.

(10) Some legislative-grant men in the House were so much in favor of vesting the power in the President that at times they came near saying it was a moral or quasi-legal duty of Congress so to vest it.

(11) For what it may be worth, one gets a majority by adding together those who favored the President-and-Senate theory presumably on constitutional grounds and those who favored the legislative-grant theory but who were dead against delegating the power to the President and Senate, and some of whom almost said Congress was bound on constitutional principles to delegate the power to remove at pleasure to the President alone.

(12) The tenure which actually resulted for all three department heads and most other officers was indefinite tenure at the pleasure of the President.

(13) Since the main argument in favor of this tenure was the need for a sanction for the administrative direction of the President, the argument did not necessarily apply, as Madison himself pointed out in connection with the comptroller, if the functions of the officer partook so much of a judicial quality as to make presidential interference with his decisions improper; and hence the way was still open to the claim that, in such cases, Congress might with full propriety determine tenure as an incident of creating the office and under the necessary and proper clause.

COMPARISON OF THE TREASURY WITH THE OTHER TWO DEPARTMENTS

FEDERALIST IDEAS VERSUS A TRADITION OF FREE GOVERNMENT. The Treasury Department was closely associated, in the tradition of free government, with the idea that control of the purse strings was an especial prerogative of the people's representatives. In the mother country the power of the purse had been a powerful weapon in the long struggle for parliamentary supremacy, the final stages of which had taken place in the first century of American colonial history.[262] This important phase of English constitutional history had been reenacted in the colonies themselves in the use of the power of the purse by the colonial assemblies in their own struggle for power with royal governors.[263] The debates which had preceded the Declaration of Independence had in no small degree centered around the colonial contention that it was against both natural law and the British constitution for them to be taxed without the consent of their chosen representatives.[264] Under the Articles of Confederation Congress, though it had had no taxing power, had been the supreme federal organ of financial as of other administration, and both the Superintendent of Finance and the Board of Treasury had been mere congressional agents.[265] The framers of the Constitution had made a gesture in the direction of the tradition when they had provided that all bills for raising revenue should originate in the House of Representatives; though even this gesture had grown primarily out of the conflict between the large and small states; and Madison had vigorously protested that the Senate's power of amendment made it no real concession to the former.[266]

Any idea, however, that legislative control of the purse included control of financial administration was in direct conflict with the Federalist idea of a unitary, independent, and "responsible" executive.[267] Indeed, these two conflicting ideas had met in a head-on collision in the Constitutional Convention of 1787, with victory for popular tradition snatched away by a last-minute reversal in favor of the Federalist idea. The story is worth recounting as a background to a comparison between the Treasury and the other two departments as established by Congress in 1789. In the report of the Committee of Detail one of the enumerated

[262] Coke was a contemporary of the founders of the first permanent English settlement at Jamestown, Virginia, in 1607, and the English Bill of Rights came in 1689.
[263] Evarts Boutell Greene, *The Provincial Governor in the English Colonies of North America* (Harvard Historical Studies, VII, Harvard University Press, Cambridge, 1898) 166–176.
[264] See Henry Steele Commager, *Documents of American History* (2d ed., F. S. Crofts & Co., New York, 1940) 58, 83, 100–101.
[265] *Cf.* Jay Caesar Guggenheimer, "The Development of the Executive Departments, 1775–1789," in J. Franklin Jameson (ed.), *Essays in the Constitutional History of the United States in the Formative Period, 1775–1789* (Houghton, Mifflin and Co., Boston, 1889) 116, 129–137, 154–160.
[266] 1 Max Farrand, ed., *The Records of the Federal Convention of 1787* (rev. ed. in 4 vols., Yale University Press, New Haven, 1937) 527–529.
[267] See references in notes 88, 94, and 106 above, and in notes 308, 321, and 328 below. See especially Lynton K. Caldwell, *The Administrative Theories of Hamilton and Jefferson* (University of Chicago Press, Chicago, 1944) *passim.*

powers of Congress had been, "To appoint a Treasurer by ballot."[268] In considering this report it had been voted, 7 states to 3, to make it a "joint ballot." Read had moved to strike out the clause,

leaving the appointment of the Treasurer as of other officers to the Executive. The Legislature was an improper body for appointments. Those of the State legislatures were a proof of it—The Executive being responsible would make a good choice.

George Mason, on the other hand,

in opposition to Mr. Read's motion desired it might be considered to whom the money would belong; if to the people, the legislature representing the people ought to appoint the keepers of it.

Read's motion to strike out lost by a vote of 4 states in favor and 6 against.[269] The clause was thus in the proceedings as submitted to the Committee of Style [270] and remained in the draft of the Constitution as reported by that Committee.[271] On the very last day of the Convention, September 14, however, it was moved to strike out this power. The mover, Mr. Rutledge, wanted to "let the Treasurer be appointed in the same manner as other officers." Gorham and King warned that the people were "accustomed & attached to that mode of appointing Treasurers." Gouverneur Morris countered that a Treasurer not appointed by the Legislature would be "more narrowly watched, and more readily impeached." Sherman wanted legislative appointment, but by separate rather than joint votes. General Pinckney said the scheme was in operation in South Carolina, but the Legislature made bad appointments and would "not listen to the faults of their own officer." The motion to strike out was carried by a vote of 8 states to 3.[272]

THE CONTROVERSY BETWEEN THE TWO HOUSES OVER THE REMOVAL CLAUSE OF THE TREASURY BILL. The House readily agreed to the Senate amendments to the Foreign Affairs and War bills;[273] but a controversy developed between the two houses on the removal clause in the Treasury bill. The House agreed to all Senate amendments except that relating to the crucial removal power.[274] The Senate then insisted

---

[268] 2 Max Farrand, ed., *The Records of the Federal Convention* of 1787 (rev. ed. in 4 vols., Yale University Press, New Haven, 1937) 182.
[269] Ibid. 314–315.   [271] Ibid. 594.   [273] 1 Annals 685, 702.
[270] Ibid. 570.   [272] Ibid. 614.
[274] Ibid. 701, 702. The House formally "Resolved, That this House doth agree to so much of the eighth amendment, as proposes to strike out these words in the seventh clause in the bill, to wit, 'The assistant to the Secretary of the Treasury shall be appointed by the President;' and doth disagree to such other part of the said amendment, as proposes to strike out the residue of the clause." The seventh section of the law as enacted was the removal clause.

THE ESTABLISHMENT OF THE GREAT DEPARTMENTS 217

upon its amendment "respecting the removability of the Secretary by the President."[275] The House called for a conference.[276] The Senate agreed to the conference and appointed managers. On August 23 Mr. Madison reported verbally for the House managers. He said that the Senate managers had stated the reasons for their amendment, which not being satisfactory to the House managers, they had submitted certain propositions, while the Senate managers had offered none. He further reported that it was the opinion of the committee that it would not be right for the House to recede.[277] Then the House voted to adhere. This deadlock was broken, however, in a way recorded by Maclay on August 26:

I forgot to minute yesterday that the Treasury bill was taken up. A number of the Senate had recanted again on this bill, and were against the power of the President's removing, and had answered accordingly. The House of Representatives sent us up an adherence, and now Mr. Morris proposed to me to leave the House. I would neither do this nor change my mind, and he was angry. . . .[278]

On August 25 the Senate notified the House that it had receded.[279] The Benson removal clause had won even with respect to the Secretary of the Treasury.

Maclay indicates that "a number" of senators who had favored presidential removal of the *other* Secretaries were at first against his removal of the Secretary of the *Treasury*. When the House adhered to its position, however, the vote of the Senate to recede was a tie of 10 to 10,

[275] *Ibid.* 705.
[276] *Ibid.* 715. The House appointed Madison as the first of the three managers for the House.
[277] *Ibid.* 808.
[278] *Journal of William Maclay* 133.
[279] 1 *Annals* 73. When the Senate considered the resolve of the House to adhere to the removal clause, the vote was 10 to 10 on the motion to recede, and the Vice President determined the question in the affirmative. So it was "*Resolved,* that the Senate do *recede* from so much of the eighth amendment as was disagreed to by the House of Representatives."
Since the yeas and nays were called for, the vote by which the Senate thus yielded is recorded as follows: yeas—Bassett, Carroll, Ellsworth, Elmer, Henry, King, Morris, Paterson, Read, and Schuyler; nays—Butler, Dalton, Few, Gunn, Johnson, Izard, Langdon, Lee, Maclay, and Wingate. This vote may be compared with the earlier vote on the same clause in the Foreign Affairs bill as given by Maclay: for striking out—Butler, Izard, Langdon, Johnson, Wingate, Few, Gunn, Grayson, Lee, and Maclay; against striking out—Read, Bassett, Ellsworth, Strong, Dalton, Paterson, Elmer, Morris, Henry, and Carroll. *Journal of William Maclay* 113-114. The comparison shows that on the *later* vote the removal clause gained the two votes of the senators from New York, who had not taken their seats when the former vote was taken (see 1 *Annals* 53; Thach 142, note 1) and lost the vote of Dalton, who was now on the other side, as well as the vote of Strong, who did not vote; whereas the opponents of the removal clause gained Dalton but lost Grayson, who did not vote.

which the Vice President broke in favor of presidential power. In this final showdown all the original presidential supporters held firm except two, one of whom did not vote. This loss was made up for by the votes of the two senators from New York, one of whom had been a framer.[280]

No Final Distinction with Respect to Removal. At the outset of consideration of the departments, Livermore asked why the Department of Foreign Affairs

was placed at the head of the list. He thought the Treasury Department of more importance, and consequently deserved the precedence.[281]

At a later point, in the removal debate, Jackson remarked that the business

had been ingeniously brought forward; for the committee have taken care to bring in the present bill, previous to the bill for organizing the Treasury, that the principle might be established before the more delicate business came into view.[282]

This implied a distinction between the Treasury Department and the other two, which is usually understood to be the distinction between the function of executing the laws of Congress under its power of the purse and the function of serving as "administrative arms"[283] of the President in the carrying out of his constitutional executive powers.[284] It is to be carefully noted, however, that by the final decision the Secretary of the Treasury was to hold office no less than the other two secretaries during the pleasure of the President. This implied that he, too, was understood to be under the administrative direction of the President. For the power of removal was meant to be the sanction of the President's power of over-all administrative direction.[285] Thach has pointed out that

the debate was on the right to remove, that this right extended to all three departments, and that the principles determining the ultimate decision were of a general character, applying to all administrative business alike.[286]

There was certainly no distinction with respect to removal in the bills as enacted finally into law.

---

[280] See the preceding note.   [281] 1 *Annals* 386.   [282] *Ibid.* 550.
[283] "The argument of convenience is strong in favor of the President; for this man [the Secretary of Foreign Affairs] is an *arm* or an *eye* to him; he sees and writes his secret despatches, he is an instrument over which the President ought to have a complete command."–Vining in 1 *Annals* 531. Italics are supplied by the present writer. *Cf.*, at the level of over-all administrative management, the *Report of the President's Committee on Administrative Management* (Government Printing Office, Washington, 1937) 4.
[284] Thach 144, 148–149, 160.   [285] *Ibid.* 158–159.   [286] *Ibid.* 144.

THE ESTABLISHMENT OF THE GREAT DEPARTMENTS

Departments and "Executive" Departments. There was, however, a distinction between the language of the acts creating the Departments of Foreign Affairs and of War and the act creating the Department of the Treasury which can hardly have been accidental. The first act began:

> That there shall be an executive department, to be denominated the department of foreign affairs, and that there shall be a principal officer therein, to be called the secretary for the department of foreign affairs, . . .[287]

The second act began:

> That there shall be an executive department, to be denominated the department of war; and that there shall be a principal officer therein, to be called the secretary for the department of war, . . .[288]

But the third act began:

> That there shall be a department of treasury, in which shall be the following officers, namely; a secretary of the treasury, to be deemed head of the department; . . .[289]

Furthermore, throughout the first two acts the secretaries are referred to as "the said principal officer," while the third act refers to the secretary of the treasury always by that title.

Thach points out this distinction, but notes something to which he attaches significance: that in the salary act entitled "An act for establishing the salaries of the *executive* officers of government, with their assistants and clerks," the first salary provided was that for the Secretary of the Treasury.[290] But while this provision shows that the terminological distinction was not consistently adhered to, the fact remains that it was made; and it is scarcely plausible to doubt that it had a purpose.

The second section of the salary act authorized *"the heads of the three departments first above mentioned"* to appoint necessary clerks at maximum salaries.[291] It will be suggested below, however, that there was here no inconsistency, since all three were *department heads*, while only the Secretaries of Foreign Affairs and of War were the *principal officers* in *executive* departments.

The source of the distinction in language between departments and "executive" departments is presumably the text of the Constitution itself. Article II, section 2, in its first paragraph, provides:

---

[287] 2 *Laws of the United States* 6.   [288] *Ibid.* 32.   [289] *Ibid.* 48.
[290] Thach 144, 158. See 2 *Laws of the United States* 50. Italics are supplied by the present writer.
[291] 2 *Laws of the United States* 51. Italics are supplied by the present writer.

The President . . . may require the Opinion, in writing, of the principal Officer in each of the Executive Departments, upon any Subject relating to the Duties of their respective Offices, . . .

The same section, in its second paragraph, declares:

. . . but the Congress may by Law vest the Appointment of such inferior Officers, as they think proper, in the President alone, in the Courts of Law, or in the Heads of Departments.

Here is the same pattern that was later followed in the organic acts, though not in the salary act, of 1789: *executive* departments with *principal officers*, and *departments* with *heads*. The repetition of the pattern in the organic acts is hardly a coincidence.

THE STATUTORY DUTIES OF THE FIRST THREE DEPARTMENT HEADS. The organic acts which created the first three departments defined the duties of the Secretaries of Foreign Affairs and of War in terms quite different from those employed in defining the duties of the Secretary of the Treasury. The act of July 27, 1789, provided that the secretary for the department of foreign affairs

shall perform and execute such duties as shall, from time to time, be enjoined on or entrusted to him by the president of the United States, agreeable to the constitution, relative to correspondences, commissions, or instructions, to or with public ministers or consuls, from the United States, or to negociations with public ministers from foreign states or princes, or to memorials or other applications from foreign public ministers, or other foreigners, or to such other matters respecting foreign affairs as the president of the United States shall assign to the said department: And furthermore, that the said principal officer shall conduct the business of the said department in such manner as the president of the United States shall, from time to time, order or instruct.[292]

The act of August 7, 1789, provided that the secretary for the department of war

shall perform and execute such duties as shall, from time to time, be enjoined on, or entrusted to, him, by the president of the United States, agreeably to the constitution, relative to military commissions, or to the land or naval forces, ships, or warlike stores, of the United States, or to such other matters respecting military or naval affairs, as the president of the United States shall assign to the said department, or relative to the granting of lands to persons entitled thereto, for military services rendered to the United States, or relative to Indian affairs: And furthermore, that the said principal officer shall conduct the business of the said department, in such manner as the president of the United States shall, from time to time, order or instruct.[293]

[292] 2 *Laws of the United States* 6.   [293] *Ibid.* 32.

THE ESTABLISHMENT OF THE GREAT DEPARTMENTS

On the other hand, the act of September 2, 1789, declared:

That it shall be the duty of the secretary of the treasury to digest and prepare plans for the improvement and management of the revenue, and for the support of public credit; to prepare and report estimates of the public revenue, and the public expenditures; to superintend the collection of the revenue; to decide on the forms of keeping and stating accounts and making returns, and to grant, under the limitations herein established, or to be hereafter provided, all warrants for moneys to be issued from the treasury, in pursuance of appropriations by law; to execute such services relative to the sale of the lands belonging to the United States, as may be by law required of him; to make report, and give information, to either branch of the legislature, in person or in writing, (as he may be required), respecting all matters referred to him by the senate or house of representatives, or which shall appertain to his office; and, generally, to perform all such services, relative to the finances, as he shall be directed to perform.[294]

Examination of these provisions reveals that Congress defined the duties of the Secretaries of Foreign Affairs and of War as obedience to the will of the President with regard to both the "line" and "auxiliary"[295] functions involved, respectively, in the conduct of foreign relations and in command of the armed services; but that, on the other hand, it defined the duties of the Secretary of the Treasury in terms of administration of the revenue, appropriation, and land laws of Congress, and of assisting that body, by information, estimates, and planning reports, in the execution of its constitutional financial powers, with apparently[296] not a word about presidential directives.

STATUTORY DUTIES OF THE SUBORDINATE OFFICERS IN THE FIRST THREE DEPARTMENTS. The acts creating the Departments of Foreign Affairs and of War provided for only one officer besides the principal officer. In both cases he was to be

an inferior officer, to be appointed by the said principal officer, and to be employed therein as he shall deem proper, and to be called the chief clerk . . .[297]

[294] *Ibid.* 48.
[295] See Leonard D. White, *Introduction to the Study of Public Administration* (rev. ed., The Macmillan Co., New York, 1939) 40–43, 73–82.
[296] The word "apparently" is used advisedly on the assumption that "and, generally, to perform all such services, relative to the finances, as he shall be directed to perform," referred to directions from Congress or either house, rather than the President. Whatever the purport of this language, however, the power of removal was recognized as the sanction of the President's power of direction. See *Thach* 144, 158–159.
[297] This is the language of the Foreign Affairs bill. 2 *Laws of the United States* 7. The wording in this respect of the War bill was identical except for the omission of a superfluous "and." *Ibid.* 32–33.

The act establishing the Treasury Department authorized the Secretary of the Treasury to appoint an Assistant to the Secretary of the Treasury,[298] whose duties were not specified, but who was obviously meant to be the administrative subordinate of the Secretary and under his orders.

Again, the salary act of September 11, 1789, provided:

That the heads of the three departments first above mentioned shall appoint such clerks therein, respectively, as they shall find necessary; and the salary of the said clerks, respectively, shall not exceed the rate of five hundred dollars per annum.[299]

Otherwise, however, there was a notable distinction between the Treasury Department and the other two. The act for collection of duties had already provided for collectors, naval officers, and surveyors, and had prescribed their respective duties in considerable detail.[300] Then in the act creating the Treasury Department, the Secretary was empowered to "superintend the collection of the revenue,"[301] and thus was made the administrative superior of these customs officers.

With respect to fiscal administration, the Treasury act created a comptroller, a treasurer, an auditor, and a register, and defined the functions of each of them,[302] as well as the functions of the Secretary. In this connection it is pertinent to quote the opinions of two members of the House. In the discussion, to be considered below, of whether the Treasury Department should be headed by a single officer or by a board, Baldwin remarked:

. . . He was persuaded there was not so much responsibility in boards as there was in individuals, nor is there such good ground for the exercise of the talents of a financier in that way. Boards were generally more destitute of energy than was an individual placed at the head of a Department. The observations of the gentleman from Massachusetts [Gerry] were of great weight, so far as they inferred the necessity of proper checks in the department having care of the public money; if they had system, energy, and responsibility, he should be in favor of them; but his experience had convinced him of the contrary. He was not an advocate for an unlimited authority in this officer. He hoped to see proper checks provided; a Comptroller, Auditors, Register, and Treasurer. He would not suffer the Secretary to touch a farthing of the public money beyond his salary. The settling of the accounts should be in the Auditors and Comptroller; the registering them to be in another officer, and the cash in the hands of one unconnected with either.

[298] Ibid. 48, 50.   [299] Ibid. 51.
[300] See above (p. 190), the section of this study entitled, "The question of the scope of the President's power of removal under the 'legislative decision of 1789.'"
[301] 2 *Laws of the United States* 48.   [302] Ibid. 48–50.

THE ESTABLISHMENT OF THE GREAT DEPARTMENTS 223

He was satisfied that in this way the treasury might be safe, and great improvements made in the business of revenue.[303]

Madison spoke to the same effect:

... He wished, in all cases of an executive nature, that the committee should consider the powers that were to be exercised, and where that power was too great to be trusted to an individual, proper care should be taken so to regulate and check the exercise, as would give indubitable security for the perfect preservation of the public interest, and to prevent that suspicion which men of integrity were ever desirous of avoiding. This was his intention in the present case. If the committee agreed to his proposition [for a single head to be removable by the President], he intended to introduce principles of caution, which he supposed would give satisfaction on that point. As far as was practicable, he would have the various business of this important branch of the Government divided and modified, so as to lull at least the jealousy expressed by the gentleman from Massachusetts; indeed he supposed, with the assistance of the committee, it might be formed so as to give satisfaction. He had no doubt that the officers might be so constituted as to restrain and check each other; and unless an unbounded combination took place, which he could by no means suppose was likely to be the case, that the public would be safe and secure under the administration. ...

If a board is established, the independent officers of Comptroller and Auditor are unknown; you then give the aggregate of these powers to the board, the members of which are equal; therefore you give more power to each individual than is proposed to be entrusted in the Secretary; and if apprehensions are to be entertained of a combination, they apply as forcibly in the case of two or three commissioners combining, as they do in the case of the Secretary, Comptroller, and other officers. If gentlemen permit these sentiments to have their full weight, and consider the advantages arising from energy, system, and responsibility, which were all in favor of his motion, he had no doubt of their according with him on this question.[304]

THE TREASURY DEPARTMENT: SINGLE HEAD OR BOARD OF TREASURY? When the Committee of the Whole came to consider the creation of the Treasury Department, Gerry thought they were hurrying too rapidly. He wanted the reasons why this department should be organized differently from what it had been under the late Congress.[305] So he moved to postpone for consideration of the War Department. Goodhue said "it was not obvious whether the department should be placed under one

[303] 1 Annals 408. May 20, 1789. [304] Ibid. 408–409.
[305] Ibid. 399–412. May 19–20, 1789. See 1 Max Farrand, *The Records of the Federal Convention of 1787* (rev. ed. in 4 vols., Yale University Press, New Haven, 1937) 111 for George Mason's assumption, on June 4 (probably), that the new government would have board organization, at least in part.

man, or a Board of Commissioners." Benson objected that postponement was against the rules, but said the committee of the whole might rise. He declared "his sentiment to be in favor of a single head of this department, rather than three; but he would have the principal officer well checked in the execution of his trust."

The next day Gerry again raised the issue of a single individual versus a board. Of a single head he said:

If he is disposed to embezzle the public money, it will be out of the power of the Executive itself to check or control him in his nefarious practices.

He then proceeded to paint a dark picture. A single head would have "abundant opportunities for peculation" and "innumerable opportunities for defrauding the revenue, without check or control." And "as the inferior officers, who might discover the fraud, are to be appointed by the principal, will they not consequently be men after his own heart?" Anyway, forming accounts would divert him from the more important duties. His proper business should be to "recommend general systems of finance, without having anything to do with the actual administration of them, because, if he engages in the executive business, we shall be deprived of his talents in more important concerns." On the other hand,

If you have commissioners, you have an opportunity of taking one from each grand division of the United States, namely, the Eastern, the Middle, and Southern Districts.

Then if your man of genius was a member of the Board, he could exercise his genius, while his colleagues did the drudgery. "We have had a Board of Treasury, and we have had a Financier." Express charges as well as vague rumors had been brought against the latter, and though they might have been unfounded, "it shows that a man cannot serve in such a station without exciting popular clamor." The noise had led the old Congress once more to use a board. Some attention had to be paid to the prejudices and wishes of their constituents, especially where they were for or against this or that mode of administration. Such an officer was unprecedented in the states. The power of issuing warrants was great; it would give him more influence than the President had, and more than it was proper for one man to have in a republican Government. Any argument for economy was insignificant when compared with securing the public treasury. Gerry then launched into the dangers of establishing such ministries:

If we are to establish a number of such grand offices as these, the consequences appear to me pretty plain. These officers, bearing the titles of minister at war, minister of state, minister for the finances, minister of foreign affairs, and how many more ministers I cannot say, will be made necessary to the President. If by this establishment we make them more respectable than the other branches of the Government, the President will be induced to place more confidence in them than in the Senate; the people will also be led to consider them as more consequential persons. But all high officers of this kind must have confidence placed in them; they will in fact be the chancellors, the ministers of the nation. It will lead to the establishment of a system of favoritism, and the principal magistrate will be governed by these men. An oligarchy will be confirmed upon the ruin of the democracy; a Government most hateful will descend to our posterity, and all our exertions in the glorious cause of freedom will be frustrated: we shall go on till we reduce the powers of the President and Senate to nothing but a name.[306]

His conclusion was this:

In short, a Board of Treasury would conduct the business of finance with greater security and satisfaction than a single officer.

So he moved to have three commissioners as a Board of Treasury at the head of the Treasury Department.

Wadsworth opened discussion of this motion with the assertion that his experience was that a board of treasury was "the worst of all institutions." They seemed to have no fixed principles or responsibility for their conduct. On the other hand, he had had transactions with the treasury under the Superintendent of Finance, and thought he had "system in his management and responsibility in his negotiations." An officer who is highly responsible must always risk his character; but a treasury board lacked the unity and decision needed.[307] Similarly Baldwin said:

[306] Here Gerry not only had to be called to order for wandering off to the question of titles but reiterated his fear of ministerial government:
". . . the Senate were constitutionally the highest officers of Government, except the President and Vice-President; that the House was about to supersede them, and place over their heads a set of ministers who were to hold the reins of Government, and all this to answer no good purpose whatever; because the same services could be obtained from subordinate officers.
". . . If the House was truly republican and consistent, they would not admit officers, with or without titles, to possess such amazing powers as would eventually end in the ruin of the Government."
[307] Benson remarked at this point: "For his part, he conceived, that it required the same abilities in every individual of the commissioners, as was necessary if a single person was placed at the head of the Department. If men competent to the undertaking are so difficult to be found, you will increase the embarrassment of the President threefold by making the arrangement the gentleman contends for. The principle upon which the gentleman advocates the appointment of a board of treasury, would apply in favor of a change in the constitution, and we ought to have three Presidents of the United States instead of one, because their business might be done with more regularity and facility; but he did not think the argument to be well founded." He and others reviewed the

Boards were generally more destitute of energy than was an individual placed at the head of a department.[308]

Boudinot compared the earlier board and superintendent to the advantage of the latter, who had created jealousy by brushing off 146 supernumerary officers in one day.[309] He thought collusion as likely in a board as between a Secretary, Comptroller, and Auditors. Vining thought a Financier and a Board, as suggested by Bland, were an "unnatural combination."[310]

Gerry lost his motion, and then Madison's resolution calling for a Department of the Treasury, to be headed by a single Secretary, was passed by the Committee of the Whole, and ultimately incorporated in the law.

Thus again, as in the Philadelphia Convention, an issue was drawn between Federalist ideas of administration and popular fear of executive control of the purse strings; and thus again Federalist ideas won out. The other point to be noted is Gerry's alarm lest the heads of departments emerge as great ministers of state who would overshadow the Senate, absorb the functions of the President, and through patronage manage the Congress. This important point came out more fully, however, in the debate to be considered in the next following section.

THE QUESTION WHETHER THE SECRETARY OF THE TREASURY SHOULD BE AUTHORIZED TO REPORT PLANS. When the House was considering

---

history of the matter under the Confederation. He also said "one officer would certainly require less salary than three." His reference to three Presidents was sarcastic; but see 1 Max Farrand, *The Records of the Federal Convention of 1787* (rev. ed. in 4 vols., Yale University Press, New Haven, 1937) 66, 88, 96–97, on Edmund Randolph's advocacy of a three-headed executive chosen from different parts of the Union.

[308] For the further remarks of Baldwin and the observations of Madison at this point, see the next preceding section of this study (p. 221).

Gerry came back in rebuttal, in the course of which he "denied the fact" that there was no responsibility in a board. His elaboration shows that he meant that each member was responsible for the act of the board, or if he denied his acquiescence, recourse could be had to the journal of their transactions. Such responsibility would of course formally obtain; but it was not responsibility in accordance with the Federalist conception, which resembles that of modern advocates of single-headed administration. Cf. Leonard D. White, *Introduction to the Study of Public Administration* (rev. ed., The Macmillan Co., 1939) 87–94. See also Lynton K. Caldwell, *Administrative Theories of Hamilton and Jefferson* (University of Chicago Press, Chicago, 1944), index, under "administration, principles of."

[309] "Was it to be wondered at," he added, "if this swarm should raise a buzz about him?"

[310] There was interesting discussion of the invitation sent by Congress in the late war to Doctor Price to come over and take charge of our finances, and of the work of the late Superintendent of Finance, who was now Senator Robert Morris. 1 Homer Carey Hockett, *The Constitutional History of the United States* (The Macmillan Co., New York, 1939) 154; 1 Annals 16.

THE ESTABLISHMENT OF THE GREAT DEPARTMENTS 227

the Treasury bill, there occurred a debate [311] which revealed a sharp difference of opinion concerning the proper relationship between the Secretary of the Treasury and the House, and indeed the proper relation of ministers generally to Congress. The bill made it the duty of the Secretary to

> digest and report plans for the improvement and management of the revenue and the support of the public credit.

Page, however, objected to this wording,

> observing that it might be well enough to enjoin upon him the duty of making out and preparing estimates; but to go any further would be a dangerous innovation upon the constitutional privilege of this House; it would create an undue influence within these walls, because members might be led, by the deference commonly paid to men of abilities, who give an opinion in a case they have thoroughly studied, to support the minister's plan, even against their own judgment. Nor would the mischief stop here; it would establish a precedent which might be extended, until we admitted all the ministers of the Government on the floor, to explain and support the plans they have digested and reported: thus laying a foundation for an aristocracy or a detestable monarchy.

Page thus feared the clause might be an entering wedge for ministerial leadership and control of the House.

Tucker agreed that the clause should be struck out. To authorize the Secretary to prepare and report plans would "create an interference of the executive with the legislative powers."

> How can the business originate in this House, if we have it reported to us by the Minister of Finance?

The House could call for all needed information.

> The constitution has pointed out the proper mode of communication between the executive and legislative departments; it is made the duty of the President to give, from time to time, information to Congress of the state of the Union, and to recommend to their consideration such measures as he shall judge necessary and expedient.

The President was responsible to the people for what he recommended, and would be more cautious than any other less responsible person. So Tucker cheerfully seconded the motion.

Benson countered that digesting and reporting plans was the most important service that could be rendered by the Secretary. He despaired otherwise of improving the revenue or supporting the public credit. He

---
[311] 1 *Annals* 615–631. June 25, 1789.

thought the subject had been well understood when Gerry had earlier said the chief financier should recommend general systems of revenue:

> For my part, I am at a loss to see how the privilege of the House is infringed. Can any of the Secretary's plans be called bills? Will they be reported in such a form even? But admitting they were, they do not become bills, unless they are sanctioned by the House; much less is the danger that they will pass into laws without full examination by both Houses and the President.

He thought the clause "not only perfectly safe, but essentially necessary," and that without it "the great object of the bill will be defeated."

Goodhue thought they carried their dignity to an extreme when they refused to receive information from any but themselves. From the nature of his office the Secretary would be better acquainted than any other person.

Page returned to the defense of his motion by saying it was well enough in an absolute monarchy for a minister to come with plans in his hands and order them to be enregistered or enacted; but this practice did not obtain even in a limited monarchy like Britain. There the minister had to be a member of the House of Commons. He was at a loss to conceive why we in our free republic "should introduce such a novelty in legislation." It did not answer to say the House had a right of deliberating and deciding upon these plans, because it might be told it would destroy the efficiency of the system if it pruned away this or that part. They would have to take or reject the whole; but in the latter event they would have to depend upon themselves for a substitute. Then why could they not do so in the first instance? Either the Secretary's reports were to have weight or they were not. In the former case the House would act "under a foreign influence," and in the latter case the clause would impose a useless duty. If any further power than giving information when requested were given,

> it will come at last to this: we, like the Parliament of Paris, shall meet to register what he dictates.

Ames stressed the presumption that the Secretary would acquire the best knowledge of finance, the fact that a public assembly is from its nature amateur [312] in public accounts, the view that "a bad administration of the finances will prove our greatest evil," and the opinion that the proposed arrangement would be safe. He continued:

---

[312] Cf. Sidney Low, *The Governance of England* (new ed., T. Fisher Unwin, Ltd., London, 1919) chap. 11 ("Government by Amateurs").

It has been complained of as a novelty; but, let me ask gentlemen, if it is not to an institution of a similar kind that the management of the finances of Britain is the envy of the world? It is true, the Chancellor of the Exchequer is a member of the House that has the sole right of originating money bills; but is that a reason why we should not have the information which can be obtained from our officer, who possesses the means of acquiring equally important and useful knowledge? The nation, as well as the Parliament of Britain, holds a check over the Chancellor: if his budget contains false calculations, they are corrected; if he attempts impositions, or even unpopular measures, his administration becomes odious, and he is removed. Have we more reason to fear than they? Have we less responsibility or security in our arrangement of the Treasury department? If we have, let us improve it, but not abridge it of its safest and most useful power. . . .

Livermore expressed the fear that it might by construction be said that the Secretary had the *sole* right of digesting and reporting plans for the improvement of the revenue. The clause would also tend to render the minds of members indifferent to the subject. He thought the power too great to be entrusted in any hands but those of the representatives of the people, unless it were to a committee specially appointed by the House for that purpose. In his opinion the clause under debate had been copied from the powers of the late Superintendent of Finance rather than those of the First Lord of the Treasury; but he reminded his hearers that the old Congress

possessed the legislative and executive power; they could abolish his plans and his office together, if they thought proper; but we are restrained by a Senate, and the negative of the President. We have no power over him, therefore we ought to be cautious of putting dangerous powers into his hands.

Sedgwick said the House members came from different parts of the Union, where the objects of revenue were different, and the circumstances and views of the people were also different and in a great degree local, and hence no one member could possess the extensive knowledge obtainable by this officer. The Secretary would also be in an advantageous position to detect systems designed to defeat the collection of the revenue and propose a remedy. He trusted

a majority [in the House] will always be found wise and virtuous enough to resist being made the tools of a corrupt administration.

They should, as wise legislators, provide such a "reservoir for information."

Boudinot insisted that if the information were sought piecemeal, by way of question and answer, then they would lose the great whole in minutiae, and instead of a system present their constituents with a structure composed of discordant parts.

In Hartley's view Boudinot had proved too much; he had proved that the House was useless, and that one person could be a better judge of the subject than the whole body of Congress:

This kind of doctrine, Mr. Chairman, is indelicate in a republic, and strikes at the root of all legislation founded upon the great democratic principle of representation.

Ames, he argued, had said the Secretary would be responsible; but how could the House detect the impositions of his plans when, according to Ames, they would need more time and leisure than fell to their lot? But Hartley merely thought the words too strong, and would be satisfied if they were modified so as to oblige him to have his plans ready for the House when they should be asked for.

Gerry remarked on

the great degree of importance they were giving this, and the other executive officers. If the doctrine of having prime and great ministers of state was once established, he did not doubt but we should soon see them distinguished by a green or red ribbon, or other insignia of court favor and patronage.

He held that the power to report plans was "giving an indirect voice in legislative business to an executive officer." "Responsibility" was made an argument "in favor of every extention of power." He "should be glad to understand the term." If the members were so uninformed, they would have to take or reject the whole. It would be "next to presumption" to prepare an alteration. They would be told it was his duty officially to present plans, and their duty officially to pass them. Then what occasion was there for a session of Congress?

Lawrence called the "effects portrayed" by Gerry "chimerical." He continued:

It is said to be giving him the power of legislation. Do we give him the power of deciding what shall be law? While we retain this power, he may give us all the information possible, but can never be said to participate in legislative business; he has no control whatever over this House. . . .

How is it said, that the power of reporting plans for the improvement of the revenue, is the power of originating money bills? The constitution declares that power to be vested solely in this House. Now, will gentlemen say a money bill is originated by an individual member if he brings it forward? It cannot be originated, in my opinion, until the sense of the House is declared; much less can a plan for the improvement of the revenue be said to be a money bill.

Gerry replied, saying among other things:

But certainly, this House contains more information relative to the proper means of supporting the national credit, and how far our constituents are capable of sustaining an increase of taxes, or what mode of assessment would yield most satisfaction. . . . It was always my opinion, that the representative body, from their sense of feeling, was a better judge of taxation than any individual, however great his sagacity, or extensive his means of information.

. . . Is digesting and reporting plans merely giving information? These plans will have to undergo the consideration of the House, I grant; but they must have some influence coming from such high authority, and if they have this in any degree whatever, it is subversive of the principles laid down in the constitution.

The gentleman says, a bill is not originated until it has obtained the sense of the House; what is it then? The bill now under consideration has not obtained the sense of the House, yet I believe that gentleman himself conceives it to be a bill; he uses the term when he is speaking of it, and will hardly deny that it has originated. I think, sir, whenever the House order a committee to bring in a bill, or give leave to a member to read one in his place, that by that order they originate the bill; and here it is that I am apprehensive of a diminution of our privilege. By this law you give the Secretary the right of digesting and reporting all plans, which is but another word for bills, for the management and improvement of the revenue, and supporting public credit. To what an extent these last words may reach, I shall not pretend to say; but certainly they may include the operations of more departments than one. If the clause will bear the construction I have mentioned, it is altogether unwarrantable. I said, I differed from the gentleman with respect to the origin of bills, but perhaps this phrase may be applicable to a bill on its passage; all bills, from the time they are admitted before the House, may be said to be on their passage; but they are originated, as I take it, at their introduction.

Fitzsimons then said he believed nobody had objected to the Secretary's preparing a plan, and giving it when it was called for; if so, perhaps harmony might be restored by changing the word *report* to *prepare*. To try the sense of the House, he so moved.

Madison thought the danger of the Secretary's deriving a weight and some degree of influence from the proposed power did not compare with that of not having well-informed and digested plans. He answered Gerry's question on the meaning of responsibility:

There will be responsibility in point of reputation, at least a responsibility to the public opinion with respect to his abilities; and supposing there is no personal responsibility, yet we know that men of talents and ability take as much care for the preservation of their reputation as any other species of property of which they are possessed. . . .

The Virginian continued:

With respect to originating money bills, the House has the sole right to do it; but if the power of reporting plans can be construed to imply the power of originating revenue bills, the constitution is inconsistent with itself, in giving the President authority to recommend such measures as he may think expedient or necessary; but the construction is too unnatural to require further investigation.

In this he was undoubtedly correct; but neither he nor any other member pointed out the simple consideration that the privilege of the House was given *in relation to the Senate,* and that accordingly the question of the *source* of the *substantive provisions* of any revenue bill passed first by the House and then transmitted to the Senate is utterly irrelevant and immaterial to the meaning of the privilege.

Livermore was glad to be confirmed by Madison that the clause had originated under the Confederation;

but he wished gentlemen to distinguish, in the manner he had attempted to do, between properties of this Congress and that, from which they might discover the impropriety of adopting it.

He remembered that this power under the Confederation had produced such "morsels" as "the five per cent. impost, a poll tax, and a land tax, if his memory served him right." Certainly one of these would meet few patrons.

Page added that the late Congress had had to submit their plans to the State legislatures, and hence there had been less danger of undue influence.

Livermore, Tucker, and presumably Page were not satisfied with the Fitzsimons compromise. Tucker asked why the Secretary should be directed to prepare plans unless it was intended that the House should regularly call for them? He admitted information might at all times be welcome, but thought advice should never come but when required. He went on:

Why have we not affronted the other branches of the Government, as well as this House? Why have we not said that the Secretary of Foreign Affairs should prepare and digest plans for the formation of treaties, and report them to the President and Senate, who are exclusively to manage that concern? . . . We ought to have given the Secretary at War an opportunity of exercising his ingenuity, in devising plans of fortifications to strengthen our shores and harbors; we ought, in every case, where we have to decide, appoint officers with the same view to aid our deliberations, and, in fine, to perform the whole duties for which we were elected.

Hartley expressed himself satisfied with the Fitzsimons compromise. Stone thought it proper for the House to give the Secretary notice of its intention if it wanted to make use of the information acquired by him. He was not afraid of authorizing him to report plans.

Sherman thought the principle of the clause so necessary that it would force itself upon them, and hence it was vain to "attempt to elude it by subterfuge." If Tucker had consulted the Constitution, he would have found it unnecessary to make a similar provision for the other two Secretaries, to assist the President. It was there made the duty of department heads to answer the inquiries of the President in writing. He did not contend for a word; if the spirit of the clause were retained, he was satisfied.

Baldwin did not see what they were guarding against by striking out the words unless they meant to introduce a prohibitory clause and declare the Secretary restrained from digesting or preparing plans. If that was an evil, he did not see how to avoid it:

Suppose the officer is a bad man, and there are others like him in this House, (for this must be what gentlemen are afraid of;) and suppose he has prepared a scheme for peculation, which he hopes to get adopted by making dupes of the honest part; how are you to hinder it from being brought forward? Cannot his friends introduce it as their own, by making and seconding a motion for that purpose? Will you restrain him from having access to the members out of doors? And cannot he infuse dangerous and specious arguments and information into them as well in the closet, as by a public and official communication? But, Mr. Chairman, can this House, or if it can, will it, prevent any of their constituents from bringing before them plans for the relief of grievances or oppressions? Every individual of the community can bring business before us by petition, memorial, or remonstrance, provided it be done in a decent manner. How then do you propose to restrain the Secretary of the Treasury?

Page's motion for striking out the clause was put and negatived; and the Fitzsimons compromise motion to strike out the word *report* and insert *prepare* was carried "by a great majority."

As finally enacted, the bill made it the Secretary's duty

to digest and prepare plans for the improvement and management of the revenue, and for the support of public credit; to prepare and report estimates of the public revenue, and the public expenditures; . . .[313]

[313] 2 *Laws of the United States* 48.

Even Tucker did not object to the word *report* in the *second* of these clauses.[314]

The act further made it the Secretary's duty

> to make report, and give information, to either branch of the legislature, in person or in writing, (as he may be required), respecting all matters referred to him by the senate or house of representatives, or which shall appertain to his office; and, generally, to perform all such services, relative to the finances, as he shall be directed to perform.[315]

Whether the Secretary was to report to the House or Senate *in person* was thus left open; but it became an issue in the very next session of the House in 1790.[316]

This is an appropriate point at which to sum up a divergence of views which emerged in the first session not only in connection with the proposal to authorize the Secretary of the Treasury to report plans, but also with respect to the prior question, whether the Treasury Department should be headed by a single head or a board, and the still broader question of the place of department heads in the system, in terms of who should possess, in relation to these officers, the powers of administrative direction and removal.[317]

It has been noted that Gerry expressed alarm lest the heads of departments emerge as great ministers of state who would overshadow the Senate, absorb the functions of the President, and through patronage manage Congress. Representative Page feared "an undue influence within these walls" and a precedent for admitting all ministers to the floor to explain and support their plans, which he considered the "foundation for an aristocracy or detestable monarchy." Ames, on the other hand, expressed admiration for the British practice by which the Chancellor of the Exchequer submitted to Parliament his annual budget. Nor did he seem to think the fact that the finance minister in Britain was a member of the House, while ours could not be, made a similar arrangement less safe for us. Baldwin added that ministerial influence could not be exorcised by formal arrangements, and could operate "as well in the closet, as by a public and official communication." The issue was between administrative planning of a financial system such as Hamilton soon undertook and, through his great influence, got Congress to adopt, and republican insistence that it was the essence of representative government for the representatives of the people to keep a firm grasp on the

---

[314] 1 *Annals* 616.   [315] 2 *Laws of the United States* 48.
[316] See 1 *Annals* 1079–1081. January 9, 1790.
[317] In the paragraphs which follow, citations of views expressed in House debates will not be given in most cases in which they have appeared in earlier portions of this study, to which the reader is hereby referred.

THE ESTABLISHMENT OF THE GREAT DEPARTMENTS 235

determination of policy, especially financial policy, in terms of the wishes and prejudices of their constituents.

Page and Livermore said the practice of reporting plans to the old Congress had been safe enough because Congress had both legislative and administrative power and could abolish both the plans and the office, and because Congress itself could not tax the people. Now, however, the representatives of the people were restrained by a Senate and a presidential veto. Gerry added that these great ministers of state might soon be given "insignia of court favor and patronage."

From the removal debate have also been quoted passages which give some insight into the views current in 1789 with respect to the legislative-executive relationship in the mother country. Smith of South Carolina went so far as to insist upon the old English idea that a public officer has a property right in his office; but he seems to have had few supporters. Yet Thach points out the assumption by some that there should be in general a "permanency" in the magistracy.[318] Even Madison asked if a President could not be impeached for unwarranted removals;[319] though others who objected to presidential removal pointed out that it would be impossible to impeach the President for doing what Madison argued he could do at pleasure.[320] There were President-and-Senate men who visualized administrative direction by joint action of President and Senate as allegedly implied by the Constitution; though they were clearly in a minority. The majority who favored removal by the President alone insisted that administrative direction either belonged to the President by the Constitution or should as a matter of policy if not of constitutional necessity be delegated to him. It was these same people who did not fear administrative financial planning. They were fond of the idea of presidential "superintendence"[321] and "responsibility."

These men appealed to the separation of powers; but those who opposed presidential removal feared it might end in the introduction of the British system. Bland thought it might allow the President to "bring about a change of the ministry." Jackson thought making officers the "mere creatures" of the President would introduce a "treasury bench" and ministerial direction of the legislature. Page attacked the conception

[318] *Thach* 148, and 1 *Annals* 397, 398–399, 491, 496, 504, 514, 517–518, 532, 540–541, 557, 559, 569, 571, 573, 590, 597, 603.
[319] 1 *Annals* 517.
[320] Gerry (*ibid.* 522, 597), Smith of South Carolina (*ibid.* 528).
[321] Ames (*ibid.* 493, 495), Lawrence (*ibid.* 504), Clymer (*ibid.* 509), Benson (*ibid.* 525), Vining (*ibid.* 531–532, 595), Sedgwick (*ibid.* 542–543). Contrast the remarks of Stone (*ibid.* 589).

of energy in the executive and opposed presidential removal as "the seeds of royal prerogative."

Lawrence, a legislative-grant man, admitted that every new President might make a clean sweep of the executive offices, but contended that it ought to be so if the President thought it necessary. He thought every President "ought to have those men about him in whom he can place the most confidence." He took pains to say that it did not follow that changes would be made "in a wanton manner, and from capricious motives"; but added that it could be presumed that changes would be made "on principles of policy and propriety only." Perhaps this was the nearest approach to a hint of party government; but nobody seems to have been assuming party government as we take it for granted today. This was because party government as we understand it was not then clearly understood.[322] "Party" was not clearly differentiated from "faction" or what we today call "pressure-group," [323] and the idea of two-party competition as a necessary technique of popular government was not in vogue.[324] Presidential removal on the basis of party policy was thus not clearly brought out by those who favored removal by the President alone, though their theories were such that this idea could fit into them neatly when it emerged.

These same men might also have written the *Report of the President's Committee on Administrative Management;* [325] though here again the purpose of an energetic Executive under the over-all administrative management of the President has changed. For men of the Hamilton school it was a means of aristocratic guidance of government; while for men of the Franklin D. Roosevelt school it is today a means of effectuating

[322] See Washington's Farewell Address, 35 *Writings* 214, 223–228; J. Allen Smith, *The Spirit of American Government* (The Chautauqua Press, Chautauqua, The Macmillan Co., New York, 1911) chap. 8. See also Henry Jones Ford, *The Rise and Growth of American Politics* (The Macmillan Co., New York, 1898) 90–161.

[323] See Madison's use of "interest" and "faction" in *The Federalist*, No. 10 (Hamilton ed., J. B. Lippincott & Co., Philadelphia, 1880) 104–112; and compare André Siegfried, *America Comes of Age* (Harcourt, Brace and Co., New York, 1927) chap. 18, and E. Pendleton Herring, *Group Representation Before Congress* (The Johns Hopkins Press, Baltimore, 1929) and *Public Administration and the Public Interest* (McGraw-Hill Book Co., New York and London, 1936).

[324] Cf. Charles Edward Merriam and Harold Foote Gosnell, *The American Party System* (The Macmillan Co., New York, 1929) 409–481; Edward McChesney Sait, *American Parties and Elections* (The Century Co., New York and London, 1927) chaps. 6–7; Peter H. Odegard and E. Allen Helms, *American Politics* (Harper & Bros., New York and London, 1938); R. M. MacIver, *The Web of Government* (The Macmillan Co., New York, 1947) 208–223.

[325] Government Printing Office, Washington, 1937. The same men might also have written James Hart, "The President and Federal Administration," in Charles G. Haines and Marshall E. Dimock, *Essays on the Law and Practice of Governmental Administration* (The Johns Hopkins Press, Baltimore, 1935) 47–93. See also George W. Spicer, "From Political Chief to Administrative Chief," *ibid.* 94–124.

THE ESTABLISHMENT OF THE GREAT DEPARTMENTS 237

democratic control of the abuses of corporate enterprise and, by the same logic, of the abuses of big trade unionism.[326]

It seems clear that in 1789 neither side wanted the British system as we understand it today, for the very simple reason that this great invention in popular government had not at that time clearly emerged.[327] It is, on the other hand, a plausible hypothesis that Hamilton looked with favor upon ministerial government *as he saw it in his day*,[328] just as Gerry seems to have feared it for the same reason. It was realized that the king had to govern with parliament, and that his ministers had to be acceptable to parliament.[329] But it was also realized that control of parliament was in practice obtained by an aristocracy or by the king through the rotten borough system, through patronage, through influence, and through bribery.[330] The future butterfly of the cabinet system was still an ugly caterpillar, but one which Hamilton probably believed to be the only way of working free government,[331] just as the simon-pure republicans regarded it as the means of subverting popular government. Those who took either view could at that time join with Blackstone[332] in

---

[326] See above, chapter 2, p. 47, section entitled, "An illuminating example of political symbolism," and especially note 155 of that chapter.

[327] George Burton Adams, *Constitutional History of England* (Henry Holt and Co., New York, 1921) 411–412, 418.

[328] See W. E. Binkley, *The Powers of the President* (Doubleday, Doran & Co., Garden City, 1937) chap. 2; Hamilton's great speech in the Philadelphia Convention, 1 Max Farrand, *The Records of the Philadelphia Convention of 1787* (2d ed. in 4 vols., Yale University Press, New Haven, 1937) 282–293; 4 *Memoirs of John Quincy Adams* (comprising portions of his Diary from 1795 to 1848, ed. by Charles Francis Adams, in 12 vols., J. B. Lippincott & Co., Philadelphia, 1874) 496–502; 5 *ibid.* 451–452; Lynton K. Caldwell, *The Administrative Theories of Hamilton and Jefferson* (University of Chicago Press, Chicago, 1944) 34–46; Leonard D. White, "Public Administration Under the Federalists," in (1944) 24 *Boston U. L. Rev.* 144, 172–173, 177–182, and notably 156–172, 177–180.

[329] See 1 *Annals* 506 (Jackson), 518 (Madison). Sherman had actually favored an executive wholly dependent on the legislature. 1 Max Farrand, *The Records of the Federal Convention of 1787* (2d ed. in 4 vols., Yale University Press, New Haven, 1937) 65, 68.

[330] See 1 *Annals* 397 (Bland), 403, 522–523 (Gerry), 506 (Jackson), 509 (Page), 559 (Sherman); 1 Max Farrand, *The Records of the Federal Convention of 1787* (2d ed. in 4 vols., Yale University Press, New Haven, 1937) 376, 381 (Hamilton), 388–389, 392 (Madison); 2 *ibid.* 284–285, 288–289 (Mercer); *ibid.* 405 (Sherman). On English parties in this and the preceding period, see 1 Sir Thomas Erskine May, *The Constitutional History of England* (Longmans, Green and Co., London, New York, Bombay and Calcutta, 1912) 396–428. On the evolution of the English cabinet system see George Burton Adams, *Constitutional History of England* (Henry Holt and Co., New York, 1921) 354 ff, notably 359–362, 365, 371, 374–376, 383–387, 397, 404–406, 410–413, 418, 434, 445, 448, 449, 463, 469–470.

[331] 1 Max Farrand, *The Records of the Federal Convention of 1787* (2d ed. in 4 vols., Yale University Press, New Haven, 1937) 289–290.

[332] 1 Sir William Blackstone, *Commentaries on the Laws of England* (in 2 vols., W. E. Dean, New York, 1851) Book I, 105, 110–112, 146–147, 199–203; 2 *ibid.* Book III, 20–22; Book IV, 212.

accepting the constitutional principle of the separation of powers. Indeed, the cabinet system as it exists today in Britain violates that principle in the customs or conventions of the contitution rather than in the law of the constitution.[333]

The course of American political development has repudiated Hamilton's principle of aristocracy, but vindicated his principle of a strong executive, not as an instrumentality of aristocratic control, but as at once the one stabilizing factor in, and the focal point of, popular government. It has repudiated the cabinet system, which would make the President a figurehead,[334] but approximated certain features of the cabinet system in that the President is himself at once the leader of his party and of the nation in the formulation of a legislative program[335] and the general manager of the executive branch.[336] For us today to weaken his all-important position by making him ineligible for re-election[337] or by making the cabinet collectively responsible to Congress[338] would be to

[333] See George Burton Adams as cited in notes 327 and 330 above; A. V. Dicey, *Introduction to the Study of the Law of the Constitution* (8th ed., Macmillan & Co., London, 1920) chaps. 14–15; 1 Sir William R. Anson, *The Law and Custom of the Constitution* (The Clarendon Press, Oxford, 1911) 1–44.

[334] Hamilton seems to the present writer, as he reads history backwards, to have endangered the position of the presidency, as the necessary spearhead of a strong executive, when, as Secretary of the Treasury, he assumed a personal leadership of Congress which tended to make a figurehead of the President, so far as policy initiation was concerned. See especially the references to Binkley and to John Quincy Adams in note 328 above. If the function of prime minister is to be effectively assumed *within the present framework of the American government*, it must be assumed, as Woodrow Wilson clearly saw, by the President. Woodrow Wilson, *Constitutional Government in the United States* (Columbia University Press, New York, 1908) chap. 3.

For an excellent short statement of the complementary contributions of Hamilton and Jefferson see Allan Nevins and Henry Steele Commager, *America: The Story of a Free People* (Little, Brown and Co., Boston, 1942) 142–149.

[335] Woodrow Wilson, *Constitutional Government in the United States* (Columbia University Press, New York, 1908) 70–72; Howard Lee McBain, *The Living Constitution* (The Macmillan Co., New York, 1929) 114–118.

[336] See W. F. Willoughby, *Principles of Public Administration* (The Brookings Institution, Washington, 1927) chap. 3, and "The Science of Public Administration," in John Mabry Mathews and James Hart (eds.), *Essays in Political Science* (The Johns Hopkins Press, Baltimore, 1937) 39, 48, 50.

[337] This idea has been a persistent one in our constitutional history. See above, chapter 6, p. 148, section entitled, "Fear of executive power: proposed amendments to Article II"; chapter 1, p. 2, section entitled, "Washington in 1788 on the question of the constitutional re-eligibility of the President"; and generally the history of this idea in its various forms right down to the present day, when a proposed constitutional amendment to limit presidential tenure has at this writing been ratified by various state legislatures despite its anti-democratic implications and potential peril to the republic.

[338] *Cf.* Howard Lee McBain, *The Living Constitution* (The Macmillan Co., New York, 1929) 125–149; Don K. Price, "The Parliamentary and Presidential Systems," 3 *Pub. Admin. Rev.* 317–334 (Autumn, 1943). While the cabinet system fortunately stands no chance of being formally adopted in our national government, another idea which has been persistent in our constitutional history is to have cabinet members sit and speak or answer questions in Congress. See above, chapter 4, note 69. Some who realize

THE ESTABLISHMENT OF THE GREAT DEPARTMENTS 239

weaken popular government and to strengthen the influence of the modern equivalent of Hamilton's aristocracy, the competing pressure-propaganda groups.[339] Hamilton and Jefferson are always with us, because Hamiltonians and Jeffersonians are always with us. They may exchange means, but never exchange ends.[340]

AN INTERPRETATION OF THE ADMINISTRATIVE LEGISLATION OF THE FIRST SESSION IN TERMS OF ITS UNDERLYING ADMINISTRATIVE THEORY

AN INTERPRETATION OF THE LEGISLATION OF 1789 DEALING WITH THE GREAT DEPARTMENTS. In conclusion, the various elements of this chapter may be tied together by offering an interpretation of the whole body of legislation of 1789 dealing with the great departments, with the purpose of showing its unity and self-consistency as the expression of the *political* and *administrative* theory of the *majority*.

That majority was Federalist in its thinking. In enacting this whole body of legislation it was divided on one, but possibly only one major point. It was united in favor of tenure at the sole pleasure of the Presi-

---

the danger in this proposal of weakening the position of the President *vis-à-vis* Congress nevertheless point out a grave defect of our system: the deadlock which may develop between the President and Congress after a mid-term election, or even otherwise, cannot be broken until the fixed date of the next election arrives. The result is always leaderless government, and crisis government which is leaderless may be disastrous. On crisis government see Lindsay Rogers, *Crisis Government* (W. W. Norton & Co., New York, 1934). In 1945 a remedy was proposed by Thomas K. Finletter, *Can Representative Government Do the Job?* (Reynal & Hitchcock, New York, 1945) 110. It so happened that ten years earlier the present writer had proposed what in one major respect was essentially the same remedy: James Hart, "The President and Federal Administration," in Charles Grove Haines and Marshall Dimock, *Essays on the Law and Practice of Governmental Administration* (The Johns Hopkins Press, Baltimore, 1935) 47, 59, 70–71, 91. See also William Yandell Elliott, *The Need for Constitutional Reform* (McGraw-Hill Book Co., Whittlesey House, New York and London, 1935) 27–40, 182–240. After hearing Price discuss the matter orally, the present writer is in agreement that the only formal constitutional or statutory change which is desirable in this respect is to make the terms of Senate, House, and President coincide. At the same time he adheres as strongly as ever to his belief that the hands of the President need to be strengthened with respect both to legislative initiative and leadership and to administrative direction. Americans still have much to learn from John Stuart Mill, *Considerations on Representative Government* (Henry Holt and Co., New York, 1882) 100–119.

[339] On pressure-groups see Arthur F. Bentley, *The Process of Government, A Study of Social Pressures* (University of Chicago Press, Chicago, 1908); V. O. Key, *Politics, Parties and Pressure-Groups* (Thomas Y. Crowell Co., New York, 1945); Edward McChesney Sait, *American Parties and Elections* (The Century Co., New York and London, 1927) chaps. 4–5; Peter H. Odegard and E. Allen Helms, *American Politics* (Harper & Bros., New York and London, 1938).

[340] See note 326 above.

dent; but half of its members preferred to consider this objective as already provided by the Constitution, and the other half preferred to regard a statutory delegation to the President as necessary for its attainment. It was the view of the *former* half which *found expression* in the acts establishing the three departments.

Accordingly, the interpretation which follows is *stated in terms of the constitutional-grant theory* of removal *in its most unqualified form*. To make that interpretation express the general *administrative doctrine* common to the *whole* majority, it may possibly be necessary merely to reword it with respect to the *source* of the presidential authority to *remove*. This constitutional-grant interpretation is as follows: [341]

The Constitution vests in Congress the delegated legislative powers,[342] and in the President "the" executive power.[343] Congress is vested with power to establish by law all federal offices not provided for by the Constitution.[344] This includes the power to define their powers and duties, fix their compensation, and arrange them in the departments assumed[345] by the language of the Constitution. It is, indeed, vested with power to make all laws necessary and proper *for* carrying into *execution* both its own enumerated powers and the executive power vested in the President.[346]

The President is vested with "the" executive power, which includes the executive powers of appointment, direction, and removal. He is *expressly* given the power to appoint to office,[347] *in order that it may be qualified*. The qualifications are two. The advice and consent of one branch of the legislature is required; and Congress may vest the appointment of *inferior* officers in the President alone, in the heads of departments, or in the courts of law.

Particular executive powers fall into two major classes: *constitutional* and *statutory* executive powers.[348] The former embrace all the executive

---

[341] See generally *Thach* chap 6, and Corwin's *Removal Power*, as well as James Hart, *Tenure of Office Under the Constitution* (The Johns Hopkins Press, Baltimore, 1930). For full citations of *Thach* and of Corwin's *Removal Power*, see note 14 above.

[342] The opening sentence of Article I vests in Congress all legislative powers *herein granted*. Eighteen but not all of these are enumerated in Article I, section 8. See also the tenth amendment.

[343] "The executive Power shall be vested in a President of the United States of America." Article II, section 1, § 1.

[344] Article II, section 2, § 2.   [345] Article II, section 2, §§ 1 and 2.

[346] "The Congress shall have Power . . . To make all Laws which shall be necessary and proper *for* carrying into *Execution* the *foregoing* Powers, *and* all other Powers vested by this Constitution in the Government of the United States, or in any Department or *Officer* thereof." Article I, section 8, § 18. Italics supplied.

[347] Article II, section 2, § 2.

[348] See *Thach* 144, 148–149, 158, 160–161; James Hart, *Tenure of Office Under the Constitution* (The Johns Hopkins Press, Baltimore, 1930) 272–373.

prerogatives vested expressly or impliedly in the President by the Constitution itself. The latter involve the execution or administration of the laws of Congress, and have their *content* defined by the provisions of those laws and such implications as flow from the officers concerned being charged with their administration.

The constitutional executive powers of the President relate to *both* classes of executive powers. For they include not only the conduct of diplomatic intercourse [349] and command of the armed forces [350] but also the power and duty to *take care* that the *laws* be faithfully *executed*.[351] By the latter clause he is vested with the power of over-all administrative management with respect to the statutory executive powers of all other executive officers.

If it were humanly possible for one man to do so much, other executive officers would be unnecessary. As it is, it is "necessary and proper" [352] for Congress to establish other executive offices and arrange them into departments, both to act as his administrative arms in the exercise of his constitutional powers in the fields of foreign relations and command, and to execute in detail (administer) the laws passed by Congress in the exercise of its delegated legislative powers relating to financial and other matters.

Here arises, however, a distinction which Congress is bound to observe. Since the powers of conducting foreign negotiations and of command are by the Constitution the President's, Congress *must* make it the duty of the Secretaries of Foreign Affairs and of War to carry out his directives in these fields. On the other hand, since the powers of finance [353] and of establishing post offices and post roads [354] are in their *legislative* aspects vested by the Constitution in Congress, and since Congress is expressly empowered to make all laws necessary and proper *for* carrying these legislative powers into *execution,* it may by law *define* the statutory executive powers of the offices it creates for such purposes.

---

[349] See 7 *The Writings of Thomas Jefferson* (Derby & Jackson, New York, 1859) 465–467; 4 *ibid.* 47, 84–85, 90–92, 99–100; 4 *The Works of Alexander Hamilton* (Federal Edition, ed. by Henry Cabot Lodge, G. P. Putnam's Sons, New York and London, 1904) 432 ff; and other references in chapter 4, above, p. 78, the section entitled, "Treaties and Foreign Relations."
[350] Article II, section 2, § 1.
[351] Article II, section 3.   [352] Article I, section 8, § 18.
[353] Article I, section 8, enumerates the powers of taxation and spending, of borrowing money on the credit of the United States, of coining money and regulating the value thereof and of foreign coin, and of providing for the punishment of counterfeiting the securities and current coin of the United States. Article I, section 9, § 7, provides that no money shall be drawn from the treasury but in consequence of appropriations made by law, and that a regular statement and account of the receipts and expenditures of all public money shall be published from time to time.
[354] Article I, section 8, § 7.

In *both* cases, however, the President has the constitutional power of administrative direction, which Congress may perhaps not constitutionally limit. For this power of administrative direction is part of "the" executive power which the Constitution vests in him. Moreover, since the Secretaries of Foreign Affairs and of War are concerned with powers which in part are constitutionally his own, he must have complete control over these officers; and he is expressly vested with the power to *take care* that the statutory executive powers of other executive officers are faithfully executed, or in other words with the power of over-all administrative management of the *execution* of the *laws*. It is part of "the" executive power to see that the laws are *faithfully* executed in accordance with *his own* ideas.

It follows that the Constitution vests in the President the implied and perhaps illimitable power to remove at pleasure all executive officers, or at least all of them whom he appoints, or appoints by and with the advice and consent of the Senate.[355] For the power of removal is part of "the" executive power and a necessary sanction of his constitutional powers of control and over-all administrative management. Indeed, it was until 1820 arguable that Congress may not even fix the terms of such executive officers; for Madison at least, the constitutional implication was that their tenure is simply and unchangeably at the pleasure of the President.

The power of removal may, ordinarily, flow from the power of appointment; but it cannot be inferred that the *President's* power of removal may be exercised only by and with the advice and consent of the Senate. For the effect would be to assume that the framers so far departed from the separation of powers as to give one branch of the legislature a share in the sanction of the President's powers of control and management, and hence a share in the control and management themselves—an assumption which is inconsistent with the very language of the opening sentence of Article II as well as with his faithful execution duty. Accordingly, the powers of nominating, appointing, commissioning, and removing officers are vested in the President; the advice and consent of the Senate to his appointments is a special exception to the separation of powers; and exceptions are to be strictly construed, and not to be extended so as to defeat the constitutional position of the President as the sole possessor of "the" executive power.

The distinction made in the language of the organic acts between

[355] See Article II, section 2, § 2, and the earlier section of this chapter (p. 190) entitled, "The question of the scope of the President's power of removal under the 'legislative decision of 1789,'" as well as *Myers* v. *United States*, 272 U.S. 52, 159, 161–162, 163–164, 176 (1926).

departments with *heads* and *executive departments* with *principal officers* remains something of a mystery. This distinction had a basis in the language of the Constitution,[356] but the only evidence that for the framers it was a deliberate one is the fact that it was followed in the organic acts of the first session. The distinction was not consistently followed by the first session; but since it presumably had a purpose, it may be ventured as an hypothesis that "departments" and "heads of departments" were the *generic* terms applicable to *all three* of the departments first created; and that "executive departments" and "principal officers" were the smaller category which included *only* those departments created to act as administrative arms of the President in the exercise of his constitutional executive powers of diplomatic intercourse and command. Under this terminology, the Departments of Foreign Affairs and War were, but the Department of the Treasury was not, an "executive" department. Thus on the one hand the Constitution authorized Congress to vest the appointment of inferior officers in department heads; and the first session vested the appointment of some inferior officers in *all three* department heads; while on the other hand the Constitution authorized the President to require the opinion in writing of the principal officer in each of the "executive" departments; and this was a power peculiarly applicable to the Departments of Foreign Affairs and of War, which were "executive" departments *in a special sense*.

This distinction is understandable in the light of the distinction between constitutional and statutory executive powers; and it might have *other* important implications in terms of the assumptions of *those who cherished legislative supremacy* and stressed preservation of the power of the purse in the hands of the popular branch of the legislature. But clearly the *constitutional-grant men* did not think of the Treasury Department as in any sense *outside* the *executive branch*. Rather was it deliberately insisted by them that it came within the scope of the take-care duty and hence of the removal power of the President considered as a necessary sanction thereof. *For them,* therefore, the distinction between departments and "executive" departments had no significance except that inherent in the distinction between constitutional and statutory executive powers.

About the manner in which the latter distinction applied to the three departments a further word needs to be said. The executive powers of the Treasury Department are *wholly statutory* executive powers, which derive their *content* from the acts by which Congress exercises its dele-

[356] Compare the language of Article II, section 2, § 1, with § 2 of the same Article and section.

gated powers of fiscal legislation and its power to *provide for* carrying those powers into *execution,* and which are unrelated to all constitutional executive powers of the President with the exception of his take-care power and his power of removal. It seems to have been understood from the beginning, on the other hand, that the *sole* conduct of diplomatic relations was part of "the" executive power of the President;[357] and the Constitution expressly makes him the Commander in Chief of the armed forces.[358] Hence in these respects these two Secretaries would be exercising, not statutory executive powers, but the constitutional executive powers of the President; and Congress could *only* give them *in these respects* the *duty* to *obey* presidential directives.

Now Corwin finds in the removal debate no necessary indication of the position, later assumed by Hamilton, to the effect that the President is not merely the sole *medium* of foreign intercourse, but also the *originator* of foreign policy.[359] Even if this is true,[360] however, one may perhaps infer that the *constitutional-grant men* reasoned as follows: the Constitution does not make clear who shall *make* the policy which the President alone may *express* on behalf of the nation. It certainly does not generally authorize Congress to enact our foreign policy by law,[361] as it may enact our fiscal policy by law; though of course that foreign policy must be made within the limits fixed by such domestic legislation as navigation, appropriation and tariff acts of Congress;[362] and clearly the President may not in the name of diplomacy make or alter such legislation. Indeed, foreign *relations* cannot *in the nature of the case* be enacted by law, but must be worked out by *diplomacy,* for the conduct of which the President is our sole medium. Even in *stating* a *predetermined* position the President inevitably *makes* foreign policy *by his very tone.* Much of our foreign policy, therefore, as a *practical* matter, *must* be *made,* within the four walls of the Constitution and laws and treaties of the United States, by the President, under whatever checks the Senate may have. As the sole channel of foreign intercourse, he alone may *negotiate* treaties, under whatever checks the Senate may have. In short, in this field there is no room for any statutory executive duties which

---

[357] See note 349, above.   [358] Article II, section 2, § 1.
[359] Edward S. Corwin, *The President: Office and Powers* (2d ed., New York University Press, New York, 1941) 209.
[360] See, however, Thach 143, 146–150, 153, 155–158, 159–164.
[361] *Cf.* John Locke, *Of Civil Government* (Everyman's Library, J. M. Dent & Sons, London and Toronto, and E. P. Dutton & Co., New York, 1924) 190–192 (§§ 143–148).
[362] It remained for Hamilton and Madison as "Pacificus" and "Helvidius" respectively to debate in 1793 the effect upon presidential diplomacy of the power vested in Congress to declare war. See citations above in chapter 4, note 61.

THE ESTABLISHMENT OF THE GREAT DEPARTMENTS

curb the *conduct* of diplomacy by the *sole* authority of the President.[363]

Neither is there room in the War Department for any statutory executive duties which *curb* the *irreducible minimum* of discretion involved in the very idea of the command power.[364] Yet in this case the Constitution expressly delegates to Congress several legislative powers with respect to the armed forces,[365] including the power to *make rules for their government and regulation*. The War Department is thus *at once* an agency of the President for the exercise of his irreducible minimum of constitutional discretion in his capacity of Commander in Chief, and an agency for carrying into execution the related legislative powers of Congress, subject to the take-care power of the President. The War Department thus stands between the other two in this respect.

In the case of officers vested with *statutory* executive powers, the constitutional-grant men of 1789 did not make explicit the manner in which the duties of such officers to the law could be reconciled with their subordination to the take-care power of the President. The solution has of course been found in the later distinction between *ministerial duties* and *discretionary powers*.[366] This was later made evident by the mandamus cases[367] on the one hand, and on the other hand by President Jackson's removal of a Secretary of the *Treasury* who refused to exercise his statutory discretion in accordance with the policy of the President.[368] It matters not whether the constitutional-grant men of 1789 clearly envisioned such a use of the removal power; for it was implicit

---

[363] This is not to deny that Congress may vest statutory executive duties in the Secretary of State (Foreign Affairs). The first session did so in giving him "home functions." See 2 *Laws of the United States* 51–52. Congress may also do so in connection with its regulation of matters within its legislative competence which impinge upon our foreign relations. But it still remains the case, in the view which is at this point being interpreted, that it could not define statutory executive duties of this officer so as to *curb* the *conduct* of *diplomacy* by the *sole* authority of the *President*, and hence cannot limit the President's sole power to remove him at pleasure.

[364] See James Hart, *The Ordinance Making Powers of the President* (The Johns Hopkins Press, Baltimore, 1925) 238–250.

[365] These include the powers to define and punish piracies and felonies committed on the high seas and offenses against the law of nations, declare war, grant letters of marque and reprisal, make rules concerning captures on land and water, raise and support armies, provide and maintain a navy, make rules for the government and regulation of the land and naval forces, provide for calling forth the militia to execute the laws of the Union, suppress insurrections and repel invasions, and provide for organizing, arming, and disciplining the militia and for governing such part of them as may be employed in the service of the United States, reserving to the states respectively the appointment of the officers and the authority of training the militia according to the discipline prescribed by Congress. Article I, section 8, §§ 10–16.

[366] See James Hart, *An Introduction to Administrative Law with Selected Cases* (F. S. Crofts & Co., New York, 1940) 440.

[367] *Ibid.* 442–448. Cf. *ibid.* 462–464.

[368] See Carl Brent Swisher, *Roger B. Taney* (The Macmillan Co., New York, 1935) 221–234, and 5 Stat. L. 266, 274 (sec. 16), April 10, 1816.

in what they decided if not in what they said.³⁶⁹ Their insistence upon tenure during presidential pleasure meant, *in necessary effect,* that the President could remove even the Secretary of the Treasury not only for inefficient, negligent, or otherwise *literally faithless* execution of the money laws, but also for the purpose of controlling that officer in the exercise of such executive discretion as the law might vest in him. The scope of the power of direction is necessarily defined in practice by the scope of its sanction.

It is hard to reconcile the constitutional-grant theory with the constitutional provision authorizing the President to require the opinion in writing of the principal officer in each of the "executive" departments. It is a rule of construction that the Constitution must be so construed as to give effect to all its provisions.³⁷⁰ Yet the constitutional-grant theory of removal reduces the opinion-in-writing clause to mere surplusage. For if he could remove all department heads, why was it necessary expressly to authorize him to require the opinion in writing of some of them?³⁷¹ The constitutional-grant men never met this objection. The best that can be said in their behalf on this score is that the framers had not thought the matter through, and that *any other* construction would be *even more* inconsistent, by undermining the independence of the Presidency and the separation of powers for which the framers had sought to provide.

It should be added, however, that the same objection does not apply to the legislative-grant theory. For if it remained for Congress to define tenure, it might, even so, have been thought proper by the framers to give the President the power to require an opinion in writing from the principal officers in the "executive" departments, which were, in any view, closely related to his constitutional powers.

Finally, it remains a fact, though the idea was neither fully developed in all its implications by Madison himself nor accepted by the House, that he suggested that officers whose statutory duties partook of a judicial as well as an executive nature should be given a different tenure from that of purely executive officers. In that area Madison favored legislative control even after his conversion.

The reader will please note that the preceding paragraphs of this section do not purport to sum up the whole history of the removal ques-

---

[369] Lawrence, at least, mentioned this point, as may be seen by re-reading his remarks as reported in the section above (p. 165) entitled, "The legislative-grant theory."
[370] 1 *Willoughby on the Constitution* (2d ed., Baker, Voorhis and Co., New York, 1929) § 40.
[371] In the section above, p. 168, entitled, "The constitutional-grant theory," it is noted that Page expressly made this objection in the House removal debate.

tion, or even the views of a majority of the House in 1789. They are merely an interpretation (with no little extrapolation, to be sure) of the constitutional *and* administrative views of those few constitutional-grant men in the House who regarded the President's implied power of removal as illimitable. The point is, however, that the extremely significant fact seems to emerge that *the same administrative,* albeit not the same constitutional, views were held by most of the House majority. It is quite true that the *formal* victory of at least a *qualified* constitutional-grant theory was made possible only by the cooperation of that core of *legislative-grant* men who also strongly favored tenure at the sole pleasure of the President. Nevertheless, these legislative-grant men probably favored all the *administrative objectives* implied in the interpretation which has just been given. *Mutatis mutandis,* that interpretation probably applies, on its *administrative* side, to them also. Indeed, Sedgwick *almost* said that it was the legislative *duty* of Congress to give the power of removal to the *President* as a sanction of his power of administrative direction. Moreover, the *formal* victory of this qualified constitutional-grant theory produced the *net result* that the President alone had the power to remove at pleasure all superior officers, at least unless and until Congress positively undertook to regulate their tenure.[372]

Still further, in the *subsequent* history of our constitutional system, the result of 1789 has normally carried great weight, and Congress has only twice, in 1867 and 1872,[373] undertaken to enact that the President might remove *heads of departments* only by and with the advice and consent of the Senate. The Tenure of Office Act of 1867 applied even to the "executive" departments; but it was modified after two years[374] and repealed after twenty;[375] its constitutionality was disputed by President Johnson;[376] and it was *in effect* pronounced in the *Myers Case*[377]

[372] Thus Corwin states Webster's position to have been in effect that the legislative decision of 1789 must be followed unless and until overridden by Congress; and Corwin himself does not argue that Congress could limit the President's power to remove at pleasure the Secretary of State. Corwin's *Removal Power* 30.
[373] 14 Stat. L. 430 (March 2, 1867), and 17 Stat. L. 283, 284 (June 8, 1872). The statutory provision actually held unconstitutional in the *Myers Case* was a rider on an appropriation act of the same era: 19 Stat. L. 80–81 (July 12, 1876). For the provisions of 1872 and 1876, see also R. S., secs. 388, 389, 3830.
[374] 16 Stat. L. 6 (April 5, 1869). [375] 24 *ibid.* 500 (March 3, 1887).
[376] See Robert W. Winston, *Andrew Johnson, Plebeian and Patriot* (Henry Holt and Co., New York, 1928) 383–384, 405–454; William Archibald Dunning, *Essays on the Civil War and Reconstruction* (The Macmillan Co., New York and London, 1898) 253–303 ("The Impeachment and Trial of President Johnson"); Lloyd Paul Stryker, *Andrew Johnson, A Study in Courage* (The Macmillan Co., New York, 1930) 438–439; Homer Carey Hockett, *The Constitutional History of the United States, 1826–1876* (The Macmillan Co., New York, 1939) 347–355. Cf. Grover Cleveland, *Presidential Problems* (The Century Co., New York, 1904) 3–76, especially 36–37, 44–45, 75–76. [377] 272 U.S. 52 (1926), and Stryker as cited above in note 376.

to have been unconstitutional, as was the act of 1872 relating to the Postmaster General. The other main instances of congressional regulation of the tenure of presumably *superior* officers have been in recent times and with respect to the Comptroller General [378] and the members of a number of quasi-judicial agencies.[379] The Supreme Court has never directly passed on the statutory tenure of the Comptroller General, and has sanctioned legislative control of the tenure of *superior* officers only in the field of quasi-judicial action [380]—a field in at least one aspect of which Madison himself thought Congress had some authority over tenure.

The legislative decision of 1789, in its bearing upon the *crucial* relation of the President to *department heads,* has thus, in any view, had profound effects upon the constitutional development of the Presidency. It is the considered opinion of the present writer that the net result has been to help save that great office from the dangerous disintegration which every *administrative* position taken in 1789 other than that of the House majority would have invited.

[378] Budget and Accounting Act, Title III, secs. 302–303. 42 Stat. L., Pt. I, 20, 23–24 (June 10, 1921).
[379] See Robert E. Cushman, *The Independent Regulatory Commissions* (Oxford University Press, New York, London, and Toronto, 1941) 760–761, for a chart showing tenure and method of removal of members of the independent regulatory commissions of the national government. See also William J. Donovan and Ralston R. Irvine, "The President's Power to Remove Members of Administrative Agencies," in 4 *Selected Essays on Constitutional Law* (published under the auspices of the Assoc. of Amer. Law Schools, Douglas B. Maggs, general editor, The Foundation Press, Inc., Chicago, 1938) 1519–1549, reprinted from 21 *Cornell L. Q.* 215 (1936); Lindsay Rogers, *The American Senate* (Alfred A. Knopf, New York, 1926) 262–271; *Power of the President to Remove Federal Officers* (Sen. Doc. 174, 69th Cong., 2d sess., 1926); Myers v. United States, 272 U.S. 52, 170–173 (1926). The reader may be interested in the analysis of the House decision contained in the dissenting opinion of Mr. Justice Brandeis in the *Myers Case.*
[380] *Humphrey's Executor* v. *United States,* 295 U.S. 602 (1935).

INDEX

Adams, John, and imitations of monarchy, 10–11, 28–54; as Vice President breaks ties on removal question, 187–188, 217–218; his notes on Senate debate on tenure, 184, n. 119; on President and Senate, 80–97; on Washington's independence in making nominations, 129–130; "the great converter" in Senate removal debate, 187; Washington on, for Vice President, 6–7

Adjournment, the President and, 151

Administration, a Federalist, 64–66, 131–133

Administrative chief, President as, 134–143

Administrative theory, interpretation of that of House majority in 1789, 239–248

Agent, private, first use of, in diplomacy, 102–104

Amendments, proposed constitutional, President and, 60

Appointments, and senatorial courtesy, 123–125; nominations and, 111–133; politics and, 125–131; recess, 125–126; Washington on, in a republic, 111–112

Appropriations, lump-sum, 63–64

Article II, and constitutional-grant theory, 168–178; interpretation of opening sentence of, by Madison, Jefferson, Hamilton, 178; Madison on opening sentence of, as grant of "the" executive power, 178–180; proposed amendments of, 148–150; its opening sentence as a general grant of power, 168–184, 201–213, 239–248

Attorney General, statutory provision for, 192; why Washington wanted Randolph as, 118

Benson, Egbert, his parliamentary strategy in removal debate, 201–202, 208

Bill-drafting, administrative, Washington and, 77

Bills, period for presidential consideration of, 61–62; Washington on veto of, 61; Washington on withholding signature from, 60–61

Board, single head or, for Treasury Department, 223–226

"By and with the advice and consent of," 94–95, especially n. 46

Cabinet, U.S.: institutional beginnings almost foreshadowed, 134–135, 137

Cabinet system, British, and Presidential system, comment on, 238–239; and views of 1789, 170, 172, 234–239; comment on, as of today, 238–239, n. 338. *See also* Leadership; Ministerial government

Chief of state, President as, 10–54; summary and comment upon, 43–47; Woodrow Wilson on, 51, n. 145

Choctaw Nation, Washington to chiefs and warriors of, 111

Commander in chief, command power, irreducible minimum involved in, 245; his relation as such to War Department, 239–247; Tucker's proposal of amendment, 148–150; Washington as, 139–141

Commissions, independent regulatory, Madison's reasoning as precedent for tenure of, 197–200, 246, 248

Communication, mode of, of President with Senate, 80–99

Compensation, presidential, constitutional aspects of, 144–148; Washington's refusal to receive, 16–17

Comptroller, tenure of, 197–200

Comptroller General, U.S., Madison's reasoning as precedent for tenure of, 197–200, 246, 248

Conduct, line of, President's, 11–15

Congress, how it got its business done in first session, 64–75; leadership from within, why it sufficed, 68–72; President and, 55–77

Conscientious objection, President Washington on, 23

Conservative, defined, 51–52

Constitutional, defined, xi–xiii

Constitutional-grant theory of removal, 155–157, 168–184, 201–214; interpretation of, in unqualified form, 239–247; Madison's historic defense of, 180–184

249

Constitutional questions, miscellaneous, raised in House debate, 144–151
Constitutional vs. statutory executive powers, 239–248
Corruption, executive, feared, 172, etc., cf. 229, 237
Corwin, Edward S., his major contribution to analysis of removal decision, 204, 206; quoted and cited, 155–214, *et passim*
Criticism of President, Washington on, 54

Deity, presidential invocation of, 20–21
Delegation of power, 150–151
Departments, administrative theory underlying legislation on, 239–248; and "executive" departments, 219–220, 242–244, 246; and tenure and removal, 155–248; comparison of Treasury and other two, 214–248; establishment of great, 152–248; heads of, in Congress, 99–102, especially n. 69; place of heads of, in governmental system, 234–239; statutory duties of first three heads of, 220–221; Washington on need for, 79–80
Direction, President's power of, 153, 163, 167, 169, 220–221, 235, 242–246, and generally, 152–248; not accidental result of removal power, 193; not extra-constitutional growth, 193. See also Management
Discretionary powers, vs. ministerial duties, 245–246

"Elective Majesty." See Title
Enacting clause, whether President's name should appear in, 40–41
Energy in government. See Responsibility
Exchequer, Chancellor of the, 229
Executive agents. See Private agent
"Executive" departments, departments and, 219–220, 242–244, 246
Executive-legislative relationship generally, 234–239
Executive power, fear of, 148–150; proposal of constitutional amendments to curb, 148-150; opening sentence of Article II as a grant of "the," 168–184, 201–213, 239–248
Experiment, American, as test of republicanism, 21

Faithful execution, President's duty of, 182, 184, 239–247
Federalist Administration, a, 64–66, 131–133
Federalist ideas vs. tradition of free government relative to power of purse, 214–216
First session of Congress, 64–75; its main tasks, 66; leadership from within, why it sufficed, 68–72; three organic acts of, 152
Fishbourn, Benjamin, case of, 123–125
Foreign Affairs, Secretary of: Acting, would give Senate needed information, 100; his statutory designation and duties, 219–221; Jay's appearances in Senate as Acting, 81, 100–102; statutory provision on removal of, 189, 218. See also Departments; Tenure of office
Foreign relations, treaties and, 78–111
Free government, tradition of, relative to power of purse vs. Federalist ideas, 214–216

Government, ministerial. See Leadership; Ministerial government

Hamilton, Alexander, comment on his legislative leadership as endangering position of President, 238, n. 334; *et passim*
Hancock incident, 17–20
Harris, poor Davy, 126
"Head" of department, vs. "principal officer," 219–220, 242–244, 246
"Highness, His, the President of the United States of America and Protector of the Rights of the Same," 36
History, defined, xi–xiii
Home Department, whether to establish a, 153–154
House of Representatives, 64–75; and Senate, 61–63; and treaties, 105–109; constitutional aspects of presidential compensation raised in, 144–148; constitutional issues relating to Executive raised in, 150–151; controversy of, with Senate, on removal of Secretary of Treasury, 216–217; miscellaneous constitutional questions raised in, 144–151; proposal in, of amendments to Article II, 148–150; grand debate on tenure of office, 155–

183, 190–214, 216–217, 239–248
Humphrey's Executor v. *United States*, 200, 248

Immunity to process, whether President has personal, 44, 46–47
Impeachment theory of tenure of office, 155–161, 201–214
Inaugural address, first, 11, 20–21
Inauguration, first presidential, 10–11
Indemnification, for executive excess of power in emergency, vs. broad executive powers, White on, 173–174
Indians, statutory discretion in calling forth militia, in relation to peace or war with, 139–141
Indian treaties, ratification of, 104–105
Inferior officers. See Subordinate officers
Intercourse with foreign governments, President as sole channel of official, 78–79

Jay, John, appointed Chief Justice, 118; as Acting Secretary, attends Senate meetings, once by order of Senate, 100–102; held over by Washington from Confederation, 134, 138; *et passim*
Judicial process. See Immunity to process

Knox, Mrs., and wicked short sofa, 33–34

Leadership, ministerial, debated, 226–239; regarded by Page as "foreign influence," 228
Leaves of absence, grant of, by President Washington, 136–138
Lee, Richard Bland, comment upon his position on tenure, 210–211
Legislation, President and, 40–41, 77, 55–58, 60–61; administrative, of first session, interpretation of administrative theory of, 239–248
Legislative-executive relationship generally, 234–239
Legislative-grant theory of removal, 155–157, 165–168, 201–214
Legislative recommendations, presidential, 55–58
Liberal, defined, 51–52
Lump-sum appropriation act, 63–64

Maclay, William, his *Journal* cited and quoted, *passim*; on controversy between two houses over removal clause of Treasury bill, 216–218; on first inauguration, 10–11; on mode of consenting to appointments, 80–86; on Senate debate on removal power, 184–189; on titles and other imitations of monarchy, 12, 28–54; President's invitations to, 130–131
Madison, James, and President Washington in first session, 58–59; as leader of House in first session, 71–72; his historic defense of constitutional-grant theory of removal, 180–184; his later constitutional objections to four-year terms, 195–197; his refutation of impeachment, President-and-Senate, and legislative-grant theories of removal, 180–184; his shift of position on removal, 165–166, 168, 178–179, 180–184, 201, 204, 208–210; his summary of four theories on removal, 156–158; his support of Benson's parliamentary strategy on removal, 201; on elastic and Protean character of legislative power, 196; on opening sentence of Article II as a grant of power, 178–180; why he shifted, 208–210; *et passim*
Management, over-all administrative, 134–143, 167, 218, 220–221, 235–237, 239–248
Marshals, U.S., given four-year terms in 1789, 192, 197
Ministerial duties, vs. discretionary powers, 245–246
Ministerial government, debate over, 224–239; rejection of, 160–161, 163, 165, 170, 180–184, 188–189. See also Cabinet system
Ministerial leadership. See Leadership
Miscellaneous officers, statutory provision for, 191–194
Monarchy, fear of, 172, 228, *et passim*; imitations of, 28–54
Money bills, origination of, by House, 226–234
Moon, man in the, 38
Morocco, Washington to Emperor of, 109–111
Myers v. *United States*, 179, 200, 202, 210, 213, 214, 242, 247, 248

"Necessary and proper" clause, in relation to administrative system, 165–169, 180–181, 219–248
Negotiations, foreign, President and, 78–80
Nomination(s), and appointments, 111–133; not given Maclay's candidate, 126; of son-in-law of Vice President, 129; only one rejected in first session, 123; political support for Wolcott's, 126–127; romance and office-seeking, 128–129; Washington on wisdom of written mesages of, 122–123; Washington's general principles in, 112–122; Washington's independence in making, 129–130

Office, public, Smith's view of property right in, 158–159, especially n. 27
Office-seeking, 112–122; by unashamed wire-pulling, 127–128; romance and, 128–129; with political support, 125–126
Opinion in writing, inconsistency between President's power to require, and constitutional-grant theory, 174–175, 246
Organic acts, 152

Party government, 236
Period allowed for presidential consideration of bills, 61–62
Permanency in magistracy, views on, expressed in House, 161, 194–195 (n. 162), 235–236
Placemen and pensioners, fear of, 172, cf. 226, 230, 237
Planner, Washington as administrative and diplomatic, 142–143
Planning, financial, issue over, 234–235
Plans, whether Secretary of Treasury should be authorized to "report," 226–239
Pleasure, meaning of tenure during, 194–197
Postmaster general, placed under administrative direction of President, 193, 196
Precedence, official, of the President, 18–20
Prerogative, fear of, 172, etc.
President, and administrative bill-drafting, 77; and a Federalist Administration, 131–133; and Congress, 55–77; and foreign negotiations, 79–80; and general principles for nominations, 112–122; and grand debate on tenure of office, 155–214; and happening of vacancies, 125–126; and leader of House, 58–59; and leaves of absence, 81, 136–138; and nominations to office, 111–130; and opening sentence of Article II, 168–180, 239–247; and proposed constitutional amendments, 60; and removals from office, 155–214, 218–220; and Senate, 78–133; and senatorial courtesy, 122–123; and treaties and foreign relations, 78–111; and veto power, 60–63; and written or oral mode of making nominations, 122–123; as administrative and diplomatic planner, 142–143; as administrative chief, 134–143; as chief of state, 10–54; as commander in chief, 139–141, 148–150, 239–247; as conductor of foreign relations and consequent relation to Department of Foreign Affairs (State), 239–247; as over-all administrative manager, 134–143; as representative of the people, 164, cf. 166, 181–184; as sole channel of official intercourse with foreign governments, 78–80, 110, n. 102; Bryce on, 51, n. 146; compared with Cabinet government of Great Britain, 234–239; compensation of, 16–17; conception of Senate as advisory council to, 80–100; constitutional re-eligibility of, 2–3, 148–150, 238–239, n. 337; constitutional significance of his replies to addresses, 21–22; first inauguration of a, 10–11, 20–21; first Thanksgiving proclamation by a, 24–25; first use by, of private agent in diplomacy, 102–104; his compensation and the Constitution, 144–148; his take-care duty, 184, 239–247; invocation of Diety by first, 20–21; issue over a title for, 34–40; Lawrence on change of ministry by incoming, 167, 236; Lawrence's view that President ought to have men about him whom he can trust, 236; legislative recommendations of, 55–58; mode of communication with Senate, 81–97; not to be his own foreign minister, 79–80; official precedence of, 18–20; period for his consideration of bills,

61–62; principles for nominations to office by, 112–122; prior consultation of Senate by, in person, 86–97, in writing, 94–95; proclamations of, 24–28; refusal of first, to receive pecuniary compensation, 16–17; right of access to, Hamilton on, 13; scope of his removal power under "legislative decision of 1789," 190–194; some pronouncements of first inaugural address of, 20–21; speech of, and addresses in reply, 28–33; style of living and line of conduct of, 11–16; symbolic character of unanimous election of first, 1–2; symbolism and, 1–2, 47–54; Theodore Roosevelt on, 16, n. 17; use and form of proclamations by, 26–28; whether federal writs should run in his name, 41–43; whether he can commit the nation by diplomacy, 109–111; whether he is originator of foreign policy as well as medium of foreign intercourse, 244–245; whether he is personally immune to judicial process, 44, 46–47; whether his name should appear in enacting clause of statutes, 40–41; Woodrow Wilson on, 51, n. 145; written nominations to office by, 122–123

President-and-Senate theory of removal, 155–157, 161–165, 201–214

"Principal officer" vs. "head" of department, 219–220, 242–244, 246

Prior consultation of Senate, in person, Washington's famous experiment with, 86–97

Private agent in diplomacy, first use of, by President, 102–104

Process, whether President is personally immune to, 44, 46–47

Proclamations, presidential, 24–28; first Thanksgiving, 24–25; use and form of, 26–28

Ratification, whether Indian treaties required, 104–105

Recess appointments, 125–126

Recommendations, legislative, of President, 55–58

Re-eligibility, constitutional, of President, comment on, 238–239, n. 337; Tucker's proposal of amendment on, 148–150; Washington on, 2–3

Religious liberty and conscientious objection, President Washington on, 23

Removal, power of, as sanction to power of direction, 193; Tucker's proposal of amendment respecting, 148–150. *See also* Tenure of office

Replies to addresses, presidential, 21–24; constitutional significance of, 21–22; examples of, 22–24

Republicanism, Washington on American experiment as test of, 21

Responsibility, Federalist conception of, debated, 166, 171, 174, 176, 177 (n. 101), 181–184, 215, 216, 225–226, 230–239

Revenue act, time limit on first, 62–63

Rubicon, Maclay crosses, 85

Sacred person, President as a, for General Schuyler, 44

Seat of government, constitutional issues relating to Executive raised in House debate on, 150–151

Sedgwick, Theodore, his near assertion that Constitution requires delegation of removal power to President, 210–211; perhaps leading exponent of legislative-grant theory of tenure, 166–168

Senate, 64–75; and House, 61–63; and nominations and appointments, 122–128; and power of removal, 155–157, 161–165, 170–177, 181–189, 216–218; and President, 78–133; and treaties and foreign relations, 78–111; Acting Secretary of Foreign Affairs ordered to attend, 100; as the great check, 175, 186; controversy of, with House on removal of Secretary of Treasury, 216–217; courtesy of, 123–125; early assumption that it was advisory council to President, 80–100, but see remark of Ames, 165; form of its advice and consent to treaties, 104–105; Jay's appearances in, 81, 100–102; mode of communication of President with, 80–100; mode of its consent to appointments, 81–86; prior consultation of, by President, in person, 86–97, in writing, 94–95; Thach on significance of its action on removal question, 189

Senatorial courtesy, first alleged example of, 123–125

INDEX

Separation of powers, 162 (n. 45), 179, 182 (n. 116), 197–200, 235, 237–238, *et passim*
Session, first, of First Congress, 64–75
Sherman, Roger, comment on views of, on removal, 211–212
Signature, why President did not allow tonnage bill to go into effect without his, 60–61
Single head, vs. board, for Treasury Department, 223–226
Smith, William, of South Carolina, leading exponent of impeachment theory of tenure of office, 158–161
"Speech, his most gracious," 29
Speech and addresses in reply, 28–33; ended by Mr. Jefferson, 32–33
"Splendor," Maclay objects to word, 31
State, Secretary of. *See* Foreign Affairs
Statutes, enacting clause of, proposal that President's name appear in the, 40–41
"Statutory" and "constitutional" executive powers, 239–248
Style of living, presidential, 11–16, *et passim*
Subordinate officers: comptroller, treasurer, auditor, register, with duties defined by statute, 221–223; power of Congress to fix tenure of, 190–194, especially n. 157
Sylvester, Peter, comment on his views on removal, 203, 205
Symbolism, and Presidency, 1–2, 11, 14, 16, 20, 33, 44, 47–54; and Washington's unanimous election, 1–2; political, an illuminating example of, 47–54

Take-care duty. *See* Faithful execution
Tenure of office, analysis of House decision on, 201–213; constitutional-grant bloc less than third of total in House, 208; controversy between houses on removal of Secretary of Treasury, 216–218; during pleasure, 194–197; historical significance of "legislative decision of 1789," 247–248; House *majority* Federalist in *administrative* views on, 239–240, 246–247; in subsequent history, comment on, 247–248; Madison's summary of four theories of, 156–158; no final distinction between departments in, 218–220; of comptroller, 197–200; opponents of presidential removal, views of those who spoke, 207 (n. 237); scope of President's power of removal, 190–194; Senate debate and action on, 184–189; summary of general conclusions on, 213–214; terms of office, question of power of Congress to fix by law, 192, 194–197, especially n. 173; the four constitutional theories on, 155–156; the constitutional-grant theory, 168–178, 180–184; the grand debate on, 155–214; the impeachment theory, 158–161; the legislative-grant theory, 165–168; the President-and-Senate theory, 161–165; the statutory result, 189–190; unqualified constitutional-grant theory of, interpretation of, 239–247; use of "to be removable," 192; whether majority of House accepted ultimate legislative control of, 205–208, especially n. 237; whether more than three men supported unqualified constitutional-grant theory of, 206; whether President-and-Senate men favored ultimate legislative control of, 206–208
Tenure of Office Act, 247–248
Terms of office, whether Congress might fix the, 192, 194–197, n. 173
Thach, Charles C., quoted and cited, 155–216, and elsewhere
Thanksgiving, President Washington's proclamation of day of, 24–25; its use to sanctify Constitution, 24–25
Tie votes, senatorial, broken by Vice President on removal question, 187–188, 217–218
Title, question of, for President, 34–40
Tonnage bill, why President did not let it go into effect without his signature, 60–61
Tour, presidential, 17–18
Treasurer, framers nearly provided for choice of, by joint ballot, 215–216
Treasury, First Lord of the, 229
Treasury, Secretary of: compared with other two secretaries, 214–248; office created, 223–226; statutory designation and duties of, 219–221; statutory provision on removal of, 189, 218; to make reports in person, if required, 234; whether he should "report" o

INDEX

merely "prepare" plans, 226–239. *See also* Tenure of Office

"Treasury bench," 172, 235

Treasury Department, compared with other two departments, 214–239; Federalist ideas versus tradition of free government, 214–216; statutory duties of subordinate officers of, compared with those of other two departments, 221–223; whether a department rather than an "executive" department, 219–220, 242–243; whether a single officer or a board should head, 223–226. *See also* Departments; Tenure of office; Treasury, Secretary of

Treaties, and foreign relations, 78–111; House and, 105–109; whether Indian, should be ratified, 104–105

Tucker, Thomas Tudor, his proposals of amendment to Article II, 148–150

Ultimatum to Creeks, and the war power, 89–97

Unanimous choice, symbolic character of Washington's, 1–2

Unique position, Washington's, 1–2

Vacancy, 125–126

Veto, presidential, which did not materialize, 61

Vice President, consulted by President on conduct and style of living, 11–15, especially n. 10; Washington on Adams for, 6–7

Vining, John, comment upon his position on tenure, 210

War, power to "make," changed by framers to power to "declare," 149

War, Secretary of: Acting, would give requisite information, 100; his statutory designation and duties, 219–221; statutory provision on removal of, 189, 218. *See also* Departments; Tenure of office

Washington, George, and administrative bill-drafting, 77; and Federalist Administration, 131–133; and alleged senatorial courtesy, 122–123; and approval of bills, 60–62; and Congress, 55–77; and foreign intercourse, 78–79; and Madison in first session of Congress, 58–59; and nominations to office, 111–133; and official precedence of President, 18–20; and parties, 6, 7, 9, 131–133, 236; and proposed constitutional amendments, 60; and Senate, 78–133; and tonnage bill, 60–61; and treaties and foreign relations, 78–111; and vacancies, 125–126; as administrative and diplomatic planner, 142–143; as administrative chief, 134–143; as chief of state, 10–54; as commander in chief, 139–141; as over-all administrative manager, 134–143; asks opinions of (acting) department heads, 139, 143; assumes President is sole channel of official intercourse with foreign governments, 78–80; attitude of, toward criticism, 54; called Cincinnatus of the West, 17; ceremonial at public ball, 33; communication of, to Emperor of Morocco, 109–111; conception of, that Senate was advisory council to President, 80–100; does not nominate Maclay's candidate, 126; embarrassed by declinations of appointments, 120–121; first inaugural address of, 10–11, 20–21; first inauguration of, 10–11; first proclamation of, 24–28; first use by, of private agent in diplomacy, 102–104; grants leaves of absence, 81, 136–138; his archival sense, 142–143; his fiscal directives prior to establishment of Treasury Department, 139, 141; his independence in making nominations, 129–130; his inexperience in politics and civil administration, 8–9, 96; his invitations to Senator Maclay, 130–131; his invocation of Deity, 20–21; his principles in nominating to office, 112–122; his pursuit of mean, 15, 60; his remark on "the public opinion," 54; his replies to addresses, 21–24; his reply to address of General Assembly of Georgia, 23–24; his speech and addresses in reply, 28–33; his tour of New England, 17–20; his unanimous election, symbolic character of, 1–2; his unique position, 1–2; holds over administrative officers, 134, 138; "indispensability" of, 4, 5; investigates delay in delivery of his letter to Governor, 142; legislative recommendations to first session of Congress, 55–57; mode of communication with Senate, 81–97; nominates son-in-law of Vice President, 129; not to be his own foreign minister, 79–80; on America's mission, 22; on appointments in a republic, 111–112; on importance of first precedents, 8–9, 12; on John Adams for Vice President, 6–7; on judicial appointments, 117–121; on nepotism, 113–114; on ratification of Indian treaties, 104–105; on religion and government, 22–23; on religious liberty and conscientious objection, 23; on sectional balance in first two offices, 6–7; on American experiment as test of republicanism, 21; on the Constitution as our *Magna Charta*, 22; on the constitutional re-eligibility of President, 2–3; on the President and foreign negotiations, 79–80; on the political prospect after adjournment, 76–77; on the Senate as advisory council in foreign relations, 97–100; on threshold of Presidency, 3–9; on why nominations should be by written message, 122–123; prior consultation of Senate by, in person, 86–97, in writing, 94–95; reflections in anticipation of Presidency, 7–9; refusal to accept pecuniary compensation, 16–17; conduct and style of living of, 11–16; success of his legislative proposals, 57–58; Thanksgiving proclamation by, 24–25; title for, 34–40; "violent fret" and "sullen dignity," 90–91, 96

Webb, Samuel Blachley, his support solicited by James Seagrove, 127–128; his unsuccessful candidacy, 128–130

Western territory, tenure of governor of, 191; tenure of judges of, 191, 196–197

Whitehead, A. N., on symbolism, 1, 47–49

Wire-pulling, for office, by James Seagrove, 127–128

Wolcott, Oliver, Jr., nomination of, 126–127

Writs, of Supreme Court, question of name in which they should run, 41–43